PRAISE FOR *The Believer*

"In this probing biography, Blumenthal, a former ̣........ .... , . Mack as a complex, deeply intelligent seeker, a man drawn equally to the mysteries of consciousness and the cosmos." —Gal Beckerman and Emily Eakin, *New York Times Book Review*

"Drop all mention of the extraterrestrials and *The Believer* remains a riveting look at the psychology of how we come to believe things. Mack's abilities, his brilliance, flaws, hubris, and mania, are anatomized with sensitivity. Readers will close the book wiser than when they opened it and painfully aware of what they do not and perhaps can never know about Mack, about extraterrestrials, and about the nature of truth." —Simon Ings, *The Times* [London]

"A compelling biography. . . . This well-researched account uses Mack's personal journals, archives, and notes, along with interviews of close friends and family members, to capture the full picture of Mack's life and genius." —Marissa Mace, *Library Journal*

"Based on fifteen years of research, interviews, and exclusive access to Mack's archival material, *The Believer* is the story of a brilliant man whose breadth of interests generated a lifetime of achievements. Believers will appreciate the book's extensive cosmic phenomena, and nonbelievers will find a unique chronicle of an unquenchable human spirit." —Amy O'Loughlin, *Foreword Reviews*

"With his access to Mack's archives and other significant sources, Blumenthal's book is a significant insight into the man, his missions, and the controversies that followed them."—Bill Chalker, *UFO Truth Magazine*

"Detailed, thoughtful, and entertaining. . . . Ralph Blumenthal is a sympathetic biographer and, perhaps, a kindred spirit."—Nick Pope, The Seminary Co-op Bookstore blog

"An inherently fascinating biography that is a 'must read' for all dedicated UFOlogists."—Able Greenspan, *Midwest Book Review*

"This extraordinary biography reads like a fast-paced thriller. It deftly weaves the detailed richness of John Mack's genius and complex life through the historical backdrop of the alien-abduction phenomena. Ralph Blumenthal has so beautifully captured the essence of Mack's soul and his relentless curiosity that by the end of the book I mourned that Mack is no longer with us." —Trish MacGregor, coauthor of *Aliens in the Backyard: UFO Encounters, Abductions, and Synchronicity*

"As a person sane enough to hold a driver's license, I say, what are we to make of Mack's findings? Read this gripping, factual account of a mental-health pioneer and truth-seeker by a soundly accredited successful author, veteran *New York Times* foreign correspondent, and reporter. Decide for yourselves and then tell me!" —Dan Aykroyd

"Anyone who is intrigued by the involvement of John Mack, a psychiatrist on the faculty of Harvard, or by the interest of psychiatrists in the anomalous in general and UFOs in particular, should not miss reading this book! It is filled with details on the topic, both pro and con, that are not publicly available in any other place that I know." —David J. Hufford, author of *The Terror That Comes in the Night: An Experience-Centered Study of Supernatural Assault Traditions*

"John Mack was one of the few prominent American intellectuals who saw and said what was, and still is, really at stake in the UFO phenomenon—reality itself. And Ralph Blumenthal is the perfect biographer to take up Mack and bring him to life, in all his humanity and complexity, on the page. A major achievement." —Jeffrey J. Kripal, author of *The Flip: Epiphanies of Mind and the Future of Knowledge*

"Ralph Blumenthal's definitive biography is beautifully written and impeccably researched, providing fascinating new insights into the professional and personal life of John Mack. What drove the Harvard psychiatrist to take alien abductions seriously? This question has never been addressed as brilliantly or as deeply as it is in *The Believer*—a must read!"
—Leslie Kean, author of *UFOs: Generals, Pilots, and Government Officials Go on the Record*

THE BELIEVER

RALPH BLUMENTHAL

THE BELIEVER

ALIEN ENCOUNTERS,

HARD SCIENCE,

AND THE PASSION

OF JOHN MACK

HIGH ROAD BOOKS
*An Imprint of the University
of New Mexico Press
Albuquerque*

High Road Books is an imprint
of the University of New Mexico Press

© 2021 by Ralph Blumenthal
All rights reserved. Published 2021
Printed in the United States of America

First Paperback Edition, 2022
Paperback ISBN: 978-0-8263-6395-4

Library of Congress Cataloging-in-Publication Data
Names: Blumenthal, Ralph, author.

Title: The believer: alien encounters, hard science,
and the passion of John Mack / Ralph Blumenthal.

Description: Albuquerque: University of New Mexico Press, 2021. |
Includes bibliographical references and index.

Identifiers: LCCN 2020038248 (print) | LCCN 2020038249 (e-book) |
ISBN 9780826362315 (cloth) | ISBN 9780826362322 (e-book)

Subjects: LCSH: Mack, John E., 1929-2004. | Psychiatrists—United States—
Biography. | Alien abduction—United States.

Classification: LCC RC438.6.M33 B58 2021 (print) |
LCC RC438.6.M33 (e-book) | DDC 616.890092 [B]—dc23

LC record available at https://lccn.loc.gov/2020038248

LC e-book record available at https://lccn.loc.gov/2020038249

COVER ILLUSTRATIONS
starry sky | Rastan | istockphoto.com
flying saucer in sky | George J. Stock | public domain

Designed by Mindy Basinger Hill
Composed in Parkinson Elecra Pro and Resolve Sans

always and forever

TO DEB,

my faithful believer

I never said it was possible, I only said it was true.

SIR WILLIAM CROOKES · 1874

CONTENTS

1

....

"THEY ARE TELLING THE TRUTH"

The Massachusetts Institute of Technology sprawls along the southern coast of Cambridge, facing patrician Back Bay Boston across a wide spot of the Charles River. On its northwest shoulder, around a bend in the river, hunkers Harvard University. But MIT alone "never really had an outdoors, not one that anyone uses," writes architecture critic Robert Campbell of the *Boston Globe*. Its 166 acres are pocketed with quadrangles of greenery and classical courts carved with the names of Newton, Aristotle, and Copernicus, but they seem superfluous. "The nearest thing to a public space, a place of social and cultural gathering, is the so-called Infinite Corridor indoors." Here MIT's scientists labor on their studies, which, to date, have been honored with ninety-five Nobel Prizes.

In this inquiring spirit, on an unseasonably hot Saturday in June 1992, an unlikely assembly convened for five days of secretive conferencing. Filling the steeply banked seats of lecture hall 6-120 in the Eastman Laboratories—where a lobby plaque pays homage to the storied MIT benefactor, Kodak photo pioneer George Eastman—were dozens of doctors, psychologists, therapists, physicists, folklorists, historians, theologians, and other specialists; a handful of trusted journalists; and sixteen otherwise seemingly ordinary folk with extraordinary experiences. All had signed nondisclosure agreements for the event that would remain under wraps for two more years—until the publication of a thick, oversize volume called *Alien Discussions: Proceedings of the Abduction Study Conference.*[1]

The conference was a professional forum about humans who believed they were, at a minimum, (1) taken against their will by nonhuman beings, (2) brought to an apparent spacecraft or other enclosed space, (3) examined or subjected to telepathic communication, and (4) could recall the experience consciously or under hypnosis. Some further recounted astral travels, ecstatic bonding with a deity or Source, apocalyptic warnings of planetary doom, and the forcible harvesting of their eggs or sperm for human-alien hybrid reproduction.

It was hardly MIT's regular fare (although the school's fabled Science Fiction Society hosted the world's largest open-shelf library of more than sixty thousand science-fiction and fantasy books and magazines), and, to be sure, MIT was not a sponsor. Rather, in the spirit of academic freedom, it only granted use of its facilities after a distinguished MIT atomic physicist, David E. Pritchard, pointed out how bad censorship would look. Renowned for his pioneering research in the wavelike properties of beams of atoms and forces of light on atoms, Pritchard, a prize-winning mentor of Nobelists, had long been intrigued by the abduction narratives, which he saw as more amenable to scientific investigation than sightings of what were long called flying saucers or, more accurately, unidentified flying objects—UFOs. He had been reading up on the subject and used his travels in physics to consult with leading investigators of the phenomenon.

At first, Pritchard thought of writing a book, but he later decided that a critical analysis of all the possibilities really demanded a conference. With a sabbatical at hand, Pritchard devoted the semester to planning it, ignoring the hostility of MIT administrators and enlisting as his partner a noted Harvard psychiatrist named John E. Mack, who had begun his own abduction investigations. Given the evident psychological dimensions of the phenomenon, Pritchard said, "I would not have had the courage to run this without a prominent psychiatrist."

Mack was a Harvard star, a heralded founder of community mental-health services in once-downtrodden Cambridge, and the author of a groundbreaking psychological biography of Lawrence of Arabia that had won a Pulitzer Prize. Commandingly tall at sixty-two years of age and with crystalline-blue eyes and a face stretched tight over his skull like the leathery mask of some totemic figure, he packed lecture halls and seminars, attracted disciples (particularly women), published prolifically, mobilized colleagues against nuclear weapons, and traveled the world on missions of peace. He had met with Yasir Arafat and been arrested at a nuclear test site in Nevada. And he was just back from the Himalayas, where he had joined a select group of professionals discussing aliens with His Holiness the fourteenth Dalai Lama.

Now Mack told the conferees at MIT why he thought the abduction phenomenon was not a psychiatric phenomenon, although that was most people's snap assumption, including, at first, his own. But any explanation,

2

he said, had to account for five elements: (1) consistency of the reports, (2) physical signs like scars and witness-backed reports of actual absence for a time, (3) accounts from children too young for delusional psychiatric syndromes, (4) an association with witnessed UFOs, and (5) the lack of any consistent psychopathology among abductees.

To the uninformed it appeared like mass hysteria fed by the culture, Mack said. Except this didn't act like a collective disorder. The experiences were too personal, involving isolated individuals not caught up in any mass movement. And they were risking ostracism and ridicule. "There is no evidence that anything other than what abductees are telling us has happened to them," Mack said. "The people with whom I have been working, as far as I can tell, are telling the truth, and this has been the impression of other abduction researchers." It was indeed a profound mystery. "Some sort of intelligence seems to have entered our world, as if from another dimension of reality."

As for the beings themselves, they were commonly described at the conference as hairless and without ears or noses, although apertures were visible. The cranium was large and bulbous, set on a thin neck like a ball on a stick. The eyes were the most striking feature—huge, opaque, and inky black with no eyebrows, lashes, or lids. The mouth was a lipless, toothless slit, not used for speaking or, apparently, eating or drinking. The chin was pointed, the jaw unhinged with no sign of musculature. The faces bore no lines or wrinkles or other signs of aging. The body, too, was devoid of muscular development, with no sign of skeletal structure, no shoulder blades or ribs. There were no visible breasts or nipples, no bulge of a stomach, no waistline, no hips, no buttocks, and no apparent genitals, just a smooth, rounded area. Nor were there any signs of male-female differentiation. Arms and legs were spindly, without joints, the limbs just bending where a knee or elbow would be. The hands had three or four fingers and an opposable thumb. The feet were covered. The skin was widely described as gray and rubbery, with no visible pores. Were they even biological creatures? Or robots? But if they were robots, they could communicate and think at least as well as humans. They could make decisions and deal with crises.

Word of the conference had leaked out, and many of Mack's Harvard colleagues were incredulous or appalled. He was lending his professional eminence to *this*?

Some were less surprised, knowing Mack as a maverick who had taken to heart the lines of the Spanish poet Antonio Machado: "Traveler, there is no path; you make the path by walking." Years of the psychoanalysis that his profession demanded of practitioners had excavated the childhood trauma that Mack himself believed lay behind his lifelong questing and openness to the anomalous. He had lost his mother at a tender age, leaving him wounded by abandonment. And so he came to tell a Brazilian therapist in a flash of insight that may have come out a little too pat, "The abduction story is a welcoming story because it means that—Ooooo, I'm getting goose pimples as I think of this—I'm not alone. There is life in the universe!"[2]

2

......

TERROR IN THE NIGHT

Behavioral scientist David J. Hufford was inclined to reject his invitation to the Alien Discussions forum at MIT, not because he was skeptical of UFOs or paranormal experiences—he had good reason to be open-minded—but because he was leery of the research methods employed, particularly hypnotic regression.[1] Abduction theory, he felt, had gotten way out in front of its data and demanded far more rigorous investigation. It was, at the very least, part of something far bigger and more unruly that could confuse people who were grappling with unresolved traumas, real or imagined. But Hufford, a folklore PhD and a professor at Pennsylvania State's College of Medicine, joined the conference after all and came to share what he knew, which was the phenomenon of awakening paralyzed in the presence of a malevolent being. He had, to his terror, unaccountably experienced it himself as a student in the 1960s, after which he had gone on to study the experience in Newfoundland, where it was surprisingly prevalent and known as the Old Hag Syndrome—nocturnal visitations by evil presences seemingly bent on strangling or suffocating immobilized victims. There were enough parallels with alien abduction to raise eyebrows. And yet, Hufford lamented, abduction investigators were overlooking connections that pointed to a larger and more complex syndrome, as explored in his groundbreaking 1982 book on supernatural assault traditions, *The Terror That Comes in the Night*. Hufford had implicated a recognized medical condition known as sleep paralysis—when the highly brain-active and dream-rich sleep stage known as Rapid Eye Movement combines with muscle atony or paralysis as people fall asleep or awaken. When he began his research in 1970, medical literature estimated the prevalence of sleep paralysis in the general population at about 1 percent. He was able to show it was about twenty times higher. In fact, he came to think, sleep paralysis seemed so central to the Old Hag visitations that it clamored for examination in abductions, although not all abductions occurred during sleep. Sleep paralysis didn't explain the paranormal experiences, but somehow they intersected.

Hufford knew that some anomalous experiences *were* conventionally explainable. A 1980s outbreak of sudden nocturnal deaths among healthy Southeast Asian men aged thirty to forty-five had been ascribed by the refugee community to threatening spirits that paralyzed victims as they slept. Hufford found it a condition of sleep paralysis turned fatal by genetically linked cardiac conduction defect, a disruption of the electrical impulses that control the heartbeat. Similarly, Hufford said, a study in the journal *Nature* of mermen sightings from medieval Norse ships found that the sightings decreased as the height of the ships grew, implicating optical distortions in transformations of walruses and killer whales into magical semihumans.

He cautioned against relying on so-called star informants, whose accounts were most alluring. The study of *disbelievers* or marginal experiencers was crucial as well. Why *didn't* they encounter what others had? He saw UFOs as part of contemporary folk belief. Not that they weren't objectively real. They were as real as other anomalous phenomena dismissed by the prevailing scientific paradigm, which couldn't, after all, *dis*prove their existence but could only hold that they didn't fit into any reality that science at the time could recognize. Abduction investigators, even someone as well trained as Mack, as Hufford saw it, were too restrictive in settling on just one manifestation of a far broader and more complex set of core experiences known to humanity since earliest antiquity. He found it curious, in fact, that investigators of alien abduction seemed almost rivalrous with those who studied, say, Bigfoot, or near-death experiences, or religious revelations, as if those were competing phenomena in a zero-sum game and not part of a bigger enveloping mystery. Hufford also distrusted hypnotic regression as a tool to explore abduction experiences or any anomalies, for that matter. It was just unreliable. "If you ask a person to remember something, they will," he said. "Some memories under hypnosis are valid, some are not."

Yet he was far from a debunker. Many who shared their experiences with Hufford had never heard of the Old Hag, so they couldn't be circulating a cultural meme. One young woman recalled waking up to a male figure pinning her to the bed. She remembered its distinctive smell, "sweaty and kind of dusty." Its face was covered by a white mask with black dots "and a red kind of crooked mouth." She tried to scream, but no sound would come out. A male college student recalled a "murky presence" like "a blob of nothing" with no real face but two holes that seemed to be eyes. Three young college women shared a Kentucky house rumored to be haunted. They described many frightening encounters including a night when one of them felt overcome with images of mass murder and struggled to resist an evil presence urging her to slaughter her roommates—she actually saw herself chopping them up. Counterintuitively, throughout her terror her dog showed no sign of distress, unlike many pets and farm animals in abduction scenarios. But like abduction narratives, Old Hag experiences often had a sexual component. The bed often rocked. Sufferers felt vibrations or out-of-body sensations of flying up and seeing themselves below. Time seemed out of joint, passing slowly. Some of the creatures seemed to shuffle or walk with a rolling gait reminiscent of aliens in abductee accounts.

Hufford had a personal reason to take the phenomenon seriously. In 1963, as a sophomore at Lycoming College in Williamsport, Pennsylvania, he had completed his final exams for the semester and collapsed into bed in his off-campus room at 6:00 p.m. Two hours later he was awakened by the sound of his door being opened and then footsteps. The room was pitch black. Hufford assumed a friend was looking for him for dinner. He tried to turn on the light but couldn't move or speak. He felt the mattress sink as something climbed up, knelt on his chest, and proceeded to strangle him. Terrified, he thought he would die. Whatever it was, it reeked with evil, leaving Hufford revolted. He fought his paralysis and then suddenly found he could move. He leapt out of bed and switched on the light. The room was empty. He ran down to the landlord, who was casually sitting and watching TV. "Did someone go past you just now?" Hufford asked. The landlord looked at him strangely and said no. Then Hufford really panicked. He told no one. But in 1970, while studying supernatural belief for his doctorate, he traveled to Newfoundland, where he found that many people had experienced the "Old Hag." It upended his thinking. He had been taught that supernatural experiences grew out of local traditions—the so-called Cultural Source Hypothesis. But he knew from his own experience that an encounter can occur with no predisposition whatsoever. He didn't want to share what had happened to him, but he now realized that strange things didn't happen to people because they believed in strange things. They believed in strange things because strange things happened to them.

7

3

THIS BUDD'S FOR YOU

John Mack had come late to the UFO/abduction game, which was a stupefying enigma any way you looked at it—newly resurfaced and yet, some said, timelessly archetypal. The phenomenon may indeed have been ageless, but the involvement of a laureled Harvard professor of psychiatry was a fresh sensation. Grappling with psychological issues from the traumatic loss of his mother in infancy, he had been studying a relaxation technique called Holotropic Breathwork—a technique in which breathing is regulated by rhythmic music with the aim of inducing altered states of consciousness. Holotropic Breathwork was developed by a charismatic Czech-born psychiatrist, Stanislav Grof, and his wife, Christina, and it opened Mack up to a range of spiritual experiences.[1] Years later he would say everything went back to the Grofs. "They put a hole in my psyche and the UFOs flew in."[2]

At a Grof training module in California in late 1989, Mack had met a fellow psychotherapist from New York who shared with Mack the story of a patient who had written an operetta set in an institution where inmates received head implants so they could be tracked. The psychotherapist, Blanche Chavoustie, who came to believe she was a victim of the CIA's Project MKUltra, the sinister Cold War mind-control experiments later devastatingly exposed by Congress, had read about abductions.[3] The composer's case offered some eerie parallels, and Chavoustie had consulted an artist friend, Budd Hopkins, who after a UFO sighting of his own had become a noted writer on abductions. Hopkins asked Chavoustie to bring her patient to his townhouse art studio in Manhattan's Chelsea section. And then, Chavoustie said, Hopkins used hypnosis to retrieve the woman's history of alien encounters. Would Mack like to meet Hopkins? Chavoustie asked.

Mack scoffed. It sounded crazy. But Chavoustie persisted. She told Hopkins about Mack and followed up with a postcard saying Mack would be in New York in January, and asking could Hopkins meet with him?

Mack forgot about it. But on a cold and blustery Wednesday, on January 10, 1990—"one of the dates . . . when . . . your life changes," Mack said later[4]—he was in Manhattan visiting his old Harvard friend and fellow psychoanalyst

Robert J. Lifton. Now Mack remembered Hopkins and, somewhat to his own surprise, called him after all. Hopkins invited him over, and Mack asked if Lifton wanted to come along. Lifton and Hopkins were neighbors on Cape Cod. Hopkins had a studio in Truro, not far from Wellfleet where Lifton and his wife Betty Jean, known as BJ, summered.

BJ spoke up for her husband. "No," she said, like a Cassandra. "Bob has a choice about getting involved in this, and you don't."[5]

Hopkins, affable and bushy-browed with a shag of lanky, graying hair, greeted Mack in his West 16th Street townhouse, which was hung with his flat, knife-bladed geometric sculptures in bright primary colors—his "Guardians," as Hopkins called them.[6] He told Mack a haunting story. A troubled woman had come to see him and spotted a drawing of an alien face—teardrop-shaped with huge, black, wraparound insect eyes. How did he know? she gasped. Know what? "My experience," she said. The picture was from someone else, Hopkins said. That really jolted her. She had been telling herself she'd suffered a nightmare. If she wasn't alone, maybe it was real after all. There were many like her, Hopkins told Mack. He had letters from his readers all over the country detailing the most unearthly encounters, too unimaginably bizarre to make up. Mack could read them for himself. Hopkins sent him off with a batch and one of Hopkins's books, inscribed in the artist's near-spastic scrawl,

For John
with every good wish
to a future—I hope—colleague
Budd Hopkins

Mack was about to leave the country, so he didn't immediately study the material. But when he did, he was indeed intrigued. He quickly collected his own circle of experiencers, a term he and others preferred as more neutral than abductee. When he heard their accounts and evaluated them as a psychiatrist, he found nothing inherently wrong with them. They harbored certain resentments, suspiciousness, feelings of victimization, and tendencies to challenge authority, and they came from homes with troubled parental relationships, alcoholism, and varied forms of abuse—that is, Mack said, they reflected a typical cross-section of humanity. In other words, they were normal. Where there was disturbance, it seemed caused by the abduction experiences, not vice versa. And with his psychiatric experience, shouldn't he know? "That's my job," he was to tell his Sikh guru, Gurucharan Singh Khalsa, a bushy-bearded Kundalini yoga expert and a disciple of the Indian yogic master Yogi Bhajan. Khalsa had been Mack's friend, counselor, and psychotherapist since they had met in Cambridge in the 1980s and bonded over a shared interest in mind-body interactions.[7] "If you're an art dealer your job would be to tell the real thing from the copy," Mack said. Anyway, he said, "what's the payoff?" Why in the world, or out of it, would anyone make this up?

"It would be wrong to say this was a sort of gradually dawning realization," Mack would later tell an interviewer.[8] He could see where it was going the moment he met Hopkins.

Mack soon introduced two women with abduction encounters to an "Affect Seminar" he was running at Harvard to explore feelings in the face of traumatic experiences. He had been cautioned by an old family friend, Thomas Kuhn, to stay skeptical. Kuhn had taught the history of science at Harvard before joining the University of California, Berkeley, and writing *The Structure of Scientific Revolutions*, his classic study on the resistance of established science to unconventional breakthroughs. "Hold on to the null hypothesis as long as possible," Kuhn urged Mack. View any hypothesis as something to be *dis*proved. Gather evidence, but postpone conclusions "until 3 smoking guns."

Yet in early 1991, barely a year after meeting Hopkins, Mack was discussing his own abduction research at a Shop Club, a Harvard dinner forum for works in progress, and he was provoking consternation.[9] Wasn't this just witchcraft? Mass delusion? Hysteria? Someone raised the dubious reincarnation claims of a Colorado housewife who had conjured a previous life as an eighteenth-century Irishwoman, Bridey Murphy. Thrown on the defensive, Mack cited the scraps of elusive physical evidence and the abductee's deep distress that to him, as a psychiatrist, had the authentic affect of a real experience and not a fantasy. Willard Van Orman Quine, an eighty-two-year-old Harvard philosopher and theoretician of abstruse mathematical formulations, had listened, stumped. How was it possible? Another listener, the philosopher, ethicist and psychologist Sissela Bok, wife of Harvard's president Derek Bok and daughter of the Nobel Prize winners Gunnar and Alva Myrdal, was also intrigued. But she objected to Mack's certainties and impatience with critics, especially since no one had the slightest idea what this was all about. Mack shrugged off her concern. In fact, he thought, it might soon be time to lay it all out more publicly.

4

THE MYSTERY

OF ANOMALOUS EXPERIENCE

Wesley Boyd, six-foot-three with a beard and ponytail, was in his final months of medical school at the University of North Carolina Chapel Hill while also completing a doctorate in religion and culture.[1] The elemental duality: science and soul, the mirror and the lamp. Now, at the end of 1991, with Boyd considering a residency in psychiatry, his professor at UNC, Jeffry Andresen, had a strong recommendation: the Cambridge Hospital, run by Harvard Medical School. That's where his favorite psychiatry teacher at Massachusetts Mental Health Center—Mass Mental, once known as Boston Psychopathic Hospital, or "The Psycho"—was teaching now. John Mack, Andresen said, was "brilliant." Tall and restless with cobalt eyes and a spiritual, intellectual, and sexual chemistry, he had been Andresen's idol. At a time when Cambridge was a blue-collar health-care wasteland where the only mental-illness problem was considered Harvard, Mack, bursting with enthusiasm, had convinced the chairman of the Harvard Department of Psychiatry in Boston to leap the Charles River and adopt the forlorn hospital. Soon under Mack the struggling community was blessed with mental-health clinics and addiction treatment centers and counseling for poor children, and the Cambridge Hospital began winning awards. Mack continued his ascent through the Harvard firmament while toiling a dozen years in England and the Middle East on a groundbreaking psychological biography of T. E. Lawrence. Even he was surprised when it won a 1977 Pulitzer Prize. Now, he said, "they'll expect me to keep it up."[2] But he did, churning out more books and scholarly articles, anointing himself an ambassador of peace to the embattled Israelis and Palestinians, and championing a physicians' movement against nuclear weapons, all the while growing in stature in American psychiatry.

Boyd applied to Cambridge but was told he was too late; there were no interview slots left. He informed Andresen, who said not to worry—he'd call his friend Leston Havens. Havens and Mack had shared the same psychiatry teacher, the legendary Elvin Semrad, who liked to tell new residency students that they would no longer be able to rely heavily on instruments and tests—the principal tools for understanding their patients would be . . . themselves. The next day Boyd got a call from Cambridge. He could come for an interview whenever he liked. He picked a day when his wife, Theonia, who was also a physician, would be interviewing for a fellowship at Boston's Children's Hospital.

Two weeks before Christmas in 1991, Boyd and Theonia drove up from Chapel Hill to check out the residency possibilities at Cambridge for the middle of the following year. Snow was lashing Boston. TV monitors were flashing images from Moscow, where Mikhail Gorbachev's teetering Soviet empire was suffering the abrupt defection of breakaway republics. Boyd was rushing to appointments in the hospital when a tacked-up leaflet of an upcoming lecture had him halt, squinting through his spectacles. He read it several times, with mounting amazement.

GRAND ROUNDS

Wednesday, December 18, 1991
12:30 - 2:00 p.m.
Macht Auditorim

The Mystery of Anomalous Experience
John E. Mack, M.D.

During the past thirty years thousands of adults and children have reported that they have been visited by humanoid beings, taken into unusual spacecraft and subjected to a variety of medical-like procedures. Dr. Mack will report his two-year experience with more than thirty of these individuals. To his surprise they appear to fit into no identifiable psychiatric or psychosocial category. He will discuss the clinical, scientific and philosophical implications of the abduction phenomenon. The presentation will include slides shown by pioneer abduction researcher Budd Hopkins of accompanying physical manifestations and a statement by an abductee who will be available to respond to questions from the audience.

The synchronicity of it! John Mack had drawn Boyd to Harvard, and here, on the very date of Boyd's arrival, Mack was delivering an astonishing talk. Residents were expected to attend grand rounds—lectures held twice a month for the hospital community and visitors—but Boyd didn't need convincing. For a twenty-eight-year-old medical student pulled between science and faith, any hospital that would host an eminent psychiatrist's talk on aliens was the place to be. Plus, he already knew UFOs existed. He had seen one.

5

"HAVE WE VISITORS FROM SPACE?"

Flying saucers had been all the rage for almost half a century, starting, by common reckoning, on June 24, 1947. Shortly before 3:00 in the afternoon, the pilot of a small single-engine plane over southwestern Washington spotted a "tremendously bright flash" and then "a chain of nine peculiar looking aircraft" approaching Mt. Rainier.[1] Kenneth Arnold, a thirty-two-year-old fire-control engineer with his own fire-fighting equipment company in Boise, Idaho, had been flying on business from Chehalis, Washington, to Yakima when he heard that a C-46 Marine transport had gone down around the southwest side of Rainier in the rugged Cascades east of Seattle, with a posted reward of five thousand dollars for finding the wreckage. Arnold was an experienced pilot with up to one hundred hours of airtime a month. He had taken his first flying lessons as a boy in Minot, North Dakota, he earned his license in 1943, and the following year he bought his own plane. He replaced that plane in January 1946 with a new three-seater CallAir, which was designed for high-altitude takeoffs and rough field use, including landing in cow pastures—something he had done, by his count, exactly 823 times. On the afternoon of June 24, as he was detouring to search for the crashed aircraft, Arnold climbed to 9,500 feet and spent an hour circling over the corrugated ridges and canyons. Not spotting anything, he turned above the old mining town of Mineral, trimming out for Yakima, the atmosphere so glassy the little plane all but flew itself. "The sky and air was as clear as crystal," he recalled. He saw a Douglas DC-4 four-engine airliner about fifteen miles away and then a sudden flash. Fearing a possible collision, he spun around looking for the source but saw nothing. And then, to the left, the nine objects: a formation of four and then five others, speeding south from the direction of Mt. Baker toward Mt. Rainier. According to the report he later gave to the US Army Air Force, Arnold assumed they were jets, but he couldn't find their tails. He watched them "flip and flash in the sun," swerving in and out of the high peaks, and as the last craft passed the snowy crest of Mt. Adams, he calculated it had flown about 1,700 miles an hour—almost three times the existing world speed record, which Arnold dismissed as impossible. He guessed they had formed a chain about five miles long and had been under view for about two and a half minutes.

Arnold had an "eerie feeling," but he continued his fruitless search for the C-46 wreckage before continuing on to Yakima, where his sighting was attributed to guided missiles. He flew on to Pendleton, Oregon, where word of his strange observation had spread and a local told him he had just spotted similar "mystery missiles" in nearby Ukiah. Arnold gave an interview to Pendleton's *East Oregonian* in which he likened the objects' movements to a flat rock bouncing up and down as it skipped across water. Reporter Bill Bequette put a short story on the *AP* wire memorializing Arnold's account of "Nine bright saucer-like objects flying at 'incredible speed.'" Headline writers later created the indelible shorthand of "flying saucers."

Strikingly, though, at least twenty other witnesses, all but two in the Pacific Northwest, reported seeing similar flying discs on June 24, the day of Arnold's encounter. One was a Portland prospector, Fred M. Johnson, who told the FBI he was five thousand feet up in the Cascade Mountains when he spotted a flying disc—and then five or six others—about one thousand feet away. He viewed one through a small telescope he carried and picked out some details. The silent objects, he said, sent his compass needle gyrating wildly.

Arnold later had seven other sightings and would run, unsuccessfully, in an Idaho Republican primary for lieutenant governor. He was often a target of ridicule, to which he reacted bitterly. "Call me Einstein, or Flash Gordon or just a screwball," he said. "I'm absolutely certain of what I saw!"

The event came to be seen as ushering in the flying-saucer era, although prodigious scholarship took the origins back to the mists of time, with ancient annals memorializing hierophanies (manifestations of the sacred) since earliest antiquity. As theology or folklore, they had been consigned to the mythical, but the modern era brought a growing technological immediacy to the ever more closely reported phenomenon. These historical experiences began to acquire a physicality. The nineteenth century saw waves of airship sightings around the United States, where no balloonlike dirigibles were known to fly yet, although patents had been applied for. Heavier-than-air–powered flight would not arrive until the Wright Brothers in 1903. Puzzlingly, these propeller-driven craft seemed to fly slowly, as if keeping just one step ahead of current know-how. More bizarrely, they were sometimes reported to land humanlike passengers for chitchats with astonished earthlings.

One mysterious visitor kept recurring, a certain "Wilson." According to research by UFO historian Jerome Clark, later author of the exhaustive 1,462-page, two-volume *The UFO Encyclopedia*, a Texas farmer named J. R. Ligon and his son saw a huge airship in a pasture adjoining their farm outside Beaumont on April 19, 1897. They described it as about 130 feet long and 20 feet wide, with wings on either side and propellers fore and aft. As the *Houston Post* reported, four men stood around the craft and requested water. One introduced himself as Wilson. They said they had just flown over the Gulf of Mexico and were returning to Iowa, where they had built their ship. Amazingly, the *Post* went on to report, J. R. then seemed to have built a replica of the machine in time to parade it through Beaumont on the Fourth of July. The tale might have been written off as a hoax but for a respected Beaumont rabbi, Aaron Levy, who while visiting New Orleans in April 1897 told the *Times-Picayune* he too had seen the original airship of Ligon's farm and shaken hands with one of its crewmen. The same day as Ligon's sighting, a Mississippi man, George Dunlap, said he had seen an airship flying over Lake Charles, Louisiana—not far from Beaumont— with an "unearthly whistle" that frightened his horses, throwing him from his buggy. The ship landed, and four occupants rushed out to see if Dunlap was hurt. The owner, Dunlap reported, was named Wilson. The next day, April 20, in Uvalde, Texas, 360 miles southwest of Beaumont, Sheriff H. W. Baylor found an airship with large fins and three crewmen near his house, according to the *Galveston News*. One introduced himself as Wilson from Goshen, New York, and formerly Fort Worth, Texas. Wilson mentioned the name of another Texas sheriff he knew—and Baylor knew him. Wilson drew water from Baylor's hydrant and flew off. Deluged with questions, Baylor later insisted he had never seen an airship, and he went on to order that the news reporter who had perpetrated the yarn be shot. But then yet another sheriff in the Rio Grande Valley told the *San Antonio Express* that he had encountered a landed airship with three men who had just come from Sheriff Baylor in Uvalde. Jerome Clark tracked down three other similar newspaper accounts. But spookily, he said, no trace of Wilson ever turned up in Goshen, Fort Worth, or anywhere else.

"If the mystery airships were not the physical aircraft of the coming twentieth century, they were not entirely imaginary either," Clark wrote. "They were only *partly* imaginary. They sailed both sides of the borderline, between the merely conceived and the vividly experienced, in the fashion of all fantastic phenomena that escape the page or the screen or the tale, to appear before us in guises that lead us to think we recognize them while yet being blind to their inscrutable and elusive identity."

As Clark saw it, UFOs were an "event phenomenon"; they were potentially explainable, although not yet explained, and accompanied by fragmentary physical evidence that never seemed to go anywhere. Clark, a devotee of the mischievous anomalist Charles Fort—who said, "accept only temporarily"—was cautiously withholding judgment on the nature of the experience, which seemed akin to ancient folktales of fairies, gods, and demons. "Nothing has ever been finally found out," wrote Fort in *The Book of the Damned*. "Because there is nothing final to find out. It's like looking for a needle that no one ever lost in a haystack that never was—"

In Clark's own case, three highly credible adult members of his family, who had vacationed years before at their cabin on Pickerel Lake in northeastern South Dakota, had looked out over the water one day to see, undulating on the surface, an immense sea serpent some fifty feet long and two feet in diameter with a head they later likened to the figurehead of a Viking dragonship. Then it slipped below the waves and vanished. The nineteenth century, Clark found, was replete with such sightings at many bodies of water. His family's encounter was in all likelihood somehow imaginary, he wrote in *Fortean Times*, but not *only* imaginary. It was both there and not there, "blurring ontological categories in defiance of all our understandings of how things operate in the world."

Before Ken Arnold's sighting, World War II pilots had reported encountering transparent metallic glowing fireballs over the European and Pacific theaters. Americans assumed they were enemy aircraft and dubbed them "foo fighters," perhaps a corruption of the French *feu* for fire, or just a nonsense term from the troops' all-purpose FUBAR (fucked up beyond all recognition). But German and Japanese pilots seemed to have encountered them too. Among those who marveled at these mysterious flying craft was a decorated veteran of Guadalcanal, Rear Admiral Donald James Ramsey. After the war, he would confide the encounters to his daughter Anne Cuvelier, who turned her family's 1869 bayside mansion in Newport, Rhode Island, into a Victorian inn where years later John Mack and Budd Hopkins and their experiencers would gather for private summer retreats to socialize free of ridicule and share abduction stories.

Within a year of the final Allied victory in 1945, a wave of sightings convulsed Scandinavia. Rumors of "ghost rockets" panicked Swedish officials, who held secret meetings with Navy Secretary James Forrestal and war hero Jimmy Doolittle, a survivor of America's first suicidal strike at the Japanese homeland four months after Pearl Harbor. Fears that the Russians were experimenting with captured German rockets proved baseless. Years later, when Sweden opened its files, reports of more than 1,500 sightings emerged. Similar accounts, forever unexplained, poured out of Hungary, Greece, Morocco, and Portugal.

The year of Arnold's sighting saw the most fabled American incident: the Air Force's reported recovery of a "flying disc" near Roswell, New Mexico. The opening facts seemed simple enough, but the affair soon "ballooned" into a mythic affair generating endless investigation, countless pop-culture touchstones, and incessant commercial exploitation. It began with a press release issued on July 8, 1947, by the public information officer of Roswell Army Air Field, Lieutenant Walter Haut, at the direction of the base commander, Colonel William H. Blanchard, later the four-star vice chief of staff of the Air Force.

The many rumors regarding the flying discs became a reality yesterday when the intelligence office of the 509th (atomic) Bomb Group of the 8th Air Force, Roswell Army Air Field, was fortunate enough to gain possession of a disc through the cooperation of one of the ranchers and the sheriff's office of Chaves county.

The flying object landed on a ranch near Roswell sometime last week. Not having phone facilities, the rancher stored the disc until such time as he was able to contact the sheriff's office, who in turn notified Jesse A. Marcel, of the 509th Bomb Group intelligence office.

Action was immediately taken and the disc was picked up at

the rancher's home. It was inspected at the Roswell Army Air Field, and subsequently loaned by Major Jesse Marcel to higher headquarters.

The *Roswell Daily Record* immortalized the event the same day with the banner headline "RAAF Captures Flying Saucer on Ranch in Roswell Region" and a surprisingly superficial page-one story notable mainly for its eyewitness account. A local man, Dan Wilmot, told the paper he and his wife were sitting on their porch the previous Wednesday night "when a large glowing object zoomed out of the sky," sending them running into the yard for a look. He described it as "oval in shape like two inverted saucers faced mouth to mouth, or like two old type washbowls placed together," perhaps fifteen to twenty feet in diameter, and glowing "as though light were showing through from inside." Wilmot remembered it as silent, but his wife recalled a brief swishing sound. They kept the experience to themselves, hoping someone else would come forward. When no one did, they decided to go public, just as the press release was issued.

But later that day Roger M. Ramey, commanding general of the US Eighth Air Force in Fort Worth, Texas, announced that the recovered object had been a crashed radar-tracking weather balloon. The striking discrepancy and conflicting reports of other witnesses, including the supposed recovery of alien bodies, as recounted in numerous books and never convincingly laid to rest, fed conspiracy theories of a government coverup that have never abated. Among those fueling the suspicions was Brig. Gen. Arthur Exon, then a colonel stationed at Wright Field at Dayton, Ohio, and later a commanding officer at Wright-Patterson Air Force Base, where recovered material and even alien bodies from the crash were rumored to have been taken according to accounts Exon said he had heard from witnesses and that he regarded as credible. He later shared the stories with a friend, who in turn passed them on to his nephew, Whitley Strieber, who would later write of one of the most popular abduction books, *Communion*. The Roswell mystique only grew with disclosure that the 509th Bomb Group that took custody of the wreckage was successor of the unit that conducted the atomic bombings of Hiroshima and Nagasaki two years before.

Over the years, as Roswell parlayed the mystery into a lucrative tourism industry, many public officials sought closure, to no avail. In a 1994 radio interview thirty years after his lost race for president, Republican Senator Barry M. Goldwater of Arizona said he had been intrigued enough to seek access to Wright-Patterson through Air Force General Curtis LeMay, mastermind of the firebombing of wartime Japan, commander of America's nuclear strike force, and vice presidential running mate of George Wallace in 1968. LeMay, Goldwater recalled, "got madder than hell at me, cussed me out, and said, 'Don't ever ask me that question again!'" Administrative records and outgoing messages of the Roswell Army Air Field between 1945 and 1949 ended up destroyed, without explanation.

But soon it emerged that the mythologized Roswell crash was hardly unique. Jerome Clark later compiled dozens of other accounts of crashed craft all over the world, followed, in many cases, by the supposed retrieval of alien bodies. They all shared one thing in common: the absence of convincing artifacts or corpses.

As the waves of sightings around the nation continued—some seven hundred were recorded from 1947 to 1951—General Nathan D. Twining, chief of the Air Materiel Command at Wright Field, called the phenomenon "something real and not visionary or fictitious." It was possible, he said, that some of the incidents could be attributed to meteors or other natural phenomena. But the extreme and suspicious operating characteristics "lend belief to the possibility that some of the objects are controlled either manually, automatically or remotely." With that, the Air Force opened its first secret investigation of the mystery, Project Saucer, soon renamed Project Sign. Its staff included a thirty-seven-year-old astronomer from the Department of Physics and Astronomy at Ohio State University, Josef Allen Hynek, who dismissed flying saucers as "utterly ridiculous." The Air Force reconstituted the inquiry as the oddly named Project Grudge under a well-regarded and open-minded Air Force officer, Captain Edward J. Ruppelt, who was credited with coining the phrase "unidentified flying object" because so many of them didn't look like saucers.

Meanwhile, *True*, the bestselling men's magazine, called in Donald E. Keyhoe, a Naval Academy graduate and combat aviator who had managed Charles A. Lindbergh's triumphal air tour of the United States after his historic 1927 solo nonstop Atlantic crossing. Keyhoe's article for *True* in December

1949, "The Flying Saucers are Real," which he later expanded into a book, proved a sensation. "For the past 175 years," he wrote, "the planet earth has been under systematic close-range examination by living, intelligent observers from another planet." He told the story of a huge, gleaming object reported by the state police flying toward Godman Air Force base near Fort Knox, Kentucky, on January 7, 1948. Three P-51 fighters scrambled to investigate. Captain Thomas F. Mantell Jr., the twenty-five-year-old flight leader and a hero of the D-Day landings at Normandy, radioed to base, "I've sighted the thing! It looks metallic—and it's tremendous in size!" He radioed that it was starting to climb and he was following it. "It's still above me, making my speed or better. I'm going up to twenty thousand feet. If I'm no closer, I'll abandon chase." The radio went dead. His plane disintegrated, scattering wreckage all over the landscape. Two days later the *New York Times* carried the *AP* story, headlined, "Flier Dies Chasing A 'Flying Saucer.'" The skeptical Hynek theorized that Mantell had been chasing the planet Venus, or perhaps a high-altitude Skyhook balloon.

Keyhoe, seen as the first to popularize the term *UFO*, and later the director of the influential and independent National Investigations Committee on Aerial Phenomena (NICAP), concluded that the saucers were indeed alien craft and that Project Saucer was set up "to investigate and at the same time conceal from the public the truth about the saucers." He appealed for full disclosure. "The American people have proved their ability to take incredible things. We have survived the stunning impact of the Atomic Age. We should be able to take the Interplanetary Age, when it comes, without hysteria."

Instead, the Air Force downgraded Project Grudge to show how little there was to get excited about. But in 1952 it reconstituted it under Ruppelt as Project Blue Book. Amid an alarming flurry of sightings over the White House, the Capitol, and the Pentagon, the Air Force called its biggest press conference since World War II. The Intelligence Chief, Major General John Samford, told reporters the sightings were optical illusions caused by "a temperature inversion" that made ground lights seem up in the air. Now the CIA mobilized. In January 1953, according to the agency's own history, it put together a UFO study panel under H. P. Robertson, a noted physicist from the California Institute of Technology, to review the available evidence as a possible danger to national security. It concluded unanimously that there was none but recommended that the National Security Council debunk UFO reports and work to convince the public via mass media, advertising, schools, and even the Disney organization that there was nothing to them.

At the height of the Red Scare, with McCarthyism rampant, the panel also recommended that private UFO groups like the Civilian Flying Saucer Investigators in Los Angeles and the Aerial Phenomena Research Organization in Wisconsin be monitored for subversive activities. Ruppelt quit soon afterward and died of a heart attack in 1960 at age thirty-seven. But Blue Book would continue to compile data through 1969, investigating 12,618 sightings out of which 701 remained unexplained.

Henry Luce's popular pictorial weekly *LIFE* had started working on a saucer article in 1949, but *True* scooped them that December. *LIFE* soon revived the project, finding an unexpectedly warm welcome in inner sanctums of the Air Force. Clearly someone very high up favored disclosure for whatever reason and was hoping, too, to gain access to *LIFE*'s intensive reporting. As one intelligence officer told the magazine, "The higher you go in the Air Force, the more seriously they take the flying saucers."

The issue of April 7, 1952, was arresting—and not just for its cover photo introducing a sexy ingénue named Marilyn Monroe. Presenting ten case studies in a long article quaintly titled "Have We Visitors from Space?" *LIFE* reported that disks, cylinders, and other luminous and solid geometric objects, including "globes of green fire," had for years frequented the earth's atmosphere. Contemporary science could not explain them as natural phenomena but solely as artificial devices "created and operated by a high intelligence." And no power source on earth could explain their startling performance.

LIFE went on to present ten carefully "checked and rechecked" case histories, including three the magazine itself had uncovered. They included the so-called Lubbock Lights of August 25, 1951, when three earth-science professors spotted a crescent of some two dozen lights flashing silently across the west Texas sky. A few nights later a student captured their images on film, showing, in several exposures, a larger luminosity "like a mother craft hovering near its aerial brood." Depending on their distance, the professors calculated, the objects may have been traveling anywhere between 1,800 and 18,000 miles an hour. The Air Force, *LIFE* reported, accepted the photos as genuine.

In another case from 1947, a top American astronomer and meteor expert who asked *LIFE* for anonymity (but was later identified as Lincoln La Paz of the University of New Mexico) was driving at daytime with his wife and teenage daughters in New Mexico when they all saw a bright, luminous elliptical object wobbling in the clouds. Its sudden ascent, the astronomer said, "thoroughly convinced me that we were dealing with an absolutely novel airborne device."

Almost two years later another prominent astronomer, Clyde W. Tombaugh, who had discovered Pluto in 1930, was sitting in his backyard in Las Cruces, New Mexico, with his wife and mother-in-law when they all saw something oval aglow with blue-green luminescence and a line of glaring windows rush overhead low and silently, too fast for a plane, too slow for a meteor. All three agreed that the object was definitely a solid "ship" of some kind.

In May 1951, three technical writers for the aerophysics department of North American Aviation's plant outside Los Angeles gaped as some "30 glowing, meteorlike objects sprayed out of the east at a point about 45 degrees above the horizon, executed a right-angle turn and swept across the sky in an undulating vertical formation." The objects, bathed in intense electric-blue light, were traveling as fast as 1,700 miles an hour, the writers estimated, and "moved with the motion of flat stones skipping across a smooth pond."

The same year, on a clear, moonlit January night, the control tower at Sioux City airport detected a bright light above the field. Captain Lawrence W. Vinther and his copilot, James F. Bachmeier (of Mid-Continent Airlines), accompanied a civilian from Air Intelligence to investigate. They were approaching the light in their DC-3 when it frighteningly dived at them before skimming silently over their nose. The two pilots lost sight of it . . . and then suddenly it was at their side, flying in tandem. It seemed as big as, or bigger than, a B-29, with a cigar-shaped fuselage and a glider-type wing set well forward. It lacked sweepback or engine housings, jet pods, or exhaust glow. After a few seconds the object descended, passed under the DC-3, and disappeared.

A year later, in January 1952, a B-29 was on a solo mission over Wonsan, Korea, flying slowly at about twenty thousand feet when the tail gunner and another crewman saw a bright, pulsating orange object about the size of a large beachball with a halo of bluish flame. It followed the B-29 for about five minutes then pulled ahead and shot away at a sharp angle. On the same night, eighty miles away, another B-29 crew reported a similar flaming ball.

LIFE concluded with a summary of what the mysterious objects were *not*.

They were not psychological phenomena, however much the Air Force liked to belittle them as illusions or delusions of witnesses.

They were not secret American experiments. *LIFE* had questioned Gordon Dean, chairman of the Atomic Energy Commission, who said, "There's nothing in our shop that could account for these things, and there's nothing going on that I know of that could explain them."

They were not Soviet innovations. "It is inconceivable that the Russians would risk the loss of such a precious military weapon by flying a saucer over enemy territory," *LIFE* said.

They were not atmospheric distortions from atomic testing, a theory David Lilienthal, the former AEC commissioner, ridiculed, saying, "I can't prevent anyone from saying foolish things."

They were not aberrations of the northern lights, magnetic disturbances, or "vertical mirages" from layers of heated air.

They were not plastic high-altitude Skyhook balloons.

They were not "fireflies in the cockpit," as one Air Force colonel suggested.

They were not auto headlights reflected in the clouds—many had been seen in broad daylight. *LIFE* had even consulted Walther Riedel, former research director of Hitler's V-2 rocket center in Peenemünde, who had joined Wernher von Braun and other Nazi scientists after World War II in the secret American intelligence program, Operation Paperclip. "I am completely convinced that they have an out-of-world basis," Riedel told *LIFE*.

So what *were* they?

"Somewhere in the dark skies," *LIFE* said, "there may be those who know."

Among the many remaining skeptics was a heralded Harvard professor of astrophysics, Donald H. Menzel, who had directed the 1936 Harvard-MIT eclipse expedition to the Soviet Union and soon after developed the first telescopic instrument in America to block out the blazing disk of the sun to study its wispy corona. Later, as acting director of the Harvard College Observatory, Menzel set about explaining away the growing waves of UFO sightings as natural phenomena (although he dabbled in science fiction and liked to draw fanciful illustrations of aliens).

"Above all, there is not the slightest evidence to support the popular fantasy that saucers are interplanetary space ships, manned by beings from beyond the earth, however much some people want to believe in this unscientific, highly publicized interpretation of saucers," he wrote in *Flying Saucers: A Great Astronomer Explains the Facts,* which was published by Harvard University Press in 1953. Call him the man who shot Santa Claus, Menzel said, but the sightings were nothing more than "optical tricks that the atmosphere and its contents can play upon our eyes." What they were decidedly *not,* Menzel insisted, were "space craft from Venus, or perhaps from Mars, controlled, according to some reports, by miniature beings 26 inches high! Little men whose powerful physiques could withstand the tremendous buffeting that the flying saucers would give them. Little men who allegedly wore no buttons on their clothes. Little men supposedly investigating the earth because they had seen our atomic-bomb blasts and were concerned whether or not the bombs constituted a menace to interplanetary space."

But the sightings continued.

After several hundred thousand people saw saucers over France in the late summer and fall of 1954, Aimé Michel, a French mathematician and engineer, discussed it with the poet and artist Jean Cocteau. "You ought to see whether these objects move along certain lines, whether they are tracing out designs, or something like that," suggested an ailing Cocteau as he was recovering from a heart attack at his villa on the Côte d'Azur. Michel went on to painstakingly plot their courses for a stunning realization he called *orthoteny,* a word derived from the Greek for "stretched in a straight line." He noted that the UFOs were witnessed flying in straight lines following the curvature of the earth. It seemed strongly probative of intelligent control, a thesis he would expound in his book, *Flying Saucers and the Straight-Line Mystery.* Carl Jung found "no certainty about their very nature" but "overwhelming material pointing to their legendary or mythological aspect," to the point that, as he wrote in *The New Republic* in 1957, "one almost must regret that the Ufos [*sic*] seem to be real after all."

6

....

THE SOURCES OF SUFFERING

If it was true that children lived the unlived lives of their parents, Mack wrote, then perhaps it was the intellectual rigor of his upbringing that impelled him later to question conventional rationality.[1]

There was a particular reason, Mack himself and many close to him believed, that he had been drawn to psychiatry and had come to risk a distinguished career chasing a disreputable cosmic mystery. It had to do with the childhood trauma that shadowed him throughout his life.

Although he was encouraged from childhood to take on the world, he grew up in a sheltered, wealthy, secular, German-Jewish home where it was assumed he was to follow his father, an English professor, and his stepmother, an economist, in the academic life. "I was raised as the strictest of materialists," Mack told the writer C. D. B. Bryan, one of the special invitees to the alien abduction conference at MIT. "I believed we were kind of alone in this meaningless universe, on this sometimes verdant rock with these animals and plants around, and we were here to make the best of it, and when we're dead, we're dead." Yet his ethnoreligious culture also embodied a commitment to open-mindedness, intellectual curiosity, and exploration—albeit short of superstition. "My parents grew up in a world from which the spirits had been banished to the supernatural or the paranormal and they did not want their children to develop irrational beliefs that would make it difficult for them to get along with other children and adults."

Mack's father's great-grandfather emigrated in the 1840s from Bavaria, settling in Cincinnati where his son, Edward, was born. Edward's son, Clarence, who was Mack's grandfather, was a whiskey salesman who often traveled to Europe. On one of his trips he ran into a girl he knew from Cincinnati, Della Aub, the daughter of a pioneering ophthalmologist, Joseph Aub, who became one of the first physicians to use an electromagnet to remove foreign bodies from the eye and left Della an estate equivalent today to more than $6 million. Della and Clarence married and had a son, Edward, born in 1904, who would become Mack's father.

Edward went to public school in Cincinnati until the family, increasingly prosperous, moved to New York, where they lived in splendor in the Sherry-Netherland Hotel on Central Park. Edward attended the exclusive Phillips Academy in Andover, Massachusetts, and then he went to Princeton, graduating summa cum laude. He worked on Wall Street, found it distasteful, and set out to become an English teacher.

Mack's mother, Eleanor, was descended from prominent German-Jewish brewers. Her great-grandfather, Samuel Baer Liebmann, owned an inn and brewery in Ludwigsburg in the kingdom of Württemberg. In the aftermath of the 1848 revolutions, Samuel and his wife, Sara, and their children left for America. They settled in Brooklyn, where Samuel and three of their sons, Joseph, Henry, and Charles, founded a brewery in Bushwick. It would be called Rheingold and would come to dominate the New York beer market in the 1950s, thanks to a catchy jingle and the annual elections to select a wholesome pinup queen as "Miss Rheingold," who sometimes got almost as many votes as the president of the United States.[2]

Henry and his wife, Emma, had seven children including a son, Walter Henry Liebman (he dropped one "n"), a New York State Assemblyman and senior partner of his own law firm. Between 1902 and 1906 Walter Henry and his wife, Lulu Waxelbaum, had two sons and a daughter, Eleanor, who would become John Mack's mother. Eleanor's younger brother, Walter Henry Liebman 2d, a lawyer, would run as a New York Democrat for Congress in 1938. His wife, Grace Koehler, a pioneering woman aviator, wrote smoke signals in the sky to aid her husband's campaign, though he ultimately lost to a Republican, Bruce Barton, who was a nemesis of President Franklin D. Roosevelt. Eleanor's other brother, Henry, who would be John Mack's uncle, suffered from mental illness and was lobotomized. "I was always interested in the sources of suffering," Mack recalled years later.

Eleanor, a luminous beauty with luxuriant bobbed hair, attended the progressive Ethical Culture School and then Vassar College, graduating at the age of twenty in 1926. The following year, the *New York Times* announced her engagement to twenty-three-year-old Edward Clarence Mack, a 1926 graduate of Princeton. The families were prominent enough to make the society pages—the Liebmans lived on Park Avenue and the Macks on Fifth. They wed in 1928 in fashionable Elberon, New Jersey, where the Liebmans had a summer estate on the shore. Once known as the Hollywood of the East, the beach community hosted stage and film stars and politicians, including President James A. Garfield, who went there to recover after being shot in July 1881 but died there three months later, the assassin's bullet still in him.

By early 1929 Eleanor was pregnant. Their son, John Edward Mack, made his appearance at New York Fifth Avenue Hospital at 8:00 a.m. on October 4, 1929—an hour Mack would later pin down for astrological readings. Twenty days later, on what came to be known as Black Thursday, the plummeting stock market set off the Crash, although the family remained well-provisioned enough to ride out the Great Depression. Generations of Macks traditionally alternated the same male names, Clarence and Edward for instance, but, the young man later came to joke, from whence came the aberrant and generic "John"? Was it a sudden parental lapse of imagination? (It became funnier when, as the liberal New York daily *PM* would report, he once heard himself hailed on the street, "Hey, John!" He whirled around, only to be curtly dismissed, "Not you, mack.")

The following June, Edward and Eleanor took an eight-month-old John to escape the steamy city for a seaside holiday with Eleanor's parents in Elberon. On June 20 Eleanor suffered an acute attack of appendicitis that went initially unattended. As her symptoms worsened, she was rushed to Monmouth Memorial Hospital for an emergency appendectomy. She developed an acute gangrenous infection, complicated by streptococcus peritonitis, an inflammation of the membrane covering the abdominal wall. Penicillin had been discovered two years before but was not yet in general use. In a week Eleanor was dead. She was not yet twenty-five.[3]

Edward, her husband of less than two years, bitterly blamed the surgeon. Others thought Eleanor may have hidden her distress until it was too late. Her mother, Lulu, was often overprotective—she was known to count the cherry pits after a meal to make sure no one had accidentally swallowed one—and Eleanor may have feared triggering her hysteria. Eleanor's father, Walter Henry, struggled with his grief for six months until his heart gave out at age fifty-six.

John, suddenly motherless, was shunted to relatives, including his grandparents Clarence and Della and his uncle and aunt, Walter Henry 2d and his wife, Grace, the barnstorming pilot. Through Aunt Grace, infant John had also acquired another set of doting relatives—Grace's mother, Carrie, and stepfather, David A. Schulte, a real-estate magnate and founder of the cigar-store chain that controlled three hundred prime street corners in the Northeast. Schulte and a real-estate partner had announced plans for the world's tallest building, a 150-story skyscraper on Worth Street and Broadway, just before the stock market plummeted. Schulte was still a wealthy man. He gave his stepdaughter Grace her first airplane, which, teaching herself to fly, she crashed. Undaunted, she would go on to fly anti-submarine missions for the Civil Air Patrol in World War II. The Schultes had their own Monmouth County manor: Telegraph Hill Farm in Holmdel, New Jersey, which was near the Bell Labs telephone research facility, where the father of radio astronomy, Karl Guthe Jansky, first discovered radio waves from the Milky Way in 1931. It was also where, after Schulte died and the property had been sold in the 1960s, the radio astronomers Arno Penzias and Robert Woodrow Wilson discovered the background radiation permeating the universe to confirm the Big Bang theory of creation, winning them the 1978 Nobel Prize for Physics.

Edward struggled with his heartbreak. But he was a twenty-six-year-old widowed English teacher with a baby son to raise. It wasn't long before he met a glamorous widow from Westchester with her own tragic past.

Ruth Allegra Prince Gimbel, a bewitching young socialite with dark, wide-set eyes, was the daughter of a Polish-born merchant/banker, Julius S. Prince, who owned a historic waterside estate—Wildcliff—on the Long Island Sound in New Rochelle, north of New York City. He and his wife, Clara Bertha Rich, had three daughters and a son; their eldest daughter, Helen, had died at nineteen of appendicitis, much like Eleanor Liebman Mack. Partly as a result, their son, Julius "Bud" Prince, went into medicine and became a pioneering public-health official in the US Agency for International Development in Ethiopia and Ghana—"the most indefatigable activist doctor I know," John Mack would later write of his step-uncle and role model.

Ruth Prince attended Barnard College, where she studied economics and was mentored by Columbia's redoubtable Arthur F. Burns. At twenty-one she married Lee Adam Gimbel, great-grandson of the founder of the department store. On New Year's Eve in 1930, as the nation slid deeper into the Great Depression, Ruth went up to Wildcliff for the holiday, expecting her husband to join her. Instead, thirty-five-year-old Lee Gimbel checked into the Yale Club across from Grand Central Terminal and leaped from his sixteenth-floor window. He and Ruth had been married barely six years and were parents of a four-year-old daughter, Mary Lee.

Two years later, after meeting the bereaved widow, the aspiring English professor Edward Mack wed Ruth Prince Gimbel in March of 1932. At two and a half years old, John Mack suddenly had a new mother and a six-year-old stepsister.

Ruth was domineering, and her adoring husband denied her nothing. Edward did not protest when Ruth banished all traces of Eleanor from the household. Growing up, young John was not allowed so much as a photo of his dead mother. He grew up haunted by her sudden death. His childhood grief, many close to him believed, found expression in his later quest for the elusive in the cosmos.

He was struggling with "the feminine in my life," Mack told one of his therapists. As a psychiatrist, he had undergone extensive psychoanalysis to excavate his earliest memories. As early as twelve, he remembered, he was searching out books on psychology in his school library, driven "by the restless hurt I felt inside." One of his favorite childhood books was *The Wizard of Oz*, about characters in search of mythic attributes that they had within them all along. Another was *Pinocchio*. He was particularly taken with Pinocchio's magical guardian, the fairy with the turquoise hair, who materializes to the boy puppet at critical moments to steer him from bad deeds. Mack would imagine his mother turning blue as she struggled to give him life. "Partly to heal the pain connected with early losses, especially the loss of my biological mother at 8 months," Mack wrote, "I embarked on a course of psychoanalytic treatment during medical school."

Susan Butler, Grace Liebman's daughter and a cousin of Mack's, was convinced that "if Elie hadn't died, he wouldn't have become a psychiatrist."

"I knew it had to do with the loss of his mother," said Vivienne Simon, an environmental activist who came to work for Mack as his abduction research was gaining traction.

Karin Austin, an experiencer and perhaps his closest confidant toward the end of his life, agreed. "If there wouldn't have been anything missing, he wouldn't have gone on this search," she said.

Phil Isenberg, who roomed with Mack at Harvard Medical School, said,

"I always felt that he was driven by the notion you could go into Heaven and find your mother."

Edward Khantzian, Mack's close partner in bringing health care to Cambridge and a later skeptic of his abduction research, saw it too, finding significance in his friend's sudden childhood acquisition of a stepmother. "He was adopted so he had an ongoing search for his origins," Khantzian said.

But Roz Zander, a therapist, life coach, and artist who had carried on an intense romance with Mack before breaking it off, cautioned against armchair analysis, finding the equation "a little too pat." Rather, she said, Mack was simply "a brilliant mind," ever courting new experiences.

The gravest of losses to a young child also became a source of strength, said his close friend Michael Blumenthal, a clinical psychologist and poet. "He knew that being wounded means remaining capable of being hurt. And all his life John was open to the wounded."

Mack's wife, Sally, would see it another way after her husband's restless search for romance, which would doom their thirty-three-year marriage. "There was always the missing woman in his life," she said. Mack didn't deny it. "It seems like my life is a never ending quest for that (those) moment (s) of bliss, connection with a woman," he confided to his journal.

Mack's therapist took note, finding that a rapturous affair with a younger woman Mack met when she was pregnant with another man's child was entangled in issues of maternal loss—"swimming in archetypes," as Mack himself put it.

That consuming love of Mack's later life, Dominique Callimanopulos, granddaughter of a Greek shipping billionaire, saw the needy side of him too. "He was so ready to believe," she recalled.

Budd Hopkins had an opposite theory. Far from traumatized, he said, Mack suffered from overwhelming self-confidence. "I think John throughout his life was extremely lucky," Hopkins said shortly before his death from cancer at age eighty in 2011. "He was cushioned financially. He had looks, personality and brains. I don't think John ever had a tough course of action. There was something blithe about the way he succeeded at everything."

One admirer late in Mack's life saw yet another impulse, a yearning for spirituality. "It is utterly fascinating to read your struggle with the reality of religious experience, or at least with experiences that seem to have a strong religious or spiritual overlay," wrote James F. Strange, a distinguished university professor and a professor of religious studies at the University of South Florida in Tampa. "It is like a man born deaf who discovers sound and Mozart on the same day, or perhaps one born blind who gains sight and sees Van Gogh in the same evening."

Mack acknowledged that it was complicated. "You know," he told his therapist, Gurucharan Singh Khalsa, "it's very hard to take a German-Jewish materialist and reprogram him into a mystic." But his upbringing was destiny, he told the *New York Times*. "I was like a recalcitrant communist who becomes a right-winger."[4]

7

MACK THE KNIFE

Half a century before Mack entered Harvard Medical School in 1951, weird science was shaking it up. "Who shall say that the ordinary experience is the only one possible?" William James told the newspapers in 1896. Later, in his influential Lowell lectures, James, a medical school graduate and revered paterfamilias of psychology and philosophy, explored psychic phenomena as part of his wide-ranging exploration of religious experience. He dared to explore cases of mediumship, witchcraft, and demonic possession, of which he said, "I am convinced that we stand with all these things at the threshold of a long enquiry, of which the end appears as yet to no one, least of all myself." He found few answers, but he ultimately concluded, "The only thing I am absolutely sure of being the extreme complication of the facts." More than half a century before, transcendentalist Ralph Waldo Emerson told the Harvard Divinity School that the world "is not the product of manifold power, but of one will, of one mind; and that one mind is everywhere active, in each ray of the star, in each wavelet of the pool; and whatever opposes that will, is everywhere balked and baffled, because things are made so, and not otherwise." Benevolence—love, justice, temperance—ruled creation, Emerson went on. "It makes the sky and the hills sublime and the silent song of the stars is it. By it, is the universe made safe and habitable, not by science or power."

But by the time of his arrival at Harvard, Mack saw the institution as a bastion of scientific materialism, with spirituality confined to the Divinity School. The most radical thing that a prospective physician could admit to, Mack thought, was a belief in God. Not that he was anything more than culturally Judaic.

He was by no means a rebel, despite a deeply progressive education. He had attended the experimental Lincoln School, founded by Teachers College of Columbia University and funded by the Rockefellers along precepts developed by John Dewey to test the latest pedagogical methods. He went on to Oberlin College, which had pioneered the acceptance of Black students and women and had been a station on the Underground Railroad for escaped slaves, fomenting an antislavery rebellion a year before John Brown's raid on Harper's Ferry. At Oberlin, Mack recalled fondly, "no one pretended to know more than he or she did." Like many of his classmates, he fell under the spell of a charismatic young history professor, Harvey Goldberg, who delivered standing-room-only lectures as improvisational as a jazz solo. In the spring of 1949 Mack won Goldberg's approval with an earnest paper called "The Soviet Challenge to American Mythology" that looked to Lenin, Trotsky, and the Bolshevik Revolution for lessons in improving American democracy, a provocative thesis at the height of the Red Scare. Among Mack's friends at Oberlin were John Kander, later the composer, with lyricist Fred Ebb, of "Cabaret," "Chicago," and other hit musicals and the Frank Sinatra anthem "New York, New York"; and John Gutfreund, later the "King of Wall Street" and the CEO of Salomon Brothers before a scandalous fall. With the rest of his "Fortunate Class of 1951" Mack, at twenty-one, was sent off by economics professor Ben W. Lewis, a Roosevelt New Dealer, who counseled graduates: "Some matters are more important than others; you're going to live a long time. Budget your decisions; save your best ones for the issues that count, and be in there strong at the finish." "When he came from Oberlin," remembered his Harvard roommate Phil Isenberg, "he was as conventional and model a medical student as you could find. He was very disciplined. He spent every night studying."

Another roommate, Lester Grinspoon, called Mack "solid as the rock of Gibraltar," so fixated on his studies that his laundry often went unwashed. A school photo showed Mack as a first-year medical student with a debonair pompadour and white lab coat concentrating on an autopsy, snipping away at entrails—"Mack the Knife," his family joked. He boasted of a distinguished forebear there. An award-winning cancer specialist, Joseph Charles Aub, a nephew of his grandmother Della's father, Joseph Aub, the pioneering ophthalmologist, had graduated from Harvard College and Medical School and by 1924 was named an assistant professor in medicine, one of the school's first Jewish academicians. That same year Aub and noted cardiologist Paul Dudley White (who would later treat President Dwight D. Eisenhower after his heart attack) happened to encounter two Bryn Mawr women on a transatlantic cruise. One of them contracted measles, and the two doctors helped them escape French immigration officers. The women, Cornelia Otis Skinner and

Emily Kimbrough, ended up writing a best seller about the caper that was turned into a popular 1944 film comedy, *Our Hearts Were Young and Gay*.[1]

In his own era, Mack recalled, Harvard's Jewish medical students were often dismissed as "eggheads if not wimps," although Isenberg had captained the football team. To counter the stereotype, Mack and other Jewish students challenged the gentiles one day to a softball game behind a student dorm. It ended in a tie, Mack recalled, but the score was beside the point. "We Jewish intellectuals, from my distorted point of view, had certainly proved our activist credentials."[2]

A confident physician-to-be, Mack gravitated to psychiatry. As he explained decades later, "I guess I sort of always felt most mental illness was the result of misery of one kind or another."[3] He was not averse to shaking things up. In his fourth and final year, he was assigned from Boston Children's Hospital to two months of surgical service at the old Peter Bent Brigham Hospital under the redoubtable chief surgeon, Francis D. Moore. "Franny," as his adoring students called him, was a legend at the medical school, renowned for his findings on fluids and chemicals in the human body. The year before, one of Moore's protégés at Brigham performed the first successful human organ transplant, transferring a kidney between identical twins. That and subsequent transplants won the surgeon, Dr. Joseph Murray, a Nobel Prize, which he graciously co-credited to Moore. Moore liked to test his students by firing out questions such as, "Mack, tell us the course and relations of the mammary artery." Mack was forced to think back to his anatomy lessons of three years before and mumble whatever came to mind. One day, feeling particularly beleaguered, Mack was scrubbed in under Moore on a sympathectomy, a surgical procedure to cut ganglia along the spinal cord to relieve the constriction of blood vessels. After Moore sectioned the nerve bundle, he told Mack to wash it, dry it, and paste it in the patient's chart. To the amazement of the rest of the team, Mack cheekily refused. The room turned deathly quiet. Moore quietly took the section of nerve-cell tissue, rinsed it in saline, and lay it down to dry. Then he turned to Mack and asked if he would be so good as to put it in the chart later. But Moore came to take a liking to Mack. Whenever he had an interesting case like a complicated parathyroid resection, he would summon Mack to the operating room, where he took pains to explain the operation. Later he wrote glowing recommendations for Mack's psych residency and other positions. So Mack was particularly mortified one day to encounter a colleague who recalled, "Oh, you were the medical student who told Franny Moore to stick the sympathetic nervous system chain up his ass." Atul Gawande, the popular writer and surgeon who had followed Mack to Harvard Medical School exactly forty years later, knew the story and speculated that Moore had been tickled by Mack's audacity. Then too, Gawande wrote Mack, "perhaps he saw you were in the 1%."

In one of his last major psychiatric papers at Harvard Medical School, Mack presaged some of the themes that would preoccupy him in years to come, while again opening a window on his fixation with his lost mother. The March 1955 paper, "Primitive Concepts of Illness and the Dilemma of the Sick Child," said primitive people associated illness with evil spirits, relying on shamanic rituals for relief. But modern children are left with no way to process their misfortune and live saddled with guilt, often blaming their own forbidden sexual desires as the cause. Evident in Mack's prodigious research was his interest in occult practices of ancient cultures, altered states of consciousness, spiritual breakthroughs, and mind-body connections that he would often later lament had been grievously devalued in an age of scientific materialism. He found Freudian relevance in his beloved *Pinocchio* story. A child, being whittled into life, turns cruelly on his father-creator, sadistically kills a cricket, and is punished with an illness that leaves him near death. He is saved by "the beautiful, good fairy mother," who offers him magic medicine, which Pinocchio deviously rejects. "When he lies to her his sexual excitement betrays itself and he becomes quite embarrassed as his nose grows several feet long." And so, Mack found, "becoming sick may play into oedipal conflicts."

Mack began his residency in psychiatry at the Massachusetts Mental Health Center, where he fell under the spell of another charismatic mentor, Elvin Semrad, a Nebraska farm boy who had earned a medical degree in the Depression and trained with Hanns Sachs, a refugee disciple of Freud's, before setting up at Boston Psychopathic. Pipe-smoking and avuncular, Semrad was beloved for his shrewd listening and knack for getting to the source of his patients' anxieties. A psychiatrist's best tool for understanding his patients, he told students including Mack, was himself.

At a house party in Cambridge in 1959, Mack caught the eye of a young woman, model-thin and radiant with dark eyes and a dazzling smile, who tried to avoid him. "I did not want to look at this guy, he was so damn handsome," remembered Sally Ann Stahl.[4] Abruptly, the tall and broad-shouldered stranger who seemed to have been shadowing her all night was at her side. "I don't believe we've met," said John Mack.

Sally was then twenty-five, almost four years younger than Mack. She and her brother Irving had been born in Oil City in northwestern Pennsylvania, where their grandparents and father, Julius, once Stalevsky, had migrated from Vilnius, Lithuania. Julius sold real estate and insurance. His proudest moment, memorialized in a prized family photo, was once shaking hands with Israeli Prime Minister Golda Meir. Sally was brought up an orthodox Jew in a Yiddish-speaking home. Refined and poised, though favoring off-the-shoulder blouses to show off her attractive figure, she won the Emily Post Etiquette Award at Oil City High School, where she graduated in 1951, the year Mack finished Oberlin and entered Harvard Medical School. Sally studied psychology and social work at the University of Michigan and was working as a licensed clinical social worker at Beth Israel Hospital in Boston when she met Mack, then chief resident of Mass Mental's Day and Night Hospital, where patients received treatment during the day and returned to their homes at night, an innovation just beginning to catch on in America. Mack's prominence was such that he had been asked to represent Mass Mental at the first national conference on day hospitals in 1958, and the following year he was named a consultant to the Veterans Administration on day hospitals.

In the face of the military draft, before meeting Sally, Mack had traveled to Washington in the fall of 1958 to discuss options for two years in the Air Force. He liked the prospect of England or France but found himself signed up for Japan. Mack asked if Sally would wait for him. No, she said. So he proposed. They wed in July 1959 in the garden of the Massachusetts home of Mack's sister, Mary Lee, and her husband, Sidney Ingbar, an endocrinologist at Harvard Medical School. Mary Stahl was delighted with her new son-in-law. "A doctor! And such nice hands!" But there were times she thought him odd, a *bissel meshuggah*. The bridal couple took a quick honeymoon trip to Colorado, where they learned their first child was already on the way. When Mack shipped out to Tachikawa Air Force Hospital west of Tokyo, Sally continued her social-work training at home then later flew to Japan to meet him. They sent over their two-tone green and white 1955 Oldsmobile and took over part of a large old Japanese-style house in the village of Akishima. Mack was chagrined to discover that the household appliances they so cavalierly imported required the rewiring of the entire village.

In April 1960 Mack was at a Japanese lesson when Sally's contractions began. He rushed home to escort her to the hospital, only to find her obstetrician unavailable. The head of the department ended up pressed into service to deliver their son, Daniel John, the proud father later confiding to his journal he was "a little disapp[ointed] it's not a daughter." When Mack's deployment was up in the summer of 1961, the family left Japan for home. Back in Boston, Mack gravitated to the psychiatric treatment of children. He returned to Mass Mental as a resident in child psychiatry, and he began training in child analysis. He was drawn to the child's world of myth and imagination. Just getting down on the floor with children kept it real, Mack found. He began training, too, with the Boston Psychoanalytic Society and Institute and commenced a study of children's nightmares that would culminate in his first book, *Nightmares and Human Conflict*. Mack joined the faculty of Harvard Medical School as an assistant in psychiatry and became the associate director of psychiatry at Mass Mental, where he began a consultation service to the Massachusetts Division of Youth Services. One of the first of its kind at the time, it provided mental-health services to youths held in maximum security and other assistance to the state's Institute for Juvenile Guidance.

Danny was twenty-two months old when he found he had company—a baby brother, Ken—and he didn't much like it. Once, as Sally was nursing Kenny, Danny tried to put a fifty-cent piece through the baby's soft skull. During nights, he would wake up crying hysterically and, brought to his parents' bed, would restlessly kick them. He would try to kiss Kenny on the forehead, then he would swing at him with his fists. Whenever attention was being paid to the baby, he would drop objects into the toilet or soak himself in the shower. Mack, seeing a rare professional opportunity, observed Danny closely, and over three days in February 1962 he recorded a detailed case study of sibling rivalry that filled twenty-one single-spaced, typewritten pages. Mack concluded that Danny had a way of using play to make sense of the traumatic loss and sudden sharing of his mother's affections.

A year later Sally was pregnant with their third son, Tony. She was in her eighth month and increasingly uncomfortable when she and her husband sought distraction one night at the movies. The theater was hot and crowded, and the desert scenes in the picture felt particularly stifling. But the long movie, *Lawrence of Arabia*, had given Mack an idea. He thought he might study up on Lawrence, and he soon embarked on a full psychological workup.[5]

8

A PRINCE OF OUR DISORDER

Though barely a mile from Harvard Square and across the Charles River from the medical school, the distressed Cambridge City Hospital might as well have occupied a different planet. The prestigious teaching hospitals all around it siphoned off the best physicians, nurses, administrators, and staff, leaving Cambridge a health backwater—a city of one hundred thousand with no adult psychiatric services.

In the fall of 1964, chafing in a middle-management position in charge of inpatient services at the Massachusetts Mental Health Center, Mack learned from his highly-placed brother-in-law Sidney Ingbar that Harvard Medical School was developing an affiliation with the Cambridge City Hospital.

Harvard saw a chance to develop a model of community-based primary health care while eliminating the embarrassment of having a derelict hospital in its backyard.[1] Making it possible was the Community Mental Health Act signed into law by President John F. Kennedy in October 1963, three weeks before his assassination. The act provided federal funds to establish local treatment centers so the mentally ill warehoused in institutions and hospitals could move back into their communities. To be eligible for the money, states had to create catchment areas to consolidate service. Cambridge and Somerville, with a total population of nearly two hundred thousand, was designated one such region.

Mack persuaded the Harvard Department of Psychiatry to adopt the Cambridge City Hospital with himself in charge of psychiatric services. He collected an eager team of nineteen fellow alums of Mass Mental along with his office secretary and assistant, Pat Carr, who would stay loyally at his side for the next four decades. For Mack it was a kind of crusade to develop a model for mental-health services. Eager to demystify psychiatry, they attended rounds and hung out in the physicians' lounge to stay visible and engage the staff, talking about the weather and world news—anything to normalize interactions. They suffered the special enmity of East Cambridge

City Councilor Al Vellucci, a Harvard hater who suggested designating the *Harvard Lampoon* a public urinal. But slowly they attracted supporters.

The unit's licensed clinical social worker, Judy Einzig, never forgot Mack's clinical approach. A twenty-two-year-old woman to whom Einzig gave the pseudonym "Patty" wandered in disheveled, drooling, and thrashing around like a wild animal in search of electric-shock treatment, which she had been unable to get at the state hospital that had been her home for the last eight years.[2] She was quickly labeled retarded. As Einzig remembered in an unpublished essay and recollections more than four decades later, the staff sent for Mack. He addressed Patty soothingly, beginning with an unexpected question: "Do you believe in God?" "Yes," Patty said. Taken off guard, she opened up and began relating her conversations with God as Mack and the clinical staff fell silent. "Our hearts opened to her," Einzig recalled. "By the end of the interview we were all in love with her." Daringly, Mack invited her to stay while they all discussed her case. "As she looked around the room, love and humanity poured toward her," Einzig remembered. "Instantly, Patty was transformed." Later, her father came to visit and was amazed, rediscovering the daughter he'd lost when his wife had died years before. Patty was able to make some visits home, but when she was away from the cocoon of the hospital she would relapse and need to return to the state hospital. Two years later she turned up for another electroshock treatment. Einzig found her strapped to a bed. But when Patty saw the social worker, she stopped writhing and smiled. "Hi, Judy," she beamed. A happy ending would have been too much to ask for, Einzig concluded. She lost touch with Patty. Perhaps she went back to her conversations with God. Yet in all the intervening years, Einzig recalled, "I've never forgotten the deep humanity of that girl. I've never forgotten the deep kindness and human dignity that Dr. Mack extended toward her."

The team continued to gain support. When non-English-speaking patients avoided the hospital, translators of various languages were recruited from the kitchen. A judge with the felicitous name of Lawrence Felony agreed to sign restraining orders all hours of the day or night. Throughout, Mack was inspired by his idol, T. E. Lawrence, whose biography he was beginning to research. He was trying to adapt Lawrence's principles of diplomacy and action to the dynamics of Cambridge, Mack recalled to a *New York Times* interviewer nearly three decades later. "I kept using his way of working."

Psychiatric nurses and addiction treatment were added. Eventually even Vellucci came around. Later elected mayor, he proclaimed Mack an honorary citizen of Cambridge. In 1993 the Cambridge Hospital would win the American Hospital Association's prize for excellence in community health care, with First Lady Hillary Clinton going on national television to sing its praises.

Mack meanwhile added to his prestige with a prescient book, *Nightmares and Human Conflict*, which he dedicated to his sons, "who showed me how important nightmares can be." It expanded on two papers he had written for psychoanalytic journals and would seem especially applicable to his later abduction research. His prodigious scholarship reached back to the ancients, who personified and sexualized the terrifying dream as a fiend that crushed the sleeper's chest, an *incubus* (or female *succubus*) from the Latin *incubare* (to lie on, as in to incubate and hatch or lay eggs). A North Borneo tribe still believed in an evil force disguised as malevolent creatures that came to women in the night to conceive children and sometimes steal away their pregnancies. The term "nightmare" itself was traceable to the Sanskrit *mara* (destroyer), which became the Anglo-Saxon *mare* (demon). The root migrated into the English *mare* (female horse), and the horse lent its symbolic sexual potency to the nightmare. Ordinary dreams occurred during Rapid Eye Movement sleep, Mack reported, but nightmares occurred during non-REM or short-wave sleep. Benign or terrifying, dreams were a way for the brain to resolve conflicts and not, as Freud said, a way of prolonging sleep. They served an evolutionary purpose, playing a part in development of the central nervous system, Mack wrote. And nightmares functioned to preserve the organism, honing a range of coping mechanisms for extreme circumstances.

How parents dealt with the children's nightmares was also noteworthy, Mack said. Parents needed to comfort their children and help them distinguish between fantasy and reality; failure to do so could be harmful. With his book, published in 1970, no one could deny Mack's expertise in matters of sleep disturbances and waking fantasy—nor could they claim he didn't know what a nightmare was. He was also embarking on another foray into the shadowlands of the mind, *Borderline States in Psychiatry*, an anthology that he edited and introduced with an opening chapter. A dense survey of the extensive professional literature on shifting definitions of mental illness, the compendium, published in 1975, showcased Mack's expertise in aberrant mental states.

He was also hard at work on the book that would crystallize his celebrity. Since the night with Sally at *Lawrence of Arabia* in 1963, Mack had been gripped by the legend of the desert-blasted, blue-eyed British warrior/statesman with a whiff of perversion who had redrawn the map of the Middle East. He was well into his own pursuit of Lawrence, one of the most quixotic figures of the twentieth century, a quest that would consume thirteen years of research and writing on three continents and culminate in a prize-winning biography, *A Prince of Our Disorder*. "It was clear this really caught him," Sally recalled more than half a century later from a hospital bed shortly before her death from cancer.

Mack felt compelled to correct the film's distortions of history. Lawrence, who stood barely five-foot-five in contrast to Peter O'Toole's six-foot-three, was no hysterical sadist in battle, Mack wrote. He may have lost control of his men at times, but he was far too self-possessed to revel in their orgies of recrimination. Lawrence was, in many ways, an anti-egotist, so averse to aggrandizement that he took a pseudonym to serve in the military. Mack was drawn to Lawrence's incessant psychologizing—could a psychiatrist find a worthier subject than someone perpetually torturing himself with self-examination? And he was astonished to realize that they were almost contemporaries. Mack was four and a half years old when Lawrence died in a motorcycle crash in 1935 at age forty-six; had he lived, he would have been seventy-five when Mack began his research at age thirty-four.

He learned that Lawrence had two living brothers in England, two others having been killed in World War I. The older brother, Montague Robert (M. R., or Bob), a religiously ethereal ex-missionary and physician, had retreated in obscurity to a rectory in southern England. Lawrence's younger brother, Arnold Walter, a professor of Hellenic archaeology, was often away in Greece. Mack tracked them both down.

He approached M. R. doctor to doctor, arranging in August of 1964 to fly to England for a meeting at the rectory. High on his agenda was an answer to the question of the source of Lawrence's guilt. Mack was ready to offer assurances that nothing would appear in print for five to ten years (it would actually be a dozen years), and he avowed the "family's right to see any thing I'd write." Mack was curious about the development of Lawrence's conscience and his high aspirations as well as his early influences at home, his young strivings and ideas, and his "unsureness & unworthiness from early evidence in childhood," which, he wrote, "may leave vulnerability." Mack wondered about Lawrence's yen for travel, particularly curious as to "why Arabia & the East"? He wanted to be sure to ask M. R. about their brotherly relationship—who was the leader?—and Lawrence's relationship with his father and mother. There was also a girl Mack had read about; was she a "lost love"?

The other brother, Arnold Walter, controlled Lawrence's archives but didn't respond. Mack traveled back to England anyway and reached Arnold by phone at home. "Nothing on that subject interests me," Arnold said. Mack said he had come all that way, couldn't they just talk? Finally, Arnold said he had a meeting at the British Museum at 6:00, and Mack could come half an hour beforehand. An hour would be better, Mack said. He would need time to thaw out. That made Arnold laugh, and he softened, eventually granting Mack the archival access he sought. Mack was also able to meet many of Lawrence's surviving comrades, who, initially suspicious, soon warmed to the big Yank with his boundless enthusiasm and ingratiating manner.

By the time Mack sat down to write, it was clearer than ever that he had chosen his subject for deeply personal reasons, "deriving from my own predilections and psychological makeup," as he wrote. "I have long been fascinated by the relationship between the inner life—between dreams, hopes and visions—and actions or activity in the 'real' world." And, notably, Mack was fascinated by what constituted heroism. Revealingly, he quoted from Irving Howe's essay, "T. E. Lawrence: The Problem of Heroism": "The hero as he appears in the tangle of modern life is a man struggling with a vision he can neither realize nor abandon, 'a man with a load on his mind.'" Mack, in fact, took his title from Howe's description of Lawrence—"A Prince of Our Disorder."

Lawrence's life began with a burdensome family secret, Mack wrote. His father, Thomas Chapman, who boasted Sir Walter Raleigh as a distant ancestor, had been married in Ireland to a vinegary cousin who gave birth to their four daughters. But sometime after 1878 Thomas ran off with the children's vivacious Scottish governess, Sarah, to Wales. They lived there, unmarried, as husband and wife, took the surname "Lawrence," and had five surviving sons. The second of those sons, Thomas Edward, or T. E., was born in 1888 and grew up with a passion for history, especially Arthurian romance. Young Lawrence was closeted in make-believe, manly deeds, and heroic fantasies that served to obscure the ignominious reality of his illegitimacy.

Mack tracked down the first and apparently only woman Lawrence had ever pursued romantically, Janet Laurie, a childhood friend two years his senior. Although she was drawn to his younger brother, Will (who would later die in World War I), Lawrence surprisingly proposed to her, taking her so aback she laughed in astonishment. Lawrence may never have recovered. Tellingly, he would inscribe the Greek words for "Does Not Care" over Clouds Hill, his small cottage in Dorset in Southwest England, and he would never again, so far as was known, attempt to form a love bond with a woman, or anyone.

Strikingly, for a figure renowned for bold action, Lawrence was essentially a man of the spirit, focused on mastery of the self, Mack said. From his earliest days digging in the ruins of Carchemish in Syria and, once the Great War broke out, as a British intelligence officer in Cairo, he seemed attuned to the Arabs and they to him. When Arab tribesmen rose in revolt against their Turkish masters, Lawrence became their guerilla commander in league with Faisal (later King of Syria and Iraq) while also serving the Crown's national interests in the field. But when his forces conquered Damascus, Lawrence returned to Palestine. "Never outstay a climax," he said. Lawrence's success, Mack wrote, was due not only to his formidable intellect and command of history, geography, customs, tribal structure, and language but also to a striking ability to influence superiors like Winston Churchill. "I have a fine taste in chiefs," Lawrence said.

Mack spent considerable effort researching two shatteringly violent events in Lawrence's life. The first was in November 1917, when he was captured by the brutal Turkish governor, Hajim Bey, and, by Lawrence's account, subjected to an atrocious gang rape. He finally escaped, but, as he later wrote, "the citadel of my integrity had been irrevocably lost." The assault haunted Lawrence for life, Mack wrote, and played a particular role in a second savage episode nearly seven months later. A column of Turkish and German troops was retreating through Tafas, raping women as they went. Lawrence's outraged Arab rebels fell upon the enemy, who retaliated by slaughtering the villagers, bayonetting many women and children. Lawrence's guerillas then counterattacked, cutting the Turkish column in three. One section got away badly mauled, but the two others were "wiped out completely," Lawrence reported to headquarters. "We ordered 'no prisoners' and the men obeyed." In *Seven Pillars of Wisdom* he quoted himself: "The best of you brings me the most Turkish dead." Some two hundred Turkish prisoners, despite the order, escaped the massacre. In a ghastly epilogue, their Arab captors then came upon one of their own men on the field, bleeding to death from a thigh wound. "In the fashion of today's battle," Lawrence recounted, "he had been further tormented by bayonets hammered through his shoulder and other leg into the ground, pinning him out like a collected insect." The dying man implicated the Turkish prisoners, who were then methodically murdered. "They said nothing in the moments before we opened fire," Lawrence wrote. "At last their heap ceased moving."

Mack found Lawrence deeply conflicted over the massacre and guilt ridden over his own loss of control. He was confronted in Arabia with an array of evils and "tried always to do the least harmful of them, and to do it so that the fewest small people were harmed by it." But the effects were malign. Lawrence's sexual humiliation at Deraa and the slaughter at Tafas, Mack wrote, somehow set off, suddenly and devastatingly, "forbidden or un-acceptable sexual, aggressive and vengeful impulses." What was until then in Lawrence a kind of rigorous self-abnegation and puritanism channeled itself exaggeratedly into a powerful need for self-abasement, a quest for penance through severe degradation. It found outlet in a compulsion for flagellation, a yearning to be whipped.

Mack now confronted a dilemma: How much, if any, of this sordid chapter was germane to Lawrence's biography? Arnold Lawrence questioned whether Mack needed to go into his brother's sexual history at all. Mack reasoned that a biographer was justified in delving into his subject's intimate life if it was vitally related to his public life and required for an understanding of his character. "In my opinion all of these conditions pertain to some degree in Lawrence's case," Mack wrote.

In examining Lawrence's psyche as a psychiatrist, Mack was struck by his close attachment to his mother, made closer by the discovery of the secret of his illegitimacy. As a youth he shied away from girls, and his one attempt at a romantic liaison, with Janet Laurie, was painfully rebuffed. Mack found no evidence that Lawrence as an adult ever engaged voluntarily in any kind of sexual relationship, with either sex, for intimacy or pleasure. It was not that he was asexual but rather that from childhood he repressed any feelings of desire and remained fearful and inhibited when it came to sex. At the same time, homosexuality troubled him less than heterosexual love—he had seen enough of it in the desert culture of Arabia—and his closest attachments were always with men.

About the time Lawrence died in 1935, Mack wrote, his brother Arnold received a letter from a young Scotsman named John Bruce, who revealed a prurient secret. Bruce had been hired as Lawrence's "personal bodyguard" to administer regular floggings. Lawrence had invented an imaginary "Uncle Ted" who was inflicting punishments for an unspecified offense, and Bruce had been paid to carry them out, believing he was truly serving the uncle. The matter lay buried for more than thirty years until Bruce sold his story to the *Sunday Times* in 1968. "How Lawrence of Arabia Cracked Up" revealed that in 1923, while writing *Seven Pillars of Wisdom*, Lawrence suffered a series of nightmarish flashbacks to his rape six years before. To expunge them, he directed Bruce to reenact the assault. The fanciful tale of the punishing uncle came later. According to Lawrence's elaborate ruse, he had stolen £150 from an uncle—the Old Man—who threatened to reveal Lawrence's illegitimacy unless he paid back the money or submitted to a regimen of severe floggings, delivered in a precise number with a metal whip on his bare buttocks until he ejaculated. And what was the crime for which Lawrence was punishing himself so heinously? Mack concluded it was Lawrence's sexual surrender to spare himself further torture at Deraa. Lawrence was convinced he had sacrificed the fundamental integrity of his very soul. More shamefully, he had derived a measure of pleasure from it, plaguing him with an insatiable desire to both put an end to it and keep reliving it.

But Mack remained careful to place Lawrence's private torment in the context of a nobler legacy, an idealistic determination to give the Arabs the land and liberty they had won on the battlefield and transform the geography of the Middle East. Back home on leave in England, Lawrence had arranged a meeting between his ally Faisal and the Zionist leader Chaim Weizmann, aimed at fostering Arab-Jewish cooperation in Palestine, a goal of Lawrence's that at the time seemed feasible. But the secret Sykes-Picot Agreement of 1916 and the Paris Peace Conference crushed those hopes as the victorious powers proceeded to re-carve the Middle East into expedient new "zones of influence," embittering Lawrence, whose promises to his warriors were thereby nullified. Syria and Lebanon went to France, Palestine and Trans-jordan to England. Mesopotamia was divided up between the two powers. "As for Irak," Lawrence wrote in 1927, "well, some day they will be fit for self-government, and then they will not want a king: but whether 7 or 70 or 700 years hence, God knows."

Lawrence's death was an accident but was not entirely accidental, Mack wrote. He was pushing his Brough motorcycle to a daredevil speed near his beloved Clouds Hill in Dorset when he suddenly overtook two boys on bicycles. He swerved past an oncoming truck to avoid them, lost control, and flew over the handlebars, landing on his head. He died six days later. "There is no evidence of a direct suicidal intent in the accident," Mack wrote. "But it is known that men who are living without hope or interest in their lives, or have suffered a recent severe loss, like Lawrence's loss of his work in the RAF, are more prone to accidents."

Mack was finishing his research on the book in the fall of 1973 when his father, Edward, and stepmother, Ruth, left New York for a weekend at their country home in Thetford, Vermont. That Friday in September, Ed drove off for groceries. On the way home he collided with a truck and was killed instantly. Once again violent death had widowed Ruth. John was plunged into existential grief. He had never stopped mourning his mother, lost to him in infancy. His beloved grandmother Della had died, along with her husband. Now his father had been struck down at age sixty-eight.

A few days later the shattered Macks—Ruth, John, Mary Lee, and other relatives—gathered numbly in the lounge of City College's Finley Student Center in Harlem for an impromptu memorial service—"brief and simple, the way Eddie would have liked it," a faculty colleague said.[3] Mourners remembered him as a "sunshine spirit," a tall, sweet soul with receding gray hair who, like his son, was an enthusiast, one to whom "today's hero was the most heroic, today's scenery was the most scenic, and today's food the most delicious ever." Academia esteemed him: Garrett Mattingly had dedicated his Pulitzer Prize–winning 1959 history *The Armada* to Edward and Ruth.

Edward was also remembered as an author in his own right, having written books on the New York industrialist Peter Cooper, on Thomas Hughes, an earlier Cooper biographer and author of *Tom Brown's School Days*, and on English public schools. His cubicle mate, the renowned Dickens biographer Edgar Johnson, recalled how Eddie would join the faculty lunch table and skip nimbly from "Tom Jones" to "The Alexandria Quartet," "Candide," Noel Coward, and the latest break in the spreading Watergate scandal. The austere and Lincolnesque college president, Buell G. Gallagher, recalled Eddie's thankless service on the Discipline Committee during the turbulent 1960s, for which he had endured indignities, harassment, and "venal cruelty." Dean Samuel Middlebrook said simply, "*Si monumentum requieris, circumspice*" (If you wish to see his monument, look about you).

In April 1977 Columbia University awarded *A Prince of Our Disorder* the Pulitzer Prize for biography, selecting it above ninety-three other submissions. "This book has such distinctive merits as to stand in a class by itself, with no serious competitors," the three-member jury decided. The *Harvard Gazette* asked Mack if there was a single theme in the book that benefited from his psychoanalytic training. Yes, he said, "the whole question of heroism and Lawrence's need to be heroic." Later Sally found him sitting with his head in his hands. "You just won the Pulitzer," she said. "Why are you depressed?" "Because now they'll expect me to keep it up," he said.

Mack was indeed haunted by Lawrence. "I have found it easy, though at times disturbing, to identify with his hopes, his actions and his pain," he wrote. Lawrence enabled him "to see possibilities that were not dreamed of before." He may also have identified with George Bernard Shaw's pointed critique in a 1922 letter to Lawrence that compared him to the headstrong and doomed defender of Khartoum, the English adventurer Major General Charles George Gordon. "You are evidently a very dangerous man," Shaw wrote. "Most men who are any good are." The following year Shaw wrote Lawrence again: "Like all heroes, and, I must add, all idiots, you greatly exaggerate your power of moulding the universe to your personal convictions."

9

"UFO CHILLER"

The Soviet Union's electrifying 1957 launch of the world's first artificial satellite, Sputnik 1, followed a month later by a second earth-orbiting satellite with the world's first space dog, Laika, turned the world's eyes to the skies. Within days, Project Blue Book was swamped with some three hundred reports of UFO sightings, a cluster of them over the west Texas town of Levelland, where multiple witnesses reported large flying objects before their car engines and lights failed. A Blue Book investigator reported that "a severe electrical storm . . . stimulated the populace into a high level of excitement." But an atmospheric physicist found no storm in the area that night.

The 1940s and '50s had taken the phenomenon beyond sightings of craft to fantastical interactions with space emissaries as recounted by a colorful new group of enthusiasts.[1] Dubbed "contactees," they claimed regular communication with Space Brothers (and occasionally Sisters), gorgeous angels in space suits on celestial missions to aid beleaguered humanity. As far back as the mid-1700s, the Swedish scientist and mystic Emanuel Swedenborg had chronicled astral travels to the moon and other bodies where he encountered enlightened creatures. Such accounts proliferated in the nineteenth century and continued into the twentieth century, notably when a Polish-born occultist and science-fiction devotee, George Adamski, described a 1952 encounter with a UFO in the desert between California and Arizona. Out of it, he said, walked a being five and a half feet tall with long, blond hair and a high forehead who let Adamski know by gestures and telepathy that he was from Venus and was here to warn humanity against its warlike ways. Many similar accounts by Adamski and others emerged, all strikingly short of convincing evidence, leaving the contactees as often-derided fringe players in a long and perplexing mystery. But other episodes continued.

In Socorro, New Mexico, Officer Lonnie Zamora was chasing a speeder in April 1964 when, he later recounted, "I heard a roar and saw a flame" in the sky to the southwest. Suspecting an explosion at a nearby dynamite shack, he rushed toward the site to find what he described as a large, egglike object supported on slender legs. "I saw two people in white coveralls very close to the object," Zamora told Blue Book. "One of these persons seemed to turn and look straight at my car and seemed startled—seemed to quickly jump somewhat. I don't recall noting any particular shape or possibly any hats or headgear. These persons appeared normal in shape—but possibly they were small adults or small kids." The policeman drove in for a closer look, but he lost sight of the object behind a hill, and when he saw it again the two beings had vanished. He got out of his car and walked closer, whereupon, he related, he heard several loud thumps like a door being slammed, and the object began to roar. "It started at a low frequency, but quickly the roar rose in frequency and in loudness." Zamora saw flames and the bottom of the object started glowing blue and orange. Fearing an explosion, he took cover behind his cruiser as the craft hovered, now silently, before it flew off, first slowly and then with gathering speed. A sergeant who had joined Zamora also saw the craft depart, and together they checked the landing spot, finding charred grass and depressions in the soil.

Later Zamora gave his account to the FBI and to an army commander at the White Sands Missile Range. Blue Book's astronomical consultant Allen Hynek also arrived to question Zamora and investigate the landing site. Long a debunker of UFO reports, Hynek was growing increasingly confused, beginning to doubt his own doubts. He left Zamora "more puzzled now than I arrived," convinced that the police officer had encountered *something*. In the end, Blue Book called the case "unsolved," meaning it could not be explained away, despite later reports of a possible student hoax. Writing in 1966 in *Studies in Intelligence*, the professional journal of the CIA, Hector Quintanilla, Blue Book's last chief officer, called it "the best-documented case on record."

In September 1965 John Grant Fuller, a fifty-one-year-old *Saturday Review* columnist, Broadway playwright, and radio and television producer who had worked on *Candid Camera* and *The DuPont Show of the Week*, read an *Associated Press* clipping from the *New York Times* on a rash of UFO sightings in Texas, Oklahoma, New Mexico, and Kansas.[2] *The Times* didn't cover UFOs much, so that was interesting right there. From NICAP, Fuller learned of a fresh case in Exeter, New Hampshire, about an hour north of Boston, not far from Pease Air Force base in Portsmouth and home to one of the nation's noblest prep schools, Phillips Exeter Academy, founded in 1781.

According to a detailed report by a NICAP investigator and former Air Force security officer, Raymond E. Fowler, two police officers had gotten a close look at a huge, floating object and there were lots of other witnesses. Fuller's *Saturday Review* "Trade Winds" column in early October told the story of eighteen-year-old Norman Muscarello, who was hitching home to Exeter on Route 150 shortly after midnight on September 3 when, he told the Exeter police, a large airborne object, bright red with flashing lights, approached him with "a yawing, kitelike motion." Officer Eugene Bertrand, out on patrol, had just stopped at a parked car on a highway overpass where two women were hysterical over a flying, red-flashing object they said had tailed them from a nearby town. Called in, Bertrand picked up Muscarello at the police station and drove him back to where he had seen the object.[3]

They parked and were walking into a field when Muscarello yelled, "There it is!" Bertrand saw it too, coming over the trees about two hundred feet away. It had five bright-red lights in a row that dimmed right to left and then left to right, "just like an advertising sign." Bertrand's first reaction was to reach for his revolver. A second officer, David Hunt, pulled up, and all three gaped at the big, silent thing floating and wobbling now just one hundred feet away. When it disappeared, they drove, shaken, back to the police station to put the whole story on the blotter. "We weren't believing our eyes," Bertrand recalled. "Your mind is telling you this can't be true, and yet you're seeing it."

Fuller crisscrossed Exeter, tape-recording dozens of witnesses with convincing tales of having encountered strange craft often hovering near the power lines. What infuriated him, and many of the witnesses he spoke to, was the Air Force's insistence that people were seeing reflections or mirages, airplanes, balloons, planets, or stars, as if the people of Exeter, many of them combat veterans, didn't know what B-52s, the moon, or Venus looked like. And what of the jets from the air base that were forever streaking around after these things? Were they chasing Venus too?

While winding up his research in Exeter, Fuller had heard about a Portsmouth couple, Betty and Barney Hill, so traumatized by an encounter with a flying craft in the White Mountains four years before that they could barely discuss it.[4] They were all the more reluctant because the husband was Black and the wife white. They were involved in civil-rights work and feared that any notoriety could erode their credibility in the struggle for racial justice.

Fuller had already talked to more than sixty people with tales of treetop sightings, and he didn't think he needed to interview any more, particularly if they were hesitant to come forward.

Several weeks later, though, Fuller was in Connecticut talking to *Look* editors and television producers about a possible documentary when calls started pouring in from Exeter. On October 25, 1965, the *Boston Traveler* broke a big scoop: "UFO Chiller—Did They Seize Couple?" It was the story of the Hills—how a UFO had followed and stopped their car in the mountains four years before, how they had been taken captive by the humanoid crew and subjected to pseudo-medical tests, and how they had been so terrorized they required hypnotherapy by a top Boston psychiatrist.

The disclosure had caught the Hills themselves largely by surprise. They had told their story to a UFO group in Quincy, Massachusetts, in November 1963—this was their first public recounting of the episode some two years prior to the *Boston Traveler* article—and a *Traveler* reporter, John Luttrell, had somehow recently gotten hold of a recording. Luttrell had badgered the Hills for an interview, but, getting nowhere, he wrote the story over their objections.

With the avalanche of publicity loosed by the newspaper's series, the Hills decided to clear the air and present their story more completely at a public meeting in nearby Dover. Fuller made sure to show up. The Hills, he later wrote, reached out to him, asking if he would write their story as a sequel to *Incident at Exeter*, and he agreed. (A niece of Betty's, Kathleen Marden, would give a slightly different account in *Captured!*, the 2007 book she and UFO researcher Stanton T. Friedman wrote about the Hill case, drawing on family accounts and other material beyond what Fuller had forty years earlier.[5]) Either way, Fuller's 1966 book, *The Interrupted Journey: Two Lost Hours "Aboard a Flying Saucer"*, based heavily on transcripts of the Hills' hypnotic regressions, became a sensation, all the more so because no one could say the Hills were copying anyone or anything—no one had ever encountered a story remotely like theirs before (although a Brazilian farmer, Antônio Vilas-Boas, had said he was forced into an egg-shaped craft to have sex with a humanoid female in 1957.) The far more elaborate Hills case would rate a top 5 out of 5 in both the quality of the witness accounts and subsequent investigation, according to a 1987 review of 270 reported abduction cases by

Thomas E. Bullard, a noted folklorist and UFO researcher at Indiana University. And it would find its way to the big screen as *The UFO Incident*, a 1975 biopic with James Earl Jones and Estelle Parsons as Barney and Betty Hill.

The Hills had initially contacted the Air Force and then Donald Keyhoe of NICAP. The UFO group dispatched investigators, who found the couple's conscious recall of the episode intriguing and suggested hypnosis as a way of accessing buried memories. A series of referrals led them to Dr. Benjamin Simon, a prominent Boston psychiatrist who had collaborated with director John Huston in *Let There Be Light*, a searing 1946 army documentary on the mental problems of returning troops that was long withheld by the Pentagon for its troubling content.

Simon saw the need for hypnosis. In cases like the Hills', he wrote, "it can be the key to the locked room, the amnesiac period." Under hypnosis, Simon said, experiences blocked by amnesia may be retrieved sooner than through other means. But there was no magic to it. Hypnosis delivered little that was not otherwise accessible. It was often seen as the royal road to truth. But it was truth as understood by the subject, which may or may not correspond with ultimate truth. What that was, Simon was to find, would prove maddeningly elusive.

10

"THE INTERRUPTED JOURNEY"

On a Sunday in mid-September 1961, John Fuller recounted, Betty and Barney Hill and their dachshund, Delsey, set off from Portsmouth, New Hampshire, in Betty's blue and white Chevy Bel Air for a quick holiday to Niagara Falls, Toronto, and Montreal. They were taking an impromptu honeymoon sixteen months after their wedding, which had marked a second marriage for both.[1] Betty, curly-haired and vivacious, was a caseworker for the New Hampshire Department of Welfare. Barney, stolid and handsome, was a postal worker and World War II veteran.

On the night of September 19, with Hurricane Esther churning up the Atlantic coast toward Cape Cod, they cut short the trip and headed home. Just south of Lancaster, New Hampshire, on Route 3, Betty noticed a bright light, and then a second one that seemed to grow bigger and brighter, keeping up with them. They first thought it might be a satellite, or a Piper Cub. They stopped to listen for the sound of an engine but heard nothing. Peering through binoculars, Barney saw what looked like the fuselage of a plane with blinking lights, although he could see no wings. Betty saw a cigar-shaped object moving erratically and flashing red, amber, green, and blue lights. In the back seat, Delsey began whimpering and cowering. Betty, remembering that her sister in Kingston, New Hampshire—just seven miles outside Exeter—had seen a UFO in 1957, kept telling Barney to take another look. It had to be a plane, Barney kept saying. But he was getting spooked. The road was deserted.

Nearing midnight, they drove past Cannon Mountain and then the rock formation and state symbol long known (until its later collapse) as the Old Man of the Mountain. Home was only a few hours away.

The thing was getting closer, now maybe only a few hundred feet off the ground. It looked huge. The blinking lights had become a steady, white glow. Betty picked up the binoculars again and gasped. She could now make out a craft of enormous size with a double row of windows. She demanded Barney stop the car and look at it. He made excuses—it would disappear by then, he insisted. But after peering up through the windshield, he slammed on the brakes and stopped in the middle of the road, leaving the motor running. He was no longer worried about oncoming traffic.

It was hovering silently just above treetop level barely a city block away—a gigantic, glowing pancake.

Barney stepped out of the car for a better view. With that, the enormous thing swung toward him. Then, for some reason he later had trouble explaining, he found himself walking across a field toward it. He remembered seeing a row of gleaming white windows and two finlike extensions with red lights on the tips. He got within fifty feet as it hovered at treetop level, looming larger than a jetliner.

Betty had seen Barney leave the car but was not immediately aware that he was walking across the field toward the object. She was worrying because they had left the car in the middle of the road. She was preparing to scoot behind the wheel to move to safety when she realized Barney had disappeared. She screamed into the darkness for him to come back.

As he approached the object, Barney put the binoculars to his eyes and halted, stricken. He could clearly see rows of windows, and behind them at least half a dozen humanoid figures in some kind of uniform were bracing themselves against the tilt of the craft. Then he watched them turn away to a control panel behind the windows—all but one of the figures, that is, who stayed at the window staring down at him. Barney remembered thinking the one who remained seemed like the leader, and he was mesmerized by its large, slanting eyes.

Overcome with terror, he thrust down the binoculars—snapping the strap and bruising his neck, he found later—and raced back screaming through the field to the car, where Betty had been shrieking for him to come back. The car was still sitting in the middle of the road, motor running. He threw it into gear and shot off, yelling that they were about to be captured. He told Betty to roll down the window and watch for the craft, but it had disappeared. She looked up and saw nothing. But, ominously, there were no stars either. Was the thing over the car, blocking out the sky? Then, creepily, they heard a series of electronic beeps from the direction of the trunk and felt the car vibrate. It was, they said later, like someone had dropped a tuning fork on the car.

All of that, Fuller recounted, they pretty much consciously remembered afterward. But from then on, their memory of the ride grew increasingly hazy. They drove on in a strange state, hearing the beeping again but somehow not talking much. Finally, as dawn was breaking the next day, they reached Portsmouth, Barney mentioning they had reached home "a little later than expected." Both their windup watches had stopped working. Barney felt dirty, and for some reason he went into the bathroom to examine his lower abdomen. Then they stood together at the window staring skyward before tumbling into bed and falling into a nine-hour dreamless slumber.

The next afternoon, Betty unaccountably packed away, in the deep recesses of her closet, the blue-and-purple patterned dress and the shoes she had worn on the trip. Barney was mystified by the badly scraped tops of his shoes. Betty, checking the car, found a dozen shiny, half-dollar-size circles on the trunk, where they thought the beeping and vibrations had come from. Wondering if they might be magnetic, she tested them with a compass; the needle spun wildly. That's when they decided to call Pease Air Force Base. Betty also checked Donald Keyhoe's book *The Flying Saucer Conspiracy* out of the library and wrote Keyhoe a synopsis of their encounter.

Ten days after they returned home, Fuller wrote, Betty was visited by a series of terrifyingly vivid dreams. On a lonely stretch of countryside, their car was halted at a roadblock. Strange men in uniforms bundled them aboard an unfamiliar craft, leading them down separate curving corridors to laboratory rooms for peculiar tests. The nightmares continued for five nights and then just as suddenly disappeared. But one day, driving in the countryside outside Portsmouth, they came across a car blocking the road. Betty was inexplicably overcome by terror. Both fell into a debilitating anxiety, setting off a series of counseling referrals that ended in the office of Dr. Benjamin Simon.

Under the psychiatrist's careful ministrations, their amnesia gave way to astounding new details—although to shield them from additional trauma, Simon ended each hypnotic session with the instruction that when they awoke they would not remember what they had said. Barney recalled under hypnosis that the figure that had regarded him from the window looked like . . . a German Nazi! It wore a black, shiny uniform with a black scarf dangling over the left shoulder and had mesmerizing wraparound eyes. Reliving the experience, Barney wept and writhed in terror, a convincing affect that Simon took as genuine.

In her hypnotic state, according to Fuller, Betty now remembered that after Barney had seen the craft and raced back to the car and they had resumed their journey, he had suddenly turned off the highway onto a narrow road, where they were halted by a group of figures. The engine died. Barney tried frantically to restart it. Strange men dressed alike pulled them from the car, but Betty kept thinking she was asleep and couldn't open her eyes. When she did manage to open them, she saw Barney behind her being sleepwalked away by two short men. "Barney! Wake up!" she cried, hearing the figure at her side asking whether Barney was his name.

Simon was surprised to hear that the intruder spoke good English. Yes, Betty confirmed matter-of-factly, but he had a foreign accent. The men brought them to a ramp that led into the craft. Betty balked and was told sharply to hurry up, that they didn't have much time. She was taken to a room, while Barney was led off elsewhere. Betty objected, wanting him there with her, but she was told they only had enough equipment in each room to do one person at a time. She remembered that they sat her on a stool, pushed up the sleeve of her dress, and examined her arm with some kind of magnifier, taking a scraping of her skin and preserving it in plastic. They put her head in a brace and shined a light in her eyes, mouth, throat, and ears, and they pulled and cut a few strands of hair. They clipped a piece of fingernail and took off her shoes to examine her feet. Then they said they needed to check her nervous system. She was told to remove her dress, but before she could pull down the back zipper, the examiner yanked it—Betty thought she could hear the stitching rip. (Later she found a one-inch tear on the left side of the zipper and, on the right, two inches of ripped stitching.) She saw an array of needles, each attached to a wire that connected to a monitor, which were run along her head, neck, legs, and back. Then the examiner returned with a longer needle that alarmed her. He was going to put it into her navel, he explained. It was a pregnancy test. She felt excruciating pain, as from a knife thrust, and cried out. The examiner ran a hand over her eyes, and the pain vanished.

Simon asked if there were any sexual advances. No, Betty said.

In a subsequent session, Fuller recounted, Betty added yet a stranger detail, a remembered conversation with the one she called the leader. Relieved at the welcome release from her pain, she recalled telling him that no one would believe her amazing story, she needed some proof, and she asked if she could take something back with her.

Like what? he asked. She fixed on a large book with strange, vertical writing. Could she have that? He said yes. Exhilarated, Betty asked where they had come from. He in turn asked what she knew of the universe. Not much, she admitted. Then there was no point going into it, he said. But he showed her a large map, a star chart, with lines showing trade routes and expeditions. Betty could make little of it.

She became aware of a commotion outside, and the examiner and others came running in. Alarmed, she wondered if something had happened to Barney. The examiner made her open her mouth and started tugging at her teeth. Why did the other one's teeth come out and hers didn't? Betty laughed and explained that Barney wore dentures. Eventually, they said, Barney was ready. The two could leave.

Then, to her dismay, she remembered, the leader reached out and took the book back. Furious, Betty said he had promised. Yes, he agreed, but the others had objected.

It was the only proof she had, Betty insisted.

That was the point, the leader said. They didn't want her to remember; they wanted her to forget.

She would not forget! Betty insisted. She would never forget!

It wouldn't do her any good, the leader said. Barney wouldn't remember, or if he did, he would remember it differently, and they would both get confused, so it would be better if they just forgot.

And then they were getting in the car and watching a big, orange ball disappear in the sky. They found themselves driving home to Portsmouth, not talking about it.

Those were Betty's recollections under hypnosis, Fuller said. Simon called in Barney next, to compare accounts.

In his altered state, Barney remembered being stopped at the roadblock by an orange glow. Two men moved him out of the car, down the road, and onto a ramp and into a strange craft. He was told to keep his eyes closed, and he complied out of the terror of seeing their eyes. He stumbled over a bulkhead. He heard a voice reassuring him that he would not be harmed. He didn't see Betty. He was put on an operating table, and he recalled that his feet stuck over the end. He felt his shoes being removed and hands examining his body, counting his vertebrae. A finger pushed at the base of his spine. To his discomfort, but without pain, he felt a narrow tube being inserted into his rectum and withdrawn. Then he was turned over on his back, his mouth was opened, and he could feel two fingers inside. Something scratched lightly against his left arm. He thought a cup was placed over his groin. (Barney later told authors Marden and Friedman that a sperm sample was taken, although he felt no sexual arousal.) Then he felt his shoes being put on and felt happy. He sensed it was over. He was at the car, and Betty was coming down the road, grinning. He thought she must have made a bathroom stop in the woods. She got into the car, and they resumed the drive home. Neither spoke.

Simon was deeply perplexed. How could two people describe, completely separately but so similarly and vividly, an unearthly encounter like nothing in human history? In one way, however, it resembled the trauma cases he had treated after the battle of Guadalcanal. The breakdowns came not during the fierce fighting with the Japanese but afterward, when the troops could afford the luxury of getting sick.

As Simon saw it, there were four possibilities: Betty and Barney were lying (unlikely); it was a dual hallucination (improbable); it was a dream or illusion, some kind of experience enhanced by fantasy (conceivable); or it actually happened (unthinkable).

Most likely, Simon theorized, Betty had dreamed these things and shared them with Barney, who adopted them as his memories as well. The psychiatrist tested this out on Barney under hypnosis.

It wasn't a dream, Barney insisted. The men in the road were real. He wished it were a hallucination.

Simon also asked Betty whether this all could have been in her dreams.

She knew when she dreamed, she said. This was different.

In the final stages of treatment, Simon, with their agreement, stopped implanting the hypnotic suggestion that, upon waking, they would forget what they had recalled. Now Barney said he remembered that the interior of the craft was filled with bluish fluorescent light that cast no shadows. Befitting a circular craft, the rooms were pie-slice-shaped, with the point cut off or blunted. The ceiling, floor, and walls were smooth and barren, no ornaments and no furniture aside from the table he was lying on. The men had large craniums, their heads tapering to a pointed chin. Their eyes wrapped around the side of their heads and seemed to follow him wherever he was. Their mouths were straight lines, without lips, and parted slightly to issue what sounded like murmurings. Their skin looked grayish and metallic. They had no hair or noses, just two nostril slits. They communicated their thoughts directly into his mind.

Betty now remembered that the beeping had sent them into a kind of hypnotic trance. She recalled struggling to awaken as she was being led to the craft and noticing a movable rim on the outside, like a gyroscope. She remembered a curved corridor with doors to different rooms and a sense that the craft was metallic. She thought, too, that the leader and the examiner were different from the crew members, maybe taller, but she was afraid to look closely. All their bodies seemed out of proportion, with oversize chests. Maybe they didn't speak English, Betty now realized, and she had just heard the words in English in her head, because when they spoke to each other they were not understandable.

Their eyes were by far their most terrifying feature, Betty said. Simon had only to say the word to send Betty into hysterics. They reminded her, she said, of a wall gecko's giant bulbous orbs and vertical-slit pupils. When they walked outside it was with a rolling gait, as if they were unsure of their balance, Betty noticed. They were strong, able to carry Barney without difficulty. Betty saw one of the crew members outside gulping air like a fish, as if the atmosphere was difficult for them to breathe.

Barney, on the medical table, saw inside the mouth of the examiner. There were no teeth, but there was a membrane, or possibly small tongue, which fluttered when they spoke in their murmuring language. The air in the craft was noticeably cool, Betty and Barney both told Allen Hynek of Project Blue Book when he questioned them under hypnosis at a special session at Simon's home. Hynek, originally a skeptic, came away deeply impressed.

As Fuller recounted, in a final hypnotic session in 1966, two years after the treatment ended, Simon asked Barney flatly: Had he been abducted?

He felt he had been abducted, Barney hedged.

Not "feel," the psychiatrist pressed. *Was* he abducted?

Yes, Barney said. He only said "felt" because he still didn't want to accept the fact.

What if, Simon persisted, he had just absorbed Betty's dreams?

He would like that, Barney said. But it wasn't true. He broke into anguished sobs. "I didn't like them putting their hands on me! I don't like them touching me!"

Simon was left with one conclusion: the whole confounding episode "could not be settled in an absolute sense."

Fuller too ended up with more questions than answers, remembering Tennyson: "Maybe the wildest dreams are but the needful preludes of the truth."

The Hills' saga took one more strange turn. Betty had made a drawing of the star map she remembered the leader showing her in the ship. In 1968 Marjorie Fish, an Ohio teacher and amateur astronomer who had read Fuller's book, correlated the pattern to the binary star system Zeta 1 and Zeta 2 Reticuli in the Reticulum constellation, which is thirty-nine light years from earth. *Astronomy* magazine took the hypothesis seriously enough to explore it in 1974, setting off a bitter debate on its plausibility.

Barney died in 1969, Betty in 2004, after ignominious final years of erratic claims that she could summon UFOs at will. In 2007 her niece Kathleen Marden gave the University of New Hampshire in Dover all their papers and artifacts—thirteen boxes containing 111 file folders, 313 envelopes of photos, 26 reels of family films, 10 audiotapes—including the hypnosis sessions—and Betty's torn blue dress. They remain open for study by anyone. Marden often shows up summers at Anne Cuvelier's Sanford-Covell Villa Marina in Newport for the annual experiencer mingle, amid the keenly felt absence of Budd Hopkins and John Mack.

11

····

THE PEACEMAKER

Mack's literary laurels gave him a special cachet at Harvard, his name to be forever paired with "Pulitzer Prize–winning." In the early stages of his Lawrence research, Mack had queried a Harvard history colleague and former Beirut foreign-service officer, L. Carl Brown, about the politics of the tormented region.[1] Brown later moved to Princeton and invited Mack to talk about Lawrence there at a 1973 conference on the psychology of the Middle East. That was soon followed by a series of other Princeton forums, including one that November, a month after the surprise Arab attack set off the short but fratricidal Yom Kippur War. While struggling to wrestle his unruly Lawrence material into a narrative, Mack delivered a paper at a conference on psychological aspects of conflict in the Middle East, a program cosponsored by the privately funded Institute for Psychiatry and Foreign Affairs, a Washington-based organization that brought together diplomats, political leaders, and military officials to discuss ways to bridge their differences. Its president was William D. Davidson, a colleague of Mack's at Harvard Medical School who, like Mack, had served in the Air Force. Arab presenters, abrim with nationalist pride from the strike against Israel, had been invited too, promising insights into the war from the other side. Before the conference, Davidson introduced Mack to a fellow panelist, Dr. Rita Rogers, a Romanian-born child psychiatrist who had survived Nazi deportation and Communist repression before fleeing to the West, while her family resettled in Israel. A short, lively woman four years older than Mack with glossy, black hair and penetrating, dark eyes, she was there to present a paper on Israel's founding father, David Ben-Gurion. They quickly bonded, beginning what would become a fruitful literary collaboration on her traumatic history.

Four years later, in November, 1977, seven months after Mack won the Pulitzer, Egypt's President Anwar Sadat stunned the world by telling Walter Cronkite of CBS that he was ready to travel to Jerusalem and address the Knesset to jump-start peace talks with the Israelis. Cronkite promptly called Israeli Prime Minister Menachem Begin, who responded, "Any time, any day he's prepared to come, I will receive him cordially at the airport." On the evening of November 20, with the Egyptian flag flying over Ben Gurion Airport, Sadat stepped off the plane to a twenty-one-gun salute and an emotional welcome by an Israeli Army officer, who said, "Mr. President, the guard of honor of the Israeli Defense Forces is ready for your inspection."

In early January 1978, in the euphoric aftermath of Sadat's visit, William Davidson, who had invited Mack to the Princeton conference and in the meantime had made two trips to Egypt, joined with Mack, Rita Rogers, and two other psychiatrists on a return trip to Cairo to see for themselves how Egyptians were greeting the historic breakthrough.[2] One thing Sadat had said resonated particularly strongly with Mack: 70 percent of the Middle East conflict was psychological.

Accordingly, Davidson and Joseph V. Montville, a career State Department officer who had served in the Middle East, were exploring innovative psychological approaches to conflict resolution through unofficial lines of communication they called "Track II" diplomacy (the official channels were "Track I").[3] Mack could help them devise a body of analytic principles as a basis for resolving ethnonational conflicts. Sally would fly separately and join him there later.

Mack's night flight from Boston began inauspiciously with an hour-long delay for an extra security check that caused him to miss his connecting flight in Paris. He got on another plane and was soon winging over the Egyptian coast at El Alamein, which gave him a shiver as he recalled the crucial World War II battle in late 1942 over a hellish field of five hundred thousand German mines. Churchill had called it the "turning of 'the Hinge of Fate'": "Before Alamein we never had a victory. After Alamein we never had a defeat." Upon landing, Mack discovered that TWA had lost his luggage. In the taxi to the Sheraton, through Cairo's tangled traffic and thick smog from factory smokestacks and blown sand, the driver beamed at hearing that Mack was an American. "America very good," he said. "French, English, German no good. Soviet very bad."

After Sally arrived they toured the cavernous Egyptian Museum enshrining Pharaonic treasures in empty galleries, so different from the mobbed Tutankhamen blockbusters back home. They squeezed in a quick flight to Luxor, where Mack imagined his Hebrew forebears laboring on colossal temples for their Egyptian slave masters. At a final gathering, grievances were freely shared. One Egyptian insisted that Uganda and Argentina had been offered to the Jews, but no, they had to settle in Palestine.

In April 1980, a year and a half after Sadat and Israeli Prime Minister Menachem Begin, prodded by President Jimmy Carter, signed their historic agreement at Camp David, Mack was invited back to the Middle East to lecture on Lawrence and consult on improving the hospital psychiatry department at the American University of Beirut.[4] In addition, Mack's Palestinian colleague at Harvard, Walid Khalidi, had arranged for a special honor.

Mack was picked up at night by Shafik al-Hout, the director of the PLO office in Beirut. Three weeks after Black September's murder of the eleven Israeli Olympians in Munich in 1972, al-Hout had told a cheering throng in Beirut, "We will continue what we began in Munich." Now, armed escorts hustled Mack into a car and sped him through checkpoints manned by glowering gunmen to Hout's apartment, where they waited. Near midnight a short, paunchy man with a trademark stubble and black-and-white keffiyeh slipped in—Yasir Arafat. Mack knew he would be meeting the "Chairman" and had come prepared with a copy of the Lawrence biography to present him.

Mack and Arafat discussed prospects for peace, Arafat envisioning an eventual confederation of Arabs and Jews, beginning with a Palestinian entity existing alongside Israel and culminating in a democratic secular state incorporating Israel, a pipedream Mack knew the Israelis ridiculed. Arafat depicted it as a compromise—Iraq and Libya were demanding the Jews be driven out of Palestine altogether. The first step, Arafat insisted, was a Palestinian state alongside Israel. How could a weak new state with no oil, no resources, and no ready army threaten the mighty Israelis? The real problem, he said, was that the Israelis felt inherently superior to the Arabs. Palestinians were becoming the dislocated Jews of the world, Arafat said. But Hout said ominously that failure to solve the Arab-Israeli conflict would have dangerous repercussions for world Jewry.

Arafat wanted Mack to tell Jewish leaders at home that the PLO sought only a Palestinian homeland on the West Bank and Gaza and not the whole of Israel. Muslims and Christians had historically been conquerors, Arafat said, but it was against the values of the Jewish religion for Jews to be the same. Mack knew that the Old Testament was replete with Israelite conquests and figured this might be a good time to end the evening.

As they left, Hout took Mack aside. He was afraid the chairman had been too frank, a common tendency of his. Hout said Mack should take care in deciding how to handle what he had been entrusted with. It carried an undercurrent of menace. But Arafat and Hout stressed that if Mack ever heard anything about the PLO that he needed to check, he should reach out to them directly. Mack could be put in touch with Arafat anytime.

The next afternoon, as Mack delivered another Lawrence lecture, the Beirut hall was rocked by a tremendous explosion outside. Having learned something from his visit, he muttered "Malesh" (doesn't matter) and resumed his talk.

12

DANNY'S GIFT

Along with his political awakening, Mack was undergoing a spiritual transformation that grew out of a spiraling crisis in his family life.

With his extensive travels, Mack was often "missing in action," Danny
remembered, although when he was around he tried to make up for it by
being passionately present.[1] Once after a ballgame at Fenway Park to see
his beloved Red Sox, he took Danny out for hot dogs. To Danny they were
just ballpark franks, but his father gushed, "These are exceptional hot dogs!
Really, tremendous!" Boston could be way ahead, but they had only to give up
a single run for Mack to moan, "Oh, God, here's where they're going to lose
it!" Kenny remembered going to see *Saturday Night Fever* with his dad. As if a
parental escort wasn't humiliating enough for a teenager, Mack, overcome at
John Travolta's heartbreaking struggles, kept up a loud running commentary
and sometimes wept. Danny was surprised one day while playing basketball
with his father when Mack blurted, "My life is just a series of obligations."

It had hardly escaped Sally that her husband was experiencing an alienating restlessness.[2] In truth, she had experienced his disengagement as early
as the birth of their boys, as Mack acknowledged in his journal: "She always
said you're away from me. You pull away into work, whatever. Not really there
with me." It occurred to Mack that Sally felt he might be jealous over her maternal bond with their sons, but he dismissed that as ridiculous. In company
with their friends and colleagues, Mack reveled in being the life of the party.
Companions found themselves disconcerted by his gravitational attraction,
a human black hole impossible to resist. At times like that Sally couldn't help
feeling he was so far ahead of her intellectually, she could never keep up. At
home, however, it was clear to her he felt something was missing. He was
no good at keeping secrets, so she knew years ago he had been taken with a
psychiatric nurse at work. Sally had suffered silently until, totally fed up one
day, she spirited her three young boys off for a quick fatherless vacation by
themselves. Lately she had seen some unfamiliar charges on the credit card
bill and some suspicious calls on the phone bill—clearly there was yet another
woman. When she confronted him, he didn't deny it. Strangely, perhaps be-

cause of his essential openness, Sally did not distrust him. She guessed he was acting out some search for the ineffable, perhaps his lost mother. "I do feel I'm selfish," Mack admitted to his therapist Gurucharan Singh Khalsa. "The whole thing is selfish. I can't seem to escape the biology of it." He was simply attracted to other women.

Meanwhile, Danny was a terror. He had resented Ken when he came along, and he later tormented their baby brother, Tony, whom Danny liked to knock down until he cried. Danny eventually outgrew bullying Tony, but adolescence brought new anxieties. Mack thought Danny might be a candidate for the Austen Riggs Center in the picturesque Berkshires village of Stockbridge, Massachusetts. Founded in 1919 by Dr. Austen Fox Riggs as the Stockbridge Institute for the Study and Treatment of Psychoneuroses, it specialized in individual psychotherapy for adults with complex psychiatric problems and had boasted Mack's idol Erik H. Erikson as a staff psychologist from 1951 to 1960. But Danny refused institutionalization, setting off a family fight. For all his training, Mack felt stymied by his own independent-minded son.

For high school, the family enrolled Danny in the elite Cambridge School of Weston outside Boston. Linked to Radcliffe College, the school took just a few hundred students and educated them in modules of individually tailored study, rather like Mack's old Lincoln School. Danny had a creative writing teacher, Holly Hickler, who assigned her students to write candidly about themselves. So when Mack was planning a lecture on teen behavior and asked his sophomore son if he knew a teacher who had access to student writing, Danny naturally thought of Hickler. She showed Mack some compositions and then a special trove—the journals, letters, poetry, and classwork of an exceptionally gifted student, Vivienne Loomis, a diarist in the mold of Anne Frank, except that Vivienne's imprisoning walls were internal. At age fourteen she had hanged herself at home, leaving behind her secret diary, which contained haunting poems like "Dream of Reality" with these lines:

What is it?
The stillness of wisdom?
The patience of doom?
That drives you to mount
That coal-black stallion?

Struggling with their grief, Vivienne's parents, David and Paulette, had asked for Hickler's help in compiling their daughter's writings as a memorial and a warning. How could the school's admissions office have read on her application essay the declaration, "I am drawn to death," and let it go without further inquiry? How could Vivienne's sister, her best friend, and her favorite teacher all have known of her self-destructive threats and yet kept silent out of respect for her privacy? Thanks to Danny, Mack and Hickler were soon collaborating on a book that would combine the girl's autobiographical writings with Mack's clinical analysis in an attempt to illuminate a growing epidemic of suicide that was killing some two thousand young people a year—a fatality rate that was second only to accidents as a deadly scourge of older adolescents. *Vivienne: The Life and Suicide of an Adolescent Girl* was published by Little, Brown in 1981 to a respectful review in the *New York Times* by a Harvard friend and colleague of Mack's, Robert Coles. He called it "a plainly written, clearheaded, wise book" and wrote that Mack's analysis was "instructively modest and tentative," adding, "He is unwilling to let the suicide's family, with its understandable feelings of guilt, transform its outpourings, inevitably confessional, into a bill of indictment."

Mack was simultaneously at work on another book, a biography of Rita Rogers, the Romanian-born antinuclear activist he had met at Princeton. Mack had been gripped by her Holocaust survival story, and he had grown determined to extract from its grim narrative inspirational wisdom on how humans surmount devastating trauma. In the summer of 1981, Rita, Mack, and Mack's nineteen-year-old middle son, Kenny, traveled to her birthplace in the Romanian province of Bukovina for the research. Inviting Kenny along had been an inspired move. He had been a struggling teen, overshadowed by his father's triumphs. But the Romania trip transformed Kenny, awakening him to something deeper in life. The book, *The Alchemy of Survival: One Woman's Journey*, would be published in 1988.

Danny, meanwhile, had been gradually discovering his own spiritual side, one that would spur his father's. In 1975 he had been in bed, fiddling with the radio he had connected to a pillow speaker, when he tuned into the Larry Glick show, a Boston-area institution known for its off-beat programming. Glick's guest that night was Dr. Benjamin Simon, the psychiatrist who had treated Betty and Barney Hill after their terrifying 1961 encounter in the

White Mountains of New Hampshire. Danny felt chills, suddenly remembering an old *LIFE* magazine that had contained images of alien spacecraft. It reinforced his growing interest in the supernatural, along with Eastern philosophy, transpersonal psychology, and alternate states of consciousness.

In the summer of 1977, he signed up with the Interlocken travel camps of New Hampshire and found himself competing in multiple games of backgammon against one of his fellow campers. She seemed to be getting an inordinate number of doubles. Danny realized that she was concentrating unusually hard. He concentrated too and realized he could counter her with his own psychic abilities. She exclaimed, "You're blocking me!" The girl then told him about Silva Mind Control, a popular training program where she had learned her skills of visualization and manifestation. Danny signed up for that course in 1978, shortly after graduating high school, and participated in multiple programs and a weekly support group. He also became more actively involved in dance and music; he had been playing the piano since age seven and had discovered dance in junior high school. He also now studied various body/mind techniques, taking multiple classes in the Boston and Cambridge area. Through participants in Silva Mind Control, he also learned about the Relationships workshop, a derivative of something called Erhard Seminars Training.

Danny had come across EST, as it became known, when the record-breaking blizzard of 1978 buried the Cambridge School, canceling classes. Bored, he had leafed through his roommate's January 1977 *Playboy*, lingering not over the lubricious centerfold but over a Dan Greenberg article, "You Are What You Est," which was about a West Coast motivational teacher, John Paul Rosenberg, who had reinvented himself as a mashup of physicist Werner Heisenberg and German Chancellor Ludwig Erhard—Werner Erhard. He preached breakthroughs in self-mastery through rigorous discipline and mind control. *Be. Do. Have.* Danny was hooked.

As he approached his high school graduation in 1978, he still didn't know his next move. His father's promptings of Harvard or Yale didn't interest him. Instead, he took a year off and made his way to San Francisco. For the academic year of 1979, he enrolled at the University of California at Berkeley.

Meanwhile, he also signed up for a Relationships workshop at a hotel in Brookline. For three and a half days, he and the hundred other participants were led to personal, emotional, and psychological transformation using techniques derived largely from Gestalt Therapy. Participants were "on the hot seat" until they had a breakthrough. One man, in a spontaneous emotional release, ejected his dentures, terrifying fellow workshoppers. Danny responded with a relish he never felt for his psychotherapy. As he felt his psyche opening up, he could visualize the constricted nature of his parents' relationship. He came home announcing to his startled father and mother, "I love you!"

When a State Department diplomat working with Werner Erhard to bring EST to Israel asked Mack in 1980 if he wanted to meet Erhard in San Francisco, Mack asked Danny if he should go. "Only if I can be invited too," Danny said. They joined up for the visit.

Twenty-year-old Danny was goggle-eyed at the Erhard mystique, the free-flowing wine in oversize glasses, the cigars. Mack was similarly entranced—"The most extraordinary person I've ever met!" he gushed to Danny. Erhard, in turn, was taken with Danny. "You opened your father's vistas," he said, offering father and son EST training at no cost. For Christmas break in 1980, Danny came home and enrolled in a workshop at a Boston hotel. Through the wall he could hear Beatles tunes from a memorial to John Lennon, who had been killed in New York earlier that month.

After two years at Berkeley, Danny spent the summer of 1981 in Japan, including a week at a Zen monastery in Kyoto. When he returned home, he vowed he would fix his family as a way of fixing himself. *He* would be *their* psychiatrist. But first he redesigned his room to conform to his new minimal Zen sensibilities. He moved out the desk and the rug. Erhard taught that your closet is your unconscious, so Danny emptied his closet and prepared to tear out the shelves until Mack put his foot down. No demolition. In the empty room Danny treated his parents to a tea ceremony. But by 1982 Danny thought it was time to leave again. He moved to Amherst, and the following year he enrolled in Hampshire College, a barely decade-old experiment in alternative higher education affiliated with Amherst, Smith, Mount Holyoke, and the University of Massachusetts.

13

"MORE ACTIVIST

THAN THE MOVEMENT"

With his trips to the Middle East, Mack had grown increasingly alarmed over the risk of world conflicts and nuclear proliferation. Moscow and Washington had signed a Partial Test Ban Treaty in 1963 and a Strategic Arms Limitation Talks Agreement in 1972, but each superpower retained enough atomic firepower to obliterate the other many times over. The Soviet invasion of Afghanistan in December 1979 and the election of Ronald Reagan the following November ratcheted up the tensions.

Mack's friend Bob Lifton had long been active in the antinuclear movement, a commitment growing out of his Air Force service in Japan, where he encountered the horrific aftereffects of the atomic bombings of Hiroshima and Nagasaki, whose total estimated casualties, dead and injured, exceeded two hundred thousand. After returning to Japan to research a book on the survivors, *Death in Life*, Lifton grew active in a group called Physicians for Social Responsibility, founded in 1961 by antinuclear activists around Dr. Bernard Lown, a developer of the DC defibrillator that could shock the heart out of life-threatening arrhythmia, and, later, a recipient of the Nobel Peace Prize. Mack, too, joined the group and was drawn into its ministry of peace and protest.[1]

The doctors group, dormant for a time, had been reactivated in the late 1970s, thanks to a kinetic Australian pediatrician, Dr. Helen Caldicott, who became an antinuclear activist after reading *On the Beach*, Nevil Shute's 1957 doomsday novel about the aftermath of a global nuclear holocaust. Caldicott had protested French nuclear tests in the Pacific before becoming a visiting instructor at Harvard Medical School and Children's Hospital Medical Center in Boston. She realized the doctor's group had an influential identity and pressed the *New England Journal of Medicine* to accept an ad by twenty-five eminent physicians warning of the dangers of a nuclear-plant catastrophe. By happenstance, it ran on March 29, 1979, a day after the reactor meltdown at Three Mile Island in the Susquehanna River south of Harrisburg, Pennsylvania—America's worst nuclear accident. Physicians for Social Responsibility suddenly attracted five hundred new members.[2] Enrollment would soar to forty thousand by the mid-1980s, just before the Chernobyl disaster.

Mack became an eager conscript, "more activist than the movement," Lifton remembered.[3] Once again, Danny was a catalyst. In Berkeley he had been taking part in demonstrations against the Diablo Canyon nuclear plant. Mack viewed nuclear weapons as a far greater threat, but Danny said nuclear plants were the place to start.

In November 1980, the physicians group and the Council for a Liveable World, an organization founded by the Hungarian nuclear physicist Leo Szilard, cosponsored a two-day symposium in San Francisco on what a Harvard public-health dean called "the last epidemic"—nuclear holocaust—for there would be no others. A thousand people attended. Mack was the only psychiatrist on the panel, tasked with examining the psychological burden of living with imminent annihilation. From Erik Erikson, he had become familiar with the concept of "pseudospeciation," the delusion that different groups of people were different species, making it easier to kill them. Nations, like individuals, Mack said, were historically locked in a self/other, good/evil, me/you duality, with differences settled by political negotiation or war. With twenty thousand nuclear warheads pointed at each other, the United States and the Soviet Union were poised for mutual suicide. Yet military strategists still talked of "fighting" and "winning" a nuclear war, a fully human reaction to the terror and helplessness of the dilemma. There was one promising development, Mack concluded. Soviet and American doctors had recently pledged to work together to avert a nuclear catastrophe. "It is not too late to begin," he said.

In the summer of 1979, Bernard Lown had invited Caldicott and a handful of other colleagues to his home in Newton outside Boston to discuss founding a new antinuclear group that would include Soviet physicians. It took two years to organize, but Lown eventually recruited Eugene Chazov, a top Kremlin partner and the cardiologist to the Politburo, including Leonid Brezhnev, the Supreme Soviet Chairman. At last the International Physicians for the Prevention of Nuclear War held its opening congress in March 1981 with doctors from eleven nations. High-level players included Moscow's leading expert on America, Georgi Arbatov, and, on the American side, the journalist

I. F. Stone and the astronomer and cosmologist Carl Sagan and his wife, Ann Druyan. The already-suspicious Soviet delegation and Lown himself were dismayed to discover that the Virginia venue, Airlie House, had been used as a conference center by the CIA. Was the congress bugged? "Of course," Lown said decades later, shrugging it off as predictable and inconsequential.

Mack, who had made his own trip with Sally to the Soviet Union in October 1979 for a landmark psychoanalysis conference in Georgia, had thrown himself into Lown's antinuclear congress, even volunteering as Lown's chauffeur. It was Mack who swayed the congress on a fateful issue. The Americans had split bitterly over whether to function as a research organization or an activist group, with Jonas Salk and Caldicott opposing activism. The doctors, they argued, should steer clear of Cold War politics. Mack argued for full engagement. "It was one of the most brilliant, emotional speeches I ever heard," Lown recalled. Mack said that an actual nuclear "exchange"—an anodyne euphemism that he deplored—would destroy human life beyond all hope of medical response. So the only sane approach was prevention. The group voted for activism. It incensed one powerful critic, Arnold S. Relman, editor of the *New England Journal of Medicine*, who decried the growing profile of the medical profession in raising concern over nuclear war. It was fine for physicians to opine about issues of medical care and public health, Relman argued in a September 1982 editorial, but "physicians have no obligation to speak out, *as physicians* on public issues on which they have no special expertise."

"But what if we believe such policies endanger the health, well-being, and lives of all peoples?" Mack countered later in a hospital lecture. "Is it not our responsibility as physicians and citizens to be sure our voices are heard? How else are we to regain control of our destinies and reverse the present course?" It wouldn't be the last time he and Relman would clash.

In the end, Lown and Chazov adroitly navigated the harsh rivalries and misunderstandings to unite the American and Soviet physicians in a consensus against the nuclear-arms race, moving the hands of the ticking atomic clock back a few precious minutes. The congress concluded with an appeal to President Reagan, Chairman Brezhnev, and fellow doctors of the world to act on the dire warnings of nuclear catastrophe. Many other world congresses would follow, earning International Physicians for the Prevention of Nuclear War the 1985 Nobel Peace Prize.

In years to come Lown would wonder about Mack's journey from anti-nuclear activism through spiritual epiphanies to alien abduction and all anomalous experience. "It made no sense," he thought at first. But then he reflected, "John's spirit roamed so wide, it was not totally surprising." His causes, Lown thought, could be seen as a succession of passionate enthusiasms.

In March of 1983 Mack organized an "Explanatory Meeting on the Nuclear Deadlock" at the Rockefeller estate in Westchester. It drew top academicians and opinion-makers including the medical philosopher-poet Lewis Thomas, the pollster Daniel Yankelovich, publisher Mortimer Zuckerman, and Werner Erhard. Later that year Mack and Lifton and other colleagues, including Roberta Snow, a Brookline teacher and principal who had founded Educators for Social Responsibility, established the Center for Psychological Studies in the Nuclear Age at Harvard Medical School. It would become the Center for Psychology and Social Change and would give rise to the Program for Extraordinary Experience Research (PEER), which would eventually evolve into the John E. Mack Institute—one of Mack's enduring legacies, enshrining his abduction research.

Mack also took time that year to anchor a scholarly anthology, *The Development and Sustenance of Self-Esteem in Childhood*. His overview noted that high self-regard, a contemporary virtue, had been condemned by early Christians. The medieval church considered pride, which it defined as "a high or overweening opinion of one's own qualities, attainments of estate; inordinate self-esteem," as the worst of all sins, fostering delusions of godliness. Mack's analysis traced self-esteem to infancy, when a child requires assurance he will not be abandoned. To be left or abandoned, Mack wrote, "conveys to the child that he is powerless." The consequences were often hostility toward the parent and a redirection of the aggression inward, toward the child.

Continuing to work for disarmament, in early May 1986 Mack arranged through scientists at Lawrence Livermore National Laboratory, which oversees the safety and reliability of the nation's nuclear deterrent, to meet the gruff, seventy-eight-year-old Hungarian-born physicist Edward Teller, widely known as the father of the H-bomb and an archfoe of the antinuclear movement.[4] Their encounter at the Cosmos Club in Washington quickly deteriorated. "If you are not in the pay of the Kremlin you're even more of a fool," Teller told Mack. He triumphantly described his "Star Wars" plan to send nuclear weapons into space to destroy incoming missiles with high energy particles. Mack asked Teller if he really thought it could work. "We might be able to save Israel," said Teller, who had fled Nazi Germany before the Holocaust. Mack beat a hasty retreat, believing Teller a complete lunatic.

Later that month the whole Mack family flew to Nevada for a protest at the nuclear test site in Mercury, northwest of Las Vegas.[5] With them was Mack's whistleblowing friend Daniel Ellsberg, a former RAND Corporation analyst who had worked with Defense Secretary Robert McNamara in the Kennedy Administration on operational plans for nuclear war before serving two years in the US Embassy in Saigon evaluating pacification efforts in the Vietnam War during the Johnson Presidency. After returning to RAND, he had worked on a classified study of the disastrous American decision-making in Vietnam. Distraught that it was being repressed, he had spent all his savings to secretly photocopy the seven thousand pages known as the Pentagon Papers and leaked them to the *New York Times* and later the *Washington Post*—resulting, Ellsberg liked to say, in the biggest federal manhunt since the kidnapping of the Lindbergh baby. His subsequent trial on federal espionage, theft, and conspiracy charges carrying up to 115 years in prison was thrown out after the Nixon Administration admitted it had illegally wiretapped Ellsberg and broken into the office of his psychiatrist, factors in the later conviction of White House aides and Nixon's pending impeachment and resignation.

Ellsberg and Mack had met at an Erik Erikson peace gathering at Robert Lifton's Wellfleet house several years before, where they had bonded over T. E. Lawrence.[6] Growing up, Ellsberg had read *Seven Pillars of Wisdom* and later recognized Lawrencian dreams of nation-building in the American intelligence operatives he had worked with in South Vietnam, if not also at times in himself. Ellsberg was further drawn to Mack as a psychiatrist who was good at listening after he confided his enduring sorrow over a childhood family tragedy: Ellsberg's mother and sister had been killed in a car crash when his father fell asleep at the wheel.

Along with Ellsberg, the Macks' contingent included Carl Sagan and his wife, Ann Druyan; Mack's former Harvard roommate, Lester Grinspoon; and Margaret Brenman-Gibson, an antiwar activist who had become one of the first women full professors at Harvard and who had pioneered hypnosis to treat traumatized World War II combat veterans. Brenman-Gibson was also a particular role model to Sally. A veteran of the Menninger Clinic, where she worked with Erikson, Brenman-Gibson later joined the eminent developmental psychologist as a psychotherapist at the Austen Riggs Center in Stockbridge, treating Mary Rockwell, wife of the artist Norman Rockwell, and later the artist as well, who was to make Brenman-Gibson's portrait. Now, together in Nevada, protesting nuclear weapons, they rallied in the 115-degree heat with some six hundred other demonstrators. They listened to speeches, sang songs, and practiced techniques of civil disobedience. After a prayer service for world peace led by a Franciscan priest, a minister, and local Shoshone Indians, they slow-marched to the base perimeter, holding hands and singing "America the Beautiful" and "We Shall Overcome." The sheriff stopped them at the boundary line. To cross it would mean arrest. The Macks and some 140 other protesters stepped over the line and were arrested, handcuffed and led to buses for arraignment in Nye County Court.

Mack, Sally, Tony, and Danny agreed to pay their fines in exchange for release. Kenny, who had been reading up on Gandhi and Martin Luther King, refused to plead guilty and insisted on being taken to the neighboring Esmeralda County jail to serve his six-day sentence. He had lately gone through a Karl Marx phase, quoting so often from *Das Kapital* that his family had started calling him "Karl." Incensed to learn that the federal civil-defense plan for a nuclear strike on Brookline was a mass evacuation to Laconia, New Hampshire, he had informed Brookline's town fathers and mobilized a Selectmen's Meeting that ended up rejecting the plan. Kenny also wrote and circulated a booklet exposing the perils of mass flight. Inspired by a group of grade schoolers in Vermont who had organized a worldwide letter-writing campaign against atomic weapons called the Children's Campaign for Nuclear Disarmament—and who had personally delivered thousands of the letters to President Reagan at the White House—Kenny had gone on Nickelodeon's *Livewire* television show, where he held the young studio audience spellbound with his knowledge of the nuclear peril. "Once I got involved, my sense of helplessness vanished," he said. "I no longer felt that scared. I realized I'm a person who can do something."

Kenny shared a cell with a Mack family friend, Richmond Mayo-Smith, the former headmaster of Boston's elite Roxbury Latin School. Sally was worried about Kenny but felt she had exorcized an old demon: growing up Jewish in wartime rural Pennsylvania, she was haunted by fears that the Nazis were coming for her family. Now she was doing something to avert another cataclysm. Mack wrote an op-ed piece on the protests for the *New York Times*. It was reprinted in the *International Herald Tribune*, where, as it happened, his beloved Oberlin professor Harvey Goldberg saw it in Paris and proudly wrote Mack, "I'm glad to see we taught you something at Oberlin."

Trying to raise money for the cause, Mack sought advice from Harvard president Derek Bok. He responded in January 1987 that "the most important problem you face is an ambiguity as to whether you are, at bottom, an advocacy group with clear convictions and preconceptions about the arms race and ways to avoid the nuclear threat or whether you are an academic group seeking objective answers to hard questions." Because their collaboration with the Soviets could be seen as amateurish or biased, they should take care to work with recognized experts, Bok suggested.

That July, Mack invited Werner Erhard to Harvard for a brainstorming session on how to woo corporate America away from a Cold War mentality.[7] They began by reminiscing about their meeting in California seven years before. Erhard asked about Mack's boys, especially Danny. "I can't believe the extent to which I grow from learning from who he is," Mack said. Kenny, at twenty-five, was the "revolutionary," Mack continued. He was working as a carpenter, up mornings at 6:00 to do manual labor. Tony, just back from Central America, was studying US–Latin American relations in Harvard summer school, Mack said. And Sally was coping with "negative energy" from her mother. "Her expertise is in mobilizing people's distress around her."

Erhard wondered if it might be worth targeting corporate bigwigs at defense firms, although most seemed to be true believers. Mack was dubious. "I wouldn't start with those people," he said. They had so much power. "We always talk about how, when we are in a happy mood, things are on our side and going our way but we don't know shit about that." Erhard thought that the defense bosses could be encouraged to at least question things. Always going with the consensus produces a Nazi Germany, he said. Mack had another idea. "Never mind citizen exchanges," he said. "Take the Congress to the Soviet Union." Erhard agreed that both sides needed to get away from rhetoric and change the climate. He paraphrased Heidegger: The power of a conversation lay not in what was said but what remained unsaid. It was not the words being spoken but the thoughts, attitudes, feelings, and actions "ontologically embedded in an already existing network of conversation." You had to know this to find a solution. It was "like trying to fix the chair working on the table," Erhard went on. "You can work on the goddamned table from now to doomsday and you are never going to fix the chair."

Erhard had meanwhile evolved his EST program into self-realization workshops called the Landmark Forum. One session in the Harvard area drew a vivacious family therapist, executive coach, and landscape painter— Rosamund Zander, a mother of two living apart from but still close to her third husband, Benjamin Zander, who was a noted conductor and a founder of the Boston Philharmonic Orchestra.[8] Roz, willowy and sensual, looked out to see a recognizable figure sitting in the back, the prominent Harvard academician John Mack. Afterward she felt emboldened to look up his phone number and give him a call. "You won't know me," she began, introducing herself. But Mack cut her off. "I know exactly who you are," he said. They made a date for coffee, began meeting regularly, and before long they were lovers.

14

"THEY PUT A HOLE

IN MY PSYCHE"

For thousands of years the rugged Pacific wilderness the Spanish settlers called El Sur Grande, the Big South, harbored a sacred site of healing mineral hot springs and cascading streams that flowed out of the granitic base rock onto the crashing ocean south of Monterey. In 1910 California physician Henry Murphy, who, as it happened, had delivered the future author John Steinbeck in Salinas a few years before, bought 375 acres between the coast and Santa Lucia Mountains for a European-style spa.[1] He got as far as some bathhouses before he died. The property fell into abandonment for half a century until Henry's grandson Michael showed up to reclaim the springs with a companion, Richard Price, and allies like Henry Miller, Hunter Thompson, and Joan Baez in what became known as the "Night of the Dobermans." Miller had been among the earliest pioneers, helping build the baths on the rebound from his traumatic breakup with lover Anaïs Nin in Paris and imbuing the retreat with a not-entirely-deserved (at least not yet) aura of sex, scandal, and anarchy. The pre-gonzo Thompson had been hired to guard the property, and Baez lived in one of the cabins, where she performed small concerts. The bar was staked out by pot-smoking mountain men called the Big Sur Heavies, and the baths were thronged with gays from as far afield as San Francisco and Los Angeles, who posted a lookout up the path to signal approaching danger with Morse code flashings of car headlights. And so it went through 1961, wrote the political scientist Walter Truett Anderson, who chronicled the compound's evolution: "Sodomy in the baths, glossolalia in the lodge, fistfights in the parking lot, folk music in the cabins, meditation in the Big House."

Soon their encampment—which they called Esalen, an adaptation of a geographic designation of one of the Indigenous tribes, the Esselen Indians (although no one knows what they called themselves)—gained renown as a temple to human potentiality, a psychic Olympia where the games would celebrate the spirit, mind, heart, and physical body. Devotees were encouraged to enjoy the springs and surroundings like their ancient forebears: au naturel. Among the many luminaries attracted early on was the émigré psychiatrist Fritz Perls, founder of Gestalt Therapy, a Zen-inflected, consciousness-expansion and healing regimen centered on "the hot seat" of psychodrama, and perhaps the only German Jew disdained by both Adolf Hitler and Sigmund Freud. Abraham Maslow, a humanistic psychologist in great vogue with the founders, wandered by in 1962 looking for a room and all but caused a worshipful riot. He stayed. Arnold Toynbee gave one of the first seminars. Aldous Huxley visited shortly before his assisted suicide (on the same day President Kennedy was assassinated), and his spiritualist writings became Esalen's ur-text. The Harvard LSD gurus Timothy Leary and Richard Alpert (later Ram Dass) offered guided psychedelic tours. The summer 1964 Esalen brochure offered "A Trip with Ken Kesey," prankster author of *One Flew Over the Cuckoo's Nest*. Mythologist Joseph Campbell arrived to lecture in 1966 and returned annually for almost two decades until his death, his archetypal journey of a hero venturing forth from the world of the common day into a region of supernatural wonder ingrained in the Esalen mythos. The Beatles came, and soon everyone else. It was the "religion of no religion" (and equally the religion of all religions), as the Esalen biographer and Rice University religion professor Jeffrey J. Kripal put it, a place where, as the Esalen ethos had it, "no one captures the flag." Perhaps Fritz Perls came closest.

In 1973 the Czech-born psychiatrist Stanislav Grof arrived as scholar-in-residence. Grof had studied medicine in Prague, and in the 1950s he was conducting research on the antipsychotic tranquilizer Melleril, produced by Sandoz Pharmaceutical Laboratories in Basel, Switzerland. Two decades earlier a chemist at Sandoz, Albert Hofmann, had synthesized d-lysergic acid diethylamide from ergotamine derived from the ergot fungus. In 1943 a trace accidentally absorbed through his fingers sent his brain exploding in kaleidoscopic colors, signaling the mind-altering psychedelic properties of LSD, the most powerful consciousness-altering substance ever discovered—up to ten thousand times more powerful than mescaline. Hofmann experimented with ingesting 250 micrograms, 25 millionths of a gram. But even smaller quantities sufficed to produce its effects; just 20 micrograms were necessary, one 1/700,000,000 of an average man's weight.[2] Sandoz provided the drug to Grof's clinic, and Grof was able to qualify as an experimental research subject. He experienced rapturous visions and, when subjected to electric impulses and strobe light, "a divine thunderbolt that catapulted my conscious self out of my body."

In 1967, an invitation from Johns Hopkins University in Baltimore enabled Grof to leave communist Czechoslovakia. Two years later, at the Maryland Psychiatric Research Center, he continued his psychedelic research on volunteers, discovering that 300 micrograms evoked forgotten infantile memories and induced powerful out-of-body experiences and transpersonal encounters with mystic dimensions of the cosmos. The results were not necessarily dose related, he discovered, but seemed affected by breathing patterns.[3] He experimented with regulated breathing in conjunction with classical music, a therapy called Guided Imagery and Music, or GIM, developed by musician and psychotherapist Helen L. Bonny at the Maryland Psychiatric Research Center.

At a party in New York in the early 1970s, Grof met Michael Murphy, who invited him to a residency at Esalen. Two years into his stay, Grof, recently divorced, met his second wife-to-be, Christina, who introduced him to Kundalini yoga and her noted master, Swami Muktananda. Grof integrated his LSD experiences into yoga practice, affirming that the drug was not a causative pharmacological agent but only a catalyst for what already lay buried in the psyche. He and Christina went on to develop Holotropic Breathwork as a relaxation technique with music to induce altered states of consciousness— better things for better living not through chemistry, as DuPont advertised, but without it. Somehow, the Grofs found, the breathing discipline altered the blood, boosting the unconscious in ways that the great Yogi and Sufi masters had understood ages ago. It was, they said, a gateway to the infinite, overturning the Western view of material reality. But hallucinogens would nonetheless permeate the Esalen experience, fostered by Leary, Alpert, and the charismatic ethnobotanist Terence McKenna, who linked human civilization to a cosmic seeding by plants containing psilocybin, dimethyltryptamine (DMT) and other psychedelics. From there it was hardly a stretch to programs on cosmic intelligence, UFOs, and alien life.

"High" on the Esalen agenda, too, was world peace, advanced by Joseph Montville, the career diplomat working on Middle East initiatives. Starting in the 1970s, and buttressed by Murphy's new wife, Dulce, and support from

83

John D. Rockefeller's counterculturist grandson, Laurance, Esalen embarked on a series of Soviet-American friendship initiatives, which only expanded in reaction to the official chill and US boycott of the Moscow summer Olympics following the December 1979 Soviet invasion of Afghanistan. The "hot tub diplomacy" reached a milestone in 1982 with a TV satellite link connecting ordinary Muscovites and Southern Californians. Thereafter Esalen became ground zero for friendly exchanges between the longtime Cold War adversaries.

In September 1987, Esalen staged a large bilateral conference on Frontiers of Health. It featured Dean Ornish on dietary approaches to heart disease; Robert Peter Gale, a bone-marrow specialist who had advised the Soviets on leukemia treatments after the Chernobyl nuclear disaster; Candace Pert, a psychoneuroimmunologist known for her pioneering mind-body work on AIDS; four Soviet physicians, including three psychiatrists; and Mack, who spoke on the imagery of nuclear war and its effect on children and adults. Stanislav Grof was asked to talk about transpersonal psychology, a vibrant spiritual alternative to behaviorism and Freudianism.[4] Grof described his experiences with Holotropic Breathwork, setting off great excitement. They quickly agreed to cancel the next day's afternoon program for a series of breathing workshops.

Mack signed up eagerly but with some trepidation, little imagining the vistas it would open and to what strange realms it would lead him. He knew that psychoanalysis depended on the recall of disturbing memories and the release of their buried affects, or powerful feelings.[5] But Freud had discovered that this catharsis by itself was not enough. The ego erected defense mechanisms against such discharges such that, improperly managed, their sudden freeing could cause damage—a failure to integrate the affective experience, or even psychosis. Controlled altered states like dreams offered normal regression. But the earliest physical experiences of birth and body awareness were so powerful that entire schools of therapy were dedicated to addressing their troubled affects. William Reich explored coping mechanisms as "character armor." Identifying an esoteric life force he called orgone, he developed cabinet-like boxes of wood and other materials as orgone accumulators to interact with a person's bioenergy and boost energetic charges in the organism. Convicted of violating a federal injunction against interstate transport of the orgone accumulators that the government called fraudulent, he died in federal prison in 1957, his devices and books incinerated by the government. Less controversial therapies explored massage and body work like Rolfing to free bottled-up energies. So what might come out of Grof's Holotropic Breathwork (which would remain a popular feature at Esalen to the present)?

15

THE TURQUOISE MAIDEN

Mack's group consisted of eleven breathers, including two of the Soviet psychiatrists, and the same number of partnered sitters positioned behind them for relaxation and safety.[1] Reclining on a mattress, Mack followed Grof's instructions: he closed his eyes and took full, deep breaths, filling his lungs completely and keeping his breathing circular, a little faster than normal, with no gaps as he focused on aligning his body with the hypnotic beats of the music. For the first half-hour, he felt nothing. He was wondering how long this would go on when he felt himself engulfed by a wave of despair. He was borne back fifty-eight years—he was an infant not yet nine months old, reliving his mother's anguished death. He was alone, abandoned. He felt his father's fathomless grief and struggle for self-mastery and the cool distancing from his son that the little boy had never understood and never quite forgave. Mack was ready to forgive him now. And then he was in medieval Russia with his four-year-old son and . . . a Mongol Tatar on horseback was *decapitating his child!* The horror ebbed, and he felt a surge of empathy for the Russians he sensed beside him. What they and their people had endured! Afterward they compared their visions. One of the Russian psychiatrists admitted, "I had an experience with God." Of course, he hastened to add, "I remain a Communist, but I understand now what they mean by God."[2]

Mack was troubled but exhilarated. Not in years of professional analysis had he come close to accessing such primal memories. And that Mongol business? Had he discovered a past life? Unlikely, he thought. More probably it showed that consciousness was fluid and could travel.

How, he asked, could he do more breathwork? Grof said they were about to start a twelve-day training module at Hollyhock Farm, a learning retreat on Cortes Island in the Strait of Georgia about one hundred miles north of Vancouver, where twice-yearly sessions alternated between there and Pocket Ranch in Geyserville in the Santa Rosa mountains north of San Francisco. Mack eagerly signed up for Hollyhock, even arranging to have his daily *New York Times* delivered to him there. (Grof, seeing him immersed in the paper, thought him rather tightly wound, someone who needed to get out more in the transpersonal world.)

"That was wonderful. Just wonderful," Mack scribbled in his journal as he emerged from trances that had carried him back to his earliest memories.[3] "It was like I was in the canal and seeing the fetus and coming thru and then I was out. But then I was her, my mother . . . I was a blue baby in my last breathing experience. A blue head came in. But she was blue. My father's story was that she was unattended at her death, which I've never allowed myself to consider what it was for her, so I got with her that she died blue . . . And then I returned to my own birth, and that I was blue, that I turned blue . . . blue at birth and she was blue and the blue came together."

With that, Mack made the connection to *Pinocchio* and his own long fascination with the turquoise maiden. "The archetype of my childhood. He keeps looking for the blue mother through the whole story. I did that. I found the blue mother in the breathing. It was obvious. She was blue. I was blue. We were together blue . . . I'm alone, this little blue baby—I'm tough as hell. I'm the toughest son-of-a-bitch, and I think my whole life is like 'I'm gonna make it!' And then I felt this flood—I cried many times, but most of the time I cried—pride & gratitude, pride that I'd made it & gratitude toward the women who'd loved me. I cried with gratitude . . ."

Mack then went on to record a particularly bizarre vision that seemed to foreshadow his later encounters with an alien world—although he would not meet Budd Hopkins for three years. "And then I got this stuff about incubators, this picture of all these abandoned fetus-infants separ[ated] from their mothers in these technology places which is the work my wife does." It brought to mind what he called "The Return of the Body Snatchers," an evident reference to the 1956 sci-fi movie *Invasion of the Body Snatchers* (or perhaps its 1978 remake). "These invaders from outer space come & they take over everyone's bodies" Mack went on. "Maybe they punish us for not loving enough. They take over our bodies. They take over the resources. They take over the plants. They take over everything—for them—and you have all these breathing creatures, these plant creatures breathing & breathing in this cold, dead suffocating way until all the resources are used up and the planet has been completely taken over. It's like for not loving ourselves enough, not giving each other enough warmth . . ."

For Christmas 1988 Mack and Sally and their three sons, now in their twenties, gathered with Mack's sister Mary Lee Ingbar and her son David at Ruth Mack's white colonial homestead in Thetford, Vermont, where Edward had been killed some fifteen years before.[4] Danny, with shoulder-length hippie hair befitting his Jesus stage, was there with his common-law wife, Adwoa, a dance-movement therapist who was expecting their first child, Ari, early in the new year. Kenny had even longer hair and the pout of a bad-boy rock drummer, and Tony had a shaggy bowl cut left over from the years when all three brothers favored Beatles coifs. Mack stood out stiffly with his unruly thatch of dark-brown hair close-shorn on the sides. The family celebrated a generic Christmas, rankling Sally and other Jewish relatives, who made sure they also celebrated Chanukah. Struggling to master a new video camera, they exchanged jokey presents, tossing the crumpled gift wrap into the crackling fire. The boys and their father donned new pointed hoodies that make them look, Mack commented, like the Black Death. Mack and Sally were presented with sexy silk pajamas amid ribald giggling over how they might be best put to use. They harmonized with Digger, the black and tan coon hound mutt that Kenny had adopted while volunteering at an animal shelter, nuzzling in to join the fun. Later, horsing around with his brothers after the others went to bed, Danny mused, "Imagine this tape in 40 years."

But the idyll was deceiving. Mack had been carrying on a tumultuous romance with Roz, the therapist he had met through Werner Erhard's Landmark Forum. They had stolen away for breathwork seminars and a weekend in Vermont at the house of a friend of Roz's. Mack was growing close, too, to her son and daughter. Roz had accompanied Mack one evening to experience MDMA, the mind-altering drug commonly referred to as Ecstasy, although she ended up demurring. Mack, infatuated, was driven to paroxysms of rapture, despair and jealousy. Sally had been on to her husband's latest affair, Mack being terrible at keeping secrets, and he had felt compelled to tell her the truth. A friend in whom Mack confided said Mack thereby "put a nail in the coffin" of his illicit relationship, but Mack responded that "it felt like there was no choice." Yet he continued to pursue Roz, filling his journal with lovesick avowals that went unsent: "This AM the pain is deep as ever. It seems unfathomable, unreparable, paralyzing—Sally, reluctantly is off to breath[work]. What do I do with myself. It is like the deepest connection, heart guts & soul have been ripped out of me. I can't work, write, create . . . sometimes I want to cry out wait for me wait for me in this life or the next . . ."

By 1989 Mack was a regular participant in Grof's breathwork modules. That March, in Geyserville, Grof gave Mack a chapter from his forthcoming anthology, *Spiritual Emergency: When Personal Transformation Becomes a Crisis.* Grof wanted Mack to read a section by Keith Thompson, a California writer and therapist adept in philosophy, quantum physics, non-ordinary states of consciousness, shamanism, mysticism, and parapsychology. As a boy in Ohio, Thompson had been captivated by a 1966 wave of Michigan UFO sightings that government consultant Allen Hynek had infamously dismissed as "swamp gas." In residence at Esalen in the 1980s, Thompson maintained his interest in UFOs, including the experiences of Hopkins, author Whitley Strieber, and the reborn Hynek, now a champion of serious research. Thompson had participated in a celebrated 1987 symposium in San Francisco—"Aliens, Angels and Archetypes: Cosmic Intelligence and the Mythic Imagination "—that found the UFO phenomenon decidedly real, a mainstay of history, and simultaneously physical and spiritual, a form of consciousness able to manipulate dimensions beyond space and time. That year, Thompson had also joined an annual UFO and abductee conference in Laramie, Wyoming, convened by Dr. Leo Sprinkle, a University of Wyoming professor whose research went back to the 1960s.

In his chapter for Grof, which he called "The UFO Encounter Experience as a Crisis of Transformation," Thompson examined the phenomenon as a rite of initiation. He was not so concerned with what was objectively true— that might never be knowable, he wrote. Rather his approach was phenomenological. He wanted to see what people reported about their experience, unencumbered by questions of what could and could not be real. Viewed in that way, the encounters resembled timeless and familiar human rites of transition or initiation, the Hero's Journey, popularized by the mythologist Joseph Campbell. First, a separation or departure from the existing state, the way a boy in an Indigenous culture might leave his childhood behind at home before entering the initiation lodge to manhood. Then, entrance into a shadow realm of marginality betwixt and between, where one is both the old thing and the new. And finally, an aggregation stage when the experiences are reassembled into a new state of being. In Campbell's epic twelve-stage mythology, the hero lives an everyday life until confronted with a challenge that summons him to his journey. He refuses it but encounters a mentor who steels him for the struggles ahead. He crosses the first threshold to a new world with tests of will, daunting enemies, and staunch allies. He suffers setbacks, forcing new strategies. He endures a terrible ordeal but triumphs to earn a reward. He sets off for home only to suffer a final trial that risks the entire journey. He succeeds again, returning to present his boon to a grateful world.

Applying Campbell's descriptions of the Hero's Journey to the UFO abduction experience, Thompson wrote that the call to adventure signifies "that destiny has summoned the hero and transferred his spiritual center of gravity from within the pale of his society to a zone unknown." The setting may vary, "but it is always a place of strangely fluid and polymorphous beings, unimaginable torments, superhuman deeds, and impossible delights." The hero (or abductee) may want to refuse the call but ultimately can not. He, or she, then inhabits a twilight state, often expressed by feelings of disbelief or unreality. These initiates, privy to the Mysterium, a realm invisible to those not similarly called, live a paradox and yet are potentially blessed as Masters of Two Worlds. As such, Thompson wrote, they may be harbingers of a momentous cosmic shift, a bridge between the death of the old gods and the birth of the new, as Heidegger said, or as Jung thought, a sign of the coming transformation of the collective psyche. But the danger, Thompson concluded, was that those ridiculed or marginalized for their secret knowledge might overcompensate by proclaiming themselves cosmic prophets. "All of us who have had extraordinary experiences should watch out for this tendency," he warned. Their special experiences do not belong to them personally. Invisibility might be advantageous. "Soul work takes time." Campbell's hero knew this. "His personal ambitions being totally dissolved, he no longer tries to live but willingly relaxes to whatever may come to pass in him; he becomes, that is to say, an anonymity."

Mack had no idea why Grof would give him Thompson's chapter. He read it with skeptical interest, all the while asking himself, "But is it true?" Were people really being contacted by humanoid beings? He saw that Thompson had skirted the question phenomenologically, but he still couldn't help wondering. Mack was still wondering later that year when he went back to

California for another breathwork module, heard from Blanche Chavoustie about Budd Hopkins, and, somewhat to his own surprise, sought him out on January 10, 1990—"One of those dates you remember that mark a time when everything in your life changes."

It was his own call to adventure.

16

"SANE CITIZEN SEES UFO
IN NEW JERSEY"

Budd Hopkins was seven years old and living in Wheeling, West Virginia, when his parents, panicked by Orson Welles's frighteningly authentic *War of the Worlds* radio play, spent Halloween eve in 1938 packing to flee from the invading Martians.[1] Little Budd cowered under his blanket. Later, at Oberlin College where he was two years behind Mack, Hopkins studied art, and in the 1950s he moved to Greenwich Village, where he worked days selling tickets at the Museum of Modern Art and spent his nights holding court at the Cedar Tavern with fellow artists Robert Motherwell, Franz Kline, Mark Rothko, Willem de Kooning, and Jackson Pollock. The *New York Times* praised Hopkins's paintings as "taut and decisive and slightly tense" and called him a fine miniaturist "especially refined in color." Hopkins had a studio on Cape Cod, where he often mingled with the busy summer colony of psychotherapists, including Robert Lifton. One afternoon in 1964, while driving to a cocktail party in Provincetown, Hopkins and his wife and another couple spotted a UFO in the clouds that seemed to keep pace with them before streaking off into the wind over the ocean. They mentioned it at the party, with other guests chiming in with their own UFO stories. Hopkins, fascinated, began reading up on UFOs. Good thing he was an artist, he thought. Nobody cared what an artist dabbled in.

In November 1975 Hopkins heard a chilling tale from his local Chelsea wine seller. After locking up one midnight, George O'Barski said, he was driving home in New Jersey when his car radio began emitting a strange, tinny sound. He was fiddling with it when a huge, bright object passed his car and landed in North Hudson Park, a 167-acre clifftop triangle of greenery about halfway between the Lincoln Tunnel and the George Washington Bridge across the river from Manhattan's West 80s. O'Barski described it as a roundish, thirty-foot-long craft with a row of vertical windows. He then watched, incredulous, as a hatch opened and nearly a dozen short figures in light-colored hooded garments descended, "like kids in snowsuits." Ignoring him, they dug into the ground, spooning earth into little bags, then returned to the ship and flew off, all within less than four minutes. O'Barski drove home shaking. The next morning, as he told Hopkins, he returned to the spot and found about fifteen small holes. Then he really got spooked. Fearing ridicule, he had kept the story to himself. But now he asked Hopkins what to do.

Hopkins found a veteran UFO investigator, Ted Bloecher—a professional singer and actor—and together they tracked down witnesses who corroborated elements of O'Barski's sighting. Four members of a family recalled running out of their house that night to get a closer look at a glowing, round, domed craft flying toward North Hudson Park. A doorman of an adjacent apartment tower remembered seeing a bright light just about the time he felt a high-pitched vibration right as a lobby window near the ground instantly spider-webbed with cracks, as from a shot. He called the police. Hopkins wrote up a long account of the episode for the *Village Voice*. The counterculture weekly ran it as a two-page spread on March 1, 1976, under the headline "Sane Citizen sees UFO in New Jersey." Suddenly Budd Hopkins was getting everyone's UFO stories.

Hopkins knew a Manhattan psychiatrist, Dr. Robert Naiman, who used hypnosis to combat smoking and overeating addictions. Could buried UFO memories emerge in an induced altered state of consciousness? Naiman agreed to try, enlisting two colleagues, Girard Franklin and Aphrodite Clamar. Franklin's first subject was a shy, intense arts professional under thirty whom they called "Steven Kilburn," although he would later appear with Hopkins using his real name, Michael Bershad. For years he had been haunted by the memory of a disturbing encounter while driving home late one night from a girlfriend's house in Frederick, Maryland. Afterward, he kept feeling like someone was watching him.

Under Franklin's gentle questioning, Steve remembered checking the car's dashboard. Then somehow the car was pulled off the road at an angle, there was a bright light, and he was walking away from the car. Then he was driving home terrified. In a deep trance, Steve recalled the car's unaccountable stopping and suddenly cried, "It's on my shoulder . . . a clamp . . . it hurts. I can't move!"[2] At that point, there was a loud click—Franklin's answering machine had just intercepted an incoming call—and Steve almost jumped off the couch. Calmed by Franklin and still under hypnosis, he went on to describe a kind of wrench that was immobilizing him while several black-clad figures observed him from a distance. One approached, sending Steve recoiling from the ugliness of its "chalkish, whitish" skin that, he said, reliving the experience, "looks like putty or something."

Later he recalled being led aboard their ship and onto a table in a curved, whitish room where a monstrous overhead instrument like the projector in a planetarium subjected him to uncomfortable medical probes. A taller figure he considered the "doctor" went over his body with a metal wand. Metal bands forced his legs apart. "I feel like a frog," he said. Later he recalled that a device had been placed over his penis, then he felt a vibration and orgasm as his sperm was collected.

Hopkins, self-taught in hypnosis, interviewed many other mystified captives. One woman he called "Virginia Horton" had a scar on her knee from what she came to remember as experimental surgery during an abduction when she was seven. She said alien beings showed her star maps from "a long ways away" and peppered her with questions about life on earth. What it all pointed to, Hopkins concluded in *Missing Time*, his 1981 book that revealed a recurring temporal feature of the abduction accounts and established his UFO bona fides, was that "a very long-term, in-depth study is being made of a relatively large sample of humans."

When *Missing Time* came out, Hopkins, Clamar, and Bloecher received a grant from the Fund for UFO Research (FUFOR), to study possible mental explanations for these stories. An experienced clinical psychologist, Elizabeth Slater, tested nine self-styled abductees. She found they shared higher than average degrees of insecurity, distrust, and wariness—perhaps arising from their experience—but no psychological disorder. They seemed most akin to rape victims.

Hopkins' pioneering abduction work had inspired another researcher, who by 1985 had been invited to sit in on some of Hopkins's hypnotic regressions to learn the technique. But David M. Jacobs was no newcomer to UFOs. A well-regarded professor of history at Temple University in Philadelphia, Jacobs, then forty-three with an Einsteinian crown of flyaway graying hair and a bristling moustache, had been a flying-saucer buff since his student days at the University of Wisconsin in the 1960s when a *LIFE* magazine article intrigued him.[3] He devoured Fuller's *Interrupted Journey* on the Hill case (he thought their weird encounter was probably a shared delusion) joined several UFO organizations, and subscribed to *Flying Saucer Review*, a high-quality British quarterly tracking the field since 1955. Although he had never seen a UFO, Jacobs ended up writing his doctoral dissertation on the history of the UFO controversy in America. Indiana University Press published it in hardcover in 1975, selling out the edition—a milestone for an academic press. A popular paperback edition followed the next year, establishing Jacobs as a leading authority on the subject. He interviewed his first abductee—Betty Hill—in 1975.[4] At Temple, Jacobs became the first American professor teaching a regular curriculum course on UFOs. In 1982 a friend introduced him to Hopkins, setting Jacobs on his own quest to unravel the abduction mystery. The business, he thought, needed a rigorous approach, strict narratives with second-by-second chronologies. By the mid-1980s Jacobs was hypnotizing his own abductees, including a professional bicyclist, a cub reporter, a lawyer, a publicist, and a twenty-six-year-old Philadelphia real-estate manager with memories of having been transported into a UFO as a six-year-old and having an object implanted near her left ovary.

Among those who wrote Hopkins in response to his book was a plus-size divorced mother in her mid-20s from a pseudonymous Indianapolis suburb. Hopkins called her "Kathie Davis," although she would later write her own book under her real name, Debbie Jordan.[5] Under hypnosis by Hopkins, she moved the phenomenon into far stranger new dimensions, explored in Hopkins's next book, *Intruders: The Incredible Visitations at Copley Woods*. In her trance, Kathie recalled that before her two sons were born, she had somehow become pregnant at about eighteen and lost the baby, although her doctor found no sign of a miscarriage. Then in a 1983 abduction, she later recalled under hypnosis, she was shown that child, a frail hybrid girl of about five with sparse white hair whom Kathie came to call Emily. "She's . . . gorgeous," Kathie told an astonished Hopkins. "She looks like an angel. She's tiny. Thin. Her skin is creamy. Her face is shaped like a heart. She has a tiny, tiny little mouth. Perfect lips. Blue eyes."

Kathie said there were eight more children—for a total of nine pregnancies of hers that had been removed and brought to term, although she was shown just two, Emily and her infant brother whom Kathie named Andrew.

Hopkins tried to fathom the staggering implications. Was it a cosmic breeding experiment by an alien race? Were "they" trying to narrow the distance between "them" and us? To what end? To someday join us on planet earth? Or escape with our genetic stock to . . . wherever they came from? There were two possibilities, Hopkins speculated. Either he had stumbled upon some heretofore unknown mental aberration that afflicted a broad cross-section of otherwise ordinary women all over the world, or these women with strangely similar stories were reporting something other than dreams, something real. If imagined, what explained the corroboration of witnesses? The mysterious scars? And the "baked" circle and lane in Kathie's yard where she said a UFO had landed and taken off on June 30, 1983? Chemical tests found no difference with the adjacent soil. But why did planted grass seed fail to sprout there? And when the snow fell, why did it melt there first, leaving the marked pattern even more visible? But if the stories were real, why was there never any medical corroboration from the women's physicians? If they *were* real, though . . . Hopkins could scarcely imagine the implications.

Staff of the Massachusetts Mental Health Center, once Boston Psychopathic Hospital or "The Psycho," where Mack began his residency in psychiatry, 1958. Mack is in the middle row, center, in a white jacket and striped tie. Photo courtesy of the Mack family.

Mack in US Air Force,
probably 1959.
Photo courtesy of
the Mack family.

Mack, early 1960s.
Photo courtesy of
the Mack family.

Mack and Sally, with Japanese household staff, in Japan shortly after Danny was born in April 1960. By the following summer the family had returned to the United States. Photo courtesy of the Mack family.

Mack and Sally, probably after returning from Japan, early 1960s.
Photo courtesy of the Mack family.

Mack (right) at the Cambridge Hospital, where he headed the Harvard Medical School's initiative to extend psychiatric care to a long-downtrodden Cambridge community in the 1960s. Second from the left is the renowned developmental psychologist Erik Erikson, whose Erikson Center was later affiliated with the Cambridge Hospital. Photo courtesy of the Mack family.

Mack and actress Lily Tomlin, Boston, August 20, 1985, the year her show, *The Search for Signs of Intelligent Life in the Universe*, opened on Broadway. Tomlin would win the Tony Award for best performance by a leading actress in a play. At the time, Mack was deeply involved in protesting against nuclear weapons. Photo courtesy of the Northeast News Service of Quincy, Massachusetts.

The Mack family protesting nuclear weapons at the Nevada Test Site, May 1986. Mack is second from the left in a polo shirt, shorts, and bucket hat. On his immediate left is his son Kenny; next to Kenny is Danny and then Tony. They stepped over a sheriff's line and were arrested, fined, and released, but Kenny insisted on serving his six-day sentence. Photo courtesy of the Mack family.

Mack (below an instructor), skydiving as part of his men's empowerment activities, October 18, 2002. With the women's liberation movement all the rage, Mack had joined a men's group headed by Robert Bly, author of *Iron John*. Photo courtesy of the Mack family.

Undated photo of Mack and Digger, the beloved coonhound his son Kenny
had rescued from a shelter. Photo courtesy of the Mack family.

17

MACK'S SECRET

Mack didn't immediately follow up the letters Hopkins had given him at their meeting in New York in January 1990. He was off on a rushed trip to Prague for his Center for Psychological Studies in the Nuclear Age with his friend Dan Ellsberg and Harvard's Margaret Brenman-Gibson, Sally's idol in political activism and wife of the playwright William Gibson, who had written *The Miracle Worker* about Helen Keller.[1] Brenman-Gibson had also attended summer conferences with Mack at Robert Lifton's Wellfleet retreat, where she held the floor with her extravagant body language, elaborate multilayer costumes, and striking classical profile, immortalized in a charcoal drawing Norman Rockwell made of her in 1962 in gratitude for the treatment she had given him and his wife, Mary, at Austen Riggs.

Mack had been eagerly tracking events in Czechoslovakia, celebrating the Velvet Revolution and the new democratic government under the beloved dissident writer Václav Havel that spelled an end to half a century of Nazi overlords and Soviet commissars. Mack, Ellsberg, and Brenman-Gibson were there to share in the jubilation and discuss ethnonationalism. But Mack, who had recently turned sixty, was heavily burdened, tormented by muscle pain, marital woes, and his rocky romance with Roz, as he recorded in his journal.

> My soul is like a wide open sewer, into which and out of all sorts of crap flows . . . If I can't find fulfillment with Sally what are my options?
> 1. death
> 2. divorce
> 3. Do the best I can and give up much of who I am.
> 4. Negotiate
> 5. Withhold some truth
> 6. Lie + cheat.

He tried to relax with bioenergetics, Prozac, and John le Carré's *The Russia House*. Although he struggled to focus on the journey, he felt alienated from his traveling companions. He wrote, ". . . don't know what I'm doing here . . . losing my mind . . . Don't know . . ."

Prague was as gray as ever, but there were smiles on people's faces now and a warm greeting at the once-grand Alcron Hotel off historic Wenceslas Square, which in its prewar heyday had welcomed Charlie Chaplin, Winston Churchill, and Nazi leaders but now was facing a court battle and closure.

Once he plunged into meetings with the triumphant dissidents, however, Mack was quickly distracted. He heard the story of St. Agnes of Bohemia, the thirteenth-century princess who was betrothed at eight years old to the ten-year-old son of the Holy Roman Emperor but instead chose a life of piety, poverty, and service to the sick. She was canonized in November 1989, more than seven hundred years after her death, in an act that fired up the revolution. Mack, Ellsberg, and Brenman-Gibson attended a ceremony commemorating the immolation of student Jan Palach, who had set himself afire to protest the 1968 Soviet invasion of Czechoslovakia that had crushed the previous liberation movement known as Prague Spring. His remains were later reinterred where he fell, outside the National Museum on Wenceslas Square. They were surprised to run into Barbara Walters, who recognized Ellsberg and whisked him off for a quick interview.

The next day Mack, Ellsberg, and Brenman-Gibson sat down at the American Embassy with Shirley Temple Black, the onetime child film star who had served at the United Nations under President Nixon and been named Ambassador to Czechoslovakia by President George H. W. Bush. Ellsberg drew Mack's attention to a photo on her wall showing Anne Frank's wartime hideout from the Nazis in Amsterdam. Temple-Black, whose trademark golden curls had turned to a serious dark coif, praised the Czech liberation struggle, which she had aided. But, she insisted, "I didn't do it, the students did it."

Only when Mack left Prague did he think back to his encounter with Budd Hopkins. Were the abductees telling the truth? Had something indeed real happened to them? He jotted speculations in his journal. "U F O—what if the horror/sci Fi fantasy stuff is not Freud projection but the effort to come to terms with the nightmare trauma of our visitations from the 'other universe,' which, because we cannot accept its reality, must come to us as buried horrors do—& this we displace in horror stories, twilight zones etc."

Mack had kept his traveling companions in the dark. Ellsberg later thought that Mack had only come across alien abduction after Prague and was shocked to learn that Mack had been captivated since first meeting Hopkins before their trip. When Mack's unusual research did emerge, Ellsberg remembered, "We all thought he went off the deep end." Not totally, though; just on that one subject. In all other areas, Ellsberg said, Mack continued functioning as a highly skilled professional. Ellsberg had talked it over later with Brenman-Gibson, and she agreed. Mack was suffering "segmented psychosis."

18

"HE'S GOT THIS GLASS JAR . . ."

Back in Cambridge, Mack thought he would confide his meeting with Hopkins to his old Harvard Medical School roommate, Lester Grinspoon, another disturber of the universe.[1] A senior psychiatrist at Mass Mental and a founding editor of the *American Psychiatric Association Annual Review* and the *Harvard Mental Health Letter*, Grinspoon was renowned for a revolutionary book, *Marihuana Reconsidered* (an old spelling), which was published by Harvard University Press in 1971. He had been an instinctive evangelist against cannabis without knowing much about it until, as he told it, he once found his friend, the world-famous astrophysicist Carl Sagan, toking up at home. He had scolded Sagan, but then Sagan passed the joint to Grinspoon. "Here, Lester, have a puff." Grinspoon, after exhaustive research, came to reverse his opposition and advocate for legalization decades before history would largely vindicate him. In the book Sagan was identified as "Mr. X."

Mack had begun trying LSD, grasping for words to capture the experience in his journal in January 1990. Exactly when and where he began or where he got the hallucinogen (which had been outlawed by Congress in 1968 and placed on the Controlled Substances index in 1970) was not recorded, but LSD remained prevalent at Harvard and many other campuses. "What is the ecsta[s]y, the surrender, the oneness: the divine," he wrote. "Why is the energy so powerful? Can people experience that who are not on LSD? What is the physical effect. The ecstatic surrender seems divine, beyond sex. All creation is there. How did we get to a place of questioning the divinity . . ."

But now Mack just wanted to talk about his meeting with Hopkins. Grinspoon listened with astonishment. Was this Mack's idea of a joke? He remembered reading a book about Betty and Barney Hill and their outlandish tale of being forced aboard a spacecraft by humanoid beings for bizarre pseudo-medical probes. Grinspoon ascribed it to a folie à deux (one person's hallucination transmitted to another), and he was incredulous now to hear Mack talk of genital probes and hybrid babies. He was dumbfounded when Mack said the aliens immobilized humans with rods and followed them with implanted tracking devices. Grinspoon even remembered Mack's intimating he actually had one such instrument, presumably from an abductee (although when pressed about it years later Grinspoon could no longer be certain of the details).

"Have you told anyone else about this?" Grinspoon asked.

"No," Mack said.

"Do me a favor," Grinspoon said. "Don't." Sagan would soon be visiting from Cornell. They should all meet to discuss it. Mack knew Sagan well and was agreeable. By all means bring the device, Grinspoon urged. Sagan could have it tested.

But when they all later sat down in Grinspoon's office, Mack didn't have it and didn't mention it. He told them about Hopkins's research and the letters. Grinspoon and Sagan were aghast. Where was evidence that any of this was real? It *seemed* real, Mack insisted. They argued for hours. That night Mack called Grinspoon and explained about the device. He would have it tested himself. "The trouble with you and Carl," Mack said, "is you're too Cartesian." What a seventeenth-century worldview of mind-body separation had to do with this, Grinspoon wasn't sure.

Not long after, Mack met again with Sagan, whom Mack accused of guarding "the gates of change." "He tried to break me down," Mack later recounted. "He got himself in more and more outlandish explanations."

Sagan, one of the world's best-known scientists with a gift for popularizing cosmology, had overlapped with Mack at Harvard, joining the faculty in 1963 as an assistant professor of astronomy (championed by UFO skeptic Donald Menzel). In 1966 Sagan collaborated with the Soviet astrophysicist Iosif S. Shlovsky on an English translation of his book, *Intelligent Life in the Universe*, which considered the plausibility of extraterrestrial contacts during recorded history. Denied tenure at Harvard over resentment of his freewheeling intellect, Sagan moved to Cornell in 1968 and became the director of the Laboratory for Planetary Studies. He chaired a NASA committee that created a phonographic record of humans for potential discovery by alien life. The record consisted of twelve-inch gold-plated copper disks containing sounds and images from earth, and these were put aboard the two Voyager spacecraft that were sent off to interstellar space in 1977—a bottle, Sagan said, launched hopefully into the cosmic ocean. Sagan's first best seller, *The Dragons of*

Eden: Speculations on the Evolution of Human Intelligence, won the Pulitzer Prize for general nonfiction in 1978, a year after Mack's Lawrence biography. In 1980 he scored another triumph with the thirteen-part television sensation, *Cosmos*, which aired on PBS. Among the most acclaimed television ever broadcast, it would earn a worldwide audience of some 500 million viewers. Sagan was consumed by the question of alien life but insisted it be pursued scientifically, as by the radio signals beamed out to the cosmos by SETI (the Search for Extraterrestrial Intelligence). He was unimpressed by Mack's accounts of people taken by aliens. Anyone could say anything, Sagan said. But where was the proof science required? A piece of an alien spacecraft, Or something that could be tested. As he often said, extraordinary claims require extraordinary evidence.

Notwithstanding the ridicule of Sagan and Grinspoon, on February 17, 1990, five weeks after Mack first met Hopkins, he was back in New York to see Hopkins. This time he went with Blanche Chavoustie and Bob Lifton.[2] Hopkins had invited four of his abductees, including Chavoustie's former patient, the operetta composer who dreamed of head implants used for tracking. In treatment she remembered undergoing abortions but couldn't say how many. Chavoustie had found that strange. What woman didn't remember her abortions? She also couldn't remember how she got pregnant. She recalled a car trip with a girlfriend in which each was driving a little sports car. In Tennessee they stopped to watch a flying disc. Then suddenly it was night, and their windshields were covered with dew. They had been chased by a single light—a state trooper on a motorcycle, they figured—but he had only wordlessly looked at their licenses and let them go. At some point the woman remembered being a child of four or five and lying under a big examining light with lots of strange people around. Chavoustie thought her patient's case masked elements of abduction, which is why Chavoustie had introduced her to Budd Hopkins and why Chavoustie thought Mack should meet Hopkins.

Another experiencer at Hopkins's townhouse was a woman who had first come forward under a pseudonym, Linda Cortile, and then later provided her real name, Linda Napolitano. She had written Hopkins about childhood memories of shrouded figures in her bedroom and the discovery of a mysterious scar in her nose. Later, under hypnosis, she recovered memories of having been floated out of her window into a spaceship over the Brooklyn Bridge.

The gathering at Hopkins's place was like a soul-baring AA meeting, Mack thought. "So I met Budd and got interested and troubled because it shakes up a lot of what I had—I like to be able to explain things and I couldn't," he told the group. "And I was troubled for the people that were going through this, and I was troubled for my profession in a sense because we haven't been available to people and I wanted to know more about it." To Mack's astonishment, Lifton admitted familiarity with abduction experiences. "I've been in on this since the early 60s, I think," Lifton said. He turned to Hopkins. "Before you were interested in UFOs." Hopkins confirmed it. "Yeah, before I even had a sighting I think, yeah, sure." Lifton went on to say, "Budd has been talking to me about his work for a long time; on a couple of other occasions I've met with some people through Budd who've had UFO experiences, and I've done a lot of work with trauma, people who've been through very severe trauma, Hiroshima, Vietnam veterans. I've done a lot of work involving that kind of so-called post-traumatic response and I could recognize some of what I found in such people in people who've been through UFO experiences and it wasn't exactly clear to me or to anybody else exactly what the trauma was."

One of the women described her night terrors in childhood. "Usually when you're dreaming you're asleep," she said, "but I was awake." Mack knew a lot about nightmares. He had written a book about them. He agreed this sounded different. "I can only say I don't know except that we have to take another look," he told the group. Several of the women asked how they could protect their children who were suffering similar night terrors.

Perhaps they couldn't, Mack said, but they should not tell the children they were just imagining it. The children know these are more than dreams and would no longer trust their parents. Tell the child, "We're worried too, we're together in this," Mack said. "We don't know what it is, it's scary, but we'll be together and we'll do our very best together."

Two days later, back in Cambridge, Mack wrote Jerome Clark, the editor of *International UFO Reporter* and a board member of the Center for UFO Studies as well as one of the field's most respected scholars. Earlier, at Hopkins's request, Clark had sent Mack back issues of *Reporter*, which Mack found eminently reasonable. He asked Clark a favor: "If from your vantage point, you could inform me about the status of serious psychiatric or psychological research or other work on this matter." By psychiatric, Mack hastened to add, he was not suggesting that these often traumatized people were suffering a mental disorder. He didn't know. "I am not invested in debunking or proving anything," he stressed. And he concluded, "Since this interest is a new one for me, and I would not wish to be prematurely discredited, I would appreciate it if you could keep this letter confidential, or use extreme discretion in deciding with whom to share its contents."

But at a dinner date with Roz at a restaurant in Rhode Island, Mack readily confided his excitement. He had now interviewed his own very first abductee who had made a strong impression, convincing him, as he gushed to Roz, "This person is not psychotic!"

Roz was taken aback but strived to be supportive. "I believe you," she said. "Go ahead."

In truth, she later recalled, she didn't know quite how to respond. It occurred to her that he was speaking as if this was all quite obviously true.

"John," she finally said, "I'm with you, but I don't think the public will be. Be careful!"

Mack soon collected additional experiencers and invited several of them to an Affect Seminar he was leading at Harvard to explore feelings in the face of traumatic experiences.[3]

Amy Anglin, a sweet-faced environmental-protection worker from Michigan, shared her strange encounters since childhood, retrieved under hypnotic regressions. At age fourteen, she and her best friend had been agog at what they remembered as the flashing red, blue, and green lights of a landed craft in the girl's backyard. Dozens of other nearby witnesses later reported similar sightings, which the police attributed to an advertising plane. "And we said that can't be right because advertising planes don't land noiselessly in your backyard," Amy recalled. Another time at a sleepover at a girlfriend's house, her parents found them missing in the middle of the night and called the police. A search turned up no trace of them, but they soon reappeared inexplicably safe and sound in their beds. Years later she experienced terrifying flashbacks. One night, she recounted, "I'm all scrunched up on my side, I see a face. These eyes come out of the darkness, very big, very round, sort of like seal eyes, you see a seal, nice soft dark eyes . . . and in the darkness he comes forward, it's a little guy, hominoid, probably about 3 ½ feet tall, he has a pretty square jaw, very flat small nose, very furrowed brow, no hair, he's dark blue green in color, sort of steely, not very bright, sort of dusty and he's not saying anything to me . . ." She had memories of being plucked out of bed and placed on a cotton-lined table, where she felt a vibrating cone-shaped device enter her vagina and push her apart, a needle painfully entering her ribcage, and her head being implanted with some object by a crystalline energy force. She also remembered being maneuvered into an arousing sexual encounter with another abductee she knew, while, to her mortification, their captors watched. Later, she had the sensation she was pregnant, but before she could see her gynecologist, ". . . I go to bed and I—before I'm even asleep, three beings are in the room with me . . . I go 'oh shit,' and we go through the ceiling of my apartment . . ." The next thing she knew, she said, she was on a table with a nursemaid and "someone we call the doctor, he's very paternal, very in charge of everything . . ." Her pregnancy is removed and "he's got this glass jar, it's got something in it . . ."

But it wasn't only terror, Amy told the Affect Seminar. She was also getting apocalyptic images of a dying world.

"This is emerging now with others that I'm working with," Mack told the seminar, "this very powerful ecological consciousness that emerges from people that would not be particularly environmentally minded or transformational but that seems to be an outgrowth of these experiences."

He continued his sessions with experiencers and, in August 1990, only seven months after meeting Budd Hopkins, exposed more of his research at one of Grof's semiannual training modules at Hollyhock Farm on Cortes Island, Canada.[4] "I've never spoken on this subject. I've never acknowledged publicly I'm doing this work," he told the group. He called it "a slight emergence from the closet—this is like private, with your private buddies here." He took a moment to recognize Chavoustie, who made no mention of her conviction that she was a victim of CIA mind-control experiments. (In 1997 she would tell the Toronto counterculture FM station CKLN that she had started receiving strange phone messages and other harassment in 1989 and that in May 1990, "I was kidnapped and taken to Cornell Medical Cent[er] in Westchester. There I was put in isolation and they tried to force me to take drugs." She would later represent a group called ACHES-MC, Advisory Committee for Human Experiment Survivors—Mind Control. Testimony before the US Senate in 1977 revealed that the bulk of Project MKUltra records had been destroyed, and with them the names of the unwitting victims, one of the most heinous scandals in the history of American intelligence. But recovered documents showed that Cornell had indeed played a key part in the experiments.) Instead, Chavoustie told the abduction story of her operetta-writing patient and how she had referred Mack to Hopkins. Yes, Mack confirmed to the group, "Blanche is very much co-responsible." There were deep questions about the phenomenon, he went on. What was its ontological status, its nature of being? What was its meaning, or purpose? And, more personally, how had he ended up in the middle of it?

His new interest, he said, overlapped astrological readings with a forty-year-old psychologist and philosopher, Richard Tarnas, who had done his doctoral dissertation on LSD, studied psychotherapy under Grof, and was completing a history of the ideas that shaped Western thought, *The Passion of the Western Mind*. After meeting Tarnas at Hollyhock Farm, Mack had invited him to speak at Harvard. Tarnas was a scholar of astrology, not the pop cliché of sun signs and tabloid horoscopes, but the more serious study of correlations between the movements of celestial bodies and life on earth. Tarnas had cautioned him of a risk that his astrological chart highlighted, Mack said. "'I don't think you would do this,' he says, 'but there's a danger of going off half-cocked with my particular chart, of getting too enthralled with something . . . something that needs to be looked at very critically.'"

He had had Tarnas do his and Roz's horoscopes as well. The match was less than perfect, Roz remembered, although Mack seemed pleased by the results.

His Harvard colleagues knew nothing of his abduction research, Mack told the Grof group, but he had discussed it with his therapist Khalsa. When Mack complained that people kept pressing him on whether the abduction phenomenon was "real" or not, Khalsa put it into his own terms: "It's like people ask me about yoga—do you float or not? Look, if I can elevate my consciousness over the crap that comes on TV, I've floated."

Now, Mack told the group, he needed their advice. His sense was that this differed from other spirit manifestations—"It penetrates our reality in a harder way."

One of his clients had suffered a searing nasal pain and sneezed out a fine thread-like object. The chief of pathology at the Cambridge Hospital was analyzing it now. Another had somehow lost her baby. She was a thirty-two-year-old mother of two with memories of being taken aboard a craft that smelled dank and "swampy." She had balked at being taken through an archway—she felt she was pregnant and didn't want "them" to take the baby. The strangest thing was, her husband couldn't have been the father. He'd had a vasectomy. "They want me to walk in by myself," she had told Mack. "It's horrible. If they want to take a baby, why don't they just take it? Why do you have to give it up?" Then, Mack said, she had answered her own question. "They said it's good for me to have to mentally let it go. The 'doctor' there, he's smiling, he says it's not my baby anyway."

"I was shaken up by this," Mack said. "There seems to be some kind of inter-species, inter-being relationship around reproduction." He saw it, he said, "as kind of a fourth blow to our collective ego." First, Copernicus displaced the earth from the center of the universe. Then Darwin dislodged man as the centerpiece of creation. Next, Freud destroyed the notion of humans as rational beings—they were ruled by their dark, primal drives. Now came the transpersonal revolution, Mack said. "We ourselves are not our own selves—other species can breed with us, do what they want."

"How do you explain your attraction to this?" someone asked.

"The short answer is, I don't," Mack said. "The longer answer is it showed up for me in the context of my own sort of consciousness exploration."

It all emerged from the breathwork, he said. "None of this would have happened except in the context of this work." He seemed to have found a pathway into some other dimension where he could experience his long-lost mother and encounter alternate realities. And so, he explained, he was professionally and personally drawn to the mystery and the plight of the abductees. "As a psychiatrist, this is an untreated, un-understood population, mis-diagnosed as an associative state and very interesting clinically, theoretically and ontologically." *They* were making a mockery of our technology, evading our radar and Air Force countermeasures while sometimes allowing astounding documentation of their presence. "We're primitive compared to what this is."

Perhaps, he went on, "the divine mind has decided we've gone far enough messing up the planet and they've given us something really to worry about which isn't so earthbound so there are potentially international political implications." Like, he said, "the narrow fight over half-dead matter called oil which we're prepared to blow up masses of people for—we could be interrupted in that preoccupation." Now, Mack said, "whether aliens are doing that or God is doing that or our own unconsciousness is doing that, it's very common on the ships that the aliens will show visions of nuclear war or visions of destructiveness. Budd Hopkins thinks they're just trying to see people's reactions."

Grof mentioned *apports*, objects that materialize in séances. "This table here is as much of a mystery as a flying saucer," Grof said. "If we believe there is matter, there has to be some point where the matter came into existence, so there is materialization. Whether it's you or the Martian what's the difference?"

"John," someone thought to ask, "before everyone goes, do you want your association with this to remain confidential when we're out in the world?"

Surprised, he stammered, "Gee, I never even thought about trusting this group. I assumed—yeah—more or less."

"It's too late!" shouted a joker.

So, someone asked, "you don't want us telling people you're really involved?"

"Well," Mack confessed, "I'd hoped we didn't get that far—I'd like some advice on the strategies of coming out. I feel a little bit sort of like in the closet."

"Don't you have something in the medical journal?"

"No," Mack said.

"Weren't you going to?"

"Yeah," Mack said. Probably, eventually.

19

"THE ABDUCTION SYNDROME"

Mack was indeed thinking of publication. It began with plans for an article in the *American Journal of Psychiatry*. Editor John C. Nemiah was encouraging. The idea stemmed from a 1990 UFO conference at the Santa Barbara Centre for Humanistic Studies where Mack, Hopkins, and David Jacobs discussed their research. As a psychiatrist, Mack said, "I think there's more to it in some of the positive experiences that people have undergone." Abductees often come to feel themselves more ethical, more empathetic. They may also feel part of something momentous—a breeding experiment or something else so important that their pain and terror become endurable. They may even feel a deeply loving relationship with another intelligence. Perhaps it was self-deception, a survival strategy to cope with overwhelming shock, he said, "but I think it's a serious question and needs to be looked at." Mack said he was not shocked at allegations of government cover-up. "I think that the government knows its helplessness, knows it can't protect us," he said. Governments were about domination, protection, and control. UFOs made a mockery of that, a trickster archetype evading radar detection, appearing and disappearing, snatching people from their beds. He cited David J. Hufford's book, *The Terror That Comes in the Night*, with its accounts of sleepers who felt suffocated by a malign entity crushing their chest. "We've got make-believe and we've got reality," Mack said. "I think we need a category of phenomena for which we have no category."

When Mack, Hopkins, and Jacobs met again in January 1991, they agreed to back Mack's preparation of "a solidly written dispassionate article" for Nemiah's journal or another publication.

By October Mack had produced a 103-page draft he was calling "The Abduction Syndrome."[1] For the last year, he wrote, he had been opening his home to monthly support group meetings, each attended by ten to eighteen people. He had ended up treating thirty-four of them, some in the same family, including a fourteen-year-old boy and three children ages seven and younger, the youngest with encounters going back to the age of two. The oldest was sixty-two. But most were in their prime reproductive years. Just over half pretty clearly met the criteria of an abductee, while the rest seemed possible or likely abductees. Almost all of the obvious abductees were women, perhaps because women were more likely than men to come forward. He had probed the memories of some with hypnotic regressions, which he defended as common practice in such treatment and necessary in order to penetrate the ensuing amnesia.

Mack began the article by decrying the scientific boycott of the subject in the psychiatric literature, which he attributed to a fear of ridicule and the subject's aura of delusion and fabrication. He said it was hard to know the prevalence of the abduction syndrome because of a lack of criteria and a reluctance of experiencers to come forward. But then he said that a California emergency medicine specialist and abduction researcher, John G. Miller, had extrapolated from Orange County cases reported to him in 1988 to estimate as many as one hundred thousand to two hundred thousand abduction cases nationwide. Others, Mack said, put the number as high as one million or more. He didn't dwell on the likelihood of these figures, footnoting only a letter to him from Miller, a Temple University survey by David Jacobs, and a Roper Poll that, extrapolating from a sample of only 119 respondents, projected almost 4 million likely American abductees, which critics would find ludicrous. He reviewed the rich history of abduction accounts, particularly the Hills case, along with Hopkins's pioneering books and Jacobs's study of the medical procedures experiencers reported. False memories were not plausibly implantable by the hypnotist nor were the accounts easily shakable, Mack insisted, in the face of considerable controversy over the issue.

In 1983 the nation had been consumed by sensational allegations of child abuse at the McMartin Preschool in Manhattan Beach, California. After one mother reported that her son had been sodomized at the school, a wide-ranging police investigation ballooned into charges that hundreds of children had been subjected by the staff to bizarre sexual violations and satanic abuse. But damning testimony in what became the longest and most expensive criminal trial in American history exposed implanted suggestions to the children by overzealous interviewers, and the case, with its increasingly outlandish accounts of implausible scenarios (including animal sacrifice and grave robbing), collapsed with no resulting convictions.

The Courage to Heal: A Guide for Women Survivors of Child Sexual Abuse, a 1988 bestseller by Ellen Bass, a poet and creative-writing teacher, and Laura Davis, an author and incest survivor, threw another spotlight on the reliability of recovered memories when critics called some of the research into question.

That same year, a Seattle-area deputy sheriff and Republican Party county chairman, Paul Ingram, was accused by his daughters and son of horrific sexual abuse, charges that progressed from molestations to torture and rape in murderous satanic rituals. Although Ingram claimed no memory of the events, and no forensic evidence was ever produced, under hypnosis Ingram readily adopted his accusers' charges. He pled guilty to rape and was sentenced to prison. He later alleged that his confession was coerced and tried to withdraw his plea, but his appeals were rejected and he ended up spending the next fourteen years behind bars. In an article in the *New Yorker* and again in a 1994 book, *Remembering Satan*, author Lawrence Wright would argue that Ingram was an innocent man victimized by his gullibility and pseudo-psychological error.

Just two years later, in 1990 (a year before Mack's abduction draft), a fifty-one-year-old former San Mateo, California, firefighter named George Franklin Sr. was convicted of the 1969 murder of eight-year-old Susan Nason of Foster City. His conviction was based on what prosecutors called a two-decade-old repressed memory of Franklin's then twenty-nine-year-old daughter Eileen. She testified that she was looking into her own daughter's eyes when she suddenly remembered her father crushing the skull of her childhood friend at a highway rest stop. "I saw my father approaching Susan, his hands above his head, a rock in his hands. I screamed. I yelled . . . I heard two blows," Eileen recalled in court. She had told investigators that the memory first came to her under therapeutic hypnosis, but then she later said she had made up the hypnosis to add credibility to her account. Yet even in the absence of any forensic corroboration, Franklin was found guilty and sentenced to life in prison. He spent six years in prison before his conviction was thrown out by a federal judge who found that the trial court had improperly suppressed evidence that all the details of the murder Eileen had produced had been available in original news accounts of the crime.

Franklin's defense had been aided by a renowned psychologist and memory researcher, Elizabeth Loftus of the University of Washington, who had also consulted on the McMartin Preschool case and many other prominent prosecutions, testifying that even well-meaning psychotherapists can implant false memories into witnesses' minds. One of her studies concerned auto accidents and how accounts of eyewitnesses could be twisted by the wording of questions—whether the vehicles, for example, "contacted," "hit," or "smashed into" each other. But Loftus, who would go on to the University of California, Irvine, as a distinguished professor and be listed by the *Review of General Psychology* as one of the most eminent psychologists of the twentieth century, would also provoke strong pushback from other professionals, including John Mack, who defended the accuracy of memories that concerned deeply personal traumas, like abduction experiences.

Mack also took issue with another challenger. Starting in 1977, Alvin H. Lawson, an English professor at Cal State Long Beach, and two of his colleagues began working with a clinical hypnotist. Together, they studied ten women and six men aged from twelve to sixty-five who had no significant knowledge of UFOs but were asked under hypnosis to *imagine* details of an abduction encounter.[2] The results were later compared with accounts by actual abduction experiencers. To the surprise of Lawson, "striking similarities emerged," their subjects coming up with details "too abundant and complex to have sprung from ordinary pop culture sources." Lawson, who distrusted hypnosis, couldn't account for the results, which seemed to suggest that abduction experiences could be readily fabricated. But he thought that both "real" and imagined abduction stories might spring from some common sensory stimulus that remained a mystery. Later he hypothesized that they grew out of remembered birth experiences.

Mack objected that Lawson's findings didn't really explain the abduction phenomenon, especially the scars and multiple-witness accounts, and even Lawson agreed that that UFO abductions seemed distinct from other hallucinatory experiences.

"The Abduction Syndrome" presented Mack's research as rigorous, backed by sixteen mental-health professionals who had seen more than 750 supposed abductees. It relied in part on a groundbreaking 1987 study of 270 cases, *UFO Abductions: The Measure of a Mystery*, compiled by the noted academic folklorist Thomas E. Bullard. But Mack put the most stock in his own core group of sixteen experiencers.

One, whom he called "Jill," had a two-year-old son who lay in his crib making flying motions with his stuffed toy and said, "Doggy fly in the sky." When Jill expressed surprise, the child said, "Uh huh, I fly in the sky," and when she asked where, he said, "To the spaceship." Given what else he had heard from Jill, Mack found this intriguingly confirmatory; the child, he thought, was unlikely to be complicit in a scam or to be referencing UFO books or movies. Another was "Will," a forty-two-year-old retired fireman who kept a "Chronicle of Alien Intervention" detailing more than two decades of encounters. There was also "Ginny," a thirty-six-year-old woman who worked with the deaf and had memories of alien beings crowding around her bassinet in infancy and recalled an abduction and invasive medical probe at age four. Ginny sometimes felt that her body did not leave the room while she was mentally projected onto the spaceship.

Abductees were frequently taken from their bedrooms during sleep, Mack wrote, but also from other locations indoors and out. "Cathy," a twenty-five-year-old employee of the US Drug Enforcement Administration, was found in a field near her flipped-over snowmobile after being missing for an hour and a half. Her coat, hat, scarf, and gloves were found neatly folded nearby. Later, under hypnosis, details of an abduction experience came back to her.

It usually began, Mack said, with the sighting of a craft that could be remembered as a helicopter, van, bus, or other vehicle; a bright light; a humming or buzzing sound; and the terrifying materialization of small humanoid figures, sometimes also appearing as deer, owls, or other animals. Abductees might feel transported on a ramp or beam of light through closed doors and windows and onto a ship, seeing their home recede below. They said they felt paralyzed, numb and powerless, and intensely afraid. Witnesses, on the other hand, were commonly "switched off," unable to interfere and often completely oblivious. But sometimes relatives or friends were abducted together and recognized each other on the ships.

The beings were commonly described as robotic or buglike "little guys" of three and a half to four feet tall with greyish, leathery skin and form-fitting grey or blue jumpsuits or robes, he said. There were also slightly larger figures, often called "doctors," who seemed in charge of the smaller beings and the abduction process. The small beings had smooth, pear-shaped heads that tapered to pointy chins and protruded in the back as well as thin lines for a mouths, holes for noses, skinny necks and arms, and hands with three or four fingers. The legs were rarely described, and the feet seemed encased in boots. The most striking features were the eyes—enormous elliptical black orbs. Communication was telepathic; "It's just in my head," Mack said he often heard from experiencers.

The craft interiors were commonly described as curved and gleaming white with slab-like examining tables. Experiencers often reported glimpses of screens, terminals, medical machines, maps, symbols, and debris. Some found the air on the ships clammy or stale. Inside, the abductees recalled being subjected to an array of invasive medical procedures with instruments often described in vivid detail.

Jill remembered "a big cylindrical thing with a little spout and a big handle . . . a spoon, a gray cloth underneath everything, a bunch of tubing, gray tubing, it's got silver stuff on it, strange things, needles, a pan . . ." The doctor figure "got the tube curled around his hand maybe three or four times and it's got silver bands on it every six or eight inches." The tube, she remembered, had a half-inch silver and blue ball on the end and a diamond-shaped form that opened like petals to deposit the ball inside her vagina, causing intense cramping. She offered Mack a novel theory on how she was transported from place to place during her encounters: "It's as though, if you want to get from point A to point B, you can take point B and twist it and just wrap it around and make it next to point A. You don't have to 'travel.' You just are right there. I don't think it's technology. I think it's more intent."

Citing Hopkins and Jacobs, Mack wrote, "A growing body of literature suggests that human reproductive functioning and sexuality is at the core of the abduction phenomenon." Both men and women "report a staggering range of experiences related to reproduction and sex which includes gynecological probing, removal and reimplantation of ova (after fertilization), removal or disappearance of fetuses up to seven months' gestation, taking of sperm samples, extrauterine incubation of embryos on spacecraft, human observation and nursing or other connection with hybrid fetuses, alien-human sexual intercourse and 'bonding' and human intercourse observed by aliens on and off the spacecraft."

"Lois," a psychiatrist with conscious memories of abductions since age three or four, believed she had lost at least six pregnancies during abductions, leaving her doctor mystified over her evident miscarriages. Ginny recalled having her eggs removed. "I saw a machine that looked like a suction machine and they would just suck them out into this long tube and into this little sack, full of like a saline solution or something where they were kept." She also described feeling "bonded" or "mated" to a particular alien doctor who had intercourse with her, but it was unfeeling, "like a ritual." The penis was "thinner and colder . . . like an erected one or something" with "a plunger or something else being inserted."

Ann, who remembered being abducted with her girlfriend, said it was worse in some ways for men because "women are more used to being powerless." She recalled finding herself on a spacecraft with a former boyfriend and being compelled to have intercourse with him as aliens watched, to her humiliation and anger. Jill graphically remembered being led to a kind of operating room where, supposedly of her own volition, she was forced to give up her baby.

"It's horrible," she told Mack. "They said it's good for me. That you have to mentally let go of it. I don't have a choice, but I have to do it by myself." Jill said she was later shown a room full of hybrid children, including her own.

Ginny offered a similar account of "a chamber where all the babies, the fetuses are being born," and even a school of hybrid children where she saw one "who looked like me." She put her arm around one. "I was the Earth kid, sort of visiting." For all the trauma, experiencers often felt an intense bonding with the aliens, Mack found.

There was another aspect to the abductions, he wrote. Abductees frequently remembered seeing apocalyptic images of nuclear and ecological destruction of the earth, as if they needed to do something about it. "I have a fear for the earth," a woman named "Shannon" told Mack. "We're killing ourselves . . . I was shown a screen. It showed droughts and trees drying up and crops drying up and people dying of famine, streams drying up, oceans were polluted . . . it was scary." Ann was more explicit. "I feel I've been told that there's something I'm going to have to do in the future when the chaos of environmental collapse comes and along with that when you have environmental collapse, you have economic collapse, government collapse, social collapse."

There was a compelling physical aspect to the phenomenon, Mack wrote. After an abduction, experiencers often found themselves oddly displaced or translocated. Cathy, the snowmobiler, had been dumbfounded to discover her missing outer garments neatly piled beside her. Jill had found herself in bed, "tucked in so hard I couldn't get up." Her husband hadn't done it; he had been asleep the whole time. "You can't tuck yourself in," Jill said. "I tried it." Others reported waking with their pajamas on backward or inside out, or naked with the nightclothes they had worn to bed nowhere to be found, or their feet caked in mud. Drivers were confused to find themselves suddenly far from where they had been, or way off the intended road, or much closer to their destination than they remembered.

Physical confirmation, however, was elusive, Mack acknowledged. Photos of UFOs were often equivocal, and soil samples from witnessed landing sites were intriguingly high in radiation but ultimately inconclusive. Abductees frequently displayed scars but couldn't fully explain their origin. Mack cited three possible implants recovered from abductees that, in the final analysis, turned out to consist of elements familiarly known on earth. In one case investigated by his friend Dave Pritchard at MIT, an object that an experiencer remembered being implanted in his penis during an abduction was found to consist of ordinary human biological material.

But who were these people? How did they differ, if they did, from other humans? They did not display any particular psychopathology. Indeed, many investigators set the absence of schizophrenic psychosis, severe depression, or neurosis as a condition of working with any abductee.

"In no case so far," wrote Mack, "have I found a way of tying the troubling events of my clients' histories to their abduction stories." Rather, he said, any disturbance seemed caused by their encounter, not the other way around.

As Mack saw it the stories were different enough to be original, so they were not copied from one person to another, yet they had a narrative consistency difficult to fake. The abductees as a group were not mentally ill. The phenomenon was associated with UFOs. It embodied a range of bizarre physical effects, from teleportation through walls to translocation, unexplained scars, and disappearing pregnancies. And even children too young to absorb cultural influences were describing eerily similar experiences.

If it wasn't mental illness, was it still somehow psychiatric? That is, was it internal, not external? But that wouldn't explain the consistency of the narratives and the similarity of physical aspects, Mack said. Was it mass hysteria or collective madness? But abductees were rarely in touch with each other before they were brought together in support groups. Indeed, they often seemed ashamed by their experiences, hardly likely to flaunt them to others. Were they picking up their stories from popular culture and mass media? An intriguing possibility, but movies like *Close Encounters of the Third Kind* and *ET* lacked the level of specificity in the abductee accounts. Were the abductees embellishing their stories under hypnosis? Unlikely, since the vivid details emerged only over intense resistance and with convincingly powerful negative affect, including weeping and terror as the experience was being relived.

What then of the long history of mythic visitations documented by folklorists like Eddie Bullard and Jacques Vallée, the French-born astronomer who compiled ancient tales of encounters with aerial craft and strange beings? Intriguing again, Mack wrote, but very different from the vividly specific accounts abductees were giving him and other investigators.

Then were they necessarily *extraterrestrials* somehow able to reach our world to abduct humans? David Jacobs, working on his first abduction book, *Secret Life*, thought so. "We have been invaded," Jacobs wrote. "The focus of the abduction is the production of children." Mack, who would write the foreword to Jacobs's book, wasn't so sure, but he agreed that no evidence had emerged to suggest that anything else was happening than what the abductees said.

But how could people pass through walls, be "switched off," or not see UFOs at all while others nearby saw them clearly? Where were the UFOs and their occupants when they were not materializing in our earth space? What planet(s) did they come from, and how did they get here? Why were the beings so humanoid and their medical procedures such a parody of ours? Where were the hybrid babies being raised? If these were literally spacecraft and alien beings, why was physical proof so elusive?

If the phenomenon was neither psychic nor extraterrestrial, Mack pondered, what was left? Jacques Vallée thought it might be interdimensional, with entities from some parallel universe penetrating our reality. It made sense to abductees like Ann. "I can really go to another time frame and can pull me from other time frames to here," she told Mack. "Rhonda" felt, "There's been times when I've wondered if I'd been put back in the wrong place for a couple of seconds. It feels . . . I don't know if I'm actually moving around through time." "Rich" put it cinematically: "When they come it is like someone shines a bright light behind the movie screen and obliterates the scene. What we perceive as the movie screen, what we call reality, they burn through, proving it's only a construct, a version of reality."

Mack sent his draft of "The Abduction Syndrome" to colleagues for feedback. "At this point," he said, "it is somewhere between a long paper and a book."

20

ALIENS AT HARVARD

Word of Mack's curious research was spreading at Harvard. In February 1991 a speaker canceled a presentation to the Shop Club, a Harvard institution since 1922 that offered a forum to senior faculty members from every school in the university to outline what Mack called "incompletely digested" work in progress once a month at the Faculty Club.[1] Mack was asked if he wanted to fill in. "Oh, no, I'm not ready," was his first reaction. Little more than a year had passed since he had learned of the phenomenon from Budd Hopkins. But then he thought, "Oh, what the hell."

And so, brushing aside Thomas Kuhn's advice to withhold judgment, Mack found himself in the stately, red-brick Georgian club before some forty colleagues, including the eminent philosopher Willard Van Orman Quine and the ethicist/psychologist Sissela Bok, daughter of the Myrdals and wife of Harvard's president, Derek Bok. Mack recounted the phenomenon, as he understood it, from beginning to end—the materialization of the spaceships, the abductions, the reproductive procedures, and the hybrid babies.

The outcry surprised him. But Mack couldn't help boasting that his talk had been "particularly well attended—perhaps even Harvard professors love a mystery." He acknowledged the hostility and Sissela Bok's reservations. Yet, he said, "if anyone thought me mad, he or she was too courteous to say." Either way, he had crossed a threshold. "But I think that as far as my engagement with this work is concerned I am completely out of the closet, I have no cover whatever in this community a[n]y more, which is both exhilarating and terrifying. It means that I am free."

Thus encouraged, he soon began planning a grand rounds on what he called the "Mystery of Anomalous Experience." Before the year was out, Mack took his presentation, this time with Budd Hopkins, to a packed Macht auditorium at Harvard's Cambridge Hospital.[2]

With medical student Wes Boyd following goggle-eyed from the audience, the program was announced by Leston Havens, the residency director and a pioneering psychopharmacologist himself who had interceded for Boyd when interviews at Harvard seemed closed. "I have a holiday treat," Havens began. He didn't need to recite the speaker's bona fides, he said. John Mack was the founder of the Cambridge Hospital's Psychiatry Department and a Pulitzer Prize winner. "He was willing to stand up and be counted on the issue of nuclear deterrence and disarmament." Mack was a man of courage, Havens said, and courage was the first of virtues to the ancient Greeks. "But it carries with it an extraordinary penalty—being thought foolish or even mad." Heads in the audience bobbed knowingly. "John has had attached to him those terms on many occasions and some of you may think that way today. I want to warn you about that because today's foolishness is often tomorrow's wisdom."

With that, Mack strode to the lectern clutching his notes and peering studiously down his nose through half-glasses.

In 1755, he began, the Prince of Tarsia in Calabria presented Domenico Tata, a professor of physics and mathematics in Naples, with a stone that shepherds had seen falling from the sky. Tata didn't believe stones could fall from the sky, and despite eyewitness accounts he held off on publishing anything for fear of the scientific elite known as the Savants. Finally in 1794 he included it in a pioneering study of what we now call meteorites. "I don't have thirty-nine years," Mack said. "I want to go forward with what I believe is the edge of this extraordinary phenomenon." A baby's wail immediately interrupted him. "*Intergenerational* phenomenon," he ad-libbed, drawing laughs. He said he had just written the foreword to a colleague's book—David Jacobs's *Secret Life*—in which were recounted some three hundred abductions of humans by alien beings. "This is a mystery," Mack said, asking the crowd to "suspend for a bit that attitude of mind that is a categorizer."

It had been thirty years since the touchstone abduction case of Betty and Barney Hill, whose astounding tale had been kept secret for four years, Mack said. Since then, "thousands have reported being taken and there may be *hundreds of thousands, if not millions.*" Whatever it was, it did not surrender its secrets readily, he said. "People ask, 'Why doesn't a UFO land on the White House lawn? Why don't we have better photographs?' I don't have the answer to that."

He started recounting "the reproductive dimension" and then stopped, as if just stuck by the absurdity. "I'm saying '*them*' as if they existed in reality," he said, "but the quotes are there because I'm not really presuming what *'they'* are in fact."

His account only grew weirder. "There's a great deal of curiosity they seem to have in staring at us, particularly in sexual situations. Often there are hybrid infants that seem to be the result of alien-human sexual cohabitation which the abductees are taken to see in later situations." The abductees helplessly suffer frightening invasive procedures, he said, but men endure a particular shame—forced ejaculation and the taking of sperm. Recovering the memory under hypnosis, Mack said, evokes unfathomable terror, "such intense rage and such expression of despair" that he was left stunned by its affective power and all the more convinced of its authenticity.

But it wasn't all physical terror, he said. Abductees were shown "visions of planetary destruction, ecological wasting," often leaving them with a heightened sense of environmental consciousness. It was a hot debate among abduction researchers—was this by design, an authentic phenomenon to re-school the human race, or some tactic by the beings to gauge human reaction?

Abductees suffered a fourfold trauma, Mack said: (1) the experience itself, (2) the isolation of knowing no one believed them, (3) the shattered sense of reality, and (4) the terror of knowing it could happen again anytime. Abductees were powerless to protect even their children.

Mack told of how he had learned of the phenomenon from Hopkins. "Since that time," he said, "little by little I have moved into that domain myself." So far he had met with more than fifteen women and ten men, plus some children, who all recalled, consciously or under hypnosis, having been taken onto a spacecraft and subjected to invasive, medical-like procedures. He was working on other cases as well—including infants. In fact, Mack said, the abductions often began in infancy and continued through the child-rearing years. And it wasn't just happening in America—there were cases all over the world. There seemed no pathology to explain it, not alcoholism, not mental illness, not sexual abuse. "Personally," he said, "it is difficult to find anything these people have in common, except they've been through something traumatic." Nor were they attention-seekers. On the contrary, they went to enormous lengths to convince themselves that they had somehow imagined their ordeal; they were even willing to be called crazy.

In a few moments, Mack promised, they would hear from Julia, "a

high-functioning woman within a healthy neurotic level of development."
He hastily turned to his attractive subject, who had jet-black shoulder-length
hair—the experiencer he had identified in "The Abduction Syndrome" as
"Jill." "You have to understand, Julia, in our community neurotic is a compli-
ment." The audience laughed. In short, Mack resumed, there was no data to
suggest that anything happened to these abductees other than what they said.
But, he admitted, "what in fact this is about is another question."

Budd Hopkins took the stage to show his slides, which began with photos
of UFOs over New Zealand, Florida, and Denmark. The images had been
authenticated, Hopkins said, by a Navy physicist and NASA scientist. Next
alien faces filled the screen—one a drawing by a seven-year-old boy which
showed him standing between two small humanoid figures surrounded by
squiggly lines that were intended to show, the child had told his parents, how
he was shivering with fear. Then came close-up photos of "scoop marks,"
distinctive body scars, usually on the lower leg, discovered after reported
abductions. "We have no idea what causes them," Hopkins said. "Very often
they heal up very, very quickly."

Next, Mack said, he would play a recent audiotape from a session of
hypnotic regression documenting the continuing trauma of a woman who
had been abducted with her roommate at the University of Massachusetts
in 1969. More than twenty years later, she was a housewife in her forties with
no children and was still terrorized by her experience. "This is very disturbing
to hear," Mack warned.

"I know," came an anguished female voice, muffled in the amplification,
"but it's still awful . . . probably is a big needle going in . . . AHH! They're
holding my head, I can't even move it! AHH! AHHH! I don't want to look
at it! Uhh! Uh! AH! AH! AH! AH! AH!" She began to weep. "Ah-huh-huh-
huh-huh-huh-huh-huh . . ." Then came a shriek that set the audience's hair
on end: "AhhhieEEEEEE!"

"Stay with it," Mack could be heard saying. "You're going to be fine. You're
going to be just fine."

"Oh no, no, no, no, NO! NO! Put this thing . . . put this thing in me . . ."
She resumed weeping. "Uhhhh. Hold me down now . . . it was just this thing,
this little thing. Oh! Huh! HUH! HUH! OooooOOOO!"

"You're going to be okay."

"I know," the woman sobbed, "I know. I know."

"What's happening now?" Mack asked.

"AH!" she screamed. "AH! OW! OW! OW! GOD!"

"Let it out," Mack said. "That's all right. Let it out."

"HOW! HOW! HOW! WOO! WOOOOO!"

He clicked off the recorder. The audience sat stunned.

"She went on to tell how her pregnancy was removed," he said, explaining that abductees of childbearing age often felt they were impregnated in the spaceships and then re-abducted for the forced delivery of a hybrid baby. "She always had dreams there was a daughter she had that she never came to have," he said. "Unconsciously she made a decision related to this never to have children."

Mack then brought out Julia.

"That tape you heard? I went through something similar last year," she began. "Not as painful, or I didn't remember the pain. I was in bed. An alien appeared and I was taken in an elevator—I can't explain this—I was taken in an elevator with a human man. When it opened up we were in a cavernous room, twice the size of this. Everybody left. I had to go into a room to give up my baby. I got to the door—that's where they do the operation. Cold. I was crying. They made me give up my child freely. It wasn't my child, I know that. It was their child. They made me make that decision by myself. They informed me that they would never take the baby. I'm luckier than the woman on the tape, but on the other hand they wouldn't let me go home until I did give up the baby." As a kind of reward, she said, "I was shown the nursery where there were a lot of other children, half human, half alien but they were quite happy."

Her husband has not been spared, she said. One night he woke her to check on the children. She was gone two minutes, but when she returned the clock showed almost half an hour had passed. "He says a group of aliens forced him to have sex with a female alien, which doesn't disturb him too much, sort of a novelty." Laughter rippled through the hall.

"Except for this," Julia said. "Basically I've been a very normal person. I'm active in the church. I'm active in my child's school. I go shopping at Stop and Shop. Nobody would ever know I've got these things going on. I don't tell a soul. You are the first people I've been brave enough to come out to." Most chillingly, she said, her children were now involved. "My daughter two months ago described a particular room with a particular type door and strange marking on the wall. I know exactly what she's talking about—I've been there."

After robust applause, Mack came out again. "So, where are you all, now?" The question broke the tension, eliciting nervous "whews" and loud sighs. He knew that colleagues were shaking their heads, wondering, "What's happened to John? He's gone off on this crazy thing." And "from that place," Mack complained, drawing sympathetic laughter, "you cannot do cross-cultural studies."

Hands shot up for questions. Could the phenomenon be neurophysiological—internal rather than external?

No, Mack said. "Any theory has to account for physical phenomena on the ground, the cuts, that it happens in small children . . ."

What about near-death experiences, demonic possession, or other spiritual phenomena that were also challenging the Western paradigm?

"We can only focus on this, given limited time, resources, and energy," Mack said. "But the Western world view is under assault from many different directions. This is one of the ones that is particularly challenging to the way we look at science and at reality."

It was finally over. The crowd shuffled out, blitzed. But Wes Boyd felt exhilarated. He knew something for sure. *UFOs did exist.* As an eleven-year-old fifth-grader in Jacksonville, Florida, he was with a classmate on the tennis courts one night in 1974 when, as he never forgot, they looked up to see a strange craft about twelve feet across and four feet high that was maybe one hundred yards away. It was ovoid, he remembered, with red and blue lights, hovering perhaps sixty feet off the ground. They stared in astonishment, as did two adults playing tennis nearby. They gaped as it flew within fifty feet of them and then zipped away out of sight. "What was that?" a shaken young Wesley asked the grown-ups, who seemed as dumbfounded as the boys. "Do you think we know?" one said. Shaking with excitement, the two boys ran home to Wesley's parents, screaming, "We just saw a UFO!" If he did end up at Cambridge, Boyd thought, he might mention it to John Mack.

"We just flooded them!" Mack exulted long afterward. "We hit them with everything!" Julia had "totally freaked them out because she's like Mrs. Everyday Whatever." He called it his "more is better" approach.[3]

21

"YOU CANNOT GO AHEAD!"

There were no immediate repercussions at Harvard, but reactions to Mack's "Abduction Syndrome" manuscript poured in, many of them negative, although the UFO community applauded it. "We are excited that you have become deeply involved with the abduction phenomenon, because your professional status lends immense credibility to this study," wrote Walter H. Andrus, international director of Mufon (the Mutual UFO Network), an organization composed of civilian volunteer investigators. But Hopkins, fearful of arming their critics, suggested many changes and cuts, starting with the opening paragraphs.[1] "State the problem: event-level reality vs psychological explanations of various kinds," Hopkins counseled. Mack had referenced "the fraudulent claims of the so-called 'contactees'" with their beautiful space brothers. Cut it, Hopkins said, along with Mack's detailed descriptions of the aliens and spacecraft smells, the surveys suggesting up to a million abductees, and any reference to fabrications and hoaxes. Because he strongly subscribed to the physical reality of abductions, Hopkins didn't like it when Mack wrote, "Ginny, who has been abducted many times, reported that she occasionally feels that her body does not leave her room but that she is mentally 'being projected onto the ship.'"

"Contradicts earlier material re being actually gone," Hopkins penciled in the margin.

But he called "terrific" the children's narratives of abductions and the graphic descriptions of adult abductees' terror. He did not care for Mack's suggestion that abductees gave different accounts of their experiences depending on whether the researcher/therapist took a benign or sinister view of the abductions, a far too subjective description of what were, to Hopkins, fundamentally real events. "Bad," he scrawled. Hopkins suggested cutting the Jacobs quote, "We have been invaded," and he didn't like Mack's speculation that the phenomenon might not be extraterrestrial after all but rather interdimensional. But when Mack wrote, "My approach as a psychiatrist has been to accept as valid and psychologically important reported experience, whether or not it causes lasting physical manifestations," and cited "the actuality of events which are so powerfully real," Hopkins gushed approval. "Good," he wrote, "this is what the whole paper should be like."

The folklorist Eddie Bullard suggested Mack should say little about UFOs at the start and introduce abduction as a "story" people tell—and a bizarre one at that. He should quickly compare the abduction phenomenon to nightmares, dissociation, and fantasy-proneness and not leave it for the end. Mack should write more on the abductees themselves, round them out as human beings. And in the absence of any artifacts of alien technology, Mack should remain skeptical of physical evidence.

David A. Gotlib, a physician psychotherapist in Toronto who also worked with abductees and had been publishing the monthly *Bulletin of Anomalous Experience*, likewise found flaws in the article. About one-third of experiencers, he said, did not undergo the "classic" encounter of disturbing physical exams, genital exploitation, and mysterious pregnancies—the so-called core abduction experience—but rather found their experiences positive and transformative.

Richard F. Haines, a NASA scientist, federal air-safety investigator, and UFO author, thought Mack gave too much information on the beings and on events inside the craft. The sexual accounts, he said, were far too weak to support the conclusions Mack drew. Haines's own interviews of some forty presumed abductees found no more than five with any such experiences, and their stories were fragmentary at best. He thought Mack's material on child abduction was the most important, and he urged Mack to report more expansively and prominently on who the abductees were *before* he went into their bizarre accounts. "Keep up the excellent work and go slow," Haines concluded. "We are all tramping through a foggy forest at daybreak and we can lose our way quickly."

A more sobering critique came from Sissela Bok, whose husband was in the process of handing over the Harvard presidency to his successor, Neil Rudenstein. She had voiced reservations at Mack's Shop Club talk on abduction the previous February. "Clearly," she now wrote him, "you cannot easily go ahead with publication so long as you do not have more incontrovertible evidence."

March 1992 brought the disheartening response from the psychiatry journal's editor, John Nemiah. "Unfortunately," he wrote, "in its present form, it poses serious difficulties." Mack's draft ran over one hundred pages, perhaps 25,000 words. Regular articles ran up to only 3,800 words, and special articles, which could run longer, were generally reserved for literature reviews and not new data like Mack's. The paper also needed "an appropriate description of methods used in the study so that others might repeat your investigation in a population of their own." In other words, shorter, with more information.

Mack threw up his hands. It should probably be a book. Meanwhile, he and Hopkins were talking to CBS about turning Hopkins's *Intruders* into a four-hour miniseries with Richard Crenna playing a psychiatrist based on Mack.

David Gotlib, the Toronto psychotherapist, saw a prized opportunity slipping away.[2] A rigorous, peer-approved article in *The American Journal of Psychiatry* on the abduction phenomenon would have had great credibility. "Of all of us," Gotlib reflected years later, "he was the one to do it."

22

IRON JOHN

Mack's personal explorations went beyond breathwork and psychedelics. Drawn to the growing men's movement, he joined a group led by the poet and mythologist Robert Bly.[1] At a time when the women's liberation movement was all the rage, Bly had found a parable for our time in the Grimm Brothers fairy tale *Der Eisenhans* about an enchanted wild man in rusty armor at the bottom of a lake who emerges to abduct a young prince and tutor him through the rituals of manhood, enabling him to break a spell and turn the wild man back into a gold-rich king. Bly had explored male empowerment with Keith Thompson in the alternative *New Age Journal* in 1982 and produced a series of pamphlets that Bly expanded into a 1990 bestseller, *Iron John*.

Bly's celebration of the lost rituals of manhood resonated strongly with Mack, who still bridled at the domineering ways of his stepmother, Ruth, as well as Sally's dim view of his extramarital adventures. In mid-1989 he had attended a week-long conference Bly convened in Mendocino, the northern California artist's colony on a piney headland overlooking the Pacific. Mack felt a great affinity with Bly, who shared his admiration for the Spanish poet Antonio Machado and his parable of the traveler: "You make the path by walking." Mack was also drawn to Bly's aphorisms, copying them down in his journal. "He who speaks the truth better have a horse at the door ready for escape." The theme of the group, Mack wrote, "seems to be men giving their power to women." He hailed his good luck. "By what amazing path do I end up with R. Bly working personally with me—how far must I open to heal?" As an exercise, he scribbled a letter to his dead father, blaming him for not standing up to Ruth "because you lived to worship her as a Goddess . . . leaving me alone to battle for my manhood." He was enthralled with Bly's "Warrior Archetype." Men, Bly told the group, were "hard-wired" to be warriors. And true warriors, Mack was especially interested to hear, "don't do love well . . ." The lesson of Iron John, Mack noted, was "where your wound is is where your genius is & where you'll give your greatest gift to the community . . ."[2]

In this macho vein, he even came to try skydiving, suited with a parachute and hurtling out of a plane under an instructor. He ended his men's group experience with an Indian sweat-lodge ceremony. He thanked his relations and ancestors and chanted a bear chant. He called on the living and dead to come to his aid and offered a prayer for the work he was to do in this world.

Now of all times Mack yearned for a more fulfilling personal life "in supportive conjunction with the professional," he told Khalsa. Following-up his trip to Prague, he had been invited to Moscow with Dan Ellsberg in March 1992 for meetings on nonviolence with historians grappling with a post-Communist world. The following month he would travel to India to consult with His Holiness the fourteenth Dalai Lama, manifestation of the patron saint of Tibetan Buddhists, who was eager to learn more about the abduction phenomenon.

Meanwhile, he told Khalsa, he had attended another men's weekend in California, where he joined male initiation rites of birth and rebirth. In one exercise, he was asked, "What's in your way of really going forward with UFOs, putting it out there?" Mack replied, "It's like, I don't have my balls. My mother has my balls." So, he related, "They set up a gauntlet of men and I had to grab these balls, these metaphoric balls. The dilemma was either I fail and don't get them back or I succeed and I have to face the terror of what I'm doing. The terror was either way. Well I won and I was dancing around really so yes, the next step of the journey is real terror."

Afterward, Mack went on, "I went to do a ayahuasca ritual with my Grof group." The powerful psychoactive brew with the "spirit molecule" DMT, used since ancient times for shamanic rituals in the Amazon, was known for its vision-inducing psychedelic properties as well as its strong purgative effects of vomiting and sometimes diarrhea. "We're sitting around this spiritual coven doing prayers and incantations," Mack continued. "I'm real open from my men's weekend. They handed out a joint to get relaxed. I took a couple of tokes and I really got panicky, really terrified. I experienced the fear of disintegration, like I was going into the unknown." He fantasized a relationship with a woman beside him as "all my jealousies and abandonment with women stuff is going on." He was still feeling vulnerable from the men's group and "struggling what I'm going to do with Sally and my partnership and I really freaked. Inside I'm really scared. Marijuana alone put me into a frightened state." In the end, said Mack, he was too afraid to drink the ayahuasca. "What was that terror really about?" It brought back, he said, "the terror of total aloneness and death in the universe"—the intense fear he had felt while glued to the television one day more than twenty years before. "What happens if they can't get the lunar module off the moon?"

Not long afterward, however, he did try ayahuasca, according to his journal. "Pain in abd[omen] becomes central. Physical pain concentrates emotional pain. Need to let go lose control, vomiting will relieve but only when ready. Fighting it. Pain like dying, accepting death. Vomiting 1st x relieved some. Pain of Elie's peritonitis = death. Letting go of that pain = letting go of her."

"The four LSD trips I did probably did more to open up the spiritual universe than anything," Mack told Khalsa. "I'm absolutely hooked up as much as a German Jew can be to the idea that there's a glory of God in this whole process."

Sally was afraid of LSD, another point of contention between them, Mack told his therapist. A friend of hers had had a bad trip. Their home life was bleak. "Do you see any hope for us?" Mack had asked her.

If he was truthful with her, she said.

"Telling the truth to you is always a disaster for me," he said.

He poured out his frustrations to Khalsa. He needed a connection to someone on an intellectual quest as he was. "I don't have that many years left."

But he said his research was going well. His monthly support group had recently started working with a twenty-four-year-old aspiring actor, filmmaker, pianist, and songwriter named Randall Nickerson, a Tom Hanks lookalike with a fascinating family history of abduction experiences whom Mack would give the pseudonym "Scott."[3] His younger sister was also an abductee, as was, possibly, their mother, who showed deep compassion for her children and their traumas. Their father, who was likely not an abductee, was nevertheless supportive. As Randy recalled under hypnosis for an earlier therapist, he was outside his house at age three when "all of a sudden, boom . . . I turned around, I was playing with my trucks, and they were there." Two beings appeared from out of nowhere and, with some kind of rod, "put me under." He ran in and told his mother, "I saw big ants out there." As he grew up he suffered headaches and strange feelings of spacing out. At age ten he saw a flying saucer outside the house, and several beings entered his room. He ran to his parents, and his father—"scared shitless"—got a gun but found nothing amiss. At twelve or thirteen he remembered a feminine figure leaning over his bed. Then in 1990, shortly before beginning to work with Mack, he saw several entities in his room and recognized them as "the same people" as when he was ten. Under hypnosis he remembered that a faucet-like device had been placed over his penis and wires attached to his testicles so that a sperm sample could be taken. But Randy also said he felt he was "prepared for" something, that some "plan" was underway, masterminded by "somebody else." In subsequent hypnotic regressions with Mack, Randy remembered he had been reading a magazine in bed when he sensed the beings were there "in my mind"—six of them with "boxy" and "angular" heads. He saw a round-tipped rod pushing toward him that touched him behind the ear and put him under so he couldn't move. Then all he saw was a TV screen "fritzing." Next he was on a table, and he saw two doctor-like figures with tan-and white-tinted skin, eyeglasses, and lab coats as well as several shorter beings in "army suits." These had deep, black, slightly slanted eyes with gray borders. He felt hatred for the way they were using him "as a father . . . taking my whatever, my babies."

Many others were also reaching out to Mack, referred by their psychiatrists as word of his work spread. A woman pastoral counselor came to him with her dreams of little alien beings sticking things into her abdomen and vagina. "Clearly an abduction!" Mack told Khalsa. "I mean, no question! Ironclad!" The woman had been dubious, but Mack was adamant. "It's the old question. I mean, how do you tell if someone is authentic or not? That's my job. If you're an art dealer your job would be to tell the real thing from the copy. You also have to ask yourself, what's the payoff?" Why, he asked, would anyone make this up?

Yet the more Mack was learning, the more puzzling it all seemed, as he free-associated in tape-recorded sessions with Khalsa. "Even the notion that here's us—humans—here's them—the aliens—the language may be wrong. We, nor they, are in charge—there's some other intelligence . . . They're in a quasi-material state and we're in a more material state and we don't even know who their handlers are. They may be asking, 'who's handling *them?*— some destructive giant is directing them to destroy their planet.'"

He kept returning to Sally. "I'm aggravated the moment I walk into the house," he said. "I cannot kick it off." He was now questioning his whole marriage, all thirty-three years. "Why did I compromise? I don't know. Fear? I was always afraid. The kids were young. There was a family life. No family life now. So there's not that to hold me. I'm not impressed that I developed new balls. I never had any balls. I was always concerned what the psychoanalytic community would think."

What to call his attraction to other women? "'Open marriage' does violence to it," he said. "'Promiscuous' does violence to it. 'Affair' does violence to it. The whole language is wrong here."

Sally had a tendency to put it crudely, he said. "You're saying you want to screw other women? Is that what you're saying?" Having gone through the household bills, she had noticed the suspicious credit card charges and phone calls to Roz. "Do you think there is really someone out there who would give you what you want and would be more appropriate for you than me?" The obvious answer, Mack wanted to say, was yes, but he stayed silent. The latest argument had been over his research. Sally couldn't stand it that he was meeting with abductees three days a week in Danny's empty room.

Mack came out with some strange things. He remembered a seventh-grade crush, Amy Jane Bunim, later Amy Lawrence. They had stayed in touch over the years. Mack had gotten her involved in breathwork, and she had sat in on some of his group sessions with abductees. Mack had even become friendly with her husband, Elliot, a noted bandleader and Broadway composer. "It turned out her mother committed suicide when she was eight months old," Mack told Khalsa, "and my mother committed suicide when I was eight months old and we had loved each other for decades before we found that out." Lawrence's mother had indeed taken her own life, a long-hidden family secret. But Mack's mother, Eleanor, had indisputably died of peritonitis, as he well knew. Years later, Khalsa recalled the strange exchange—he even remembered that Mack may have made the same assertion several times—but he didn't know what to make of it.[4]

Mack complained that he felt stuck. Roz had left him for someone else, deeply wounding him. His private life was getting more complicated than his alien research. "This is harder than presenting my UFO grand rounds," he despaired. "You ask me, do I ever solve the personal? That's been my difficulty."

Mack also groused about his health. He was suffering from high cholesterol and an elevated prostate-specific antigen level. He agonized over whether he was even healthy enough to press on with his work. "My knee cleared up but I have arthritis in my back, only when I have stress." He was taking on his experiencers' battles and paying the price. It was genetic. "The back in our family was the vulnerability organ, where information gets stuck, so to speak," he said. "I'm going to have lockjaw of the whole body before I'm through with this thing."

On top of that there was discord in his group, newly renamed the Center for Psychology and Social Change after six years as the Center for Psychological Studies in the Nuclear Age. He had just hired a new director, Vivienne Simon, a winsome environmental activist who had worked for Greenpeace. Mack had liked her immediately, admiring her coolness and amusement when she arrived to find him stomping around the office in a fit of sexual jumpiness he explained as "a Kundalini awakening," an arousal of the snake coiled at the base of the spine that releases tremendous sexual and spiritual energy.[5] Simon was no stranger to anomalous phenomena, as Mack was to learn, and she had an endearing way of bursting out with whatever she happened to be thinking at the moment, which posed challenges for an organization involved in conflict resolution. For her part, she adored his piercing blue eyes and infectious enthusiasm—like a little boy, she thought, who discovers something like a water faucet for the first time. But all was not well. Simon's hiring had brought to tears another woman in the office who had wanted the job. Mack sought to smooth it over, worried that the drama might expose the secrets he was keeping from his staff. "I didn't want anyone to know I was working on this alien business," he told Khalsa. But Simon had sniffed it out. "She says she's more interested in that than international relations dialogue," Mack related. It was all giving him a headache. I'm tired of being in so much melancholy," he said. He needed a break. "I'm going away to Mexico. Sit on a beach and meditate ten days."

And yet, he confided to Khalsa, it wasn't all bleak. He had met someone else.

Dominique Callimanopulos was one of three daughters of the first wife of a playboy shipping tycoon, Gregory Callimanopulos, and a granddaughter of Pericles Callimanopulos, founder of Hellenic Lines. Bypassed on the family fortune, she had gone to Wesleyan, where she had once spotted a UFO on the football field, and she went on to work overseas on cultural-anthropology projects before landing in Boston.[6]

"I don't know quite how she's come into my life," Mack told Khalsa. They had danced but barely talked at a 1991 holiday party thrown by a staff member at his Center for Psychology and Social Change. He had run into her again a few times before she asked him to another party. Once she was accompanied by her two young children from an early marriage that had ended in divorce several years before. It all seemed mysterious to Mack. "I keep asking her: 'Who are you? Where do you come from? Where do you live?'"

She had been staying in an apartment on Martha's Vineyard with a man who never seemed to be around when Mack phoned. "She's like a waif," he said. "There's a kind of un-anchored fluidity about who she is. Although voluptuous, with chestnut hair and pillowy lips, with "earthy, sexy energy," she "didn't seem like someone I would fall in love with," Mack said. So she seemed somehow safer. "I noticed how caught up I still am in this courtship male-female game," he said. "Sort of a dance of life."

He agonized over the consequences. "If I'm really dissatisfied enough with my marriage, I ought to consider leaving." But, he said, "the idea of really breaking up my marriage seems like such a major undertaking." Sex was secondary—it was the thrill of the chase he craved. Physicality even seemed a hindrance. "It's an old-fashioned model, the body," he said. "I get intimations of that in the height of psychedelic experience. Maybe the body really is a drag."

There was a pattern to his behavior that he saw. "A woman says, 'I'm interested in you and what you're doing' and if it involves a sexual interest, all the better."

He had another worry, Mack told Khalsa. Harvard's Psychiatry Department had a new chairman. "I felt I should see him and tell him what I'm doing so he doesn't just read about it in the newspaper."

23

HELLO, DALAI

Robed in his trademark maroon and orange, his eyes glinting impishly behind his spectacles, Tenzin Gyatso, His Holiness the fourteenth Dalai Lama, welcomed Mack and his longtime assistant Pam Kasey and eight colleagues to his modest Namgyal Monastery in April 1992.[1]

Their visit to Dharamshala, India, in the foothills of the snowy Himalayas—home in exile to the spiritual leader of Tibetan Buddhism and Nobel Peace laureate—had been arranged by David Cherniack, a Canadian documentary filmmaker.[2] Cherniack had been in Dharamshala making a film on Tibetan Buddhism when the Dalai Lama offered him the rare opportunity to film a possession ceremony of the Nechung, the State Oracle of Tibet, a spirit that had inhabited a succession of fourteen mediums who had served as advisors to the Dalai Lamas over four centuries. Cherniack's camera was rolling as the last Nechung, Thubten Ngodup, went into a violent trance. At one point the medium locked eyes with Cherniack and next, as Cherniack remembered, "something I can only describe as a force shot through my body, practically blowing me off the steps." The film, *The Oracle: Reflections on Self*, would not be released until 2010, but in 1992 Cherniack got the idea to invite a small group of American medical professionals and social scientists for a three-day conference on UFOs and alien abduction. Cherniack began with David Gotlib, the Toronto psychotherapist and a fellow Canadian, and Mack was soon added to the list. He brought Pam Kasey to record and transcribe the sessions for Cherniack, and Sally traveled with them. The event was to be low-key in deference to the Buddhist leader's sensitive political position since a Tibetan revolt against the Chinese Communist takeover of their homeland had sent him and his followers fleeing to India in 1959. But Mack would retain a transcript of the proceedings for his files.

In his simple quarters hung with colorful prayer flags—a far cry from the thousand-room hilltop Tibetan palace he had fled—the fifty-six-year-old monk sat with a translator, although he spoke passable English. The sessions—there would be seven in all—opened with a brief introduction by

Gotlib, who began by explaining close encounters of the third kind, "where there are intelligent beings that are seen in the ship or that are seen to leave the ship and interact with people."

"I wish to see such thing!" the Dalai Lama interjected.

"Me too!" Gotlib said when the laughter died down.

Mack posed the question that was on many minds: "I was wondering if you would be willing to say what . . . there was about this subject that you found interesting or important enough now that you were willing to meet with us for these days."

"One says this kind of thing just nonsense," the Dalai Lama said. "Don't pay any attention. Just a few individuals, you see, feel or experience this due to something wrong with their mind or brain. And others say there's something really, how do you say, not only fact but something really, something really valuable."

Buddhists speak of three realms, he said. The physical world of the five senses; an in-between world of form and meditation; and, finally, the highest realm, that of subtle mind—"No ordinary body so no sound but the seed of sound, the seed of body . . . the formless realm." The body of flesh, the consciousness of grosser matter, cannot ordinarily communicate with the subtle mind, he said. But sometimes, "through dreams or through certain experience, the grosser level of our mind becomes inactive so at that moment there's more chance to communicate, sometimes to see."

Mack outlined his own involvement with some forty to fifty abductees so far in monthly meetings. He described his methodology and findings, including the physiognomy of the aliens.

"Quite beautiful!" the Dalai Lama commented. And these small creatures, he asked, were they male or female?

Both, Mack said. They had no evident sexual characteristics or gender-specific dress, but abductees seemed to intuitively distinguish male and female. The aliens were deeply interested in human sexual activity, Mack went on, sometimes watching staged intercourse between abductees. But beyond the traumatic dimensions of the experience often lay spiritual growth and a greater sensitivity for the fate of the planet, he said.

Then, apologizing in advance for the bad language, he played a tape of a hypnotic regression of one of his earliest subjects, a married man in his thirties he would later identify as Peter Faust. A telegenic former restaurant and hotel manager in the Caribbean and later a healer in the Boston area, he had grown up in Hawaii, where at about nineteen he felt himself taken by beings out of the window and onto a ship for traumatic sexual procedures that he terrifyingly remembered in sessions with Mack.

"You can't do this to me!" Faust was heard crying on the tape. "I want to say, 'No you can't do this to me! You can't do this to me any more. Stop it! I'm so fucking tired of it.' They just do this any time they want."

Suddenly he shrieked, "They're taking it! They're taking my semen! They have control over me. I'm just laying there. They're taking me! They have control over my genitals. Over me. They have a cup over me. They have a cup over my cock! They're just taking me!"

"Fuck you! . . . AAAHHHHHH!"

His Holiness seemed puzzled. "This person, when not focusing on that memory, usually his mental situation, something normal?"

Completely normal, Mack said.

He had heard of Tibetans taken by "small elves," the Dalai Lama said. Spirits were the accepted explanation, and he was sometimes called upon to banish evil forces. He had no special powers to do so, he said, but "I stay there, and I visualize these negative forces . . . they also have selfish, selfish feeling, they also have every right to be happy."

Next, Peter M. Rojcewicz (pronounced Ro-sevich), a folklorist on the faculty of the Juilliard School at Lincoln Center, explained his research into a particularly shadowy corner of the UFO phenomenon, the so-called Men in Black. For years, witnesses to UFO events reported ominous visits from mysterious dark-clad figures who seemed eerily cognizant of their encounters and intimidated them into silence. Some took the visitors for government agents, but their sudden appearances and disappearances gave them an unearthly air.

Rojcewicz was less concerned with the ultimate reality of UFOs than with their meaning for people who have had these experiences, he said. "Why do some of these people prosper, why do their lives seem to flourish as a result of these contacts, while other people's lives seem to fall apart? It's been going on for all time, throughout history," Rojcewicz said. The myths of the flooded continents Atlantis and Mu; annals of flying palaces and airborne chariots and celestial cars known as Vimanas in the ancient Sanskrit scriptures called the Vedas; the Old Testament's cylinder-shaped cloud and the pillar of fire that led the Jews out of Egypt, as well as the radiance around the Ark of the Covenant, too fearsome to look upon; sightings of fiery aerial crosses that pre-date Christianity; bloody shields in the sky that terrified the warring Anglo-Saxons; and spectral schooners seen sailing the skies of colonial America—what was to be made of these?

Folklore was also replete with abductions, Rojcewicz said, from the Frankish and Cajun loup-garou or werewolf that waylaid the unwary to cattle-snatching witches, incubi that copulated with humans at night, and diminutive fairies bereft of human warmth that took human children and replaced them with deformed replicas that often quickly died. They seemed an obvious parallel to the abductees' fetus stories. In the last years of the nineteenth century, before there were airplanes, Rojcewicz said, witnesses were reporting phantom airships, as if they somehow lay embedded in the collective psyche as an imminent new technology. "Human abductions, kidnapping, people being seized, people losing control, is as old as the human soul is old," Rojcewicz said.

He presented another hypothesis, the Jungian psychic anatomy. Archetypes rising from the soul into consciousness were incredibly powerful, overwhelming the ego, the folklorist said. Like UFO experiences, they had a dual nature, both benign and fearsome. The Zen masters knew it as satori, a psychotic episode yielding enlightenment. Archetypes were subtle bodies from the soul that became conscious to us. Perhaps, Rojcewicz concluded, UFOs were mind-generated psychokinetic manifestations of the consciousness of nature, what the Greeks called Gaia, the living earth.

Another participant, Mario Pazzaglini, a clinical psychologist and neurophysiologist from Delaware who had manned a "bad trip" drug tent at the 1969 Woodstock Festival, documented references to spacecraft and aliens from earliest antiquity. A specialist in cryptic writing and peculiar symbols recalled by abductees, Pazzaglini drew parallels to the mysteries of a fifteenth-century illustrated Italian codex known as the Voynich Manuscript, which contained images of heavenly objects and women undergoing various bodily procedures. It was written in an indecipherable language that has defied cryptographers for centuries.

"I think these things very much material of previous life," the Dalai Lama said. If you believed people had just one life, a relationship was harder to prove, he said. "But the previous life, something happen, so traces of that experience deep down still there."

Maralyn Teare, a marriage and family counselor and a clinical instructor of psychiatry at the USC School of Medicine, ventured an intimate question. "What is the strangest experience that you've had personally, that might be of the nature that you couldn't explain but it held a mystery?"

The Dalai Lama paused. "I don't know." Earlier, Teare had shown pictures of clouds and speculated on their relationship to UFOs. His Holiness had looked on quizzically and remarked, "You know, sometimes some things in nature are just nature. Sometimes cloud is just a cloud."

Toward the end, the Dalai Lama turned to Mack. "What you think?"

"I think we have a lot to learn from each other," Mack replied, referring to aliens and humans. "I think they connect with us to get knowledge of the heart and the spirit and of us, but we learn from them that there is a spirit world, there is a universe beyond this narrow one."

24

ALIENS AT MIT

Two months after his return from India, Mack joined a larger group of experts at the long-planned "Alien Discussions" Abduction Study Conference at MIT.[1] The gathering, from June 13 to 17, 1992, featured fifty-one authorities invited to submit papers, including the MIT physicist Philip Morrison, who had helped hand-assemble the first atomic bomb on Tinian before it was dropped on Hiroshima. There were also close to a dozen experiencers themselves, several notable skeptics, and ten television and print journalists selected for their discretion and open-mindedness, including C. D. B. Bryan, author of the Vietnam War best seller *Friendly Fire*, who would turn the conference into a book, *Close Encounters of the Fourth Kind*. Dave Pritchard's wife, Andrea, a painter and tapestry maker who shared her husband's fascination with alien phenomena, was there with Mack's assistant Pam Kasey to edit the proceedings, which would be embargoed for two years. Two popular headliners were Budd Hopkins and David Jacobs, with Jacobs's recent exposé, *Secret Life: Firsthand Documented Accounts of UFO Abductions*, listed as required reading for conferees. Mack had contributed the foreword, drawing the ridicule of the *New Republic*. "Mack, once known for his touchy-feely approach to assuaging nuclear anxiety . . . warns of 'a huge, strange interspecies or interbeing breeding program that has invaded our physical reality and is affecting the lives of hundreds of thousands, if not millions, of people and perhaps in some way the consciousness of the entire planet.'" It concluded, "Oliver Stone, call your office."

"My job at this point is just to welcome you—so, welcome to this extraordinary event!" began Mack. He stood, slightly stooped, in the lecture hall before a triptych of blackboards wearing a baggy, dark suit with a white shirt and striped tie. He went over all the reasons the abduction phenomenon could not be dismissed psychiatrically—the consistency of the accounts, the incidence among young children, the mysterious scars, the occasional witness corroborations, the sometimes physical absence of experiencers, and the notable lack of any evident psychopathology among them.

Offering a note of caution as a physicist, co-organizer Pritchard said there was one way to prove the reality of abduction: through physical evidence, specifically an artifact with "out-of-this-world" performance or properties. One promising attempt, he reported, involved a forty-five-year-old former taxi driver who remembered being abducted at age eight near Troy, New York, by uniformed aliens from a landed saucer. The cabbie, Richard Price, who was at the conference, had recounted watching on a wall screen as the aliens removed an object from a dish and implanted it in his penis. Many years later, in 1989, it began protruding from the skin and soon dislodged with the sensation of an electric shock. He brought it to MIT for testing. It appeared to be a cottonlike cylinder about one by three millimeters. But, Pritchard reported, after exhaustive microscopic examination and secondary ion mass spectroscopy, it was found to be of organic elemental content—a biological object that grew in the body. "The analysis shows nothing unterrestrial about it, quite the opposite," Pritchard said. He couldn't prove the artifact was *not* manufactured by aliens. Perhaps they were clever enough to make their devices look like products of the human body. But he said it would be better to set aside an extraterrestrial hypothesis for now.

The results hadn't surprised atomic scientist Phil Morrison. "You will do two years of work," he had predicted to Pritchard, "and at the end you won't have anything probative." Morrison told Mack that these abduction accounts were being filtered through the most complex, most subtle, and least understood instrument imaginable—human beings under stress. From that you could infer almost nothing. "We have enough trouble using our telescopes."

Academic folklorist Thomas Eddie Bullard, known for his groundbreaking study, *UFO Abductions: The Measure of a Mystery*, outlined patterns in his 451 cases since 1985. They broke down evenly by gender, though men led in highway and outdoor abductions and women in household and repeat abductions. Two thirds of Bullard's reports came from North America, principally the United States, while South America reported some of the most bizarre cases. Scandinavian abductees for some reason didn't encounter the small gray individuals commonly reported elsewhere but rather tall Nordic types (also widely reported in Britain) and beings with two antennas or divided heads or other abstract features.

Bullard cited a case from the University of Connecticut near-death researcher Kenneth Ring involving a woman who had passed out in front of her husband. While fully visible to him, she experienced looking out of a round window into darkness, then being on an operating table in the presence of tall, thin figures communicating telepathic messages. She saw herself looking down on earth before rushing toward it and reentering her body.

Yet there were cases of physical disappearance as well. Bullard cited one of Australia's leading aviation mysteries, the case of twenty-year-old pilot Fred Valentich, who vanished with his plane during an encounter with a UFO over Melbourne in 1978. Valentich had radioed that a long, shiny object with landing lights was "orbiting" above him. His last words were, "It is hovering and it's not an aircraft." Nine years after Valentich vanished, he reportedly reappeared at the bed of an Australian teacher recovering from a broken foot who was later spooked to find she was living in his former house. Under hypnosis, she recovered her own abduction experiences. Was it a ghost story, or something else?

Abduction and ritual-abuse cases had their similarities, said California family psychologist Gwen L. Dean. Devil worship and human sacrifice also seemed preposterous. Both involved secrecy, leader figures and followers, forced breeding, examining tables, surgical instruments, physical wounds, esoteric writing and symbols, geometric emblems like circles and triangles, post-event amnesia, and visits by mysterious Men in Black who seemed to track abductees. Both employed tracking devices, staring eyes, bright lights, hooded garments, restraints, and electrical energy. Reptilian creatures appeared in both. Striking, too, were the consistency of the accounts and the accompanying affect—ritual-abuse survivors gave every impression they believed their accounts and were telling the truth. Yet they were different too. Abductees were not subjected to cannibalism, forced to copulate with cadavers, or kill anyone.

As for the Men in Black, software engineer Joseph Nyman presented a bizarre story. A Massachusetts woman named Marie had reported a 1983 UFO sighting to Mufon, and the case had been assigned to a volunteer, Jules Vaillancourt, who sent Marie all the forms to fill out. Vaillancourt never heard back. Five years later Marie contacted Vaillancourt again, and the case was referred to Nyman and a partner to check out. They met with Marie and asked her why she had never returned the forms to Vaillancourt. Oh, but she had,

Marie and her husband, Mike, insisted. Vaillancourt had even telephoned to make an appointment and had visited them in May 1984. He had arrived, they told Nyman, in a dull-gray Mercedes with a gray interior, bearing the forms Marie had sent in to Mufon. He was five-foot-eight or -nine, slim, with brownish hair, a mustache, and a pointed chin and nose. He wore a brown jacket and tie and old-fashioned brown wingtip shoes. Later, under hypnosis, Mike remembered offering him a drink and hearing in his mind something like, "This is none of your business, keep out of it," whereupon he retreated to the kitchen. He realized, too, he had seen that face before—as a hooded figure in a recurring nightmare. When Marie finally did meet Vaillancourt, she registered surprise. "Gee, you're not tall." He had no mustache, and he didn't drive a Mercedes. Who, or what, was impersonating Vaillancourt—or why—they had no idea.

The reported medical procedures in the spaceships differed notably from earthly exams and were unlikely to be ordinary doctors' visits misremembered, said California physician John G. Miller. The aliens seemed to focus on the cranium and nervous system, skin, reproductive organs, and sometimes joints. They largely ignored the cardiovascular and lymphatic systems and the respiratory system below the mouth and nasal cavity. Human doctors liked to check the heart, lungs, liver, spleen, stomach, and pancreas and palpate the axilla, or armpit, looking for enlarged lymph nodes; the aliens scarcely bothered with any of that. Human doctors didn't remove a patient's eye and then put it back. They didn't open patients' chests to examine them. They didn't collect sperm or jab long, sharp objects up a patient's nose, crunching into the brain to deposit a BB-size implant, as many experiencers reported. Aside from providing a possible parking spot for an implant, Miller said, the nasal cavity housed the olfactory nerve, which might be of special interest for its sensory ganglion cells similar to those found in some lower animals.

Alien exams also often seemed to include probes into the rectum without so much as an initial insertion of a gloved finger. The gynecological-type procedures on women represented a particular puzzle, Miller said. Human doctors commonly performed a bimanual pelvic exam, placing one or two gloved fingers inside the vagina and palpating above the pubic bone to feel the pelvic contents. The aliens preferred inserting long needles into the navel—years before invention of the laparoscope, which, in any event, required an incision.

Here Miller had a suggestion. In laparoscopic surgery, doctors insufflated the abdomen with carbon dioxide to separate the organs from the abdominal wall. The gas lingered for several days. Had anyone ever checked whether women recounting alien needles in the abdomen had any residual carbon dioxide that could provide verification of an actual medical event? But as for the supposed harvesting of fetuses implanted by the aliens, physicians were mystified by the women's claims. None had yet found proof of any anomalous disappearing pregnancy. That had to be telling.

After Jacobs presented a portrait of the beings from experiencer accounts, the man becoming known as the godfather of alien abduction, Budd Hopkins, sought to quantify the phenomenon, presenting the "Roper Poll on Unusual Personal Experiences," financed by a fellow conferee, the billionaire developer and aerospace entrepreneur Robert Bigelow. It seemed obvious that no one would answer honestly if simply asked, "Have you ever been abducted by an alien?" Instead, the poll of some six thousand people in the continental United States, excluding those under eighteen and the incarcerated and military populations, was more roundabout. Based on five "indicator" questions about having experienced missing time or unexplained lights, having woken up paralyzed with the sense of a strange presence in the room, having experienced sensations of flying, or having suffered unexplained scars, the survey found that 119 participants, or about 2 percent of the 185 million covered by the survey population, gave positive answers to four of the five questions. That, Hopkins said, translated to about 3.7 million adult Americans "highly likely to be UFO abductees."

It set off an uproar.

Conferees erupted with objections, attacking the questions as unscientific and the extrapolation as unreliable. Hopkins stood his ground, responding that the figures jibed with Gallup and other surveys that found as many as 14 percent of respondents answering yes to whether they had ever seen a UFO.

His case was buttressed, Hopkins said, by his work with the youngest abductees, children who could not have been influenced by the cultural milieu. He displayed his "Hopkins Image Recognition Test." It consisted of ten cartoonish illustrations: a policeman, Santa Claus, Batman, a clown, a witch, a boy, a girl, a skeleton, a Ninja Turtle, and a big-eyed alien. Children with tales of awakening to strange figures at their bedside and flights in the sky often readily picked out the alien, he said. Children with no known abduction history, the control group, ignored that picture. The questions, however, had to be carefully worded. When Hopkins asked a five-year-old California girl with unexplained scars if she knew any of the people in his pictures, she said no. But when he reworded the question, she readily picked out the alien she had "dreamed" of. She just didn't *know* him.

Again, the hall rang with objections. The images lacked the credentialing of a standardized test. There was no consistent methodology.

"Credentials have been a problem for a long time in my work," Hopkins conceded. "Originality has been my strength." But, he argued, "the test has proved its effectiveness."

Hopkins said abductees sometimes found themselves returned to the wrong locations, or with their clothes wrongly put on, or in the wrong clothes altogether. One experiencer awoke with both legs stuffed into the sleeve of her pajama top—the bottoms were on the floor, neatly folded. It happened rarely, perhaps in fewer than 5 percent of the cases, he said. Did the aliens sometimes screw up? Was Murphy's Law truly *universal*? Unless, of course, they weren't mistakes at all, but deliberate acts as unfathomable as everything else.

Then Hopkins introduced his latest sensation—"the most important UFO abduction case that I've ever worked on"—the teleportation, reported by witnesses, of a woman from her twelfth-floor apartment overlooking the Brooklyn Bridge into a hovering spacecraft on the early morning of November 30, 1989. He had previously told Mack of the case, and Mack had met the woman at Hopkins's townhouse with Bob Lifton and Blanche Chavoustie. She had first come forward under a pseudonym, Linda Cortile, but she later provided her real name, Linda Napolitano. Now Hopkins played a tape from one of the purported witnesses, a security guard who called himself "Richard." The witness recounted how he and his partner, "Danny," in their stalled car under Manhattan's FDR Drive had spotted "an oval shaped object hovering over the top of an apartment building." Richard had watched with binoculars as "a little girl or woman wearing a full-white gown sailed out of the window in a fetal position," looking, he said, "like an angel or a Christmas tree doll." Above and below her were "three of the ugliest creatures I ever saw," big-headed, hairless, thin, white figures that escorted her into the craft, which then flew overhead before plunging *into* the East River near Pier 17. But Richard and Danny couldn't come forward publicly, they said, because they had been escorting a VIP to the heliport from an all-night meeting.

There was no time to give details, Hopkins said. He would lay it all out in his third book, *Witnessed: The True Story of the Brooklyn Bridge UFO Abductions.* But the case had grown ever weirder. While he had not yet been able to identify the two supposed witnesses, who had signed only first names, or the unnamed VIP they were escorting, Hopkins had asked them to send him a tape recording of their account, and they complied. Now Hopkins had their voices along with other interviews on tape. Later, as Hopkins wrote in *Witnessed,* their account took an even more astonishing turn. After they saw the object splash into the East River, Dan wrote Hopkins, their VIP wanted to swim out to save her. They stopped him, but suddenly—having apparently been abducted themselves—all three found themselves on an unfamiliar sea-shore with Linda and the beings, who were shoveling sand into small boxes. Linda approached the three with a dead fish, demanding, "Look and see what you have done." Then suddenly Richard and Dan were back at their car under the FDR, with the VIP clinging to the roof. Hopkins wrote that Richard later mailed him two bags of sand that Hopkins sent off to the University of Nevada for analysis. It turned out to be mostly common silicon with some slight anomalies that seemed inconclusive.

(All of this would all lead nowhere, as usual. Despite help from a private eye referred by his Cape Cod neighbor, constitutional lawyer Leon Friedman, Hopkins would be crucially unable to uncover the true identities of the two security agents, one of several major flaws that would ultimately dash his hopes of breaking the greatest abduction case in history and doom it to UFO limbo. Nor would the "high muckety-muck" they said they had been escorting—later identified as the UN Secretary General Javier Pérez de Cuéllar—ever offer any satisfying response, fending off inquiries with oddly phrased denials.[2] Peculiarly, his UN successor, Boutros Boutros-Ghali of Egypt, was sabotaged in his bid for a second term by the CIA and Britain's MI6, which planted stories portraying him as a believer in UFOs and alien life, according to former British intelligence operative Richard Tomlinson.)

Later in the MIT program, Cincinnati physician and abduction researcher Brian C. Thompson reported on his studies of the effects of electromagnetic radiation on biological systems. There was reason to believe, he said, that abduction accounts could be transmitted from investigators to experiencers, and among experiencers, by telepathy. As far back as 1930, the celebrated writer and social activist Upton Sinclair reported in his book *Mental Radio* on his own telepathic experiences with his wife, Mary Craig Kimbrough, who was able to copy pictures from his mind. It carried a foreword by Albert Einstein, who wrote, "In no case should the psychologically interested circles pass over this book." Subsequent research, Thompson told the conferees, suggested that the dream state enhanced telepathic communication to the point where two people might have the same abduction dream, possibly explaining shared abduction experiences.

Seeking a skeptical perspective, Pritchard and Mack had invited Robert Sheaffer, a California author from the Committee for the Scientific Investigation of Claims of the Paranormal (CSICOP). Sheaffer saw a clear subjective basis to the abduction phenomenon. The bulk of reports came from North America, where the small gray individuals predominated. Brits tended to be abducted by tall, blonde Nordics, and South Americans by the most bizarre creatures. Had the Galactic High Command split the world into Alien Occupation Zones? Abductees seemed divided, too, by hypnotist. Seeking a gentle, uplifting alien experience? Consult Dr. Leo Sprinkle. Aliens that stole sperm, eggs, and fetuses; deposited implants; and left scars sent you running to Budd Hopkins. Sheaffer also claimed to find abduction elements from the Betty and Barney Hill case prefigured in such science fiction classics as the 1953 film, *Invaders from Mars*, and the 1930 comic book, *Buck Rogers in the 25th Century*. UFOs, like ghosts, ESP, and Bigfoot, must be "jealous" phenomena, Sheaffer said, always managing to slip away without evidence. Given the large numbers of UFO sightings and abductions in populated areas, why was no unambiguous evidence like alien garbage ever left behind? Didn't the witchcraft mania of medieval and colonial times look familiar? Now the human race was supposedly at the mercy of secret sex rituals by otherworldly beings—and only specially trained inquisitors could draw the story out. Conferees thanked Sheaffer for braving a hostile milieu but then attacked his arguments. Why expect all aliens to act alike? The differences between investigators were more subtle than Sheaffer portrayed, and the geographic anomalies probably relatable to sample bias. If abduction was a cultural phenomenon, what about the accounts by young children "who don't have time to absorb all the information adults do?" For another thing, said Eddie Bullard, witch finders had thumbscrews and the rack. Budd Hopkins obtained results without torture.

Carl Sagan had been invited, along with NASA scientists, to present the scientific Search for Extraterrestrial Intelligence (SETI), but the association with aliens and abduction drove them off. Instead, Paul Horowitz, a Harvard physics professor and experimental astrophysicist, agreed to detail the radio search for cosmic intelligence. It was relatively cheap, he said. A dollar's worth of electricity would send one word traveling a thousand light years, almost one-hundredth of the diameter of our Milky Way galaxy, where it would reach about a million stars like our sun. So, he said, "there ought to be a reasonable likelihood of folks that we could communicate with."

McGill University psychology professor Don Donderi ridiculed Horowitz for "nothing but noise." The whole conference had been about alien signals. Hadn't Horowitz been listening?

Donderi's anecdotal evidence was not what he was looking for, Horowitz said. "I'd like to see a thing that I can hold in my hand, like the piece of the landing gear of a UFO, or a cigarette lighter."

Mack took a dim view of the SETI project. Why assume that other civilizations would recognize our radio signals? It seemed so hubristically anthropocentric. You might as well, Mack thought, search the heavens for a good Italian restaurant.

"I object to the either/orness of this," he said. Why couldn't aliens be real and not real at the same time, inhabiting some liminal zone? Modern physics was replete with contradictions, as in quantum superposition, where chunks of matter could occupy two different places at the same time. In any case, he said, the phenomenon could not be explained psychiatrically. "The people with whom I have been working, as far as I can tell, are telling the truth."

As the five-day Alien Discussions concluded, physicist Mark Rodeghier, Scientific Director of the Center for UFO Studies, announced he had been looking for a direction and had found one. "I think I know exactly where we should go from here," he said. "We should follow John Mack!" The hall echoed with applause.

"The conference was great for me," an ebullient Mack told C. D. B. Bryan in a long, taped interview afterward. But please, he beseeched Bryan, "you could really make me sound like a nut on this thing." Bryan told him not to worry, but to make sure he let Mack edit the transcript with changes, comments, deletions, and additions.

David Hufford, who had studied supernatural-assault traditions, found the conference disheartening.[3] He had argued that sleep paralysis, which cropped up often in hypnosis-enhanced abduction accounts, was a far more complex condition than abduction researchers credited. He didn't claim that sleep paralysis explained abduction encounters, although he was open to the possibility that the condition might be involved in some experiences. But he was dismayed that "much of the abduction community had a very narrow view of all 'paranormal' experience apart from alien abductions."

Hufford was also put off by the Roper Poll, although he found that its estimate for the prevalence of abduction jibed generally with his calculations of the prevalence of sleep paralysis. He said that in his interviews he used the same primary index question about waking up paralyzed with the sense of a strange presence in the room. But he left the details to his subjects to fill in, unlike Mack, Hopkins, and Jacobs, who favored prompting respondents with queries about "a strange person or presence or something else in the room."

Hufford's skepticism of hypnotic regression grew when he listened to David Jacobs presenting his findings on abduction. When other conferees objected that they weren't getting the same pattern from their subjects, Jacobs replied they should keep regressing them—they'd get the same pattern eventually. Hufford thought that Mack might be more cautious. But Mack, he realized, seemed also prone to "conclusion-jumping."

The overall danger, Hufford thought, was that the 20 percent of the population with a sense of having at some point awakened paralyzed with a threatening presence in the room—a "common and entirely normal" episode of sleep paralysis, by his account—could be misled into adopting a traumatic history of alien experimentation, sexual abuse, or other repressed horror. Nor, he said, should abduction be automatically implicated in other common paranormal events like near-death experiences, reported by around 20 percent of resuscitated cardiac patients. In combat veterans, the figure was close to 50 percent. And a third of Americans reported visits from deceased relatives. Altogether, he said, over half the population experienced reported anomalous encounters like these. So it would be sad indeed, Hufford concluded, if by hypnotic regression or other means these people were to become "convinced of a personal tragedy that they may not have had!"

It was left to Dave Pritchard to write a somber conference postscript. They had tried to find the answer but had failed, predictably, ending up with more questions than they had started with. Now, said Pritchard, they were heading back to a suspicious and hostile world. They had "a very interesting, very challenging, sometimes frightening problem" that they would keep trying to figure out. Maybe they would still learn something "and have some fun in the process." But deep down, Pritchard had lost faith, not in the scientific method but in its ability to get to the bottom of whatever was going on here. The whole business had damaged his reputation, he said years later, but going forward was the problem.[4] He had heard many fantastic things, none of them proven. "It's the tar baby," he reflected. Scientific progress was measurable. "I can't say the same for the spiritual." Some things, like love, just eluded science. "I'll never do anything like that again," he said. "How was I ever suckered in by the thought I had any chance of making this discovery?"

25

"GOOD EVENING, DOCTOR"

As far afield as the Alien Discussions ranged, scholars besides David Hufford also felt the scope was too constrained given the broader contours of anomalous experience and its anthropological dimensions. Another leading critic of the prevailing abduction narrative was a French-born astronomer, computer scientist, author, and venture capitalist with a daunting intellectual pedigree. Jacques Vallee had studied mathematics and astrophysics before helping develop the first computerized map of Mars for NASA and designing experimental computer links for the Defense Department's Advanced Research Projects Network called ARPANET, which eventually gave rise to the Internet. With a long interest in UFOs following several personal encounters in France, he had already written close to a dozen books on the phenomenon, relating it to folkloric myths of fairies and demons.[1] He had also served as the model for the French researcher Claude Lacombe, played by François Truffaut, in Steven Spielberg's *Close Encounters of the Third Kind*. Charter member of a low-key network of investigators called the "Invisible College," Vallee may have been, as the scholar Jerome Clark would say, "the single most intelligent human being to direct his attention to the UFO question" (Clark himself being a likely rival), but his independent ways could be off-putting. Vallee was excluded from the conference at MIT after refusing, as he said, to submit his data for vetting in advance. He liked to call himself the only expert who didn't know what UFOs were, too many others being all too certain they were spacecraft from another planet. Vallee acknowledged he was not easy to categorize, as he himself summed it up: "One moment you talk about UFOs as if they were real, physical material objects. And in the next sentence you talk about them as psychic effects, producing paranormal phenomena in and around the witnesses." This was a fair criticism, Vallee said. "I can only answer that this ambiguity is genuine, and that it lies in the data."

At another 1992 symposium, this one in Albuquerque and which he *was* invited to, Vallee said he believed that a genuine, physical UFO phenomenon existed. He speculated, but couldn't prove, that it involved a nonhuman form of intelligence. He called ufology a forbidden science—doubly so, with skeptics refusing to entertain possibilities averse to their rational universe and UFO advocates fearing that the scientific method would expose their research incompetence.

The problem with the conventional abduction narrative, Vallee said, was what it left out—all the data that didn't fit, creating the false impression of a consensus. Many incidents were not traumatic, and many didn't involve short gray beings, medical exams, or anything resembling spacecraft. Witnesses, furthermore, had complained to Vallee that investigators often imposed their preconceptions, distorting the accounts. In some cases, Vallee suggested, the deception was part of a disinformation campaign to use the abduction phenomenon to mask other activities, perhaps secret military research. He knew of one especially bizarre case, "even more chilling," he said, where alien imagery had been planted into the mind of a woman as an "overlay" to conceal another terrifying experience altogether. Furthermore, the numbers were implausible, Vallee said. At the rate of abductions projected for the United States, the worldwide figure would be something like 200 million abductees. The aliens would be poor scientists indeed if they needed that many human experimentees.

Whatever the phenomenon represented, it was not outside the realm of science to explore—no problem was by nature unscientific provided it was approached properly, Vallee said. He called for more rigorous investigation and reporting, better exchange of data among researchers, and better fieldwork, including the study of metallic residues and other samples collected at sites of UFO activity. Most of all, he cautioned, sensational theories should be put aside in favor of continued careful study. He took as inspiration the perspective of the sci-fi writer Philip K. Dick, who experienced communications from a life force he could not identify. "Some living, highly intelligent entity manifested itself inside me and around me, but what it was, what its purpose was, where it came from—I have tried a thousand theories and all work equally well, but at the same time each theory leaves some datum unexplained . . . and I know this is not going to change," Dick wrote in 1978. "I have the impression that a master game-player and magician and trickster is involved."

Bestselling author Whitley Strieber, whose book *Communion* helped set off much of the alien abduction frenzy of the late 1980s, also found the core narrative simplistic. Mack himself had acknowledged as much later at a UFO conference they both attended in Brisbane, Australia, Strieber remembered. But Mack had explained that his role as a physician was to stick to what he was hearing from people struggling with an inexplicable trauma. "He very intentionally did not want to look too deeply into the anomalous aspects of the reports," Strieber recalled. "He felt his approach as a physician should be to not look beyond the narrative but to approach it as a source of information about the individual's state." But there was more to it than abduction could encompass, as some quarter-million letters from Strieber's readers testified. His wife, Anne, tried to read them all and decided, "If it's not weird, I don't trust it."

Strieber's experience *was* indeed hard to categorize.[2] A forty-year-old Texas-born novelist with a string of popular thrillers like *The Wolfen, The Hunger,* and *Catmagic*, he was celebrating a snowy Christmas 1985 with Anne and their son in their wilderness cabin in the Catskills near the upstate New York hamlet of Accord, when he awoke to a strange swirling sound, as if people were moving around downstairs. The burglar alarm was set but hadn't gone off. He settled back in bed only to see the bedroom's open double doors slowly swinging closed. Then, terrifyingly, in the dim glow of the reflected snow and the alarm-panel lights, he caught sight of a small figure bending around the closing doors to look in. Its face was hidden, or perhaps Strieber was afraid to look closely. It was strangely clad, with a sharply etched wide-brimmed hat and what looked like a breastplate or armored vest patterned with concentric circles. Then the figure rushed into the room.

The next thing Strieber remembered, he was naked and flying, or being carried, out of the room. He found himself sitting in the woods. The snow had disappeared. Out of the corner of his eye he could see a small figure in a grayish-tan bodysuit with two dark holes for eyes and a round hole for a mouth—he thought it might be a mask. He couldn't move. To his right another figure he couldn't see but thought might be female seemed to be doing something with his head. Then he felt branches and saw he was flying high above the forest until he found himself in a small circular chamber with clothes strewn about. It felt messy and stuffy. Little figures were scurrying around. He felt trapped. He remembered being shown a small, gray box with a sliding lid and curved lip. A small being opened it to reveal a glittering, hair-thin needle that Strieber realized, or was told, would be inserted into his brain. He grew crazed with terror and must have struggled to resist because he remembered hearing a female voice say, "What can we do to help you stop screaming?" Absurdly, he heard himself saying, "You could let me smell you," and then he felt a hand against his face that was strangely comforting. It smelled, he thought, like cardboard, faintly sour, not human but nonetheless alive. Then he felt a bang and a flash and realized they must have used the needle on his head. Next he found himself in a kind of operating room with a realization of having encountered four distinct types of beings—child-size robotic figures; short, stocky beings with wide faces, pug noses, and dark blue coveralls; taller, nonhuman-looking figures, slender and delicate, with large, mesmerizing, black slanted eyes and barely a nose or mouth; and still other entities with buttonlike round black eyes. He felt alarmingly passed along as if by ranks of insects, although their hands felt soft, even soothing. His legs were spread apart. He was shown an ugly, gray triangular object, scaly and nearly a foot long, sprouting wires. Somehow, as with a life of its own, it swarmed into his rectum. Strieber, with a rush of fury, felt raped. The last thing he remembered was a painless incision being made into his right forefinger. He awoke the next morning with only a nagging sense of anxiety and a vague memory of a barn owl outside the bedroom window, staring in.

He grew short-tempered with his family; he was hypersensitive, paranoid, and easily confused. He came down with chills and a fever and suffered rectal pain and an infected finger. He thought he had a brain tumor or was losing his mind. Then, as with Proust, it came back with a sudden sense memory. He recalled their smell. It made him think he was not going crazy after all. He began reading up on UFOs. Strieber couldn't put a name to his experience. It was real, but the source was unknown. It was not physical but projected into the physical realm. Without answers, the critical thing, he felt, was to keep the question open.

The same year of Strieber's Christmastime encounter, Kary Banks Mullis, a California biochemist who would share the 1993 Nobel Prize for Chemistry for his invention of the polymerase chain reaction allowing a section of human DNA to be copied billions of times in a few hours, was driving from his home in Berkeley to his rustic country place in Mendocino.[3] As Mullis, an avid surfer not unfamiliar with psychedelics, would recount in his quirky

1998 memoir, *Dancing Naked in the Mind Field*, he got to his cabin around midnight, dropped his bags, picked up a flashlight, and headed down the hill to his outhouse in the woods. On the way he saw something glowing and shined the light on it. It looked like a raccoon. But then, Mullis said, it spoke to him. "Good evening, doctor." The next thing he knew, he said, it was early morning and he was on the road near his house. He had no memory of the night, but his clothes were dry and clean. The flashlight was missing, never to be found. Mullis returned home, slept for a few hours, and decided to clean out a pipe that fed stream water into his pond. But in the woods he suddenly grew terrified and fled. He had no idea why.

Sometime later, he said, he came across Whitley Strieber's *Communion* and felt troubling vibes from its black-eyed alien cover. While he was reading it, his daughter, Louise, called. "Dad, there's a book I want you to read. It's called *Communion*." "I'm reading it right now," Mullis said. And then Louise told him about her experience in Mendocino. She had gone to the house one night, walked down the hill, and went missing for three hours. She found herself later on the same road as her father, also with no idea of how she had gotten there. He was a scientist, Mullis reflected, but there was no way of testing his experience scientifically. It was anecdotal and couldn't be reproduced. It wasn't, as far as he could tell, an abduction. But whatever it was, he said, "it happened."

"Things first look like weeds when they begin to push their way up in cracks and unintended spaces," wrote anthropologist Susan Lepselter in *The Resonance of Unseen Things*.[4] "But the roots are deep." Lepselter, an associate professor of anthropology at Indiana University, Bloomington, spent time in Texas and Nevada with people who accepted their anomalous encounters as just another strange thing in a strange and alienating America, where the humanoid face on the cover of Whitley Strieber's *Communion* triggered buried angst. "Fantastic stories, like ordinary personal memories, arise amid experiences of class, loss, race, gender, and the body's unmoored location in a world of accelerated technological change," Lepselter wrote. "But those experiences aren't always articulated. Their shapes as stories are only partially visible from wherever one stands."

American experience was replete with genuine historical abductions— African slaves transported to the New World, pioneer women taken captive in Indian raids, Indian children kidnapped to boarding schools, "overlapping call signs" that produced a powerful resonance, Lepselter said.[5] "We're standing on piles of stuff on the cutting room floor." She herself was not immune. She was at the Las Vegas airport waiting for a flight home when a stranger sat down beside her. He was short with a jaunty moustache and a dapper black suit and spoke in "a clipped accent." He presented himself as a vitamin salesman and asked about her work, which seemed to delight him. "I see you have in you the sociological imagination!" he said, before squeezing her hand hard and evaporating into the crowd. Somehow, he seemed to know who she was. It then hit Lepselter. She had met a Man in Black.

The anthropology of the paranormal also resonated strongly with Luise White, a professor emerita in the University of Florida's Center for African Studies. She had spent years in East Africa investigating the deeply held belief that the fire brigades employed vampires that abducted people to take their blood for the white colonialists. When she asked why white colonialists would need their blood, terrified Africans answered, "Ask them." Often, the rumors went, victims were taken in sleep and immobilized with injections in the head or rendered helpless with wands. They were carried off by blood-red fire engines or other vehicles with the back seats ominously removed. These weird experiences varied yet seemed generally congruent. White later presented her research in a book, *Speaking with Vampires: Rumor and History in Colonial Africa*.[6] When White, back home, saw a TV show about alien abduction, she almost fell off her chair in astonishment, blurting, "Oh my God, that's a vampire story!"[7] She saw similarities in the tubes and needles cited in both cases. She also saw a strong sexual component to the abduction accounts, which seemed farfetched. "Human reproduction is not that hard to figure out," she said. Aliens capable of traveling the cosmos shouldn't need to conduct all those repetitive experiments—"you could get a hygiene manual." The unlikelihood of human-alien interbreeding, she said, recalled colonial-era debates about whether whites and blacks could propagate. Was it a reflection, too, of declining male virility—"that when real men have bottomed out, you acquire a lover from another galaxy?" Mack's involvement in alien abduction cases seemed also hardly accidental, White said. "They came to him—not another psychiatrist," she said. "You have this experience you don't understand and you happen to go to a psychiatrist who also believes in aliens."

26

STUCK

Throughout Mack's Affect Seminar, his two campus talks on aliens, and much gossip, Harvard had left him largely alone. Lots of university research was unconventional, after all. But in what Pritchard called a breached promise of confidentiality, the *Wall Street Journal* published a page-one article pegged to the May 1992 debut of the *Intruders* CBS miniseries (which featured Richard Crenna playing Mack) that broke the news of the upcoming conference at MIT under a derisive headline.

A HARVARD DOCTOR

OFFERS TRAUMA RELIEF

FOR UFO 'ABDUCTEES'

EXTRATERRESTRIALS PLAY ROUGH

SO THERE ARE MANY INJURIES

FOR JOHN E. MACK TO HEAL

The article, which also lampooned Pritchard, Jacobs, and Hopkins as well as some of their abductees, quoted a UC Berkeley professor who scoffed, "There's no evidence that even a grand jury in a DA's pocket would take seriously that UFOs have visited the earth, much less abducted somebody." The acting head of Harvard's Psychiatry Department, Malkah Notman, defended Mack, for now. "Many great ideas sound offbeat at the beginning," she told the paper. "There is some concern, but by and large I think the department feels it's useful to encourage creative work, as long as it doesn't get in anybody's way or do any harm." The article caused an uproar, Pritchard remembered years later. "All the crazies started calling my department head."[1] Everyone with a certain solution to this mystery demanded to be included in the Alien Discussions conference. Pritchard and Mack, having carefully screened participants for credibility, held firm.

The *Journal*'s exclusive had tipped off other media, and the Knight Ridder chain had weighed in with a brief story that noted the recent appearance of Mack, Hopkins, and Jacobs on *The Jane Whitney Show*. Whitney, a former news reporter and Philadelphia broadcaster who was being mentioned as a possible replacement for Johnny Carson, had booked Mack and Hopkins with some of their abductees for her syndicated *Night Talk* program. But shortly before the taping, an ABC producer in Los Angeles told Mack he was off the show—there were too many people.[2] Hopkins was outraged. No Mack, no show, he insisted. Mack soon got a call: What time should the limo pick him up? The segment, "Abducted by Aliens," aired in June with three abductees, including the shy arts professional called "Steven Kilburn" in Hopkins's book, *Missing Time*. On the show he revealed his real name, Michael Bershad, and told the audience—some of whom were snickering—of how he was subjected to a shameful ejaculation that the aliens forced in order to collect his sperm. Mack, looking awkward, acknowledged his initial doubts on abduction. "When I first heard about it, I didn't believe it," he said. While he couldn't explain what the phenomenon meant, "it certainly means something." When Whitney brought on a skeptical space engineer, James Oberg, to ridicule the accounts, the experiencers were mortified. "We got sandbagged," Mack said later.

The experience heightened Mack's worry about how his superiors were taking this. He made a point of showing up at a medical school reception where he could pretend to bump into the medical school dean, Daniel Tosteson.[3]

"I guess you're fairly uneasy about all this, you know, front page *Wall Street Journal* this 'n' that," Mack began.

"Yeah, John," Tosteson said. "I get the *Wall Street Journal*. People do call about what's going on."

He didn't look happy, Mack thought. "Maybe I should come and see you and talk to you about it," he said.

At Tosteson's office a few days later, he outlined his research. Tosteson, a physiologist who had established Harvard's Department of Genetics as well as the Departments of Cell Biology and Biological Chemistry and Molecular Pharmacology, suggested a double-blind study to see if supposed abductees could be differentiated from nonabductees. Mack was dubious. Tosteson was being "super-Western-science-y," Mack later told his Sikh therapist Khalsa.

Over the following months, Mack agonized over laying it all out for President Neil Rudenstein. More than a year and a half after he had introduced experiencers like Georgia and Amy to the Harvard community, his Affect Seminar was still going strong. Mack had even used sessions in June and July 1992 to give a presentation on the confidential abduction conference with the Dali Lama. He had told Tosteson, and now he thought he should tell Rudenstein as well. But time and again he picked up the phone only to panic at the thought of explaining it to Rudenstein's assistants. Each time, he would shakingly hang up.

But as he told Khalsa, he was more convinced than ever that he was on to something momentous. The next time he gave a grand rounds, he would not tolerate a discussion of whether the phenomenon was real or not. He may have been unable to determine what exactly it was, but it was real enough. "These smoking-gun physical things are very hard to come by," he told Khalsa. "The one thing the West cannot stand is traffic from the astral level into the hard physical plane." A woman flying out of her window—with witnesses! "Talk about blowing the Western mind." It could be a celestial awakening, Mack said, God's "sledge hammer approach."

His marriage was shakier than ever, Mack also confided. He felt the same powerlessness as his abductees. "I have not come to terms with the feminine in my life and Sally is one of the major manifestations and I don't know what the fuck to do with it," he told Khalsa.[4] He would have to do something soon, but, he confessed, "I have not the balls to make a choice about it." Their latest spat was again over psychedelics—Sally wouldn't partake. Some of his friends and their wives were getting together that Friday to "maybe do some substances," as Mack put it, but "Sally is making herself scarce, she doesn't want to do that. She is not a partner to me." Age was creeping up like "a terror—it feels like a kind of dread through my body." He could understand what the people he was seeing were going through. "Powerlessness is what I'm dealing with every day with the abductees," he said. "They're helpless." It had come out again in California, during his alternate states of consciousness. "I would disintegrate, dying to death, dying to death, dying to death." He had once again felt himself stuck in the birth canal, struggling to be born. It was like his marriage. "I'm stuck with Sally, unborn. She keeps me in the womb." He heard himself and stopped. "Not fair I'm blaming her," he said, it was "the dynamic." Still, he repeated, "I'm in the womb with Sally, resenting it, depressed—stuck in there with her. What decision can I make? That's the terror." Morosely, he added, "the strategy is not to be born." He felt trapped. "Being in this kind of nebbish arrangement with Sally is terrifying," he continued. "It's depressing is what it is. I feel anxiety right now, scared of making decisions and anger at Sally and the games she plays. 'Poor me—you don't help me.'" Why, he despaired, was he having so much trouble with Sally?

"Forget about Sally," Khalsa said. "What about you?" Mack was being too reactive. "The novice skates to the puck," Khalsa said. "Wayne Gretzky skates to where the puck is going to be."

His deepening relationship with Dominique, nearly thirty years younger, haunted him too, Mack told Rick Tarnas, whom he had been consulting for astrological guidance.[5] "I am thinking of making a life with this person, not just an affair." He also confided in Roz after running into her on the street one day. He was still hurt by their breakup but decided they could be loving, if unromantic, friends.

But there was a complication: Dominique was pregnant. Already the mother of an eight-year-old daughter and a seven-year-old son from her dissolved marriage, she and the new child's father had what she called a "complicated" and nonmarital relationship that was no secret to Mack. She assured him it was no impediment to their love. Mack was her man. He found it naturally disturbing but convinced himself it was part of some peculiarly emancipated Greek tradition. Nor was Sally in the dark. She saw her husband repeatedly rushing off to the hospital as the date approached for Dominique's cesarean. Finally Sally gave him a choice—it would be one of them or the other. The ultimatum plunged Mack into new despair. With the coming birth of Dominique's baby, his own unresolved maternal issues, and the stories he was hearing from his experiencers of stolen pregnancies, he told Tarnas, "I'm swimming in archetypes!"[6]

He and Sally separated in January, 1993. He moved out of the house and stayed with a friend, Honey Black Kay, a therapist who had also studied with Stan Grof.

Tarnas had reviewed their natal charts. Astrology, he believed, recognized that the sun, moon, and planets had a basic cosmic connection to forces that influence human existence. The planets did not *cause* anything to happen, any more than the hands of a clock caused the time to be 7:30 p.m. The entire universe was pervaded by "a fundamental holistic patterning," Tarnas said.

The circumstances of birth were not random but karmic, from a higher level of spiritual consciousness. So, Tarnas told Mack, their charts were of interest.

For Sally, "this year will have its challenges," he said. "She has structurally profound transits going on this year." But Mack's and Dominique's charts were powerfully connected. Right now, Tarnas said, Dominique had Pluto conjoining her moon at an aspect, or angle, of less than 10 percent, making for a strong effect. Pluto, God of the underworld, symbolized subconscious forces.

It made sense to Mack. "We have a lot of power struggle stuff," he said. Dominique also had a Saturn-Pluto conjunction. "Kafka was born with that conjunction," Tarnas noted. Michelangelo had painted *The Last Judgment* under it. "Just as you're a moon-Uranus person," Tarnas said, "she's a sun-Uranus person, hard to pin down, free spirit."

"Drives me crazy," Mack agreed. Not long before, he had joined Dominique on the Greek isle of Hydra, where she had often harbored while cruising on her father's yacht. The vacation had been idyllic until she asked when he was going to leave Sally. He didn't know. The mood had turned sour, and Mack flew home in a funk.

"You're born with a very tight Mercury square Pluto," Tarnas said, reading Mack's chart. "When you get interested in something, it becomes an obsession. There's a desire to transform other people's thinking."

Mack's abduction work was on growing display at Harvard. He had begun leading a Harvard seminar in non-ordinary states of consciousness aimed at examining "other experienced realities than those given in the culture." He drew freely on his own experience, including "this abduction thing—why I think it's got me so powerfully and why I was sort of a sitting duck for it." It was the confounding duality of it, he told the seminar.

This empirical left brain side of me that believes things are only real if they show up in the physical world—I've got that side of me [Mack said, gathering speed as the words flowed mesmerizingly]. Then I've got this sort of emerging consciousness spiritual side of me. And this does both. It should stay out there in the spiritual world—and then it shows up in the physical world. That's what you got to do to people like me. We can't all be

Buddhist meditators. I'm not built that way. But this stuff from person after person telling me there are entities smashing through into their world, roughly or spiritually, whatever, cuts and scoop marks, and UFOs happening, independently viewed—all that data which the left brain simply rejects out of hand, it doesn't fit—I think the data for that is overwhelming.

A big part of the seminar session was devoted to hypnosis, with guest appearances by the turbaned Khalsa and Wesley Boyd, who had attended Mack's 1991 Harvard talk on "The Mystery of Anomalous Experience" and was now a promising young psychiatrist with his own patients. Mack had referred Randy Nickerson to him.

Mack's taped freewheeling sessions hurtled from William James to LSD, magic mushrooms, and Carlos Castaneda, from Jung and Bill Wilson of Alcoholics Anonymous to Wittgenstein's theories of ineffability and the role of light in near-death experiences, from yogic techniques to John Mack himself. "I have a love-hate relationship to psychoanalysis," Mack confessed. "It saved my life and ruined my life." He faulted Freud for his epic reversal of his original seduction theory—that his patients had suffered actual sexual trauma—in favor of the belief that they were fantasizing to cover up forbidden Oedipal desires, a fateful fork in the road in psychiatry highlighted by the contemporary anti-Freudian renegade Jeffrey Moussaieff Masson. "What makes Masson's work so dangerous," Mack said, is how it showcased Freud's shifting of blame away from the pathogenic role of others onto the victim. That "blaming the victim system" had its counterpart in distrust of the abduction experiencer. Similarly, Mack said, abduction was in no way a screen memory of sexual abuse or rape, although, he granted, he was treating people who were both sexual-trauma victims and abductees. But the first had not caused the second.

Word of Mack's research was spreading quickly. A certain television producer, Chris Carter, had taken note of the Hopkins poll that ascribed abduction experiences to a large portion of the population. Now he was creating a TV series centering on two FBI agents who investigate cases of the paranormal. Fox would begin airing it in September 1993 as *The X-Files*.[7]

The *Journal of Irreproducible Results* also found the subject irresistible, announcing in October 1993 that it was awarding its "Third First Annual Ig Nobel Prize in Psychology" to John Mack and David Jacobs. The science humor magazine ("first make people laugh and then make them think") cited the two as "mental visionaries, for their leaping conclusion that people who believe they were kidnapped by aliens from outer space, probably were—and especially for their conclusion that, in Professor Jacobs's words, 'the focus of the abduction is the production of children.'" They shared the dishonors with three urologists recognized for their painstaking medical paper, "Acute Management of the Zipper-Entrapped Penis." The research was all genuine, as if to demonstrate that in science, nothing was too ridiculous to be studied. Mack took it with good humor. Jacobs said he was proud to share any laurels with John Mack.

27

"THE WHOLE BLOODY SNOWSUIT"

Mack had expanded his rejected abduction paper into a book for Scribner's. *Abduction: Human Encounters with Aliens* was slated for release in the spring of 1994. As he exulted to Khalsa, "I ended up with a quarter of a million dollar advance!" The *New York Times* Sunday magazine secured the prepublication exclusive. "My editors want me to lead readers through your psychological process by which you became convinced," reporter Stephen Rae told Mack.[1] They were also interested in the reaction of Harvard and Mack's colleagues to his work.

Mack held little back. "We're just talking here," he blithely told Rae. He had learned a lot from T. E. Lawrence, he said, which helped him in his dealings with Harvard and the Arabs. "I kept using his way of thinking. His struggles with his mother were somewhat similar to mine. He had certain confusions of identity similar to mine." He finally caught himself. "You got to be careful how you say it," he said, naively telling Rae to put it "in a way that doesn't make me look like a flaming egotist."

He also confessed, "I don't know how to deal with Werner and EST in this process. I'm afraid if we put too much EST stuff in here—you don't want to give people unnecessary targets to shoot at. I don't mind it being mentioned but if it's stressed it's going to affect credibility, that's all, because EST doesn't have public credibility."

Could he bring up psychedelic drugs? Rae asked.

"We sort of have to pick our issues," said Karen Wesolowski, director of Mack's new Program for Extraordinary Experience Research (PEER), an offshoot of his Center for Psychology and Social Change. They moved on to family life. He had been married for thirty-four years to a psychiatric social worker who was "very supportive" of his abduction work, Mack said, although "it's not a primary interest of hers." Actually, he and Sally had separated earlier in the year.

He recounted his momentous first meeting with Budd Hopkins. His own interest was no "gradually dawning realization," Mack said. "I really knew when I first talked with him." But he differentiated himself from Hopkins and Jacobs, who, he said, didn't take the phenomenon's transformative aspects seriously—"the way we deal with each other, destroying the earth." He recounted an argument he'd had with Jacobs. "David, how can you say this is the real experience, this is the reality, the reproductive baby-making aspects, and the rest is secondary when we don't know what reality any of this is taking place in?" The staggering thing, Mack said, was how the supernatural was "crossing over and being experienced by ordinary people." It was "epochal arrogance" that humans should claim to possess the only intelligence in the cosmos, he said.

Mack kept calling abduction a mystery, but to Rae it seemed like Mack had already made up his mind. He asked if Mack led his witnesses.

"Co-creation," Mack admitted. "I can really be attacked around that because that would imply that I'm sort of creating the ideas with them. I cannot deny that somehow my presence, what I'm known for, would not have some power to draw forth this material rather than that material. In that sense I'm co-creating." But, he said, "that is not the same as leading somebody. These people are very hard to lead, by the way."

"I was raised with the notion that there was no intelligence that gave a damn about the earth or us or anything else—we were alone," he said. "I was like a recalcitrant communist who becomes a right-winger."

Days later, he spoke with *Psychology Today*'s reporter-editor Jill Neimark, who had long been insistent on an interview, saying that the magazine was increasingly covering "spiritual issues."[2] Neimark's eclectic output included an erotic thriller, children's picture books, and a recent article on her uncle, Philip John Neimark, a Chicago commodities trader who had become a high priest (or *babalawo*) in Ifá, an eight-thousand-year-old West African religion of oracular deities and animal sacrifice similar to Santeria and voodoo.

When Neimark arrived at Mack's cramped third-floor hospital office decorated with a Buddhist thangka and an Egyptian scroll rendering his name in hieroglyphics, she noticed that his eyes matched the blue of his slightly wrinkled button-down shirt. She was struck too by his boyish sincerity and sense of helplessness. "My editor wants to get *you* in there, *your* path, *your* upbringing, *your* identification with Lawrence," she said. Mack suggested they talk through lunch. He produced bagels, a gallon of peanut butter, and Mars bars.

Neimark began by asking Mack if he'd had any abduction experiences of his own. No, he replied, "but I suspect that if I did and went around saying I know what this is about because I had it myself I would lose my credibility." Why did he think he had been spared? Perhaps, Mack said, because he was past his prime reproductive years.

She asked about proof. "The most robust stuff are the cuts," Mack said. But "trying to rely on physical proof is a dead end. The plan is subtle."

Didn't that bother him?

No, he said. "In fact you could say the phenomenon by its very nature is trying to get us off this pure reliance on physical artifacts and evidence for experiencing something as true. It's about that." When he first heard about the implants he got very excited. But the pathology tests found no foreign substances—she could talk to Dave Pritchard. "Which makes sense," Mack said. "If you have this technology that they can do all these things to track people, there's no reason why they couldn't accommodate with some subtle energy thing using tissues not that distinct from the body's tissue."

Neimark asked if the abduction stories might be generated out of sexual guilt.

It looked sexual, Mack granted. But with forty-two years of psychiatric experience he could say he had not found any connection between these people's abduction experiences and their psyches, histories, or emotional lives. Anyway, Mack said, his real interest was not abductions per se but "the ontological and conscious-raising questions this raises, astrology, near-death"—he stopped. "Don't put in astrology. It's going to compound the problems."

What did Mack's family and Harvard colleagues think of all this? she asked. His wife was "supportive, interested, maybe a little anxious at times," Mack said. Their sons were encouraging, although their middle boy, Kenny, studying international relations at Columbia, liked to joke, "Dad, I've got to get my career going before they find out I'm your son." His colleagues were variously tolerant and skeptical.

Finally, Neimark asked, "Why did it capture you?"

"Why would it not capture anybody as the most interesting story going on the planet now?" he said. The resistance came from the "elite culture." The vast majority of the population, the grass roots, had no problem accepting UFOs, polls showed.

Why did the elite resist so much?

"Vested interests," said Mack. Huge investments in weapons, mass culture, advertising, and the scientific establishment; universities would be jeopardized as trivial if extraterrestrial life started showing up. "That changes the research base. It's very threatening. I run into that a lot at Harvard."

Neimark asked about his hopes for his book.

"It can really make an impact," he said. "Or undermine my credibility. It's kind of a race, nip and tuck." In the end, he said, "I hope this can have some effect on raising the question of our place in the universe."

But where did it end? Neimark asked. "Do we have to embrace everything beyond the paradigm? Do you have to put on the whole bloody snowsuit?"

"I don't think we should abandon the scientific paradigm," Mack said. He was only questioning whether "the subject/object, materialist dualist structure" was the best way to understand matters that didn't seem to fit the physical, four-dimensional Newtonian-Einsteinian universe. He had invested hundreds and hundreds of hours, Mack told her, "before I finally said, 'Y'know, the truth is that I think there's some other intelligence at work here and I'm going to own that.'"

Did he ever ask himself, Neimark asked, "Why am I doing this?"

"Yeah," Mack said. "All the time."

28

PEER PRESSURE

In late October 1993, Scribner's began sending out bound galleys of Mack's book. One went to Budd Hopkins with a note: "I hope you'll agree that *Abduction* is a unique and startling book that shows us how to see the alien abduction phenomenon in a new and valuable way." But the publisher had mistakenly released an early version of the manuscript that had not been fact-checked or approved. It contained errors as well as actual names of some abductees instead of agreed-upon pseudonyms and had to be hurriedly recalled.[1]

Hopkins had immediate objections. Debunkers should be given "no easy foothold in the wall of evidence," he wrote Mack. "I'm afraid that the image you unconsciously present in the book is that of a well-meaning but gullible person, a man with a deep hunger to believe and to trust everyone who claims to be 'an experiencer.'" He wisely pleaded with Mack to delay publication so a skeptical psychiatrist could critique the book.

Hopkins had just finished the letter when Mack phoned to read him his dedication: *TO BUDD HOPKINS, who led the way.*

One of Mack's prime experiencers, Peter Faust, identified in the manuscript only as Peter, was also wavering. "Admitting openly in your Book that I had sex with an Alien, at this moment it all seems too much," Faust wrote. But then he thought it might help others. "So with my best wishes & only a few corrections & insertions I give you my Blessing." He later went public with his full name.

Mack was entangled in another difficult case he had written up as a chapter in the book. "Sheila," a forty-four-year-old Massachusetts psychiatric social worker, had recovered a flood of abduction memories. As young children, she and her brother remembered two small creatures in their bedroom at night. She thought there might have been a spaceship outside the window. Her main experience occurred years later when she was asleep next to her husband and awoke to an ear-piercing screech and flashing red lights. Her husband seemed dead, switched off. She saw beings coming down the corridor toward her and standing over her, and then she could remember nothing more. She consulted two psychiatrists and eventually Mack. He gave her permission to say what she believed was real to her and gave her life back to her, she said. Like the French physician Philippe Pinel, who freed the mentally ill from their chains in the 1790s, Sheila wrote Mack, "You have helped us all by lifting that burden and giving us the freedom to express our experience."[2]

What made the case more unusual was the willingness of one of Sheila's previous psychiatrists, Fred H. Frankel, a colleague of Mack's at Harvard Medical School, to continue discussing it with Mack. He disputed Mack's treatment of her but nevertheless agreed to a joint grand rounds on the case in September 1993 at Boston's Beth Israel Hospital, where Frankel was the psychiatrist in chief.

Frankel had been critical of Mack's therapeutic approach, as he wrote Mack: "Despite your proclaiming yourself as not fully understanding the nature of this phenomenon, you make it perfectly clear from the way you handle these unfortunate people that you not only do not disbelieve them, but that in some way you convey you are comfortable with viewing them as what they claim to be, abductees." That, Frankel said, "seems like much more than neutrality to me." Frankel also voiced surprise that a writeup of Sheila's case that Mack had sent Frankel and his colleague turned out to be the draft of a chapter for his book, and he disputed some quotes that Mack attributed to them. (Mack would use them anyway, identifying the two only with initials and noting their denials.) Mack would lay some of Frankel's hostility to the fact that Sheila left treatment with Frankel for him.

Two months before publication, Mack and Dominique and their PEER team sat down with a media consultant to prepare for likely hostile interviews on the book. Recruited by the Laurance Rockefeller–funded Human Potential Foundation, Norie Huddle, a published author, environmentalist, and antinuclear activist like Mack, had made an art of living off the grid, surviving, she boasted, on just a thousand dollars a year. In 1979, after hearing a voice while driving on the New Jersey Turnpike—"You will found the Center for New National Security"—Huddle did just that, setting up the small progressive think tank in Washington, DC.

Now, meeting with Mack and his PEER circle, the forty-nine-year-old Huddle told him his body language gave him away.[3] Sometimes he was scrunched up like he carried the weight of the world on his shoulders. Other times he seemed nimble enough to float away. "The first game rule is tell the truth," Huddle advised. "The second is come from love and respect."

"There are going to be people gunning for me," Mack said, "personal dirt, personal issues. Maybe we should get to that personal vulnerability." That meant, they agreed, questions about Dominique. People were sure to ask why Mack was not with his wife.

"For John's support," Dominique suggested. "John wants me there for support."

Simmering tensions at PEER quickly surfaced. Mack's research director, psychologist Caroline McLeod, complained that Mack was often remote, focusing on big philosophical issues while leaving staffers to struggle with details.

"Is there a feeling that Dom and I get to do all the good stuff and everyone else is stuck with the shit?" Mack asked.

"Yep!" came the prompt chorus. One of the women, overcome with emotion, burst into tears.

"Let it go!" said Huddle.

They continued peppering Mack with sample questions. "Are you creating a new religion, Dr. Mack?"

"Are you asking if there's a spiritual element to this?" Mack answered. "I would say yes. Spirituality to me is rediscovery of what is sacred in nature, something beyond ourselves."

"What about spaceships?"

"The more important question," Mack responded levelly, "is where do they come from? I don't know. We are not good at 'I don't know' in this country."

"Government coverups?"

"Not an area I know much about. You'd think someone with as high a profile as me would attract government attention. I haven't heard anything from the government."

What made him an expert in hypnosis?

He wasn't, Mack said. "I had to dust off my training and bring back my skill. I was trained in the '50s."

"Is it possible you're creating these 'memories'?"

"Excellent question! It raises this question: Where are these memories located? In the brain?"

Huddle suggested he say, "For further study."

"I like that!" Mack said.

His work was deeply affecting, he said. "I come out of there sweating, quite shaken and disturbed."

Huddle stopped him. "I wouldn't use the word 'disturbed.'"

Randy Nickerson, one of Mack's first experiencers, had joined the session, and he tested Mack with a question of his own about abductees. "There are 3 to 4 million people at home thinking they're crazy. What can you say to these people?"

Mack called it "a fundamental question." Some seventy-five to eighty people, he said, "show me they have experienced some kind of energy, beings, whatever we call it, entities that entered their world and those accounts, so tightly similar among people not in touch with each other all over the country and as far as I can tell as a psychiatrist, the only thing that can do that is an authentic real experience. As reluctant as I am to believe such a thing was possible, that in fact seems to be occurring."

The drill turned to questions about drugs. What about his use of LSD?

"Some of these agents, used in a research context—" Mack began.

"No!" Huddle cut him off.

Mack tried again. "The use of psychedelics for research would be perfect for another show, but that's not what we're here to talk about."

Was he a cult leader?

"It depends how you look upon cult—"

"WAIT! WAIT! WAIT!" Huddle said.

"One final question, Dr. Mack," came a shout. "I hear you've been married thirty-four years and are now sleeping with a young associate."

"I'm not sure my personal life is relevant here," Mack began. "My wife and I are on good terms. We've been separated over a year now, that's true."

"Hardly an anomaly in America," Huddle prompted.

"Not unusual in America," Mack echoed.

Was Mack suffering a midlife crisis?

"You're not the first one who said that," Mack answered. "I'm sixty-four, I like the midlife notion."

29

ALIENS IN BRAZIL

Amid prepublication fever, Mack and Dominique set off in February 1994 on a rushed week-long trip to Brazil, where in October 1957 the twenty-three-year-old farmer Antônio Vilas-Boas had become the world's first well-publicized abductee.[1] According to his account, while he was working one night on his tractor, he had watched an egg-shaped craft land nearby, where it disgorged small figures that pulled him inside. He was stripped and covered in a thick, odorless liquid, and then he found himself having ecstatic sexual intercourse with a beautiful naked female not entirely earthly in appearance with whitish-blonde hair, a pointy chin, and huge, blue, ovoid eyes. Afterward she pointed to her belly, smiled, and pointed to the sky. Vilas-Boas said he got a tour of the ship and observed the other creatures, who spoke in "growls, like dogs," before he was ushered out. He watched the ship shoot away into the sky. He suffered sleeplessness and nausea and eventually told his story to a journalist.

Mack and Dominique had an introduction to Gilda Moura, a Brazilian psychologist, astrologer, and author of a popular new book on alien contacts, and Moura's mother, Irene Granchi, one of Brazil's leading UFO investigators, who had translated records of the Vilas-Boas case.[2] Moura, a vivacious Carioca with tinted skin, thick, dark hair, and carmine lips, had seen a spaceship as a child and later met a special being that ignited her interest in the paranormal. Wristwatches stopped in her presence, and unusual synchronicities propelled her to a career of investigating UFOs and abductions.

In Minas Gerais, the southeastern Brazilian home state of Vilas-Boas, named for its rich colonial gold, gemstone, and iron mines, they visited a spiritual house where mediums in trance states treated the sick. There they gained entry to a "disobsession" service, where mediums summoned energies to rid sufferers of troubling spirit influences.

Mack and Dominique joined nearly a hundred women who sat barefoot, hands in their laps, palms up. At a table set with candles and Christian icons, mediums dressed in white sat under a hanging portrait of an Amazonian

Indian, the presiding deity. The room echoed with groans, sobs, handclaps, and finger snaps. Some mediums went through an elaborate cleansing ritual, tearing at invisible fields around their bodies and shaking off unseen burdens, while others perfumed the air with swinging cans of incense.

Dominique looked up from her chair to see a medium reaching out and tracing her contours. Then suddenly the woman began to weep, tears streaming down her face as if detecting something heartbreaking about her. As the woman again reached out her hands, Dominique closed her eyes and concentrated on beaming her a stream of loving energy. As if blasted back, the medium reeled against the wall. "You have an entity," Dominique was told. "A water entity. From the rivers or the sea. You are a medium."

Dominique was then asked to work on someone herself. Hardly realizing what she was doing, she closed her eyes and felt herself going into a trance. Her hands fluttered around a small woman who had stepped forward, and Dominique began to feel energies passing through her and meeting the woman's. Dominique could sense the different regions of the woman's body as she herself felt powerful yet strangely hollowed out. Other mediums surrounded Dominique, waving their hands around her body to remove negative energy and transmit positive energy. Mack marveled at Dominique's expression—ecstatic and transcendent.

The other mediums decided Dominique should work on Mack. As she concentrated, onlookers shouted, "Tell him the message!" It reminded her of an evangelical revival meeting. Mack, too, was pronounced a medium, although encumbered with several lifetimes of black magic that he would first need to eliminate.

One evening Mack took time away to be hypnotized by Gilda Moura.[3] He felt anxious, he told her. "I feel fear right through my body."

"You are here, you are safe," she said.

Mack visualized a room with a table, a TV turning itself on and off, a child's nursery table—"I'm sort of halfway there," he said. He was going down a hallway past a desk with a tiny black-haired receptionist. "Then it's blocked," he said.

Go on, Moura said.

"I could go into space, free, travel anywhere," Mack said. "I hear ringing in my ears now, high-pitched."

"Don't try to make up a story, Mack," Moura said. "Let it happen."

". . . like a ketamine trip I took once," he free-associated. "I'm in this blue space but too small, like a planetarium space . . . temple walls . . . I'm floating, ancient. I'm keeping it blocked up."

He stopped. "I'm afraid I'm stuck. There's something I'm supposed to do but I don't know what it is. I'm afraid I'm not doing this right."

Moura counted, "one, two, three—you can see, Mack."

"Strange world that I'm picturing," he resumed, "bright light coming into my mind . . ." Now he was seeing a huge object, not a spaceship, but a surface with squares. "I feel so cold."

Strange, Moura said. "Here it's too hot."

Mack felt a vastness all around and grew scared, remembering his anxiety when the astronauts flew to the moon. "I was always afraid they'd be lost in space," Mack said, "lost in multiple realities, never able to get back."

"Feel safe that I'm with you," Moura said.

"Why don't they freeze when they're out in space with no clothes on?" Mack asked. "Must be some energy protecting them."

"Go on a trip," Moura said.

He was in an enclosure, "very small like an eggshell made of porcelain." Then he thought, "I'm out in the desert . . . I don't know why it's so cold—it could be another planet." He felt so alone. "There is nobody, no God. I'm scared to be alone. I'm terrified of aloneness."

He had an image of characters from *The Wizard of Oz* tramping through the Judean wilderness. "I feel lost there, lost in space, like a terror of death, that for me death won't be joined by joy of loved ones. Death will be utter aloneness in space."

Suddenly he perked up. "I just got an idea," he said. "This is like an insight—why I'm interested in abductions. Can I say this or stay on the journey?"

"You can say that," Moura answered, "and then continue the journey."

"Because," Mack continued excitedly, "the abduction story is a welcoming story because it means that—Ooooo, I'm getting goose pimples as I think of this—I'm not alone. There is life in the universe! It may not be, you know, familiar, traditional Christian life or Jewish life but it's some kind of life. The universe has beings in it. You know, maybe they're not nice to humans. They come, they do this and this but there's some kind of population out there, you know, in the universe."

Moura nudged him back to his journey.

"It's the fear of aloneness in this life, the fear of aloneness when I'm dying," he said. "It's like my mother. It's like, where did she go when she died? It's funny, the whole thing, I see why I'm so interested in this abduction story—because it's the opposite of my belief system . . . it's the welcome opposite to my conscious belief system, 'cause I was raised to believe in a universe with nothing in it, no God, no intelligence, no life, no nothing . . ."

Moura eased him out of his trance. It was February 24, 1994, in Rio. His body was coming together, and all his fears would disappear. She counted up to ten and snapped her fingers.

In the following days, Mack and Dominique attended an abductee support group at Irene Granchi's house with an astrologer who had analyzed the charts of more than 250 abductees. They talked to a psycho-surgeon known for performing knifeless operations. They met the director of the International Institute of Projectiology and Conscientology in Rio de Janeiro, where people are taught how to project their consciousness to accelerate their communication with the cosmos and their spiritual evolution through successive embodiments interrupted by periods of death. They met with an American researcher studying abductions in Brazil's UFO-ridden northeast—a poor, backward, and superstitious region where people were afraid to leave their homes for fear of botched abductions by often hapless aliens. "It's as if they sent their worst ones to the Northeast," the researcher told them. They then flew to São Paulo, where they met a prominent businessman who told them how he had stolen some stones from a sun temple in Machu Picchu, Peru. That night he heard a voice commanding him to return the stones. The voice dictated a message that, when he wrote it down and had it translated, turned out to be in Quechua, an indigenous language of the Inca empire. At another abductee support-group meeting, they heard from a former nautical engineer in the Brazilian Navy who told of seeing a gigantic spacecraft buzz his ship before plunging into the sea. They spent the weekend in the mountains of Minas Gerais, stopping in the village of Baldim near the state capital of Belo Horizonte, where people had demanded streetlights as protection from all the

UFO activity that locals attributed to the mineral mines. A shopkeeper told them of his encounter with a spacecraft he had seen land. He had watched "dwarves" exit the ship, and he grabbed one, wrestling with it before it slipped out of his grasp. It had tough, leathery skin and a face "like a helmet." The ship had tried to capture him with a pincer at the end of a chain, catching him by the pants and hauling him up as he held onto the hatch, struggling to break free, before he was dropped to the ground. The ship, he said, sent out streams of gold and violet light stronger than a lamppost. Another witness, a field hand, said he had seen too many spaceships to count. They came in four shapes: coffin, pipe, tower, and saucer. He recounted a conversation with a tall stranger, balding with a fringe of blond hair, after which he was suddenly able to read and write. A farmer in the mountains told them of a night the previous July when he smelled something bad he thought was cat shit. In the bedroom he found four foul-smelling little gray men with four-fingered hands, webbed feet, and huge eyes that he felt pierced his very soul. A former boxer and police chief, he tried to punch the smallest one and was zapped painfully in the arm by its two forefingers, causing paralysis. He still suffered pain and had terrible nightmares. He asked Mack to hypnotize him in hopes of recalling more. In a relaxed state he began to shake, terrified and cold. He recalled being in a round, white enclosure with a splitting pain in his ears, as from a turbine. He felt his eyes aching like they were being pulled out, then a sensation of floating and a sudden terror of death. He grew so upset, gasping for breath, that Mack brought him out of the trance, whereupon he threw up. He remembered nothing of what he had said. They asked his wife if she had her own encounters. No, she said, but she had many out-of-body experiences and sometimes sleepwalked, often waking on the road with no idea how she got there. Mack and Dominique asked her to keep good notes of subsequent events and send them to Cambridge.

Brazil was alien ground zero, but they had to get home.

30

THE *TIME* BOMB

The Sunday *New York Times* curtain-raiser on Mack's book, appearing a month before *Abduction*'s April 1994 publication date, was illustrated with an eerie photo of Mack under a skylight in the low, canary-yellow PEER office building in Somerville, just a few minutes' walk from Mack's office at the Cambridge Hospital. Mack thought it made him look like "a cadaver."[1]

Parts of the article also gave him pause. It led with a lurid quote from Peter Faust: "I didn't realize that I was having sex with aliens until a few months ago." It segued to the anal probes and forced sperm collections and fetus removals, saying "the sex was nonstop" and making the phenomenon sound, Mack thought, like an orgy. Rae's article called Mack "mystically detached and certain that he is right." It said that Mack's interest in his patients would not have caused a stir, "except that he believed them." It also said Harvard's Macht building might have been named Mack if his colleagues hadn't feared he had gone mad.

While the *Times* article disappointed Mack, Jill Neimark's earlier article in *Psychology Today* had shocked him.[2] "One of the best and the brightest," it began, "a Pulitzer Prize–winning psychiatrist, has made himself into a high priest of what is politely called 'the abduction phenomenon.'" Neimark ridiculed Mack for believing Hopkins's claims that some abductees were returned to earth in the wrong clothes. Would aliens smart enough to traverse the universe screw up like that? And, she wrote, "Hopkins' reliability began to crumble like old cake" over his Brooklyn Bridge abduction case, which she asserted had been convincingly debunked by UFO researchers, although the debunking was itself later debunked. She questioned what it meant for Mack to attach himself to Hopkins given their differences. "Hopkins is an artist, but Mack is a high priest at a most sanctified temple of science: Harvard Medical School. He also happens to be a man with a halo of perfection about him, an honorable man given to just causes, a man with a reputation for kindness. Mack, more than anybody needs to be rigorous in his research. Otherwise he may become a kind of Pied Piper, seducing and perhaps terrifying us with visions of a world that may not exist." What proof did he offer? None really, Neimark said. The mental normalcy of experiencers had hardly been as verified as Mack claimed, and hypnosis was fraught with pitfalls.

"Mack is the most frustrating type of true believer: congenial, intelligent and absolutely impenetrable," she concluded. "The real disappointment is that he brings us no closer to the truth—even though he could."

Mack had one more big interview to do, with *Time* magazine.

James Willwerth, a former Vietnam war correspondent and one of *Time*'s stars, had a longtime interest in mental health and had been looking into Mack for some time. He saw a great story in the distinguished Pulitzer Prize-winner who had taken on aliens. "It's a natural, I would say," Willwerth later recalled.[3]

He began by asking Mack about his "psychobiography" of Lawrence. "I wouldn't call it that," Mack said. "I tried to write a biography that was psychologically infused." With PEER's administrative director Karen Wesolowski and research director Caroline Mcleod listening nervously, he quickly grew expansive, telling Willwerth about his transpersonal research with Stan Grof, who had shifted out of psychedelic drugs. "He found breathing could do it," Mack said. "After half, three-quarters of an hour, you experience the psyche traveling to another country. You know other languages, identify with animals, gods and goddesses and travel around the cosmos."

Skeptics like Carl Sagan demanded proof, Mack said. "I'm not against proof. But every case I've got in the sense of hard proof is faulty." He described something of the abduction experience and added, "This is where my clinical background comes in and where I hope you'll treat me well." He scoffed at Neimark's description of him. "The high priest! I'm as confused about this stuff as you are." The media loved to portray him as gullible. "The *New York Times* has never had an article that wasn't totally snotty on this subject," he said.

"When you decided to get into this did you set up a research design?" Willwerth asked.

"Now how am I supposed to study this?" Mack said he asked himself. He had a full-time academic appointment, so he didn't have a private practice to devote to abduction. Those consultations were not reimbursable, although he was fortunate to have a two hundred thousand dollar grant financed principally by Laurance Rockefeller, ostensibly for studying interspecies communication. "I take no direct salary," Mack hastened to add. His book advance also helped finance his research.

He started to relate his warnings from Thomas Kuhn to remain skeptical, then he caught himself. "I'm not sure I want this on the record, depending on how you use it."

Willwerth asked again about Mack's scientific protocols—had he set up "the standard bureaucratic models?"

There were no models for his research, Mack said. He had submitted a paper to the *American Journal of Psychiatry*, but they had wanted extensive revisions, so he had decided to do his book instead.

"You dealt with this on your own?" Willwerth pressed. The National Institute of Mental Health was not involved?

There was no standard conventional model for this kind of research, Mack repeated.

Willwerth then met with Mack's staffers. As a writer on scientific research, he had never seen anyone with the credentials of Mack approach a subject like alien abduction, Willwerth said. "Harvard hasn't given you any trouble at all?" he asked Vivienne Simon, the director of Mack's Center for Psychological Studies in the Nuclear Age who had helped set up PEER.

"Harvard has asked all the right and all the difficult questions," she said. "John is one of the genuine pioneers, willing to engage in a genuine mystery. He's okay with not knowing. He eagerly embraces the mystery of life."

Willwerth had long hidden his antipathy, but now was letting it show. "Keep in mind," he said, "I'm also talking to people who don't think this is such a great deal."

Willwerth had one more major interview, with experiencer Randy Nickerson. Willwerth knew that Nickerson was "Scott" in Mack's forthcoming *Abduction*, and he wanted to reveal the connection. Nickerson was reluctant. "I can't put my life out there for people to walk on me."

"I don't take a side on this," Willwerth assured him. "I don't write articles people necessarily like. I just write what I find out." He led Nickerson through some options, such as speaking off the record or not for attribution—printable but with his name withheld. "I've been doing this twenty-seven years now," Willwerth said. "I make gut-level judgments."

Nickerson said he had been burned before by a TV producer who had promised one set of questions and asked another. Willwerth tried to craft a statement that Nickerson would subscribe to, but he got nowhere. "What bothers me," Nickerson said, "is sensational bullshit, pardon my English."

Willwerth later called Mack with a few last questions. Did Mack know someone named Donna Bassett? Of course, Mack said. She was one of his experiencers, with a particularly interesting history. He barely heard Willwerth's last words: "Donna made the whole thing up."

31

OPRAH

Mack now courted a vast and voracious new audience, the tabloid television world of the Oprah Winfrey Show. A few months before, Oprah, destined to become America's richest woman and the first black female billionaire, had snagged the reclusive Michael Jackson for the most-watched television interview in history, drawing some 90 million viewers. Mack agreed to tape Oprah's show in Cambridge and Chicago for broadcast two days before the publication of *Abduction*.[1]

It opened with a clip of Mack in a gray suit striding self-consciously out of Harvard Yard. "He is an eminent psychiatrist and he has been cited on numerous occasions for his scholarship," Oprah began. "He's even won the Pulitzer Prize. His recent work with people who believe they've been abducted by aliens has even caught the attention of the respected *New York Times*."

The camera dollied to Oprah, svelte in a butterscotch-yellow jacket and leggings and white boots. "For the last four years," she continued, with upraised eyes, "Dr. Mack has studied about one hundred patients who claim they have been abducted by aliens. He believes them when they say aliens have inserted foreign objects into their bodies. He believes them when they say they have been on the aliens' space ships. And Dr. Mack believes them, he says, when they say that they—have—had—children—with—aliens. Uh-huh!"

Mack was splayed in a chair with his trousers riding up over his argyle socks. Beside him sat Peter Faust, tall and debonair with a neatly trimmed beard and glossy, swept-back hair, "a typical thirty-six-year-old guy," as he described himself.

So, Oprah turned to Mack, what did it all mean?

Mack recited his litany—the uniformity and universality of abduction accounts, the involvement of young children, the absence of any evident psychopathy, and the scraps of physical evidence. "The only thing that behaves like that is real experience," he said. "When I first heard this, I thought they must be mentally disturbed, but they're not. Of thousands of abduction cases, there's not a single one that turns out to reflect some other kind of problem."

He described a typical abduction, oblivious of how it might strike a dubious audience.

"A powerful blue light or energy comes along," he began, recounting the switched-off witnesses, the short beings with big black eyes, the examining tables, the doctor figure, and the probing and testing. ". . . Sperm samples may be taken," Mack continued, "eggs from a woman . . ." These, he said, were often later reimplanted for pregnancies that were removed in subsequent abductions. Finally the abductees were taken to visit their fetuses or hybrid babies on the ship.

Oprah wondered if they might be spiritual beings, or something only quasi-physical.

"We want to have it one way or the other," Mack said. "It's not that simple."

Oprah turned to Faust. "What do they say to you? What do you think they want with you?"

"They wanted connection," Faust said. "They wanted to make contact. They wanted me to connect with them."

"Why you?" Oprah asked.

It wasn't just Faust, Mack said. Housewives, scientists, psychiatrists, diplomats—all kinds of people were being taken.

What was the message?

"That it's not just traumatic," Faust said. "There is an aspect that is traumatic, but that something good comes out of it."

Mack was exasperated. "Why is it every other culture in the history of the human race has believed that there were other entities, other intelligences in the universe? Why are we so goofy about this? Why do we treat people like they're crazy and humiliate them if they're experiencing some other entities, some other intelligence that's coming across?"

Mack and Faust were soon joined by the Nickersons—Randy and his ethereally pretty younger blond sister, Glynda. Their mother, Marcia, watched from the audience.

Oprah asked about proof.

"I wish I had it," Randy said. He had tried to take photos. Glynda said they had even set up trip wires, to no effect. The phenomenon defied photography.

"First of all," Mack said, "there *is* physical evidence. These people have cuts, scoop marks, lesions on their bodies. They are witnessed to be absent by other people." Furthermore, he said, "there is burned earth outside where ships have landed." It might be less than satisfactory proof, but it was something. What was going on was subtle, Mack said, but "this phenomenon stands a chance to break us out of that box that Carl Sagan would keep us in."

They were soon joined by two more experiencers—a studious-looking psychotherapist called Joe who said he knew he had a sixteen-month-old hybrid alien son, and a well-coiffed woman, Eva, whose last encounter occurred the day before, she said, on the way to the studio. "I can sense them."

"We want to believe we have some measure of control over the world, and we don't," Joe said. "The world you live in is dying."

"We're not here to convince anybody," Eva said. "We're just bringing things to the public to make them aware that this is happening and this is very real. It's as real as it can get. All we're asking is for you to go home and think about it."

Oprah brought out a prominent skeptic, Nicholas P. Spanos, a professor of psychology and the director of the Laboratory for Experimental Hypnosis at Carleton University in Ottawa. "If you convince them that something happened and regress them, they will believe it," Spanos said. "You can create experiences and they'll elaborate on them if you provide appropriate expectations."

That didn't explain the memories consciously recalled, without hypnosis, the experiencers objected.

Spanos cited sleep paralysis as another possible explanation, setting off a cacophony of argument.

"You don't have to be crazy to be imaginative," Spanos said.

Oprah turned to the audience for a snap poll. Who believed what these people said happened to them actually happened to them? And who didn't? The two rounds of applause sounded similar.

A woman in a red sweater said she wanted more information about Faust's hybrid babies. How had it happened?

In other words, Oprah interpreted, "Was it a normal sexual thing?" Oprah said there was no time to go into it now, "but after the show I'll make sure to give you step by step what happened."

Joe resumed talking about his hybrid son, ". . . half human, half very humanoid, smaller, very large head, very listless—they're obviously starting to mix them and us, I mean that's real clear."

"What is it about you that makes you a UFO or alien abduction expert?" a last questioner asked Mack.

"Well, I wish I knew," Mack said. "What got me involved was . . ." The credits scrolled up the screen as he continued talking. He was still talking when the program cut out.

32

"THE MAN FROM OUTER SPACE"

With the publication of *Abduction* imminent and the Oprah segment about to air, Mack was increasingly uneasy. How would Harvard take this? He sent President Neil Rudenstein an author's advance copy with a note: "I know that this book has been generating a good deal of 'Harvard' attention in the media, some of which is quite distorting of what I've done. I hope you will have a chance to read it and we might then talk about what this means."

Rudenstein replied promptly. "It certainly looks like an intriguing book, and I look forward with great interest to reading it very soon."

Abduction was built around the case studies of eight men and five women experiencers, selected from the seventy-six Mack had studied to date. Their identities were masked, although Randy Nickerson and Peter Faust had gone public. "This book is not simply about UFOs or even alien abductions," Mack said in the preface. "It is about how this phenomenon, both traumatic and transformative, can expand our sense of ourselves and our understanding of reality, and awaken our muted potential as explorers of a universe rich in mystery, meaning, and intelligence."

But clearly Mack regarded the experience as fundamentally real. "The pioneering work of Budd Hopkins and David Jacobs has shown what is amply corroborated in my cases, namely that the abduction phenomenon is in some central way involved in a breeding program that results in the creation of alien/human hybrid offspring." The back cover sported flattering blurbs from Keith Thompson, Rick Tarnas, and George Vaillant, a colleague of Mack's at Harvard Medical School. Tarnas had read a draft and provided a stirring endorsement, calling the book "a landmark work." But after going through the published pages, Tarnas had second thoughts. Mack had failed to convey the requisite degree of doubt for the reader. He asked Mack to omit the quote from the paperback.[1]

James Willwerth's article, "The Man from Outer Space," detonated in the April 25, 1994, issue of *Time*.

"Psychologists and ethicists do not question Mack's sanity so much as his motives and methodology," it said. "They charge that he is misusing the techniques of hypnosis, trying to shape the 'memories' of his subjects to suit his vision of an intergalactic future, and very possibly endangering the emotional health of his patients in the process."

There wasn't much worse you could say about a physician than that he was harming his patients. But *Time* struck another blow. The experiencer that Willwerth offhandedly mentioned to Mack in a last phone conversation, Donna Lee Rice-Bassett, had told the magazine that she was an "undercover debunker" who had run a sting on Mack, hoaxing him with a bogus abduction story that he had completely fallen for. While in a therapy session in a bedroom of Mack's house, she said she remembered meeting President John F. Kennedy and Soviet Premier Nikita Khrushchev on a spaceship during the Cuban missile crisis. Khrushchev was supposedly crying. She had sat in his lap and comforted him. Mack was so excited by the story, *Time* quoted Bassett, that he leaned too heavily on the bed and it collapsed.

Bassett claimed that Mack's work was "riddled with scientific irregularities" and lacked a formal research protocol and the necessary consent forms legally required from research subjects. Mack had provided her UFO material to read prior to her hypnotic sessions, she said, which, if true, would violate proper professional practice. *Time* also said Bassett had discovered that Mack was improperly billing insurance companies for his research, listing it as therapy.

The story blindsided Mack. Willwerth had offered few clues to his mindset. He had not warned Mack, as Willwerth acknowledged years later, "I hear you're full of shit."[2] But he had come convinced that "this guy is irresponsible—I won't say a nut case." It also didn't escape Willwerth that Mack's staff was largely female, and attractive at that—a "groupie situation," as Willwerth later called it, with Mack "a rooster in the barnyard, that was clear." Willwerth had no patience for the experiencers either, he acknowledged, calling them "absolutely nuts."

He had been put onto the story, he later revealed, by Donna Bassett's husband, Edward, who had been a fellow reporter in South Vietnam writing for *United Press International* and *Aviation Week and Space Technology*.[3] When Ed called Willwerth out of the blue one day to ask if he would be interested in a story on a psychiatrist who was misusing his mystique in harmful ways, Willwerth said yes. He flew to North Carolina to meet with the Bassetts. They struck him as eccentrics with exceptional research skills, Willwerth recalled.

They showed him transcripts of Donna's abduction-therapy sessions, including the one with the Kennedy/Khrushchev episode. She told Willwerth she had made it all up, that she had collected a large library of abduction books to concoct an identity as an experiencer and then had written Mack a letter with all the right cues. "Like a fat fish in the river, he took the bait," Willwerth recalled. "She totally hornswoggled him and the whole thing was totally false. She took him to the cleaners. It was the beginning of the end of John Mack."

But Bassett may have hoaxed Willwerth as well. If she had fabricated an experiencer history, she had done it long before meeting Mack. Or perhaps she really was an experiencer all along, as she told *Communion* author Whitley Strieber almost a year before meeting Mack. In December 1991, according to documentation later collected by Mack, Bassett wrote Strieber, saying, "I come from a family that has had experiences such as those you've described on and off as far back as anyone can remember (several centuries)." She came from Oak Ridge, Tennessee, "radioactive gophers and all," she wrote, in a rambling screed on the dangers of radiation poisoning from a nuclear disaster.

The following September she wrote Mack, introducing herself as a research analyst who had worked with the government and military and saying she had been encouraged to contact him by a variety of sources. "My background includes multiple events that are now being referred to as abductions," she said. "This is an ongoing situation and has been a factor in my family for many generations." These experiences dated back, she said, to the fourteenth century. In 1974, she went on, "an anomalous object was removed from my left sinus cavity." She noted that she was living in Oak Ridge at the time and that the alien phenomenon seemed linked to sites of "social activism." She signed off, "Good luck with your efforts."

When Bassett and her husband ran into Mack, either by happenstance or design, at a UFO event in New Hampshire shortly after writing him, she seemed already highly informed about the abduction phenomenon. Mack also later recalled that Ed was offering to share his technical expertise as an aviation journalist with the aim of gaining Mack's help for Donna as an experiencer. Mack was willing. In preparation, he sent them both—not just

Donna, as *Time* had reported—some material on abduction, well before any discussion of a therapy appointment for Donna.

They met at the Charles Hotel in Cambridge, with Mack scribbling notes that he later recorded. Donna was then thirty-five. Born in Murfreesboro, Tennessee, she was an only child born premature at seven months with a leg deformity. They later moved to Oak Ridge. She had been married before—her first husband had been into Nazism and satanism. Her maternal great-grandmother saw "angels," and Donna, at age five, saw "balls of light" in the house. At two and a half she wandered into a neighbor's house to snoop, and the neighbor punished her by plunging her hands into boiling fudge. Donna was healed by an apparition, "Jane," who continued to protect her from danger. She recovered to play eight musical instruments and type one hundred words per minute. At five a boy tried to rape her but was chased off by Jane. At six or seven her shortened leg was cured by a visitation that her great-grandmother attributed to angels. Growing up she was able to finish people's sentences—some called her a witch. On and off throughout her life she had "gone someplace else" with missing time. One night during puberty, without having sex, she woke up bleeding and in pain, feeling pregnant.

Bassett further told Mack, as he noted, that the Oak Ridge National Laboratory near her, where a water-cooled reactor produced the plutonium for the first atomic bombs, had been drawing alien visitors who shared their concern over the bomb making and radiation that endangered the planet.

Mack, with assistant Pam Kasey, met with the Bassetts again several days later, and in October, at Mack's home-office in Brookline, they interviewed Donna about her experiences. They did it again the following month, when Bassett, in a hypnotic regression she later said she faked, spun the outlandish tale of meeting Kennedy and Khrushchev in a spaceship during the Cuban missile crisis. Bassett pretended at first not to know who the bald man was. "He looks like that guy with the shoe at the UN," she said. Then, seeming suddenly to remember, she continued, "He looks like Khrushchev! That can't be! That can't be!"

"Don't worry about how foolish or crazy or impossible it seems," Mack told Bassett. "Just notice. Who's there?"

"What's the other one?" Bassett said. "It's Kennedy! It can't be Kennedy!"

Mack pressed her for more. "Was McNamara—did you see him?"

"McNamara, yes," she said. "And Rusk. I thought Rusk was also there."

Mack seemed glad to hear it. "Well, we certainly needed some kind of intervention in 1962."

The sessions had been taped, and Bassett showed Willwerth transcripts. Mack did not feel free afterward, whatever the circumstances, to disclose a patient's therapeutic session. But Mack's lawyers later made part of the tape available to counter *Time*'s insinuation that there was something untoward going on in the bedroom. Mack had been using Danny's empty room for his interviews. Pam Kasey had been present. As Bassett was about to sit up, Mack cautioned her to do it slowly, because earlier "we knocked a piece of the bed down." Bassett said she was sorry. It wasn't her fault, Mack said. "This is part of the comedy."

In March 1993 Bassett and her husband were moving to North Carolina.[4] By now she had become a trusted member of Mack's nonprofit self-help Group for Research and Aid to Abductees, or GRAA (pronounced "gray"), created for the experiencers the previous year with a name too good to pass up. Bassett was preparing to take over publication of GRAA's newsletter and quarterly magazine and was aspiring to replace the treasurer, Amy Anglin, who was one of Mack's first experiencers and whose contact with him went back to his time with the Affect Seminar at Harvard. Bassett had become a dissident member of the group, insisting that Mack was involved in some nefarious mind-control activity he was refusing to acknowledge.

In early July 1993, Bassett deposited into a North Carolina bank account a GRAA check made out to the organization for $2,840. It displayed Amy Anglin's signature as treasurer, but Anglin said later she had not signed it. Bassett said years later she couldn't recall if she had ever acted as the group's treasurer. She remembered depositing a check for GRAA "in good faith" but was vague about what account it went into. "I would have spent it on the group," she recalled. "I certainly did not pocket the money."

Either, Mack said later, she had lied her way into his confidence, or, as he believed, she had lied about lying and really *was* an experiencer—which was worse?[5] In a letter he wrote to a sympathetic news reporter in September 1994 but ended up not sending, Mack said, "These two have caused relentless damage not only to me personally but to the whole effort to legitimize the abduction phenomenon and explore its depths."

The whole episode disgusted Budd Hopkins.[6] He saw Mack falling victim to his gullibility and tarnishing their cause. Khrushchev! Kennedy! Hopkins was still incredulous nearly two decades later. Mack, he thought, should have asked Bassett if Alexander Haig had been on the spaceship too. If she'd said yes, Mack would have had her. Haig wasn't involved in the Cuba crisis then.

33

"A REVIEW OF YOUR WORK"

Mack's book particularly enraged one critic, James Gleick, a former editor and science reporter for the *New York Times* who had written bestsellers on chaos theory and the physicist Richard Feynman. Calling alien-abduction mythology "one of the country's tawdry belief manias since the 1960s," Gleick opened a slashing attack on Mack in the *New Republic*, likening him to the fans who watch rigged wrestling bouts, some gullibly believing the fakery in the ring is real, others knowing it is fake but relishing it as entertainment.[1] Mack was something of both, Gleick said. Headlined "The Doctor's Plot," his piece ridiculed a Roper poll that yielded an extrapolation of nearly 4 million abductees from 119 respondents and called Mack's anecdotal case histories "grossly lacking in respectable methodology."

Mack was different from "the standard flying-saucer nut," Gleick wrote—he had authority. Adopting some of Donna Bassett's claims to *Time*, he disparaged hypnosis as a conspiracy between hypnotist and willing subject and faulted Mack for not establishing controls or explaining how he had selected his thirteen case studies. For all Mack's claims of starting out as a skeptic, Gleick went on, he was clearly a believer, and wasn't it funny that his aliens talked about saving the planet—just like Mack with his affinity for Werner Erhard and Esalen? Actually, Gleick said, there *was* an abduction phenomenon—hallucinations of gods and spirits went back far into human prehistory. This was worth study by cultural historians, Gleick said, citing Carl Sagan, but skeptics like the Committee for the Scientific Investigation of Claims of the Paranormal (CSICOP), had mostly given up trying to reason with believers like Mack. In the end, Gleick maintained, "Our memories cannot be trusted—not our five-minute-old memories, and certainly not our decades-old memories. They are weakened, distorted, rearranged, and sometimes created from wishes or dreams."

To counter critics like Gleick, Mack and his PEER research director, Caroline McLeod, sent the Cambridge Hospital Institutional Review Board a proposal for a pilot study of the psychopathology and personality characteristics of a sample of people claiming UFO-related abduction experiences. The hypothesis was that anomalous experiences might be related to an individual's ability to enter dissociative states. As Dean Tosteson had suggested, the study would compare forty people who had reported abduction experiences to PEER to a forty-member control group recruited from the public. The interviews would be conducted by McLeod, Pam Kasey, and Roberta Colasanti, a licensed clinical social worker recently hired by PEER who bore more than a passing resemblance to the young Elizabeth Taylor. Colasanti felt well-equipped for the role. Her father was a forensic detective; she had learned how to unmask a liar.

Later, other critics poked fun at Mack, claiming abduction could be explained by imagined memories. Mack staffers urged a frontal counterattack. Mack sought to calm them. "We had an old saying in my youth that you don't need a baseball bat to fuck a fly," he said, "but as an addendum to that you do need to have an effective fly swatter."[2]

So sensing it was time to clear the air with Harvard, Mack made an appointment with the executive dean for academic programs, S. James Adelstein. When he got to Adelstein's office on June 1, 1994, however, he saw he was too late. Adelstein, a medical biophysicist, radiologist, and specialist in nuclear medicine, handed him a letter dated the day before.[3]

Dear John,

During the past several weeks, we have received several inquiries concerning your work on alien abduction that relates to protocol formulation, informed consent and patient billing. I am writing to inform you that Harvard Medical School is appointing a committee of senior faculty members to undertake a review of your work on alien abduction in response to these concerns that have been raised in the press and elsewhere. The review will not be in the nature of a scientific misconduct inquiry. Instead, we will ask the committee to examine both the clinical care and research aspects of the work to assure its compliance with standards expected of a faculty member at Harvard Medical School.

Finally, let me emphasize that in undertaking this review we are mindful of the right of any faculty member to espouse controversial or unpopular views. The subject of your work is not at issue here. Instead, our concern lies in accounts we have read as to how and under what circumstances the work was carried out and what safeguards were in place for the subjects. We believe those issues are of sufficient weight to warrant the action being taken.

The panel, Mack was told, would be composed of Arnold S. Relman, an emeritus professor of social medicine and, until recently, editor of the *New England Journal of Medicine*; Allan M. Brandt, a professor of the history of medicine; Miles F. Shore, a professor of psychiatry; and Margaret L. Dale, the associate dean of faculty affairs.

Through his shock, Mack heard that he could object to any of the members, but he chose to say nothing, fearing it wouldn't change anything and would just come back to haunt him. He had some objections, starting with Relman as chair. A dozen years earlier, he and other activist physicians had drawn the ire of Relman, who questioned the rising profile of the medical profession in voicing alarm over a growing danger of nuclear war. Physicians had no obligation to speak out *as physicians* on general public issues, Relman had written. Mack had rebutted Relman in a hospital lecture shortly afterward, asking if it made a difference if physicians believed that such policies presented grievous danger to public health? Was it not then their responsibility as physicians and citizens to sound the alarm? After the rejection of his article for the *American Journal of Psychiatry*, Mack had approached Relman's *New England Journal of Medicine* but was informed by the associate editor that the subject matter made such an article unpublishable. Mack later submitted a revised version only to have it returned to him in its original sealed envelope, as if to emphasize that it had definitely not been reconsidered or even opened and looked at.

As Mack walked out in a fog, Adelstein said that he would not be in this situation if, instead of challenging accepted concepts of reality, he had just said he had found a new psychiatric syndrome of unknown etiology. But to Mack, that was hardly the case.

A week later, the *Harvard Crimson* was out with an article headlined "Med School's John Mack Believes in Wicked Aliens." The Cambridge morning paper, the nation's oldest continuously published college daily going back to 1873 (with past editors including Franklin D. Roosevelt and John F. Kennedy), said Mack was convinced of the aliens' existence by evidence like "the common phenomenon of people who awake upside down in bed." Mack, caught off guard, responded, "I'm telling something which involves some kind of truth but it's not something I can prove."

Mack with His Holiness, the fourteenth Dalai Lama, in Dharmsala, India, for a week's conference with fellow professionals to discuss aliens in April 1992. Mack kept a detailed transcript of the confidential proceedings. Photo courtesy of the Mack family.

Mack, ill, in the Amazon, 1996. He had attended Stan Grof's International Transpersonal Conference in Manaus and then interviewed witnesses to an alien sighting in the coffee-processing city of Varginha. Afterward he joined Gilda Moura and others in a trip into the Amazon, where he suffered diarrhea and other ailments. Photo courtesy of the Mack family.

FC0697 114 NNNN 10. 3

A UFO conference in 1997 at the historic Medway Plantation in South Carolina (owned by a former World War II OSS spy) drew Mack, sitting between benefactor Laurance Rockefeller and Trish Pfeiffer, later Mack's coeditor of a consciousness anthology. At the far left in the big sun hat is Whitley Strieber, author of the abduction bestseller, *Communion*. Strieber said Rockefeller revealed he knew UFOs were real from high-level contacts in the US Government. Mack inscribed the photo, "Laurance of America." Photo courtesy of the Mack family.

Mack and Budd Hopkins at the International UFO Congress, in Laughlin, Nevada, 2002, where Mack spoke on "Transcending the Dualistic Mind." He and Hopkins collected an EBE film award (for "Extraterrestrial Biological Entity") for the home-video release of *A Dialogue on the Alien Abduction Experience*, hosted by Christopher Lydon with Mack and Hopkins on March 7, 1997, at the John Hancock Hall in Boston. The statuette depicts a big-headed, grey alien holding a motion-picture camera. Photo courtesy of Stuart Conway.

Mack, in his seventies, taking a break with his two dogs in the hills near his house in Thetford, Vermont, early 2000s. Photo courtesy of the Mack family.

Undated late portrait of Mack. The sign in the background reads, "Subvert the Dominant Paradigm." Photo courtesy of Stuart Conway.

Undated late portrait of
Mack. Photo courtesy
of Stuart Conway.

Undated late photo of
Mack with colleagues
Roberta Colasanti (left)
and Karen Wesolowski.
Photo courtesy of the
Mack family.

Mack and writer Leslie Kean unwind at the International UFO Congress in Laughlin, Nevada, 2002, where Mack and Hopkins collected an alien trophy for the home-video release of their 1997 Boston dialogue with Christopher Lydon. Photo courtesy of Stuart Conway.

Mack and Sally at
Stonehenge, England,
1970s. Photos courtesy
of the Mack family.

Drawings by unidentified pupils at the
Ariel School in Ruwa, Zimbabwe, where
Mack and Dominique traveled in November
1994 to investigate reports of a UFO
landing and alien contacts with the children.
Mack made an extensive video record of
his interviews. The striking episode itself
remains unexplained. Photos courtesy
of the Mack family.

34

NOT AN INQUISITION

Foolishly, Mack realized later, he had imagined his first visit to the Harvard committee in July 1994 as a collegial conversation.[1] Instead he felt himself in the dock before an array of accusers. They were a fact-finding body, began Arnold Relman, the chair; their job was to gather information about Mack's work and report back to the deans, not "to conduct an inquisition into your beliefs and opinions—that is none of our business and the University has no business in determining what a member of the faculty should think or should not think and we are not in any way going to infringe on your freedom to think and write and say what you believe."[2] But Mack, as a Harvard physician, was not free to practice medicine any way he wanted, Relman said. So the committee would explore his conduct with the so-called abductees or experiencers.

The university was also concerned with Mack's actions as a clinical scientist—governed by rules of scientific behavior—and how much of his work was clinical care as opposed to research. These might be in conflict when it came to data handling and informed consent, so there were possible "ethical issues" at stake.

Was that clear?

Yes, Mack said, although he wondered about supposed "rules of scientific behavior" and Relman's ominous use of the word "inquisition" to say what it was *not*.

Was Mack acting primarily as a clinician/therapist or a scientist/investigator?

A clinician/therapist, Mack said, but when he came across material of special interest that he could not account for he tried to chronicle and document it—in the narrative tradition of forebears like Freud, Jung, and Erikson. Figuring it might carry some weight with the panel, he cited his recent proposal to the Cambridge Hospital for a controlled pilot study of the psychopathology and personality characteristics of people claiming abduction experiences.

He further acknowledged that he might sometimes be on "an investigative adventure" with his clients.

A "co-investigation?" Miles Shore asked.

"Something like it," Mack agreed. "We are looking at it together." But his primary responsibility was their well-being.

Asked about his book, Mack said he was "mapping out the territory" of a phenomenon not taken seriously by clinicians, which left the field to outsiders like Budd Hopkins and David Jacobs.

Wrapping it in a joke—"I say this enviously"—Relman asked how much Mack expected to earn in book sales.

No more than sixty thousand dollars, Mack said. He would basically break even. He expected no income from the book next year.

Did Mack charge his abductees? Relman asked.

While he didn't consider them psychiatric cases, Mack said, they were undeniably stressed, and he could treat them for that. Some had insurance coverage, and in those cases he billed the companies. The money all went to GRAA, his self-help Group for Research and Aid to Abductees.

Relman was puzzled. They weren't patients because there was nothing intrinsically wrong with them apart from the trauma of their experience, yet Mack was treating them as a physician—rather like victims of sexual abuse, correct?

"Fair enough," Mack said.

How much of Mack's practice concerned abductees?

Almost all of it, he said.

Of the people who came to Mack as abductees, how many did he eliminate as falling outside the category?

About a third, Mack said. To be included, someone needed to have conscious or retrievable memories of seeing unusual beings and of being taken into some kind of enclosure for various procedures, and the presence to recount these with suitable emotional affect.

But was there an abduction spectrum from definite yes to definite no? Relman asked.

Here was where he parted company with Hopkins and Jacobs, Mack said. There *was* a continuum. It was a subtle phenomenon. To Hopkins and Jacobs, it was not an out-of-body experience, it was an "out-of-house" experience—that is, it was definitely physical. He was not so sure, Mack said. He had cases of children who had discovered their parents missing at night while the parents were experiencing an abduction, and also cases where people were seen in place while their consciousness traveled to some other plane or dimension, including a spacecraft. So he was not in the either/or mainstream of abduction. In other words, without stronger evidence it was hard to argue that it was always literally true that people were floated out of their beds, through walls, and into the sky.

How did he know the people weren't just asleep and dreaming these experiences?

Some were multi-witness cases, Mack said. Others occurred during the daytime, while people were driving—in one case a snowmobile.

How did he rule out substance abuse?

He collected their medical histories, Mack said. It didn't seem to be a factor, though it was worth checking.

Asked about his therapeutic techniques, Mack said he used *modified* hypnosis—he didn't like the word for its negative connotations. It was just a relaxation technique, easily applied because their memories were so close to the surface that they emerged with powerful intensity. Sheila was a good example.

What about Grof breathwork?

He used that too.

With sexual abuse there was a standard protocol for treatment, Allan Brandt noted. Was there something similar for abduction?

There was an important difference, Mack said. Traumas like rape and war were unmitigatedly hurtful. Abduction did not normally shatter human relationships to that extent. It was traumatic, certainly, but it was not *just* traumatic.

Relman homed in on a core concern. Was it Mack's primary role to let his patients express themselves and to assure them they weren't crazy. "I mean, are you there simply as a neutral soothing observer or does the therapy—your therapeutic role as a physician—require you to some way co-experience with them or contemplate the same mystery?" In other words, Relman asked, "How much of the treatment is simply your giving them a chance to have a sympathetic ear and someone who is not judging them?" Or did Mack think there really could be aliens abducting them?

"I think it is both," Mack said. "I mean, I wouldn't use the phrase, 'yes there are aliens abducting you,' I would never say that to somebody. What I would say is, 'yes, there are many people who have had these experiences and I don't have a way psychiatrically to account for it' . . ."

Mack didn't sound like someone describing what he was seeing and struggling to understand, Relman said. "You talk about what these aliens are trying to tell us and you talk about, you know, the implications about the future of the earth."

Reading Mack's book, Relman said, "one cannot escape the impression that you accept the basic premise that they have been in contact with an alien world of some kind through means we don't understand." So Mack was not simply a clinician trying to take these people with unexplained and disturbing feelings and observe and comfort them to examine the data. Rather, Relman said, "you at some point early on appear to have decided that you were treating people who had this experience and you're trying to help them, that is true, but you are also trying to understand what it is the aliens are telling us."

Yes, he took it seriously, Mack said. "I may have gone too far in terms of not being tentative enough . . . but it was just such a consistent pattern of accounting that I was getting. I just thought I would lay it out and invite other people to see what they find."

But all this stuff about missing fetuses, disappearing pregnancies—Mack hadn't reported any evidence, Relman said.

"Not evidence of physical proof," Mack conceded.

"It is not even proof. There is no evidence. *There is no evidence!*"

There *was* evidence, Mack insisted, in the sense of consistent experience. But if this was happening in another reality—and here Mack admitted he was on slippery ground—then the evidence would never be available in this physical world. "I mean, I acknowledge that over and over again. It's not going to yield what we would consider to be evidence, as purely physical evidence."

"Where is the evidence?" Relman repeated.

There were scars and lesions, which Mack called intriguing but admittedly equivocal. A quadriplegic abductee displayed wrist wounds that could not have been self-inflicted. "I think we should continue to look for evidence in this physical world as we have it," Mack said, "but I don't think we are necessarily going to get it. . . . I don't think that this phenomenon, by its very nature, is going to yield the kind of . . ."

Relman easily finished Mack's sentence. "It is never going to be demonstrable in modern scientific terms."

Scientists were trying to unravel the mysterious aerodynamics of UFOs . . . , Mack began.

"No, John, with all due respect," Relman interrupted. This was not about how UFOs flew. Mack was a physician. His patients were telling him that things were getting stuck inside them and babies taken from them. "Now these are not things that require an advanced knowledge of physics or astronomy to deal with. These are statements being made by your patients which can be verified. Now maybe you say that verification is not important."

"It is important," Mack said.

"Okay," Relman said. "Well then why aren't you doing that?"

Because he wasn't a dermatologist or a gynecologist, Mack said. The best he could do as a psychiatrist was point to these experiences and say, "I cannot account for it," and leave it to others to follow-up.

"Could it be purely psychological?" Relman asked.

"I mean of course it could be," Mack said. But clinically it felt like something had happened to these people.

Then Mack was not ruling it out? Relman said.

"I can't rule it out."

35

"WHAT IF YOU'RE WRONG?"

When Mack's nephew David Ingbar, a son of his step-sister Mary Lee and a Harvard-trained physician himself, learned Mack was meeting with the panel without a lawyer, he was appalled.[1] "Don't you see," he said, "they're setting you up." It was more than foolhardy, Ingbar told his uncle. It verged on martyrdom. Was he channeling Lawrence of Arabia?

Mack was stunned. Was it that bad? He quickly reached out to Carl M. Sapers, a partner at Hill and Barlow, one of the staunchest of Boston's white-shoe law firms. About to celebrate its centennial, it boasted a founder who had appealed the murder convictions of the anarchists Sacco and Vanzetti as well as an elite roster that included three Massachusetts governors and a longtime Justice Department prosecutor, Robert Mueller. Sapers, who was also a professor in Harvard's Graduate School of Design, had done legal work for Mack and his family. Mack sent him a long memo about his abduction research including his confidential thoughts on the inquiry. Sapers then met with Relman and the staff attorney and advised Mack to cooperate.[2]

When he was called back before the committee, Mack was pressed on why he had not looked harder for conventional explanations of his clients' abduction accounts.[3]

There didn't seem to be any, Mack said.

"What if you're wrong?" Relman asked. Mack got the feeling Relman was really asking whether Mack might be right.

Mack provided him a newly compiled transcript of the 1992 Abduction Study Conference at MIT, and physics professor David Pritchard offered to appear before the panel to describe his search for implants and other physical proof. The committee interviewed Dr. Fred Frankel, the psychiatry professor at Boston's Beth Israel Hospital, where he and Mack had conducted an adversarial grand rounds on the case of Sheila the previous September.[4] Frankel criticized Mack's use of hypnosis and said he could unwittingly be using his patients to further his own viewpoint. Mack found it troubling that the panel's chief witness on hypnosis was Sheila's former psychiatrist, whom she had left in favor of treatment with Mack. Another psychiatrist who had treated Sheila before Mack, William Waterman, was supportive, testifying that she had undergone "a remarkable improvement" after Mack's hypnosis.

The panel also interviewed Dr. Notman, who was the acting head of the Department of Psychiatry and had defended Mack to the *Wall Street Journal*.[5] She did not think his clinical relationships or funding were inappropriate. Mack might not be helping his patients by believing them, but he was not delusional. Notman called him "an eternal questor" and suggested the inquiry be kept "low key." Notman had met with Mack and three of his experiencers. "I think they are sincere and have had some kind of experience which has subsequently been organized around the ideas that these were 'real' visits from 'beings' from outer space," she said. "I saw no evidence that any of them were delusional or that these were or are delusions."

Dr. Joseph Coyle, head of the medical school's Consolidated Department of Psychiatry, had no problem with the subject of abduction—psychiatry often studied strange experiences, Coyle said.[6] But it was Mack's manner of study that concerned him. Mack seemed to entertain only two possibilities: the person was either crazy or had actually seen aliens. Were there no other explanations?

In late July the panel began meeting with experiencers themselves, starting with Sheila.[7] The panel also interviewed a prominent businessman whom Mack called Arthur. He was another of the thirteen case studies in *Abduction*, and he attributed his considerable success to spiritual enrichment from alien encounters. Arthur commiserated with the committee, he told Mack afterward. "If I were sitting in Relman's seat, I wouldn't believe it." The panel also met with Randy Nickerson and his mother, Marcia, who had been on the Oprah Winfrey Show with Mack. When Randy was asked if he could accept an explanation other than alien abduction for his trauma, he replied yes—as long as it could explain why he went into shock when he felt an alien presence, why he had marks on his body, why he had the memories he did, and why other people, including little children, said the same thing. If there was another explanation for all that, he'd be relieved to hear it.

The panel interviewed Peter Faust and listened to the chilling tape of his hypnotic regression.[8] They also called in Mack's assistant, Pam Kasey, who helped screen his cases and often sat in on his sessions.[9] She said that she herself had long struggled with the question of the reality of the experiences but realized she did not need to know the answer in order to help these people. In any case, she thought, Mack was backing off his "enthusiasm."

The panel barraged Mack with questions. Did he have informed, written consent from the abductees? How much did he get in grants from Laurance Rockefeller and any others? What were PEER and the Center for Psychology and Social Change? Had he been reporting on his work to anyone at Harvard?

At Mack's suggestion the panel interviewed one of his fellow professors of psychiatry, George Vaillant—"My only friend in court," Mack called him.[10] Vaillant compared the committee to the Star Chamber, the oppressive English court from the late 1400s to 1600s, and questioned the due process involved. While he himself thought the abduction phenomenon was more of a temporal-lobe issue, Vaillant called Mack "a highly moral person" whose crusades, like revitalizing the Cambridge Hospital and engaging Yasir Arafat, "sometimes work." Mack needed to be taken seriously "in the same way that Martin Luther needed to be taken seriously," he said.

Mack was getting new legal advice as well. Santa Barbara art professor Ronald Robertson, a friend of Mack's from his Air Force days in Japan, had heard of his problems at Harvard despite the official blackout and knew someone who might help—Daniel P. Sheehan, a graduate of Harvard College and Harvard Law School with training too at Harvard Divinity School.[11] A firebrand attorney with a mop of silvery curls, Sheehan was renowned for his leadership of the Christic Institute, a public-interest law firm that had used the courts to battle the Ku Klux Klan and expose the Reagan Administration's secret arms deal known as the Iran-Contra scandal. He had also helped defend the *New York Times*'s publication of the Pentagon Papers leaked by Daniel Ellsberg, and he had won a $10.5 million judgment (later reduced to $1.38 million in a settlement agreement) for the estate of the chemical worker and union activist Karen Silkwood, who was killed in a mysterious 1974 car crash after raising alarm over plutonium contamination at her Kerr-McGee plant in Oklahoma. Sheehan, whose portfolio had also spanned Watergate and Wounded Knee, was particularly close to the Jesuits, having studied for the priesthood himself.

Robertson invited Sheehan to dinner. What, he asked the lawyer, did he know about UFOs? Quite a bit, it turned out, although Sheehan didn't advertise it. In 1977, through contacts with the Vatican Observatory, where astronomers took seriously the prospect of extraterrestrial life, he had been given access to confidential material at the Library of Congress that detailed secret parts of Project Blue Book, the Air Force program designed to officially debunk flying saucers. In one box, Sheehan found what seemed to be photos of Air Force officers examining a crashed UFO that had plowed a path into the earth. He could make out a bulbous dome and what looked like a frieze of weird symbols running around the base. On a small, yellow legal pad he was not supposed to bring in, he scribbled some of the symbols, which looked like nothing he had ever seen before (although the pad with the symbols was later destroyed in an office flood). So, yes, he did know something about UFOs. Robertson told Sheehan about Mack and his unusual research. Would Sheehan take Mack's call? Of course, Sheehan said. Mack called several days later. Sheehan said he was coming east, and they arranged to meet in Cambridge.

Mack had been having doubts about his counsel, Carl Sapers. His law firm had done work for Harvard, Mack learned, and while Sapers himself said he never represented the university, his appointment in the Graduate School of Design made for a potential conflict of interest.

Sheehan, hearing Mack's account of the case so far, was outraged, especially by Sapers's advice that Mack cooperate with the inquiry. Mack was in far more legal jeopardy than he realized, Sheehan said, and he offered to help. His first step was to call his old Harvard Law School professor, Laurence Tribe, an eminent constitutional-law scholar who had clerked for Associate Supreme Court Justice Potter Stewart and had counted among his research assistants at Harvard a young law student named Barack Obama. Tribe suggested that Sheehan partner with the leading Boston civil-liberties lawyer Harvey A. Silverglate, who was known for his representation of academic plaintiffs. Silverglate was tied up on cases, but he suggested an activist colleague, Roderick "Eric" MacLeish Jr., the son of novelist Rod MacLeish and the grandnephew of the poet Archibald MacLeish. Eric MacLeish was acquiring a reputation representing men and women who claimed they had been sexually molested by priests of the Boston Archdiocese.[12] Three years before, MacLeish, who himself had been abused as a child at a British boarding school, had met with a Rhode Island private detective who said he and eight others had been molested as children in the 1960s by Father James R. Porter. By 1992 MacLeish was representing seventy men and women who claimed Porter had sexually abused them in three parishes in southeastern Massachusetts. In December 1993 Porter pleaded guilty to having abused twenty-eight victims as young as eleven and was sentenced to eighteen to twenty years in prison. MacLeish would later be presented in the *Boston Globe*'s Pulitzer Prize–winning "Spotlight" series, as well as in the subsequent 2015 Oscar-winning best picture of the same name, as a champion of sexual-abuse victims—though critics complained that he was over-inclined to quietly settle client cases for large cash payouts in exchange for secrecy.

MacLeish was eager to sign on to Mack's defense team. Sheehan, meanwhile, sent Mack a twenty-page Proposed Litigation Plan that laid out the lawyer's fiercely combative strategy in ripe and overflowing verbiage.[13] What made Mack's case special, Sheehan wrote, "is the fact that the Administration of Harvard University has decided to undertake to silence you in your effort to set forth *your side* of this all-important, dare we say 'historic,' debate."

Sheehan was only getting warmed up. "Let me state to you, flatly, that I view the potential contact by the human family with Beings from any extraterrestrial source of intelligence to be the single most important potential event in the history of the human family in effectuating a transformation of the consciousness of the human family from the present state of our evolution of consciousness to the next." He compared Mack's revelations to those of Galileo and Darwin, hailing his challenge of "the entire Newtonian-Cartesian scientific-materialist paradigm upon which your critics' very status and stature as professionals directly *depends*." Moreover, Mack was "dashing headlong into the spiritual world of reincarnation and life after death, not to mention alien-human interbreeding."

"You certainly do not make your lawyer's task an easy one," Sheehan wrote. "I must know *exactly what you believe* is being communicated to the human family via these experiences which you are studying." He had to know, too, what all of Mack's experiencers believed was being communicated to them and what message the aliens were bringing humans. More pragmatically, Sheehan continued, they needed to exploit every legal theory and tactic to fight Mack's case. He advised Mack to hire MacLeish at a retainer of $2,500 and fee of $225 an hour. He himself, Sheehan proposed, could be paid by outside donors, possibly Laurance Rockefeller. He urged that they demand a halt to the report the panel was preparing pending a host of new defense submissions.

Sheehan's confrontational twenty-one-point action plan culminated in a threat that they could go public with the secret proceedings and bring a state or federal civil-rights lawsuit against Harvard, although he and Mack agreed it was not in anyone's interest to air the dispute openly.

On September 14 the two lawyers showed up with Mack, unsettling Relman, who asked what had happened to Carl Sapers. Mack said he wanted a second opinion. MacLeish noted later that Relman was "extremely provocative," convincing them that "he does not possess the temperament or character to consider these matters in any type of dispassionate fashion."[14] MacLeish challenged the committee process as unfair, and Relman countered that it was not a legal proceeding and no specific rules or regulations pertained. The lawyers also pressed him on whether the reality of UFOs was an issue for the committee. Relman replied, "Of course the issue is relevant," before realizing his mistake and trying to retract the statement.

Sheehan was particularly determined to turn the proceedings into a forum to counter the government's historic duplicity on the UFO issue and offer evidence for the existence of extraterrestrial life. When a member of the panel objected that it would not be turned into a circus, Sheehan took umbrage. "John, let's leave," he said. When the committee was ready to proceed, Sheehan said, they would return.

36

ALIENS IN AFRICA

Meanwhile, more than 7,600 miles away, strange events were unfolding in southern Africa. At 10:00 p.m. on September 14, 1994, Tim Leach, the BBC correspondent in Zimbabwe's capital, Harare, got a call from the principal immigration officer. Something large, quiet, and very weird had flown over his house about an hour before. Air Traffic Control confirmed that something had been hovering over the airport before it shot away with amazing speed to the Zimbabwean cities of Bulawayo and Mutare then headed toward South African air space.[1]

Leach, a forty-two-year-old veteran war reporter, clicked on his tape recorder. "It was so low," the immigration officer reported. "I thought they were meteors, you know?" Then he thought it might be a plane. It left a kind of trail before clouds obscured it. When it emerged, he saw light behind and above it. "Now I thought, well that's no—that's nothing like any plane I've seen, you know, there's something very odd here," he said. "And the shape of it I would say is like a, it was, it was more like a, a zeppelin, you know? But going quite fast. But it was, it was the absence of noise I didn't like." He thought it might be a squadron of helicopters flying in close formation. But no, he immediately decided. "They're too close, they're too close for this time of night." And then whatever it was went past. He had called his friend out of the house in time to hear a big bang. "I've never seen anything like it in my life," the officer told Leach. "You know a meteor normally comes down in a, in a, in a sort of arc. And these were going, these were just flying along, you know, parallel to the ground sort of thing." Leach asked if it might have been an American stealth bomber. That didn't seem right, the officer said. "I can't think of a, of a, a plane without configuration, you see?"

Leach started frantically calling around for other witnesses. Eventually he reached a group of Zimbabweans who had been hosting a visiting quantum physicist and spiritual teacher from England, David Ash. They had been outside on the veranda about 9:00 p.m. when massive shooting stars, or so they seemed, flashed across the sky right to left, north to south. They looked like a formation of about ten, and it dawned on the group that they couldn't be meteorites—they weren't burning out and their color was radiant white. They seemed very high and far away, so they must have been massive, some sort of craft. "Whatever those lights were they were not meteors," Ash said.

It was quickly all over ZBC 92.8, whose popular radio host Praxedes Dzangare announced, "I don't know what to do about this strange object. Some think it's really out of this world, that it's fantastic, it's fabulous, it's amazing, but somebody, some people have seen it and they keep phoning." She added an appeal. "Tim Leach is from the BBC—and he's desperate for somebody to, who might have taken photographs or who might have seen this, might have a clear description, if it all is what we think it is, to get in touch with him. Now Tim is welcoming calls any hours of the morning and the night." She gave out his phone numbers.

Two days later Leach had learned more and talked to Cynthia Hind, Mufon's Continental Coordinator for Africa. She suggested Leach call John Mack at PEER in Massachusetts.

It was morning on America's east coast, and Leach got a recording. He left his contact numbers and a short message: "This concerns a UFO mothership plus or minus fourteen to sixteen other craft sighted. The latest sighting was over a school where it hovered, landed, a black man got out, possibly somebody's gardener or local person from Africa. There've been other sightings. It's been going on for three days now. Our phones have been jammed. The story will probably be with you tonight, but of course we're having difficulty being taken seriously in spite of being the BBC. Please call me as soon as you can. Thank you." He hung up, muttering, "Fucking hell! Close encounters of the first kind."[2]

Pam Kasey was the first to retrieve the message and called Leach back right away. He said there had been sightings in neighboring Zambia, over Victoria Falls on the Zambia-Zimbabwe border, in Botswana, and in South Africa, where the Pretoria government tried to suppress news reports. That morning at a school in Ruwa, a small agricultural crossroads fourteen miles southeast of Harare, administrators herded two hundred children inside after they said a strange craft appeared at the schoolyard. A black man got out, and the object flew off at tremendous speed. Leach told Kasey that the BBC was taking the matter seriously, collecting interviews but still searching for good video.

Kasey wrote quick notes to Mack relating the conversation and asking if he wanted to speak to Leach himself. Just as she was about to fax Mack, a fax from Leach elaborated on the story. "I have since got copious tape recordings of sightings and now there seem to be abductions and CEOTFK." Kasey puzzled over the strange word until someone figured out it stood for "close encounters of the first kind," UFO-speak for sightings of craft within 150 meters.

The schoolchildren, Leach's fax went on, had been pulled off the playground at break time between 10:00 and 10:30 a.m. "while a strange small craft hovered over the trees and then landed and let out a 'Black man' possibly an indigenous Zimbabwean." A local man who had called Leach to say he had a photo of the UFO had not been heard from again. Since the radio appeal, Leach wrote, he had been inundated with calls and was investigating the case of a three-year-old girl who saw a "lion" outside her bedroom. But "when she drew a child-like picture it was no lion," Leach recounted. "Lions do not stand up." He had loads of material, he said, but barely thirty seconds of amateur video "of pix that look like someone with a torch drunkenly looking for a toilet in the dark!"

Leach's last appeal to Mack was the strangest of all. "Please advise how I get to contact the visitors—I gather there are two types—friendly and the reverse."

37

"HAVE GOOD MANNERS!"

Mack was too busy with his lawyers to immediately deal with Leach. They had been greatly surprised to hear that the inquiry into Mack's conduct hung to some extent on whether UFOs were real or not. MacLeish was demanding the "policies, procedures, guidelines or regulations" governing the Harvard inquiry, along with any other professional or university standards on sponsored research. He asked for tapes and transcripts of the proceedings to date, a list of all witnesses, and the credentials of the panel members. There would be a lot to go through.

Then, in need of distraction, Mack began going over the reports from Zimbabwe. Shortly before 8:00 p.m. that September 14, hundreds of people all over the country reported bright lights moving across the sky. Witnesses from farm workers and fishermen to pilots and technicians described seeing a silent object, brilliant white with an orange-red trail, about the size of a Boeing 747. Some thought it was on fire and about to crash, but it leveled off, flying at treetop level and rising to avoid the hills at Lake Kariba on the Zambian border northwest of Harare. Two people viewing it from underneath said it had a flat belly. One thought he could see two engines in front.

Cynthia Hind, the African Mufon investigator who had put Leach in touch with Mack, was in her study in central Harare that night when she heard what sounded like an explosion.[1] Hind had served in the South African Women's Army Air Force in World War II, married a Royal Air Force pilot, and moved to England before relocating to what was then Rhodesia. She began investigating UFO sightings for Mufon in 1981, published a book, *UFOs: African Encounters*, in 1982, and for the last eight years had been issuing *UFO Afrinews*, a newsletter with global fans. After hearing the noise, she quickly tuned into the radio reports that were flooding the airwaves and phone lines but thought the meteorite explanation dubious. A sonic boom from a falling meteor was not impossible, but she had read nothing about a predicted meteor shower.

Five days later, having rounded up Leach and a BBC television crew and a friend with a makeshift Geiger counter and magnetometer, she headed for Ruwa outside Harare, where reports said children at an elite private primary day school had gotten a closeup look at something two days after the mass sightings across Africa.

The progressive Ariel School, started only three years before by religious parents of varying denominations, served 230 first to seventh graders, ages six to thirteen. The children were a cross-section of modern Africa—tribal black, tawny mixed race, Asian, and post-colonial blonde and freckled British white. The headmaster, Colin Mackie, told Hind that at about 10:15 that Friday morning, the children were in the playing field when, as roughly sixty of them later reported, three silver balls appeared in the sky over the school. They disappeared with a flash of light and reappeared elsewhere, repeating again until they started to move down toward the school. One of the objects then hovered over or landed at an overgrown tract about a hundred meters away where the children were not allowed.

Then, several of them reported, a small man about one meter tall in a tight-fitting black suit appeared on top of the object. He walked across the rough ground, saw the children, and disappeared. Then he, or another small man, appeared at the back of the object, which took off swiftly and disappeared.

The teachers had been closeted in a staff meeting and shooed away the children, who excitedly tried to summon them. Some were crying in fear. Several had run to the snack shop to alert Alyson Kirkman, one of the volunteer mothers, but she too blew them off, afraid to leave the food and money unguarded. When one little girl shouted, "Aliens!" Kirkman told her, "Just calm down! Have good manners! If there are aliens there, make sure they think earthlings are nice."

Headmaster Mackie had the presence of mind to herd the children back into the school to draw pictures of what they had seen. One child had drawn a picture of a large ship and four or five other ships buzzing around it. Several children said the two figures they saw had big heads with eyes like rugby balls and seemed to be wearing tight, black, rubber-like outfits.

The parents picked the children up as usual at 1:00—Fridays ended early—and heard the excited chatter, after which the episode quickly leaked to reporters. Mackie said it had put the new school on the map. Some parents who came to scout the school for the upcoming term seemed titillated, one asking if the school could promise another UFO next year. Mackie said he would try.

In the ninety-degree heat, Hind and her group checked the ground but got no special radiation or magnetic readings and found no sign of bent grass. Heedless of the waist-high thorn bushes, bamboo stumps, and snake holes, she walked alone for a distance following the electricity pylons, still seeing nothing amiss. Maybe it was the heat, but when she got home she had a headache, her feet ached, and she felt disoriented. Was she suffering from a mild dose of radiation? she wondered.

Hind had taken photocopies of some of the children's drawings and given them to Leach to fax to Mack. A television producer for the South African Broadcasting Corporation, Nicky Carter, had a half-brother at the Ariel School. He was out sick that day but quickly heard about events from his classmates and told Nicky. She soon arrived with a TV crew.

Mack and Dominique weren't far behind. After nearly half a year under Harvard inquiry, Mack didn't need much to get him out of Cambridge—the Ariel School story was more than enough.[2] They stopped in Johannesburg, where they were whisked off by a member of the local UFO group to a TV studio for a program called *Agenda* on aliens and abduction. One of Mack's fellow guests, appearing remotely from a studio near his home in northwest South Africa close to the Botswana border, was Credo Mutwa, a celebrated South African *sangoma* (medicine man) known as "Vusumazulu" (awakener of the Zulus). Then seventy-three, the portly Mutwa, with his thick glasses, tribal skins, and gaudy bling, was just the indelible character to enrapture Mack. The shaman had only to display the statues he had made of small extraterrestrial creatures that he said had been familiar to Africans over thousands of years for Mack and Dominique to arrange a quick visit to his home in Mafeking (now Mahikeng), site of a celebrated siege during the Second Boer War. Born to a Zulu mother and a Christian father forced apart by religious strife, Mutwa began life under the stigma of illegitimacy. As a teenager in a rough mining town, he was attacked and sodomized by miners before discovering his powers as a healer. Finding faith in his African roots, he devoted himself to building a living museum of ancient African culture only to be denounced as an apologist for apartheid. Although long suspicious of white people, he found a kindred spirit in Mack, sharing stories of his own traumatic

211

encounters with evil beings he called *mantindane* (star monkeys) and becoming one of Mack's most iconic and colorful experiencers. By November 30, Mack and Dominique were in Harare, where Mack spoke on abduction at the local Sports Club, drawing an overflow crowd of three hundred—twice the expected audience.

Then he and Dominique headed to the Ariel School in Ruwa, where they plunged into filmed interviews at the school, starting with Headmaster Colin Mackie. "You must realize we are talking about children here," Mackie said. "And sometimes the imagination can get carried away with them." Of the 230 children in the yard, he said, about 60 reported seeing the UFO and later drew pictures of it. But only a handful had seen beings.

Mack talked with a seventh grader named Emily, who was about to turn thirteen and wore blonde braids tied with scarlet ribbons. "I think it was quite unusual that the aliens came at the same time that the teachers were in the staff meeting," she said.

So the children saw actual creatures? Mack asked.

"Yes," Emily said. "I saw—there was about two little Black men. They were all in like tight black suits kind of thing and there was a big kind of like mother craft, ship, and it had a saucer around. And there were lots of little ones around it." They were just hovering, she said, and then they suddenly vanished "like the speed of light."

How many creatures were there? Mack asked.

She saw two, Emily said, but other children saw more. They were about her size.

How tall was she? Mack asked.

"I have no idea," Emily said.

One of the creatures was staying by the door of the mother ship, "kind of like guarding," Emily said. The other was running back and forth. "It ran just like people. But it was like more bouncier as if, like, a human would be on the moon." She said they had oversize heads, eyes that were all black, no nose—just two holes—no mouth that she could see, and long, wavy, curly black hair.

Any sense of what they were doing there? Mack asked.

"Maybe they were running away from astronomers in space and they came there to hide," she said.

What if, Mack asked, a scientist would come along and say Emily was just making it up?

"I would tell them," she said, "that he can believe that, but it's not going to change my idea of what I've seen and what I know."

When these beings were looking at her, Dominique asked, did she have any idea of what they were thinking?

"They were kind of astonished," Emily said. "Well, just looking at us, just like staring. In wonder. Just staring, just to see what we were and what we were like."

Nathaniel, a tall eleven-year-old in shorts and a monitor for the younger children, said he had herded them back from the UFO, which he described as all silver with a ring around it. He saw two figures running around. "The hair was a bit like Michael Jackson's and they had black suits like Michael Jackson's," he said. "They had short legs and quite a long top. They had big heads and eyes that are bigger than ours."

Mack asked if he doubted what he saw.

Yes, at first, Nathaniel said. But the next day he and another boy saw a UFO again. And, he said, two girls saw one just the day before yesterday.

Could it have been just a regular airplane with passengers getting off?

Nathaniel didn't think so. "If kids my age got dressed up in funny suits, then maybe. But it couldn't be adults. Unless they're dwarfs."

Nathaniel said that he thought they looked dangerous. "That they could just pull out a laser gun and—"

And what? Mack asked.

"Kill us," Nathaniel said.

Why did he think they had come?

"Just to inspect," Nathaniel said. "To see what was happening. To see if they could build any sort of secret place around here."

Mack mentioned he had written a book about UFOs and alien beings. A girl named Emma perked up. "How many pages are there?"

About four hundred, Mack said.

"Have you ever seen a UFO?" she asked.

"I never have, no. I'd like to," Mack said.

Lisil, a petite eleven-year-old in a pale-blue dress, recalled running to the enclosure to see "a silver thing" and a little man with pointed eyes and long hair. There were smaller ships flying around with green, yellow, and purple lights coming out of the bottom, and they kept vanishing and reappearing. She felt scared.

What was scary about it? Mack asked.

"Well I felt scared because I've never seen such a person like that before," Lisil said. "At first I thought it was just a gardener. Then my friend showed me that his eyes were quite big and then I said it must be a UFO."

How did it make her feel?

"Sometimes I think that they want to tell us something," Lisil said. "Something in the future."

Like what? Mack asked.

"Maybe they were telling us the world was going to end," Lisil said. "Because maybe because we've got to look after the planet, the air, properly." She added, "I felt all horrible inside."

When did she feel the horribleness?

"When I got home," she said. "It was like the world, all the trees would just go down, and there'd be no air and people would be dying."

Mack wondered if Lisil might be an abductee. Had she ever seen a strange light in her room at night? Had her mother ever come into the room and found her missing?

"No," she said. But she did get afraid at night. She thought the little man might kill her.

Did she tell her mother how scared she was?

"Yeah."

And?

"She wouldn't believe me."

"Would you like to see him again?" Mack asked.

"Yes," Lisil said.

And if she did, what would she do?

"I'd ask him some questions," the girl said. "I would ask him what is he doing on earth and what does he want with us."

Mack asked about her feelings for the little man.

"He looks interesting," she said.

Was there anything people could do to take better care of the earth? Mack asked.

"No," Lisil said.

Why not?

"I think that in space there is no love and down here there is. It just feels that there is no love. The way he looked at us was just like looked sad, looked sad."

And how did that make her feel?

"I felt sorry for him," she said.

Another little girl said she called visitors "Martians."

Where did she get that idea? Mack asked.

"Just from watching TV," she said.

Next Mack sat with the teachers. Most initially thought the children were making it up. How many still thought so? he asked. A single hand went up.

"I find that absolutely fascinating that no adults were there," Mack said. "You could argue it's just one of those odd coincidences or you could argue that whatever this intelligence is, that somehow they planned it that way." But he had given up trying to figure out alien psychology.

Mack thanked Mackie and the teachers for putting up with the disruptions of his filmed interviews. He had encountered the phenomenon all over the world, Mack said. But Ruwa was exceptional—a large group of children all witnessing the same thing, not only seeing a craft but also its inhabitants, the actual beings. "I think that's a planetary first."

A student had a last question. If they had nightmares, "could we come and, we could contact you?"

Did she have nightmares? Mack asked.

"No," the student said. "I just wanted to ask you."

Mack said he lived far away, but if they had nightmares they could come and see him.

38

"OH GOD!"

In twenty-seven sessions since July 1994, the Harvard committee had examined Mack and thirteen other witnesses, including four experiencers and the mother of one of them, Marcia Nickerson; listened to twenty-five to thirty hours of audio tapes of Mack's hypnotic sessions; and read Mack's book, many of his published articles, and the proceedings of the Abduction Study Conference at MIT. It had also reviewed Mack's proposal for a PEER personality study of experiencers. Now, in mid-December, a week after Mack and Dominique returned from Zimbabwe, it presented its thirty-page draft report to Deans Tosteson and Adelstein, with copies going also to Mack and his lawyers for any comments and corrections.[1]

The good news for Mack, as Harvard counsel Anne Taylor noted, was that the draft report included no recommendations for immediate action against him. "I am in a position to tell you that the committee does not believe Dr. Mack's conduct provides a basis for referral of the matter to the Medical School committee charged with adjudicating allegations of misconduct nor does it believe that there is a basis for taking action to alter Dr. Mack's status as a permanent Professor of Psychiatry on the Medical School faculty," Taylor wrote. But it was hardly vindication. The deans could still impose sanctions.

Although the committee applauded Mack's planned study as a sign that his approach was becoming more scholarly, it couldn't decide whether Mack's work was research or therapy or whether the people he saw were subjects or patients. It ended up calling them, rather awkwardly, "S/Ps." As for UFOs, it adopted debunker Curtis Peebles's conclusion in his recently published book, *Watch the Skies: A Chronicle of the Flying Saucer Myth*, that most sightings had been proven explainable by natural or man-made effects, or else they were just fraudulent.

Any sanction of Mack would be up to the deans. But the report was severely critical. It found that his manner with S/Ps reflected "a persistent pressure" to get them to accept that they had really been abducted by aliens, to the exclusion of other possible explanations. "In none of the tapes we listened to," the panel said, "was there evidence of a serious effort to seek clinical data that might support alternative explanations of the phenomenon." It said he dealt with the S/Ps' stories "as if they were accurate memories of actual events, not simply psychological phenomena" and that he considered their emotional symptoms "to be a reaction to the trauma of the 'abduction' experience."

The report was particularly critical of Mack's failure to produce documentation to back up his claims of physical evidence—burned earth grass from UFO landings, skin lesions, and missing pregnancies. It faulted him for not subjecting his work to peer review, for not obtaining the S/Ps' informed consent as research subjects, and for not responding fully to questions about his financing. In short, Mack's clinical approach to the S/Ps "does not conform to accepted standards of sound psychiatric practice." The report ultimately called his approach to supporting evidence "unscientific and unscholarly."

In answer to the deans' question of whether Mack's abduction work met Harvard's standards, the committee's answer was no. "In our judgment, neither as a clinician nor as a scholar and investigator has Dr. Mack shown the judgment, the intellectual rigor or the professionalism one would have expected of a Harvard professor of psychiatry dealing with a puzzling and controversial phenomenon," it said. Harvard Medical School also bore responsibility for not properly supervising him.

Far from mollifying Mack and his lawyers, the draft report's silence on any disciplinary action, coupled with the condemnatory language, ignited their outrage over the inconsistency. It impelled Sheehan to redouble his efforts to find witnesses who could back up Mack's approach. He thought MacLeish, in a conciliatory style typified by his priest-abuse settlements, might be signaling that they were seeking a settlement, thereby pushing the committee into a tougher stance in order to better negotiate a compromise.[2] Sheehan, on the other hand, felt there was nothing to compromise—this was Mack's golden opportunity to prove the reality of abductions.

As Sheehan later recalled, he told MacLeish when presenting the matter to his co-counsel, "They're accusing John of eating a shit sandwich and you're saying there's no evidence he even likes bread. You've got to get into their face."

They did agree on another concern. Relman had just been appointed to the Massachusetts Board of Registration in Medicine, the agency in charge of licensing and disciplining physicians. In addition to being Mack's prosecutor, Relman could now also be his judge, MacLeish said. They resolved to attack the report.

In early January 1995, Mack sent his lawyers a fifty-page rebuttal—almost twice as long as the draft report itself.[3] He questioned the panel's competence and independence and said he felt "morally sullied." Just reading the report, he said, made him feel like a sewer worker—"It was necessary for me to come up periodically, as it were, to bathe and cleanse myself." Aside from its endorsement of his proposed personality study, "only the negativity is expressed and there is a relentless steady attack upon me. Bias is evident over and over again." Relman's disparagement of UFO sightings and reliance on the Peebles book showed their determination to dismiss Mack's work as mythology, Mack said.

There was no inherent conflict between therapy and research, he insisted—findings in psychodynamic psychiatry have come through clinical interviewing, which was both therapeutic and investigative. He never claimed abductees were literally removed from the earth "in our objective reality." For all its listening to tapes and reading of his book and articles and the MIT proceedings, the committee showed little sign of taking the information into account. Yes, Mack billed insurance companies for trauma treatments because he wanted money for the self-help group, GRAA. He discontinued the practice when lawyers said he should not bill people with insurance unless he was also billing everyone else. He never put "persistent pressure" on patients to accept the reality of abduction. There was no data to support alternative explanations of the phenomenon—at least none had emerged in thirty years of research.

Yet Mack—unlike Sheehan—was eager to make one distinction. Nowhere was he claiming that abduction stories were accurate accounts of real events, Mack said, but neither could they be easily explained away. The consistency of the S/Ps' stories had nothing to do with worldwide publicity—the stories began long before the phenomenon gained widespread attention. Children's accounts were particularly persuasive. Could a two-year-old really be contaminated by pop culture? As for "co-creating" the memories, he tried to be open to people's experiences, but he didn't impose his own views on them. It was simply not possible to understand anyone's experiences by taking "an objectifying distancing subject/object approach." Anyway, he hadn't had any beliefs until he spent hundreds of hours listening to people's stories. To accuse him of harming children and adults by allowing their pathologies to go untreated was "slanderous." If anything, by offering support and validation, he helped people feel less isolated and improve their relationships, as many confirmed.

There was a reason he didn't stress physical evidence of abductions, Mack said. There *was* no smoking gun. He wasn't enough of an expert to validate skin lesions or missing pregnancies. The phenomenon was subtle and didn't yield the kind of proof the Relmans of the world were demanding. To dismiss UFOs altogether as mythology only revealed the committee's prejudice.

Mack did concede he should not have used the word "evidence" to describe cases in his book in which aliens supposedly healed abductees. It was, he said, "probably the weakest passage in the entire book." He should have said "reports."

Sheehan disagreed with Mack's apologetics. "He was a strangely humble guy," the lawyer recalled years later, "always exploring what he could have done differently." But in terms of dealing with the committee, Sheehan found Mack's honesty risky. "I said, 'Don't make concessions. They're not being objective. They're going to drive a truck over you.'"

Mack did defend his efforts for peer review of his research. He had in fact published a summary of his work in *Noetic Science Review* in August 1992. He had submitted an article to the *American Journal of Psychiatry*, but the demanded revisions would have taken weeks of work, with questionable results. He had even twice attempted to publish in Relman's own *New England Journal of Medicine*, to no avail. Instead, Mack said, he decided to try to reach a large public audience with his book, a judgment all but guaranteed, he now saw, to bring down the wrath of the "small-minded" Harvard Medical School. As for withholding some information from the committee, Mack disputed the relevance of certain financial requests, like dragging in the name of Laurance Rockefeller, who had specifically asked for anonymity for his gifts of $250,000 a year to the Center for Psychology and Social Change. By questioning his financial support, Mack said, "they are casting doubt upon my integrity."

Pressed by Sheehan, Mack insisted on his right to present more witnesses, arguing that, secrecy notwithstanding, they too should be shown the draft report. Harvard's attorney, Anne Taylor, would not approve showing it to outsiders. And if Mack refused to be forthcoming about financial issues, "so be it," Taylor wrote, concluding with a veiled threat: "I would have thought there would be an advantage in honesty and openness at this stage, rather than running the risk of additional future investigation by another body." Mac-Leish responded that the committee was on a "witch-hunt" against Mack and his supporters.

The way things were going, MacLeish recommended they retain an outside psychiatrist who could testify that Mack's contacts with his patients were not harmful. His rate would be $270 an hour. And with the growing legal workload, they needed to put another member of the firm on the case. MacLeish felt compelled to warn Mack, "Your legal bills will be quite high."

Sheehan, increasingly outraged, weighed in with a blistering nineteen-page strategy memo that began, "I think that it is time that we *all* get *pissed off!*"[4] He called the draft report a travesty and Taylor's requests for respect and confidentiality "utter horseshit." He too called it a witch-hunt. "This whole procedure is total due process BULLSHIT." They would demand time to present their full case, he said, under threat of blowing the inquiry's secrecy. Sheehan said he was not a "reasonable doubt" type of criminal-defense attorney—he didn't believe you won acquittals by arguing that prosecutors failed to prove guilt beyond a reasonable doubt. If you didn't do it, say you didn't do it, Sheehan said. If you did it, say you did it, and that you were right to do so. It was foolish for Mack to argue, "It is not *entirely clear* that I was *wrong.*" Instead, they should present other physicians and witnesses to tell the committee, "THEY TOO POSITIVELY BELIEVE THAT THIS ET, UFO, ALIEN ABDUCTION PHENOMENON IS *REAL* AND THAT YOU WERE *RIGHT* AND *COURAGEOUS.*"

His Christic Institute had learned this lesson during the Iran-Contra scandal, Sheehan said. So had Socrates, Galileo, Jesus, and Karen Silkwood.

And then the inquiry leaked.

On February 9, still seeking witnesses to aid Mack's case, Sheehan, on his own, had faxed potential supporters a letter announcing that "Harvard University has secretly convened a 'Special Faculty Committee' to evaluate

John Mack's work in the field of Extraterrestrial Intelligence, Unidentified Flying Objects and the reported Abduction of a number of individual human beings by Beings allegedly piloting such Unidentified Flying Objects."

Sheehan said the inquiry "grossly violates all accepted standards of law and academic freedom." He quoted findings from the committee's draft report and called on recipients to request to testify on Mack's behalf.

The first Mack got wind of it was five days later, when he was handed a copy of Sheehan's faxed appeal. He scribbled his shocked reaction on top. *Oh God.*

It quickly escalated. One of the Mufon experts who received Sheehan's appeal, Dennis William Hauck of Sacramento, a mathematician studying UFO phenomena, was so outraged by the Harvard inquiry that he posted details on a local computer bulletin board. Subject: "Secret Committee Seeks to Expel Dr. John Mack." Hauck wrote, "I thought the issue important enough to take the soapbox for a moment and ask that anyone with academic credentials contact Daniel Sheehan"—and here he gave the lawyer's address and phone number—"to see how they might be of assistance." Hauck summarized Sheehan's findings "by this kangaroo court" and added, "The whole affair reminds me of the persecution of Galileo in the hands of an equally short-sighted Catholic Church." He urged everyone interested in scientific ufology to contact Sheehan or himself. "Those who remain quiet will only share in this travesty of academic freedom." Someone who saw the post put it on the Internet.

The repercussions came swiftly. Mack's assistant, Pat Carr, received a call from a man in Vancouver, British Columbia, who had seen it on the web. He wanted to know if it was true and how he could help. Mack quickly learned what had happened and scrawled a note to MacLeish: "Eric, please quiet down before you call me about this. John. I did not see these letters in advance and I did not authorize the 'Mufon Expert Witness Panel.' It is important that this be understood."

Mack tried frantically to reach Sheehan by phone and finally sent a fax. "I deeply appreciate the efforts which you have undertaken on my behalf over the past six months," he wrote. But as angry as he was with Harvard, he had always wanted the inquiry to be dealt with quietly. "I have decided that I must take action to remove you as my counsel immediately."

Anne Taylor called Sheehan's letter "outrageous." It knowingly misrepresented the panel's deliberations, she said, charging that "Dr. Mack knew about the letter for some time before it was disclosed to us and took no action to stop or correct it."

MacLeish denied Mack's complicity. Mack took no action to stop it because he did not see it before it went out. Sheehan, profoundly apologetic, said he understood Mack's need to insulate himself from the affair. Looking back later, Mack wrote he came to realize that Sheehan's strategy all along was "to make this a big Swopes-like case" (he meant Scopes, the celebrated 1925 "Monkey Trial") while "MacLeish and I wanted to keep the notoriety and expense to a minimum and get the thing to go away." But in the end, Mack reflected, "the publicity probably helped me as it brought forth an avalanche of press coverage, mostly negative for Harvard, accusing it of a witch hunt, stifling my academic freedom, etc." He would later reconcile with Sheehan, engaging him to represent PEER and plan for a Worldview Institute at Harvard, a visionary scheme that would never be.

Their formal response to the committee's draft report ran eighty pages, not counting reams of supportive testimonials and patient affidavits in response to Sheehan's solicitation.[5] It challenged the propriety of the inquiry and the committee's commitment to due process. MacLeish called the case an affront to academic freedom and the proceeding "a moral disgrace" violative of Harvard's own procedures and recognized professional standards.

Far from harming anyone, MacLeish wrote, Mack exemplified "passionate devotion to the care of others." It was the committee and its inquiry that had traumatized his patients. Allies also weighed in. Roberta Colasanti, a Master Clinician in the Behavioral Medicine Program of the Harvard Community Health Plan who had sat in on nearly two dozen of Mack's experiencer interviews, swore she had never seen him plant suggestions of abduction or exert pressure to accept the reality of abduction.

K. Danner Clouser, a professor of humanities and a biomedical ethicist at the Penn State College of Medicine, told the panel there was no fraud or misrepresentation in Mack's work—"His methods are out in the open for all to see." Mack may well have been wrong, but science and medicine were full of blind alleys. In any case, medicine was aimed at relieving suffering. Unlike pure science, if an approach worked, it didn't need to be investigated out to the fiftieth decimal point. Had Mack harmed his patients? Unlikely. They came away relieved. Did he prevent them from seeking "proper" help? Many had already seen other psychiatrists to little avail. And yes, his patients consented to their treatment. They consulted him freely and came back again and again.

Mack's Harvard colleague George Vaillant appealed to president Neil Rudenstein to replace the secretive disciplinary proceeding with open academic debate. If anything, he said, Mack was guilty of heresy, like Jung, Freud, William James, and Conan Doyle, who dabbled in the occult yet did not practice bad medicine. The inquiry was dangerous for Harvard, Vaillant said. No one would win this battle. Harvard should not be a church judging the belief systems of its members.

It soon hit the papers. The *Harvard Crimson* exposed the inquiry in mid-April, citing an anonymous source. The university refused comment. The student newspaper linked the leak to Sheehan's widely circulated appeal soliciting support for Mack. It had obtained a copy and spoke to people who knew of Sheehan's dismissal. It also interviewed David Jacobs. "Temple University considers me to be an embarrassment also," he said.

MacLeish blamed a committee leak. His dismay grew in May when the *New York Times* published its own long article, "Harvard Investigates a Professor Who Wrote on Space Aliens." Reporter William H. Honan, a former *Times* culture editor, somehow knew that the committee was about to present the dean a final report sharply critical of Mack. Tosteson was concerned not only for Harvard's reputation, Honan said, but also that Mack's cases "may have been a result of hallucinations for which his discussions with the subjects amounted to treatment that was not appropriate." Honan didn't fail to mention the collection of sperm and eggs and forced sex with aliens. The final word, he said, would be up to the dean, Mack's lawyer, "and perhaps some diminutive, large-eyed gray beings who claim tenure."

Amid the uproar, Scribner's and Ballantine Books released the paperback edition of *Abduction*. It included a new preface and two new appendices that added or expanded information that critics said Mack should have included originally. Mack now conceded that "my growing conviction about the authenticity of these reports, together with a sense of their great potential significance, resulted in a tendency to write as if the fact or reality of the experiences was established before the case had been made. In so doing, I may have denied some readers, especially those who would be naturally skeptical, the opportunity to make up their own minds." Accordingly, he had revised the language to clarify that he was reporting the experiences of abductees and not presuming that he was accepting everything they recounted as literally true.

After eleven months of investigation, the committee completed its forty-one-page final report by early June 1995.[6] MacLeish had noticed a considerable change in the attitude of Harvard lawyer Anne Taylor. She became "extremely nice" and "unbelievably friendly," MacLeish told Mack, who kept notes of the conversation. The committee presented the report to Deans Tosteson and Adelstein on June 8, with copies going also to Mack and his lawyers.

The panel acknowledged Mack's efforts to sympathetically support his "subject/patients." But, echoing the draft report, it found his work "deviates significantly from that of a clinician seeking to understand his patients' experiences and their implications." He failed to rule out mental disorders and other psychiatric factors. He influenced his S/Ps to accept the reality of their experiences. The report faulted Mack for dealing with the S/Ps' stories "as if they were accurate memories of actual events, not simply psychological phenomena." Mack's failure to seek other explanations, the report went on, exposed his S/Ps to harm from undetected but treatable emotional disturbances—an egregious charge against a physician, particularly when it involved children. The committee condemned Mack's failure to produce the evidence he cited to support abduction accounts—body implants, skin lesions, and missing pregnancies. It scoffed at the UFOs Mack found often associated with abductions, dismissing most sightings as "proven" errors or hoaxes and giving, as its footnoted source, *Watch the Skies*, the debunking Curtis Peebles book. The report also claimed that Mack had failed as a scholar and scientist to present his work for peer review, dismissing his protestations that he had tried and been rebuffed.

In short, the committee wrote, asked by Tosteson to determine whether Mack's work met the standards required of a faculty member of Harvard Medical School, "We have regretfully concluded that it does not." The committee also charged Harvard Medical School and the Department of Psychiatry with failing to adequately supervise Mack's Center for Psychology and Social Change and PEER.

Mack and his lawyers were furious. MacLeish complained that the committee failed to credit the testimony of Mack's licensed clinical social worker Roberta Colasanti, a leader of the Harvard Community Health Plan. She had detailed their prescreening procedures to rule out psychopathology as a source of abduction experiences. She was certain Mack had not injected his personal beliefs into his clinical interactions and had abandoned hypnotic regression in favor of simple breathing and relaxation exercises to explore his clients' recollections. But none of this was reflected in the final report.

Mack had also asked the committee to interview Rudolph E. Schild, an astronomer at the Harvard-Smithsonian Center for Astrophysics. They had become friendly since being introduced to each other by Schild's good friend Roz Zander and discovering that Mack was living across the street from Schild's lab, although Schild joked, "I can't be seen with you. If what you're discovering is true, it could threaten all this." Schild had read a chapter from Mack's forthcoming book and grown intrigued. "So, I took up my cross and followed him," he said. The panel found no need to interview Schild.

Residents and interns who had trained under Mack in the Department of Psychiatry at the Cambridge Hospital wrote Relman to express their "great concern and apprehension" over the investigation. They could testify that Mack had the utmost respect for his patients and students.

Also rallying to Mack's defense was the legal gadfly Alan M. Dershowitz, the Felix Frankfurter Professor of Law at Harvard and a columnist for *Penthouse* magazine. Any formal investigation of a professor's ideas threatened academic freedom, Dershowitz wrote. "Will the next professor who is thinking about an unconventional research project be deterred by the prospect of having to hire a lawyer to defend his ideas?" In the end, Dershowitz predicted, Harvard probably wouldn't do anything to Mack, nor would Mack be deterred from his research. But the principle of an investigative committee was troubling—"a sword of Damocles, hanging over the head of every professor who drifts outside the mainstream, especially in politically sensitive areas."

At the end of July 1995, after more than a year of investigation and seven weeks after receiving the committee's draft report, Mack was called to a meeting in Tosteson's office. Adelstein was there too. Tosteson handed Mack a two-page letter dated ten days before. Mack scanned it hurriedly and fastened on the last page.

John, I hope you are aware that it is not my intention to keep you from the study of a group of individuals whose perceived experience is hurtful to them nor to prevent you from treating their emotional distress. Nor do I wish to deny your right to postulate a syndrome with a heterodox etiology. I am concerned, however, that in your enthusiasm you do not violate the high standards for the conduct of clinical practice and clinical investigation that have been the hallmark of this Faculty.

Walking a line between the rights of members of the Faculty to inquire freely and the rights of patients and subjects is sometimes not easy. As stewards for the Faculty of Medicine we need to protect both. I hope you will help.

It was over.

Mack exhaled with relief. Tosteson and Adelson seemed to relax as well.[7] The deans went over the letter paragraph by paragraph with Mack, who still felt compelled to defend his clinical work. But when they got to the part about his enthusiasm, Mack had to agree—yes, the excitement of discovery may have left him, at times, "insufficiently cautious." They bantered about billing practices, Mack reminiscing about his pioneering days across the river when innovative financing kept funds flowing to the struggling Cambridge Hospital and out of the hands of the profligate and sticky-fingered municipality. Mack confessed he quite liked Tosteson's "syndrome with a heterodox etiology," as if anyone might understand he was defending Mack's right to investigate abduction's unconventional cause. And Mack admitted that appearing on Oprah with his experiencers could have been perceived as provocative, although he had turned down Geraldo Rivera. As they said good-bye, Adelstein told Mack, "I know this hasn't been pleasant for you, but I think we are in a better place now." Mack agreed and turned to Tosteson. "Dan, I think this may have been painful for you as well."

Harvard prepared a terse press release saying Mack had been cautioned not to violate Harvard's high clinical standards but reaffirming his "academic freedom to study what he wishes and share his ideas without impediment." And it concluded, "Dr. Mack remains a member in good standing of the Harvard Faculty of Medicine."

Maybe abduction was "nothing but total bullshit," science writer Mary Roach quoted David Jacobs in *Salon* several years later, although Jacobs didn't think so. In any case, Roach asked Harvard spokesman Bill Schaller if Mack was an embarrassment to the university. "They're all weird and embarrassing one way or another," he said.[8]

39

"WE WATCH THE X-FILES"

Sorely needing a respite in early 1996, Mack was off to Australia with Dominique. The Harvard inquiry had left him psychologically and financially drained. He and Sally had formally separated shortly before their thirty-sixth anniversary, and she had already filed for divorce. The house would be sold and their property divided. Their legal agreement lay no blame on either party. Sally seemed averse to bitterness. She knew all about Domi and had once run into Roz at a party. "I'm sorry," Roz had confessed. Sally was gracious. "I was angry for a while, Roz," she said, "but not now."[1]

Mack had been invited to address the Australian Transpersonal Association in Sydney, which would give them a chance to investigate UFO sightings in a remote aboriginal reserve in Arnhem Land.[2] His last trip to Australia had been a disaster. The previous June, oppressed by the committee's deliberations, he had signed up for a meditation and energy-healing workshop in rural Victoria, southeast of Melbourne. It was as far away as he could get. He and Dominique had been feuding. She had driven him to the airport in a toxic mood, quite willing, as she said, to "let you have a nervous breakdown." It was, he had realized too late, winter Down Under. He developed a series of bladder infections that kept him running to doctors and the hospital for catheters and tormented him with frustrating dreams.

This trip was different. He was with Dominique now, their romance had rekindled, and the Australian summer was in full swing. In Sydney they interviewed Peter Khoury, the Lebanese-born director of an abduction-support group. Khoury's own history of alien encounters emerged after he came across Whitley Strieber's *Communion*. One retrieved memory involved a recent sexual encounter with two female beings that left Khoury with a blonde hair retrieved, he said, from his penis. Genetic tests later linked it to a rare human type of Chinese Mongoloid. Khoury and an Australian UFO investigator, Bill Chalker, who was investigating Khoury's case and would detail it in a book, *Hair of the Alien*, appeared with Mack and Dominique at the forum. Peering through half-glasses perched at the end of his nose, Mack drew laughs when he described the alien phenomenon as "an outreach program from the cosmos to the spiritually impaired." Mack and Chalker compared notes about their frustrations over coverage by the mainstream media. "Fuck 'em," Mack said.[3]

Afterward Mack and Dominique headed north to Croker Island in the Arafura Sea. Despite prearrangements, no one was there to meet them. They hitched a ride in the bed of a pickup for the ten-mile journey to the island village, which consisted of cement-walled houses with corrugated tin roofs, a health clinic, a store and post office, and a two-room air-conditioned shed for guests. Knowing no one, the pair sat down on a bench in the middle of the village and waited, saying hello to anyone who wandered by. Soon a curious crowd gathered. Mack introduced himself and Dominique and explained their research mission. "Well, you see, people in the United States have been reporting seeing strange beings . . ." He got no further before someone piped up, "Oh yeah. Alien Abductions. We watch *The X-Files* every week."

A few months later Mack was off again, this time alone, to Brazil for Stan Grof's International Transpersonal Conference in the Amazon capital of Manaus. He and Dominique had been to Brazil two years before, and Mack was eager to return. For one thing, he was invited to give a talk, which he titled, "Connections Between Earth and Sky Beings: Cross Cultural Perspective." For another, the conference theme, "Technologies of the Sacred," promised a full examination of psychedelic substances, particularly ayahuasca, the "vine of the soul" in the Quechua tongue and a mainstay of some of the local syncretic religions, including Santo Daime, which blends elements of Catholicism, shamanism, and animism.

Then, too, Gilda Moura, the exotic Brazilian ufologist who had hypnotized him on his last visit and would also be a conference presenter, had tantalized him with a new sensation in Mina Gerais, the southeastern state where they had conducted their earlier research.[4]

As revealed by the Sunday television news show *Fantástico*, the Brazilian sisters Liliane and Valquíria Fátima Silva, and their friend Kátia Andrade Xavier, were taking a shortcut through a vacant lot in the coffee-processing city of Varginha on January 20, 1996, when they spotted a wobbly, foul-smelling, rubbery-looking brown figure with a large head and large, red eyes. They fled, telling their mother they had seen the devil. The story—which the

Wall Street Journal, quoting Canadian ufologist Stanton Friedman, would later mockingly call a "cosmic Watergate"—soon raced through the town, with others reporting a crashed spaceship and a second creature captured by police and firemen. According to local news accounts, both beings had been supposedly whisked off to military hospitals where they died, to be studied at the medical school of the University of Campinas near São Paulo.[5]

Mack arrived in mid-May and quickly made for Varginha with Gilda Moura. They were able to arrange interviews with the three witnesses, including twenty-two-year-old Kátia.[6] As Moura translated, Kátia, a plain, religious young woman, said she and the Silva sisters were taking an unfamiliar way home to avoid a group of troublesome boys when Liliane suddenly called her attention to something only ten or twelve feet away. It was a creature with an enlarged chest—she thought it was a heart—red eyes, and three hornlike bumps on the head. She couldn't see a nose, mouth, ears. or neck. It was crouching, bent at the knees and at the waist, with its arms on its knees. Kátia was paralyzed with fear. The red eyes gripped her. She screamed, and the creature turned. She thought it must be the devil, but the devil was supposed to have hair, and this had no hair. Its skin looked shiny, oily, and soft, like a balloon.

The sisters had run off, leaving Kátia alone with the red eyes that looked, she thought, like something external, glued on. She felt they were going to reach out and attack her. But she also felt a strange stirring of pity. She felt the being was suffering and needed help. But then the eyes spooked her again, and she thought, "This creature is going to take me." At that moment she suddenly felt free to move and ran away.

But Kátia said the experience made her more sensitive. She was anxious and afraid of sudden noises, but she felt strangely better afterward. In any case, Moura translated, "Her head is completely turned." Kátia said she couldn't describe her transformation, she was just different.

Mack left Varginha convinced it had happened. As he later told the BBC, "The usual cover-up followed." Perhaps the authorities were afraid of panicking people. The head of the university's medical department, Fortunato Antônio Badan Palhares, who would have conducted the alien autopsies, later derided the accounts as ridiculous lies.

When Moura and some forty-three others said they were heading further into the Amazon for a week, Mack joined them, traveling to the forest settlement of Boca do Acre, a stronghold of the Santo Daime, where Mack happily "got stoned" as he noted in his journal. He took a swim, forgetting he was carrying his prostate drug Hytrin. The vial opened, and he lost his pills. Then he came down with diarrhea. They were in Céu do Mapiá, a primitive riverine village where the privies were nothing more than square holes in the ground.

Still, on top of his Tylenol, Imodium, and electrolyte fluids, he drank ayahuasca, the thick and often vomitatious hallucinogen that lit him up with visions of geometric crystals and fantastic primal creatures. In one trance he saw all the ancient gods squeezed into a long trough into which they had been forced, waiting for humanity to call them back.

Some of the group planned a hike into the jungle to do ayahuasca there, but Mack was too weak to join them. He tried to find time to write in his journal, but everything was an ordeal. The boats taking them on the river kept breaking down. Their hotel lost water.

And then he may have come close to seeing what he had never seen before. He was constantly hearing from his traveling companions about strange lights he had just missed. Everyone was seeing them but him—it was becoming a joke. He would come running out at their summons only to see nothing and be told, "Oh you should have been out here a few minutes ago, it was much brighter."[7]

That night he was standing with Gilda Moura and two Japanese visitors on the veranda of their remote Amazon farmhouse. There on the horizon was a small, red object. It went one way, then another way. It disappeared and then reappeared.

Had he finally seen a UFO? He didn't know.

40

THE LIGHTHOUSE

Back in Cambridge in 1996, Mack was soon defending his work in a respected professional forum he had long craved. *Psychological Inquiry*, a quarterly published since 1990 by the British firm of Taylor & Francis with roots
going back to 1798, had run a provocative article by two skeptical psychologists offering a nonalien explanation of the phenomenon—taking abduction
accounts "seriously but not literally," as they said. The authors, Leonard S.
Newman of the University of Illinois, Chicago, and Roy F. Baumeister of
Case Western Reserve University in Cleveland, did not believe that people reporting alien abduction were liars or mentally ill. But neither, they
wrote, were the accounts to be taken as literally true. If Budd Hopkins's
poll was to be believed, since the Betty and Barney Hill case of 1961, an
average of 340 Americans were being abducted by aliens every day—with
no persuasive physical evidence whatsoever. "It is necessary to admit at the
outset that we do not believe in the literal reality of these experiences, and
so our explanatory efforts are devoted to explaining them as fantasies and
false memories," Newman and Baumeister said. Rather, they hypothesized
in their paper—"Toward an Explanation of the UFO Abduction Phenomenon: Hypnotic Elaboration, Extraterrestrial Sadomasochism, and Spurious
Memories"—the "parsimonious" explanation involved a psychological escape
into masochism.[1] First of all, they said, abduction accounts rarely emerged
unaided. The narratives were elicited and often shaped by professional fa-
cilitators—believers, like Mack. They were reinforced as the experiencers
self-protectively banded together in like-minded groups. And even without
hypnosis, the presence of authority figures reinforced a certain version of
events. But why would people construct false memories of horrific events?
For the same reason, the authors argued, that many people pay to be tied
up, humiliated, and subjected to pain. Abduction experiencers were engaged
in an escape from self-awareness and sought comfort in a loss of control and
submission to others—in this case, imagined beings. There was an overlap
in experiencer and masochist populations, Newman and Baumeister found.

Both were largely Western, white, and socioeconomically upper class. Even some of the purported alien instruments sounded like accoutrements for a dominatrix, they said—a faucetlike device to collect sperm, a metal gizmo to cup the testicles. "Like masochistic rituals," they concluded, "UFO abduction experiences could remove the person from his or her ordinary network of concerns, relationships, and strivings and then strip away many of the centrally defining features of the person's identity, deconstruct the person's familiar structures of self and world, enforce cognitive immediacy through a mixture of pain, pleasure, and suspense and then finally return the person to his or her ordinary life with a sense of having had an extraordinary transforming experience during the timeout."

Mack, along with PEER's research director, Caroline Mcleod, and a colleague, Barbara Corbisier, countered with a coauthored rebuttal in *Psychological Inquiry*, their article called "A More Parsimonious Explanation for UFO Abduction."[2] Although grateful for Newman and Baumeister's "well researched and carefully considered" piece, they found it "skewed" by a lack of firsthand clinical information and cultural biases. They chided Newman and Baumeister for declaring from the outset their belief in the nonreality of the phenomenon—shouldn't that be a matter of investigation, not belief? Abduction accounts could not be dismissed as constructs of hypnosis, because nearly one-third were adduced without hypnosis. They could not be ascribable to sleep paralysis, as a good portion occurred in the waking state. Abduction was not just a Western cultural phenomenon, either—witness the experiencers in Brazil, the Zulu shaman Credo Mutwa with his "star monkeys," and many others worldwide. Abductees as a group were not convincingly more prone to fantasy than the general population, and they did not, contrary to Newman and Baumeister's claims, gravitate to self-fulfilling groups. Rather, they were distinctly uneasy about congregating. Finally, Mack and his coauthors argued, abduction experiences scarcely fit the rubric of masochistic fantasy. Masochism associated sexual gratification with limited pain, loss of control, and humiliation. But the beings were not following any such understandable playbook. Their unwilling victims were terrified, deriving no pleasure from the experience, least of all sexual pleasure. And any pain was usually quickly assuaged. So the most parsimonious explanation was that there was no explanation, not one that science could offer.

Seven years after Mack had first learned of abduction from Hopkins, from whom he was painfully estranged for some of that time since Hopkins's critiques of Mack's abduction theories and his book, they reunited at John Hancock Hall in Boston in early March 1997 to offer contrasting perspectives in a benefit for PEER and the Intruders Foundation. Many of the 1,100 seats were filled, three by relatives of Laurance Rockefeller.[3]

Moderator Christopher Lydon, a public-radio host at WBUR, said the dialogue would focus on two central questions: Was the abduction phenomenon primarily a traumatic or transformational event for experiencers, and did abductions occur in a physical or spiritual reality?[4]

To robust applause, Hopkins rose from his red-plush armchair first. He called the abduction experience a signal event in human history. He found the aliens deceptive, clouding human minds with screen images of owls or deer or other creatures to mask their malign intentions. They were not evil per se, but they operated in a realm beyond simplistic human dichotomies. Yet humans were deeply traumatized. Like rape victims, abductees exhibited low self-esteem and low levels of trust. He was adamant that evidence showed that the abductions were real, occurring on a physical as well as a paranormal plane.

Mack followed him to the lectern, professorially unfolding his notes. He agreed with Hopkins that the experience was intrusive and traumatic. But there were other effects. An informational aspect that provided the experiencer with insights on ecological damage to the planet, telepathic communication, and hybrid breeding. A spiritual aspect that fostered a sense of oneness with the Source or God. Experiencers also developed an attachment to the beings.

In any case, society was reeling from the ontological shock of a challenge to the dominant paradigm, a crossing over of the physical into the spiritual and the spiritual into the physical. The mystery could not be fathomed from within existing structures of knowledge, Mack said. The notion of reality needed to be expanded to accept different forms of knowledge. Proof might never materialize, but gradually perhaps the experiences would be accepted as genuine.

With both back in their chairs for a dialogue, Hopkins reiterated his view that the aliens were not to be trusted. Humans did not need any extraterrestrial prodding along the evolutionary path. They needed to remain vigilant and resistant.

Mack responded that the trauma led to something greater, an opening that non-Western cultures seemed to understand.

When it came time for questions, audience members lined up behind two standing microphones in the aisles. One was a sprightly young woman who said she was an experiencer currently working with Mack.

Karin Austin, then twenty-nine, had endured a troubled childhood in the Tampa area. Her father disappeared shortly after her birth, and her mother cycled through three successive husbands. Austin's anomalous experiences began not long after infancy, quieted at eight, and then resumed at twenty-five, coming "hard and fast" over the next four years. She could remember somehow arriving with other humans at a clearing in a forest to be presented with their hybrid children, and she felt a dual-soul connection to a home planet in the Orion Belt whose astronomical features, despite her limited education, she could describe astonishingly well. She knew she wasn't crazy and began researching her experiences. In the yellow pages she found a Florida therapist who prescribed medication. Austin fled. Then she came across Mack's book and moved to Boston. Mack soon became not only her therapist but the father figure she never had.

Austin called him "a wonderful man and a wonderful listener" who had provided her "an opportunity to stand or sit down in a room for a couple of hours and get rid of a lot of stuff that I can't tell to anybody else."

She had not been predisposed to the phenomenon, she said, identifying herself originally as "Rush Limbaugh–watching, right-wing, very square-box, very three-dimensional." Abduction, she said, "didn't have anything to do with my reality . . . I didn't watch television shows with almond-eyed alien things . . . what I would like to say is that I think that each experiencer who's going through this knows that this is very much an individual experience . . ." Experiencers, she said, "don't have any answers—we have nothing but questions." Still, she said, "something is obviously definitely happening and if we close ourselves to it, we will be missing perhaps one of the most incredible experiences that mankind is to develop . . ."

A month later Austin repeated her message at a meeting of Friends of the Institute of Noetic Sciences, dedicated to consciousness research and founded by astronaut Edgar Mitchell, the lunar-module pilot of Apollo 14 and the sixth man to walk on the moon.[5] In the audience was Mack's primary benefactor, the eighty-six-year-old Laurance Rockefeller. Throughout Mack's ordeal at Harvard, Rockefeller had remained a bulwark, the financial mainstay of PEER as well as the world's foremost billionaire interested in UFOs. Rockefeller had commissioned a study called *UFO Briefing Document: The Best Available Evidence,* and he sent a copy to the White House for President Clinton. He had also tried to enlist the support of Carl Sagan, writing the Cornell astronomer in October 1996, "We continue to share your interest in assessing the probability of extraterrestrial life." Sagan's search for radio signals from the universe through the SETI program had yielded nothing to date, in contrast to extensive evidence of UFOs under intelligent control. "Thus," Rockefeller said, "we believe other avenues are worthy of serious scientific inquiry." Sagan was dismissive. "My view is that no amount of anecdotal evidence, unsubstantiated by physical evidence, is worth a single substantive bit of physical evidence." Less than two months later, Sagan died of bone marrow disease at sixty-two.

Now at the Noetic Sciences gathering, Rockefeller listened to Austin deliver an emotional summing up. "I believe our future is not as yet determined," she said. "I refuse to accept that we are destined to continue on our current path of callousness, fear and anger. I believe we can change how we view our earth, our nations, our families ourselves. I believe this because the universe reached out and touched me." Surely, Austin went on, this was akin to a birth. There was so much pain because there was so much beauty. Once again, humanity was at a crossroads, facing a fateful choice. "Couldn't we this time, finally, make the right one? Couldn't we simply reach out and embrace this experience and all that it brings with it? Including the terror, as well as the questions, truth and beauty." It would tell who and what we were and the nature of our connection to the Creator and the Universe. "Please," she appealed, "can't we this once choose the path that will finally set us free? Free to love, laugh and cry. Because after all it is our ultimate destiny to live in the joy of being alive. I, for one, am ready to live in a world like that. Aren't you?"

Moved by her words, Rockefeller invited her and Mack and other members of PEER to his penthouse triplex on Fifth Avenue overlooking the Central Park Zoo.[6] But he had sharp words for Mack. "You're just doing too much," Rockefeller told him.[7] As a role model, he cited Bill Moyers, the public-television innovator. Moyers spent at least half his time fundraising, Rockefeller said. "You need to cut back significantly," he chided Mack. "You're one of my beacons of light that I put out into the universe . . . I hear about these experiencers you are seeing: why? You're not a clinic. If you want to go out there and raise consciousness cut back; get yourself solid first. Get the earth beneath you so you can reach for the stars." He soon added, "You look like a young man; life can't be that difficult John." And then, "Stop being the answer to everyone's prayers. It's fine for all these people to call—who says you have to respond? I'm paying the bill for you to be a lighthouse." Rockefeller concluded, "I have confidence in you; you should have confidence in you. I'm pulling you down, John; I'm grabbing your feet and pulling you down to earth."

41

ABDUCTION AND DIVINITY

The Relman committee had made one good suggestion, Mack realized.
In April 1999, almost four years after Harvard ended its probe, Mack and
twenty-two colleagues gathered at Harvard Divinity School to follow-up on
a recommendation of the medical-school inquiry urging Mack to involve
fellow academicians in his abduction work. Mack now convened a two-day
conference with a multidisciplinary group including several other psychiatrists and psychologists, among them Gilda Moura, Harvard's Richard J.
McNally, PEER's Caroline McLeod, astrophysicist Rudy Schild, optical
physicist Dave Pritchard, Tulane philosopher Michael Zimmerman, and
a psychiatrist-theologian, Jeffrey Rediger—plus six experiencers, including
Karin Austin and Peter Faust.[1]

In the imposing halls they again grappled with the same nagging questions.
During abductions, was the body actually taken somewhere? Did it matter
either way? Why were people taken and brought back without anyone else
seeing? And what investigative paths seemed most promising?

As to whether any psychopathology characterized the experiencers, Mack
said no. Only three of the two hundred or so experiencers he had worked
with became so troubled they required brief hospitalization in psychiatric
units, but that was undoubtedly an effect of the abduction experiences, not
the cause.

Rich McNally, a Harvard professor known for his research into anxiety
disorders, suggested sophisticated testing and measurement of experiencer
body reactions. Rudy Schild urged study of the physics of passing through
walls and traveling on beams of light.

The solution was more science, Pritchard urged, although he was depressed to report that since their groundbreaking conference at MIT, research
into the abduction phenomenon had dwindled. Every time they thought they
had a possible alien implant or other piece of physical evidence, it turned out
to be a terrestrial artifact or another dead end.

Ultimately, the Divinity School conferees recommended further research. Once again they ended with more questions than answers. Mack sent a transcript of the conference to Arnold Relman.

Responding six months later, Relman said he was "disappointed by the limited range of attendees" and the inclusion of abductees whom he claimed had inhibited frank discussion.[2] He faulted Mack for inadequate attention to what he called the central issue—were the abductions "real physical events rather than simply psychological phenomena within the brain of each subject?" He found Caroline McLeod's study of forty experiencers and forty matched controls that had detected few personality differences "disturbingly imprecise." Had it been peer-reviewed and published? "I was hoping to see some evolution in your own thinking about 'abduction,'" Relman complained, "but it seems as if you and PEER have not moved off square one in elucidating this phenomenon." Relman enclosed an article from the CSICOP magazine *Skeptical Inquirer* by the Dutch theoretical physicist Gerard 't Hooft, who had shared the 1999 Nobel Prize in Physics for his findings in quantum mechanics. His article, "Physics and the Paranormal," argued against alien abduction as a physical event, consigning it to the realm of the mental.

Mack responded seven months later. The conference was not designed to marshal scientific evidence to prove the reality of abductions. There *was* evidence, though not enough to make the case by itself, but it was not the reason for the gathering. The real reason was to explore the nature of the phenomenon and its meaning for experiencers and to seek methods of future study.[3]

But the biggest difference he had with Relman was over the meaning of "real." To Relman, anything that couldn't be readily anchored in the material world had to be "simply psychological phenomena"—as if anything about that was simple.

It wasn't, agreed Jeff Rediger, the psychiatrist-theologian who held a Master of Divinity degree from Princeton Theological Seminary. Rediger, who would later become the medical director of the Harvard-affiliated McLean SouthEast Adult Psychiatric Hospital in Middleborough, Massachusetts, was a noted researcher of spontaneous remission of disease and the mind-body connection. He saw Relman's harsh subject/object dualism as simplistic. So-called objective reality did not always have to be tangible, Rediger said.

Another psychologist at Mack's conference, Tulane's Michael Zimmerman, said a multidimensional universe could explain "all sorts of paranormal phenomena." Schild, the astronomer, said one abductee's account of an alien home planet circling a double star system matched verifiable esoteric facts that could not possibly have been researched, guessed at, or made up.

Mack thanked Relman "for helping me sharpen my thinking."

42

"PASSPORT TO THE COSMOS"

Mack had long been looking for a sequel to *Abduction*. He and Dominique thought they had it in the story of the 1994 alien uproar in Zimbabwe, but Mack's agent found it too narrow. Instead, Mack opted for a more philosophical approach. *Passport to the Cosmos: Human Transformation and Alien Encounters* came out in late 1999 from Crown's Three Rivers Press with just Mack's name on the cover, although he credited Dominique with helping come up with the title. "From my perspective it is about the best and most important thing I've written," Mack wrote a friend.

From the preface, which quoted astronaut Edgar Mitchell ("Who are we? How did we get here? Where are we going?") *Passport* offered a broader reframing of the abduction phenomenon. Now, Mack declared, "I do not consider that abduction reports necessarily reflect a literal, physical taking of the human body." He was no longer seeking to establish the material reality of the alien-abduction phenomenon. "Rather, I am more concerned with the meaning of these experiences for the so-called abductees and for humankind more generally." He was more careful this time to attribute the "reports" of his "experiencer participants."[1]

Mack wrote that he had come to regard the alien-abduction phenomenon as only one of the mysterious crossovers confronting human consciousness, along with near-death and out-of-body experiences, animal mutilations, crop circles, apparitions of the Virgin Mary, and shamanic soul flights. He cited William Crookes, a British scientist of the nineteenth and early twentieth centuries later knighted for his discoveries with cathode rays, radioactivity, and helium, who had been sent to debunk a celebrated spiritualist, Daniel Dunglas Home, who was then astounding Europe with his mediumship.[2] Crookes witnessed Home materialize body parts in séances, levitate his body, and play a locked-up accordion without ever touching it. He emerged a believer. When told that what he had seen was impossible, Crookes replied, "The quotation occurs to me—'I never said it was possible, I only said it was true.'"

As he examined the phenomenon from the wider new vantage point of *Passport*, Mack was struck by how much it had to do with extraordinary energies, particularly vibratory beams of light so often associated with the Divine. Karin Austin had described passing out during teleportations through her solid walls or ceiling into a ship. It was as if someone had plunged her hand into a light socket. "It's like going 30,000 miles an hour . . . these sparks scream off you." She was never the same afterward—it made her telepathic. It was not simply that she could hear people's thoughts. She heard the entire universe resonating within her.

In *Passport* Mack puzzled over the light. Was this where theoretical physics and spirituality met? It was a better question than whether he believed in aliens and what planet he thought they came from. Dave Pritchard, however, had thrown up his hands. The abductees' light didn't behave like any light physicists recognized.

But if there was no room for this in Einstein's four-dimensional universe, there might be in dimensions yet undiscovered, Rudy Schild at the Harvard-Smithsonian Center for Astrophysics told Mack. More than a century and a half earlier, Michael Faraday discovered how electromagnetism affected light, opening the way to James Clerk Maxwell's findings of physical lines of force and vibrational waves. The universe offered vibrations of all kinds, and light was a manifestation of vibration, Schild explained. But *what* exactly was vibrating? Photons, the quanta of light, had no mass, nor did light, although it had energy, and energy was another form of mass, as Einstein's equation showed. Was light its own thing, God's third creation after heaven and earth?

In line with the more spiritual approach of *Passport*, Mack explored the apocalyptic messages that experiencers recounted getting from the aliens. Julia was one of the first to alert him to these alarming visions of the future. She saw herself in a rural area in charge of distributing greenhouse food after a nuclear war or other cataclysm had destroyed the planet. Mack had been stunned to hear similar dark prophecies from his other experiencers.

"Astonishingly," he wrote, risking the more cautious note he set for *Passport*, "the damage we have been inflicting upon the Earth's life-forms appears not to have gone 'unnoticed' by whatever intelligence or creative principle dwells in the cosmos, and it is providing some sort of feedback to us, however strange its form seems to be."

To receive these warnings of environmental catastrophe, abductees felt they needed to adjust their "vibratory rates" to be "reprogrammed" to take in the information, Mack said. It was imparted by telepathy or eye-to-eye contact with the beings, on electronic screens in the ships, inscribed in libraries of alien books or literary plates, or delivered by balls of knowledge-filled light.

Even without being abducted, Mack wrote, the Ariel School pupils told of receiving messages of "something that's going to happen." Of all his experiencers, Austin was the most upset, seeing visions of meteors or nuclear warheads showering destruction on Earth "like God's wrath exploding." Weeping, she saw smashed cars and the bodies of dead dogs, the waters poisoned with sewage, a vengeful Second Coming. "This is the stuff the Bible is talking about," she said.

But was it *this* planet, or the aliens' own? Sometimes the message seemed to be that *they* had suffered a catastrophe that served as a warning to humans. Austin thought they were telling her they had destroyed their planet with strip mining, forcing them underground. Their eyes had grown huge in the darkness and their bodies atrophied; they were unable to reproduce and needed to breed a new race. She recalled an encounter during which a being seemed to disintegrate before her eyes. "His face looks like he's dead," she reported. "It looks like he's been rotting." The message she got was, "'This is what will become of your race. This is what is happening to you.'"

If these weren't just fantasies projecting personal fears, what were they? Mack thought they could be manifestations of the real crisis afflicting the planet—archetypes of world-ending destruction. At the same time, experiencers told of being shown scenes of breathtaking beauty of the earth at risk—ancient forests and oceans teeming with fish only to see them succumb to blight and pollution.

In 1997, Mack wrote, experiencers began to tell a different story, one of more successful interbreeding. Austin, too, recalled meeting a bunch of her growing children, including one that she could cuddle. "The tall one tells me that these are mine," she said. He told her they were a new race, "and they will know love and happiness like humans know, and they will know their soul and their consciousness like we don't know, and they will inhabit the planet and take care of it and make it a beautiful place."

Mack struggled to make sense of it.

"I am convinced that the reproductive narrative is powerfully real for the experiencers," he wrote. He could find no Freudian or other psychodynamic explanation for why anyone would fabricate such intricate accounts. But there was no solid evidence that any of this was occurring on the material plane. The mating was in no way human—how could it be? Even Austin sensed it was happening in another "vibratory dimension." Perhaps the so-called hybrid project was less a matter of breeding and colonization than an evolution of consciousness, Mack wrote. The success of which experiencers spoke was not the creation of a new species but a dawning awareness of the peril to the planet and the urgent need for intervention—not by aliens but by humans.

In the rest of *Passport* Mack did what critics faulted him for not doing in *Abduction*—he put the phenomenon in the context of other mystical encoun-ters and archetypes that carried experiencers farther away from the world of material reality to a realm well-known to Native cultures.

Why did deer, raccoons, cats, panthers, owls, eagles, snakes, and spiders figure so often in abduction narratives? Shamans knew they embodied sym-bolic power and had much to teach humans. The beings might also take var-ious forms depending on an experiencer's consciousness, Mack wrote. Was it a coincidence that after a loutish crowd of construction workers plagued Austin at the bar where she was working, she encountered a new race of beings—repulsive lizard-like reptilians that also showed up in other abductee accounts?

To Mack, the deepest message of the encounters was not in their trauma but in their transformational aspects. Was it intended that way? Perhaps God inflicted such pain to teach lessons to humans. "Virtually all the experiencers with whom I have worked feel in them a spiritual power or the potential for personal transformation," he wrote. But the spiritual growth was not an end in itself, Mack wrote. It was a pathway to the Divine, the Source, the One, the Great Spirit to Native Americans, or simply Home.

Mack noted a shift in the accounts of his experiencers, who now reported a desperation and sadness in the beings, finding them deprived of love. In any case, sex with aliens was nothing like its earthly counterpart. It's not that it wasn't erotic—it was, often intensely so. But it was strangely disembodied, freed of the usual human machinery while still exuberantly fulfilling, a rush of pure, radiant love. Some experiencers felt bonded to an alien mate they would repeatedly encounter. Whitley Strieber confided such a secret relationship, along with a hybrid child. His wife was resigned to it, he told Mack.

At the end of *Passport* Mack was left with the same persistent question. Was any of this real? But that wasn't the most important question, he wrote. The most important question was what the phenomenon said about the power of the experiences to signal other dimensions of reality.

Mack steeled himself for an inevitable new uproar over *Passport*, but nothing happened. The media, he wrote a friend, "seem to be greeting it not with attacks like last time, but with a wall of silence."

43

A COSMIC MARRIAGE

What did he think of death? asked Shirley MacLaine.

The sprightly redheaded actress had long been interested in past lives and UFOs. She had sought Mack out early in his research, sparking a continuing friendship. In February 2001 they were on the phone "blue-skying," as Mack liked to call his freewheeling flights of fancy.[1] He had started off wondering how you established the truth of something you couldn't prove. You depended on the accounts of witnesses, he concluded.

"Why do we need mechanistic proof of anything?" MacLaine said.

It all began with disappointment in God, Mack said. To the ancients, nature was a destructive force. They needed to conquer it with science. In the process, spirituality was lost.

Did humankind suffer from a collective guilt over the civilizations it had destroyed? she asked. "I've gone back to previous lives. I remember my body being androgynous, translucent, being completely in touch with the divine, when I look back and remember what went on in Atlantis and Lemuria."

"You're speaking as a witness, a sacred witness," Mack said.

"And I'm considered sane," she added.

"Abductees will say in some past lifetime they made an agreement that they would come and be here in this material plane to help awaken and bring a different consciousness," Mack said. "I've seen them weep on my couch about being separated from the Godhead. It's possible that none of us are material at all—that we are basically spirits that have gotten hooked up with a body to have the experience of being embodied but that's not truly who we are."

Like angels, aliens didn't understand maternal instincts and sexuality, Mack said. "They envy our physicality, as if they once had it and lost it."

Everything was spiritual, MacLaine said, even a grain of sand.

"Everything is divine, everything is sacred," Mack agreed.

For the abductees, the hardest thing was to live in both worlds. The biggest question they kept asking him, Mack said, was "now that I'm aware of my divinity, my connection with the divine, that these spirit beings that have been with me all my life are real—now how do I work with my parent-teacher association? My church group? Or shop in the supermarket or buy my children's clothes?"

MacLaine had heard on talk radio that people could live to be 150 "with little attention to the consequences, good thing or not." But wasn't death just another form of being? Didn't Mack yearn to go "home"?

"I'm not quite there yet," he said. "Maybe I still have the idea I've got more things to do here or something. I still have a bit of that arrogance left over." For one thing, Mack said, "I have to restrain some experiencers from killing themselves either directly or indirectly because they do long so much to leave this plane and return Home. Home with a capital 'H' is what I hear from almost all of them." He was still wishing for a shift of methodology, some acceptance that "our heart's mind is the principal way of knowing."

MacLaine agreed. "The sky is full of wonders, but it's also the interior, who we are."

"But it's all over," Mack said. "We're the sky. It's us."

"If you look within, it's vaster than the cosmos itself," MacLaine said.

"I believe that," Mack said.

It was a painful time. He and Dominique had drifted apart. After another of their spats, he had stewed before writing her: "What seems to occur is that a grievance of the moment, small in itself, triggers the larger stuff that's not far below the surface, and the conversation quickly goes to hell." They had been talking about her moving out, which, it hurt Mack to write, "might be best for you and would serve the trajectory of your growth." He was not, he said, "falling on my sword in a sort of American *seppuku*. It's just a bit of truth-telling, what I see, painfully, when I go inside." He struggled to find the right words to close. "I'm sorry," which was true enough, sounded rather thin. Better was, "Much love."

In September 2001, at Dominique's suggestion, he enrolled in a weekend Landmark Forum. Werner Erhard's self-realization and relationship program had been licensed to a new group of presenters. In his application, Mack had to list his goal: "To overcome anxiety related to fear of rejection which inhibits communication especially in high stake intimate relationship." One of the program's exercises was to write, but not necessarily send, a letter to Dom about what he hoped to achieve. "I am committed to the transformation of our relationship. This does not mean making it better. It might mean separation with truth and dignity . . . in conclusion, whatever the outcome, I want you to know that I love you deeply and wish to stand guard over the treasures of your soul." He had borrowed his closing from Rainer Maria Rilke, one of his favorite poets, who had written, "I hold this to be the highest task of a bond between two people: that each should stand guard over the solitude of the other."[2]

But the growing emptiness between them—a relationship "flat" and "pro forma"—was undeniable. He was soon writing her, "It may seem as if I have been avoiding seeing you, and in a sense this is true." He should have written before, he said, but it had been a time of reflection, "a kind of waking up." He reassured her that his love for her and admiration for her heart, spirit, and sensitivity were boundless. "But there is a residual of trauma that I want to try to explain, for hurts of the ten years flooded back upon me when over the summer I reached a still place in myself." The Forum had taught him to come to terms with the past lest it become the future, and he wanted to prevent that. "Maybe my early mother loss made me slower, more needy, less able to give up, but I don't want to make much of that now." Now, he went on, she asked for them to be friends. It was true they had a deep soul connection. But after all they had shared . . . *friends*? He didn't think he could do that. He had hoped the Forum would bring them together, but it was not to be. "You know how much I will miss you," Mack wrote her. "I have loved you from the bottom of my heart."

The last day of his Landmark Forum, September 11, 2001, had evaporated in the mayhem of the terrorist attacks. Mack struggled to place the shattering events in his emerging cosmology, scratching out notes for an impromptu talk shortly after the World Trade Center Towers fell.

It could be argued that the events of Sept. 11, rather than representing a unique incident, reflect rather a larger? growing energy? Planetary crisis. Behind the attack itself and the apparent social, political and economic causes that seem to have given rise to it, there is a deeper problem. We in the West are trapped in dualistic worldview that allows us to reduce reality to simple division of good and evil. Explorations of the center over the past two decades, especially the study of anomalous experiences, are revealing to us the possibility of a unifying cosmology that transcends this dualism.

To help him run his household after Dominique moved out, Mack brought in Karin Austin, but lest anyone get the wrong idea, Mack spelled it out in an email to his friend Michael Blumenthal, the psychologist and poet. He and Austin were housemates and companions—"no sex." Austin quickly got busy, rearranging the furniture and cleaning up Mack's messy desk, angling it so he could see the turning leaves outside. She also thought the house could use a dog or two. Mack's faithful hound Digger had died years ago, and Mack still missed him. Soon the household rang to the yelps of two Australian shepherd pups, Ivy for him, Bree for her. Austin also knew that Mack had always mourned his mother, Eleanor—all traces had been banished by Ruth's decree. But Austin had found photos of Eleanor in a closet and asked Mack if she could borrow them. She soon presented him with a framed collage of Eleanor's pictures. Mack broke down and wept.

Now, confronting his own mortality, Mack had plunged into a timely new interest that dealt with the survival of consciousness—life after death.

Through a mutual interest in Buddhism, he had befriended a brilliant young California psychiatrist and brain researcher, Elisabeth Targ, born to intellectual and psychic royalty. Her father, Russell, a laser physicist, had co-founded a parapsychology program at Stanford Research Institute in Menlo Park, California, that in 1972 reported astonishing success with remote viewing and other feats of extrasensory perception. Funded by the CIA, it used the instrument of the mind to envision secret Soviet installations deep behind the Iron Curtain. Russell's father, William Targ, Elisabeth's paternal grandfather, had been editor in chief of G. P. Putnam's Sons, where he had purchased Mario Puzo's *The Godfather*, sight unseen, for five thousand dollars in 1968 after two other publishers had turned it down. Elisabeth's mother, Joan, was the sister of Bobby Fisher, perhaps the greatest chess grandmaster ever. She had taught her little brother the game.

As a child, Elisabeth was able to describe the contents of Christmas packages before opening them. She trained on her father's ESP machine, intuiting which of four colors was about to flash onscreen. And in playing hide-

and-seek with friends, she used remote viewing to find them. She graduated from high school at age fifteen, taught herself Russian so she could follow paranormal research there, and studied neuropharmacology at Stanford. When her father traveled to the Soviet Union in 1983, twenty-one-year-old Elisabeth translated for him and briefed the Russian Academy of Sciences on his remote-viewing experiments. She also assisted him at his Parapsychology Research Group, which he had founded in Palo Alto, California, in 1962 and where she would meet her life's soulmate.

Mark Comings, the son of two biologists, was reading novels in kindergarten and science texts in the second grade. As a freshman at Berkeley in the late 1970s, he experienced a mystical epiphany, his heart suddenly unfolding to a universe of love-filled radiance and infinite possibility. He quit college to study, on his own, advanced physics, alternative energy, consciousness, and spirituality. But fearing him to be mentally ill, his father, a geneticist at a California cancer hospital, committed Mark to psychiatric hospitals, where he underwent tormenting treatment. Once free, Mark made his way to Russell Targ's Parapsychology Research Group, where his dramatic psychic journey drew the interest of researchers including Elisabeth, who was then recently out of Stanford. But feeling intimidated by her brilliance, he kept his distance. They wouldn't meet again for fifteen years.

By the 1990s Elisabeth was running the Parapsychology Research Group as president when Mark, sun bronzed from six weeks in India, showed up there again, brimming with tales of his spiritual adventures. She was captivated. They shared an interest in Buddhism and, at the time they met Mack, were spending hours together in the Tibetan meditative practice of Vajrasattva. They were two fledgling practitioners striving to master the understanding of subtle bodies and purification.

Elisabeth's most famous experiment involved twenty AIDS patients under hospital care. Half were randomly assigned to also receive the distant prayers of forty spiritual healers, from rabbis to medicine men. No one knew beforehand who was in which group, but after six months all ten who had been prayed for were still alive, including one who had developed a particularly lethal brain cancer called glioblastoma multiforme. Four of the ten in the other group had died.

Elisabeth soon designed a larger and more exacting confirmation study. It came up with similar astonishing results. She didn't know how or why prayer worked, and she refused to speculate.

She remained intrigued by the recovery of her AIDS patient with a glioblastoma. Could distant prayer actually shrink a deadly brain tumor? In 2002 the National Institutes of Health approved a $1.5 million grant for her to restudy the effects of distant healing on AIDS and cancer patients.

Elisabeth was forty years old, and she and Comings were eager to start a family. They set a wedding date in May.

As she began in vitro fertilization treatments, she began noticing some deficits—a difficulty in pronouncing some words, a numbness on the left side of her face. She thought it might be related to the egg implantations, but emergency-room doctors found nothing. Her symptoms persisted. She got an MRI, which she could read for herself. A brain tumor. Tests confirmed glioblastoma, grade IV, the most malignant and, at that stage, inoperable.

Clinging to her macrobiotic diet, Elisabeth began a regimen of psychic healing. But, with time running out, she elected for surgery. Afterward Mack reviewed the histological slides at the University of California Medical Center. Malignant astrocytes, the star-shaped cells that make up the supportive tissue of the brain, were cascading down the lines of her surgical incisions and spreading through her brain. It was clearly hopeless, and heartbreaking.

An army of healers converged on Elisabeth's bedroom. A Lakota sun dancer, a Russian psychic, an acupuncturist. She ruled out radiation treatment, then reluctantly agreed, then stopped it, then restarted it.

She and Comings took their vows in Tiburon on the water north of San Francisco. Their officiant was J. J. Hurtak, the humanist founder and the president of the Academy for Future Science and the author of *The Keys of Enoch*, which he presented as the revealed teachings of messengers of universal intelligence. After the ceremony Elisabeth went back to the hospital. In her final days she returned to her mother's home in Palo Alto, where Joan Targ had died of a cerebral hemorrhage at age sixty in 1998 amid a flurry of paranormal phenomena. The house lights had flicked on and off during the night, with no one touching the switch. Now Elisabeth lay surrounded by her husband, her family, and her friends in a field of love consecrated with ceremonies from various traditions. She slipped away on July 13, 2002, less than three weeks before her forty-first birthday.

But within days of her death, family and friends reported receiving strong messages from her. Mack compiled a list. Three nights in a row, the house lights went on and off by themselves three times, as they had after Elisabeth's mother had died there. A friend of theirs had a dream that Elisabeth was speaking to her husband in what sounded like Russian. Upon waking, the woman, who knew no Russian herself, wrote down what it sounded like. Comings had it translated. "I love you, I adore you, eternally." Comings received calls on his cell phone from mediums he didn't know who said they had gotten messages to call him. He had a dream that Elisabeth, lying in bed beside him, rolled over to say Mack was upstairs waiting to go out for breakfast. Comings got dressed and walked out of his room to find Mack coming down the stairs, ready to go out for breakfast with him. "Elisabeth is working with Mark from the other side," J. J. Hurtak declared. It was indeed "a cosmic marriage."

Mack and Comings agreed to collaborate on a book to be called *Elisabeth and Mark Before and After Death: The Power of a Field of Love*. "I will provide evidence that Elisabeth Targ has in some important ways survived her death," Mack wrote his literary agent, Tim Seldes. It would be a fitting next step after alien abduction. Was it any stranger that the dead may live on as spirits? "There is perhaps no more important question to human beings than what happens to us after we die, whether or not our individual consciousness continues in some way after we have 'passed over to the other side,'" Mack wrote. But here too he had to acknowledge, "it is unlikely that we shall ever be provided with material proof that will altogether satisfy the demands of science."[3]

44

THE HOLY GRAIL

The year 2002 closed with a doleful milestone. Ruth Gimbel Prince Mack, the woman John Mack came to call mother, died on December 30 at ninety-nine, having long outlived two husbands tragically killed and, in her later years, a companion, Edwin H. Koehler Jr., who had died at ninety-eight just four years earlier. Curiously, he was the brother of Grace Koehler, John Mack's pioneering aviatrix aunt and the sister-in-law of Mack's birth mother, Eleanor. Three months later the family gathered for a memorial at Terrace in the Sky on the Columbia University campus in Ruth's longtime neighborhood of Morningside Heights—she always did love a good party, everyone agreed.[1] From the high windows overlooking Ruth's alma mater, Mack and Mary Lee could see the Lincoln School they had attended as children. Mack's son Tony remembered his grandmother as "brutally honest," although, he said, "she struggled to be as tactful as she could be." Kenny recalled her taking potshots at varmints with her rifle in Thetford. Danny told of the cabin she had insisted he build there as a teenager—"the enforcement of me becoming myself."

It wasn't just the end of Ruth, Danny said, "it's the end of an entire era." Others cited her fondness for candied ginger with sharp cheddar, the smell of her pipe, the way she twisted her lemon and set it on fire before dropping it into her vodka, her maniacal driving, her sunrise swims and horseback rides, how she called all her housemaids "Nora" (not remembering their names), and the perils of living under "Ruth's Rules of Order." A friend recalled how Ruth announced one day at ninety-three, "I think I've got it." "Got what?" he asked. "Life," Ruth said. "I think I figured it out." Sally said her mother-in-law was "first and foremost her own person—she really challenged me." And then Mack, in a blue shirt and multicolored tie, took the microphone. His hair cut short with his ears sticking out and bags under his eyes, he looked worn. "I learned a great deal about myself today," he began. He ruefully remembered Kenny asking him, "Jeez, dad, how did you do it? How did you survive and grow up?" She was loving, he continued, "but she could also be extremely tough." He recognized her insistence on courage, which he said she undoubt-edly got from her domineering father, Julius Prince. "She instilled that in me," Mack said, "not to be afraid of anything or anybody." He remembered running home from a fight at school. "She made sure I went back and con-tinued the fight until it was over," he said, while acknowledging that it might be apocryphal, "what you call in psychoanalysis a screen memory." But what was true, he said, was "this John Wayne quality, this True Grit thing she had."

Little now seemed too offbeat or uncanny for Mack. His media adviser, Will Bueché, sent him a newspaper article about six-year-old James Leininger of Lafayette, Louisiana, who suffered searing nightmares about a World War II fighter pilot shot down near Iwo Jima in 1945 and seemed to have a scarily encyclopedic familiarity with the most obscure details of the pilot's life. Had little James been, in a past life, that pilot—a "Soul Survivor," as a book would call him? Intrigued, Mack emailed back, "O.K., but am I now on the horizon for any reincarnation story?"

When Mack heard about David Ray Griffin's conspiratorial book *The New Pearl Harbor*, which claimed US complicity in the 9/11 attacks, he made sure to get a copy. He also ordered a new book about a strange case of pol-tergeist possession, *Unleashed*, that had sent a young Georgia woman, Tina Resch, to prison for life for the murder of her daughter, when the real cul-prit, the book suggested, may have been supernatural forces. Then, as Mack wrote a friend, he "devoured" *The Ghost of Flight 401*, which was about an Eastern Air Lines TriStar jet that crashed into the Everglades on December 29, 1972, killing 101 of the 176 passengers and crew aboard. In the telling by John G. Fuller, author of the UFO classics *The Interrupted Journey* and *In-cident at Exeter*, the flight and aftermath were replete with spooky anomalies like reported encounters with the dead pilot and the flight engineer on later flights. "How can anyone doubt that consciousness survives bodily death after reading this?" Mack said.

Mack had his own full plate of literary projects. He and a colleague, Trish Pfeiffer, were planning an anthology on consciousness. He was writing a cri de coeur centered on his Harvard ordeal, "When Worldviews Collide: a Paradigmatic Passion Play," although his agent, Tim Seldes, was having no luck finding a publisher. Mack set aside the draft as flawed and produced a thirty-page proposal that he thought better presented his ideas. It drew interest from Michael Briggs at the University Press of Kansas, but Briggs frowned on the subtitle as too Mel Gibson-ish. Mack even gave consideration to Dominique's "wise ass" suggestion of Harvard University Press. He asked Harvey Silverglate, who had found him his lawyer Eric MacLeish, to read his proposal. He also went back to Seldes, and with his blessing he took the project to another agent, Jane Dystel, who didn't believe she could sell it as a trade book, through bookstores. "This is not a book about UFOs, or for that matter, about alien encounters," John Mack wrote. Rather, it was to be a book about ideology and intolerance and what he saw as his struggle against a dominant Western materialist paradigm stuck on a fixed and constricted idea of reality—in short, about his search for intelligent life on earth. As he once half-joked to longtime assistant Leslie Hansen, "I didn't think people would believe me, but I didn't think they'd get so mad."

He was also working on the life-after-death book on Elisabeth and Mark as well as an essay about the Middle East conflict. "I've never had so many balls in the air," he told Seldes.

He was getting a bounce from a new documentary on abduction featuring him and Karin Austin and other experiencers and colleagues. The idea for the sixty-five-minute film, called *Touched*, had been suggested to the filmmaker Laurel Chiten by Mack himself, who had admired her last film, *The Jew in the Lotus*, which was about a historic dialogue between two kabbalist rabbis and the Dalai Lama and was based on the book by Rodger Kamanetz. At first, Chiten was dubious; she thought the whole abduction business rather silly. But then she met some of the experiencers. "I was mesmerized," she wrote in her film notes. "I feel that I was abducted by John Mack." She wasn't sure about the alien business, but she didn't *not* believe it. Mack played himself, as did Austin, Peter Faust, Alan Dershowitz, the Vatican ufologist Monsignor Balducci, Gilda Moura—and even Arnold Relman. Mack had quietly fronted ten thousand dollars toward the film's nearly three hundred thousand dollar budget. It was screened at Harvard, where sixty juniors and some professors gave it a warm reception.

In November 2003 Mack addressed an abduction conference outside Florence, where he gave students of the *Gruppo Academico Ufologico* his latest thoughts on establishing a science of human experience. "We have to start with the 'holistic way of knowing,'" he said, "a knowing of the heart and a knowing of the spirit." The Vatican took UFOs seriously, Mack said, because it credited the notion of "reliable witnesses."

Back home in Cambridge, he was quickly swept up in a financial crisis at his Center for Psychology and Social Change, which was struggling to meet its budget of more than eight hundred thousand dollars a year. He had naively guaranteed a one hundred thousand dollar loan from his bank to the center, which had been paying the interest but no principal. Happily, he had attracted back an old supporter, Richmond Mayo-Smith, the former headmaster of Roxbury Latin School in Boston who had shared a cell with Kenny when he and the Macks were arrested protesting nukes at the Nevada Test Site in 1986. Now, Mack said, Mayo-Smith should review the Center's books "such as they are." Mayo-Smith quickly began thinking of creative solutions. He had just read a piece in the *Exeter Bulletin* by the religion chair of Phillips Exeter Academy, who was then on sabbatical in Africa. The early Christian missionaries had imposed square houses on the Zulus, although they preferred their traditional round dwellings. Everything was round—the sun, the moon, the circle of life. Why have lines and angles? Just so, Mayo-Smith wrote Mack, perhaps the Center should be a round organization without sharp distinctions of title and pay grade? Mack liked that. He was preparing a lecture for the International Transpersonal Association that would relate UFOs (round) to the Grail chalice (round). And what about the tremendous power of the ring (round) in Tolkien's film trilogy?

Mack was also captivated by crop circles (round), the mysterious geometric patterns that began proliferating in English wheat and grain fields in the 1970s, some laid to hoaxes, others defying explanation. "It is, in my opinion, the ultimate shatterer of the materialist worldview," he emailed friends on the last day of 2003.

Within weeks he was arranging a summer's trip to England to explore the phenomenon for himself. He had been gripped by it since meeting Barbara Lamb, a regression therapist and marriage and family counselor from Claremont, California, who had been studying crop circles and running summer tours for a 2001 book, *Crop Circles Revealed: Language of the Light Symbols*, with her coauthor, Judith K. Moore.

Lamb had also been counseling abduction experiencers almost as long as Mack. She remembered being abducted in 1994 by three aliens who took her into a craft to show her the making of a crop circle, she said. She had also encountered a reptilian in her living room in 2000, as she had told Mack at a UFO conference. "I was walking through the house and there was standing this reptilian being. I was alert and awake. It was not night time. I was startled someone was there."[2] Normally, she said, she was repelled by snakes and lizards, "but he was radiating such a nice feeling, I went right over and put my hand out. He was taller than I, this close to me, with yellow reptile eyes. Then he was suddenly gone." She had a colleague regress her and remembered more. "He said telepathically, 'Ha, Barbara, good, good. Now you know that we are actually real. We do exist and have contacts with certain people.'"

"Tell me every moment, Barbara!" Mack had begged.

Mack seemed open to most anything strange now. In early July a Romanian-born research physician and experiencer sent him an article from a Romanian magazine purporting to announce the "galactos," a new cosmic currency "to represent Terra in its financial relations in the Universe." Mack forwarded it to a friend.

He had also heard of mystical experiences with a translucent bottle-green rock called moldavite, formed some 15 million years ago from the impact of a giant meteorite in southern Germany. The crash ejected vitreous fragments of the wormy-looking tektites along a river the Germans called the Moldau in Bohemia in the present-day Czech Republic. It was believed to be imbued with supernatural properties, even reputed to adorn the Holy Grail that early Christians believed had caught the blood of the crucified Christ, or by some accounts to be the Grail. Moldavites were said to have an unsettling tendency to vanish, only to turn up somewhere else. Mack might have thought little of it but for a startling synchronicity. After hearing of moldavites, he had discovered a long-forgotten letter in his files from a friend of one of his experiencers who had bought a piece of moldavite at a crystal shop in New Mexico and kept it on her night table. One morning she found it missing. Three months later she was lying on her couch meditating. When she got up, something fell from her chest onto the floor. It was the moldavite. Mack was taken enough with the stories to deliver a paper on moldavite at the twenty-first annual meeting of the Society for Scientific Exploration in Charlottesville, Virginia, in May 2002. And leaving no stone, or crystal, unturned, he ordered a piece from a Vermont gemstone dealer to present to a young niece.[3]

On a Sunday morning in July 2004, Mack set off in a rental car with Karin Austin, Barbara Lamb, and Anne Cuvelier (of Newport) from Heathrow Airport for Wiltshire, a crop circle hotspot near Stonehenge, where Mack had been booked to deliver a lecture on paranormal phenomena later in the week. They headed first for Windmill Hill in Avebury in Southwest England, home of the largest Neolithic stone circle in the world—three concentric rings of ditches built nearly six thousand years ago as a possible festival site or animal marketplace.

Meeting up with Shawn Randall, a crop-circle researcher and channeling teacher from California, Mack told her he had pretty much left alien abduction behind to explore continuity of consciousness.[4] But aliens and crop circles seemed linked, he said.

Randall was dubious. It was hard for her to imagine that the beings who so terrified humans would create the ineffably beautiful and transitory landscape patterns.

Anyway, Mack said, "it's all from Source, isn't it?"

They were walking into their first crop circle before he knew it. When Randall pointed it out, Mack jumped back as if struck. "Wow!" he said. "The power that it took to make this!" Mack sprawled over the flattened stalks, the better, he said, to imbibe the energy. "God, I feel so restored!" he exclaimed. Later, some of the group's photos seemed to show a vapor rising around him.

Austin was guarded, finding the whole business a bit of a hype, to her annoyance, which in turn annoyed Mack. She kept pointing out farm equipment that could have been used to fabricate the patterns.[5]

"There isn't anybody in the world who's going to convince me this is man-made," Mack insisted.

After Wiltshire they went on to Glastonbury, the spiritual center of Britain, rich in Neolithic history and Arthurian legend, where the town bookstores overflowed with New Age material. As the keynote speaker, Mack sought to tie together crop circles, UFOs, and the Grail quest. Like the holy chalice, the crop circles "invite us to stretch our very souls to higher possibilities," he said.

A week after returning from England, he drove to Newport for what was billed as the Tenth Annual Newport Alien Festival at Anne Cuvelier's Sanford-Covell Villa Marina on the historic cobbled waterfront. Codesigned in

1869 by a cousin of Ralph Waldo Emerson's, the blue Victorian inn on Narragansett Bay had been in Cuvelier's family since 1895, when her great-grandfather purchased it as a summer retreat even though he lived just blocks away. Remembering her father's stories about the mysterious objects that had buzzed their fleet in the wartime Pacific, she began opening her inn to experiencers for private summer retreats in 1995.

Besides Mack, the August 2004 guest list included Budd Hopkins and his soon-to-be third ex-wife, Carol Rainey, as well as his next and last partner, Leslie Kean, a UFO journalist and niece of the former New Jersey governor Tom Kean. There were strains between Hopkins and Rainey; she would soon accuse him of fabrications in his abduction research. Also there were the divinity-trained psychiatrist Jeffrey Rediger and a handful of experiencers including Randy Nickerson and two brothers and their friend, Jack and Jim Weiner and Charlie Foltz, who had undergone a terrifyingly remembered 1976 abduction on Eagle Lake in the forbidding Allagash wilderness of northern Maine as recounted by Raymond Fowler in *The Allagash Abductions*.

Mack had been brought to Newport by his assistant, Leslie Hansen, who he'd originally hired to transcribe his treatment tapes. With experiences of her own, she knew of Cuvelier's retreats and beseeched Mack to attend.

"What's this going to cost me?" he had asked, suspicious.

"John," she said, laughing, "you're a guest."[6]

After all the strains between them, Mack and Hopkins re-bonded, splashing around in Cuvelier's pool with towels on their heads as Nickerson snapped photos. In communal meals and cocktail hours on the sunset deck, the visitors laughed over incomprehensible events, secure in knowing that here at least they were spared the world's ridicule. They twitted Mack about his shift away from the absolute reality of abductions and his new after-death focus that he called "life on the other side."

Mack despaired of solving the mystery of abduction. "Do you think we will ever understand this?" he asked.

"We will," said one of his experiencers he called "Nona," "at some point, after death or before."

"Okay," Mack said. "I guess I don't have to worry about it." But would he ever really see a UFO?

"Probably you're not patient enough, John," Nona said.[7]

As Mack described his after-death research, Nickerson confessed his fear of dying.

"You never know when it will be your time," Mack said. "We could all go at any time. I could walk out on the street and get hit by a car."[8]

45

THE RUNE OF DOOM

Mack had cut it close. He left the Newport gathering before its end on Friday, August 6, 2004, to drive to Cape Ann, Massachusetts for the weekend wedding festivities of his son Kenny and his Kazakh bride, Aliya Suleimenova, a lovely young multilingual lawyer he had been dating for three years in Kazakhstan. The prewedding dinner and traditional gift-giving ceremony was in the historic fishing town of Gloucester, in the gray Victorian Castle Manor Inn, built in 1900 for a partner of LePage's Glue, a fixture of every schoolroom across America for generations. Mack beamingly donned a Kazakh brocade robe that he had been presented, making him look like an ancient wizard. The wedding ceremony was the next day. Conducted by a rabbi who mixed Jewish and Kazakh traditions, it took place in an even older rented seafront duplex in the quaint tourist mecca of Rockport. Afterward, Mack put up Aliya's parents and brother and sister, as well as the bridal couple, in his home. The parents spoke little English, which made for some awkward comradeship, but all in all, Mack enthused, it was a great time, overshadowed only by the realization that Kenny and his bride would soon depart again for Almaty. The couple were organizing a traditional Kazakh celebration for October at home and were hoping Mack and Sally would fly over for that, but Mack was not so sure. "I'm still in good health but clearly slowing down," he wrote friends. To Ken, Mack wrote, "I personally would have a problem leaving the country before the November 2d election, as I want to spend as much time as possible working on regime change. Maybe after the election, I'll feel I have to leave the country. I hope not." Meanwhile, he had heard back from a crew of ABC filmmakers who had crashed the gathering in Newport for a forthcoming Peter Jennings special. "It's clear to us that your perspective is an important one for our documentary," wrote Associate Producer Justin Weinstein, "and we would like to be able to film an interview with you, as well as any experiencers that would be interested in sharing their stories and experiences with us." On August 18 Mack wrote Stan Grof, "My house is crawling with people from ABC." The Peter Jennings crew of

Life in the Universe was keeping the extraterrestrial aspect quiet, Mack said. "The producers I have spoken with seem to be doing a responsible job, but who knows what they'll end up with." (The show aired on February 24, 2005. Now re-titled *Peter Jennings Reporting: UFOs—Seeing is Believing*, it drew on close to 150 interviews with scientists, investigators, and experiencers. But Mack had been cut out.)

Laurence Rockefeller had died, at age ninety-four, on July 11, 2004, and several weeks later Mack joined an overflowing crowd of grieving family, friends, and beneficiaries of his extraordinary largesse at Harlem's soaring Riverside Church, the gothic temple of ecumenical worship known by the Rockefellers as "Father's Church," having been built by John D. Rockefeller Jr. in 1930 for what would be, in 2004, nearly $300 million. It had played host to Fidel Castro and Nelson Mandela and the Rev. Martin Luther King Jr., who had preached his famous sermon against the Vietnam war there a year and a day before he was assassinated in Memphis. Laurance had been strikingly generous with him, Mack reminisced to a friend, supporting his work in preplanned diminishing amounts through 2000 but then coming across with a badly needed twenty-five thousand dollars. He had had the courage to support "leading edge people and projects," Mack said. He had last called the ailing Rockefeller on New Year's day. Laurance had answered feebly, but Mack soon had him gossiping and laughing about women they had known. Whitley Strieber memorialized Rockefeller on his website, praising his sponsorship of the 1995 *UFO Briefing Document* that expertly marshalled evidence of the phenomenon. Strieber recalled attending a conference with Rockefeller in 1997 at the 6,700-acre Medway Plantation in South Carolina, owned by the then ninety-five-year-old Gertrude Sanford Legendre, a former 1920s socialite adventurer and World War II OSS spy who had barely escaped getting shot by the Germans. Strieber said Rockefeller had revealed that his private contacts in the government knew UFOs were real and that it was a heavily guarded secret. He told Strieber too that he had briefed President Bill Clinton and Hillary on UFOs and the need for disclosure when they visited his JY Ranch in the Grand Tetons of Wyoming in 1995. Rockefeller said the Clintons had not immediately commented but that Hillary had later asked him, out of the president's presence, not to raise the subject again. "If there's nothing in it," Rockefeller had said with a twinkle, according to Strieber, "why would that be?"

Mack's Center for Psychology and Social Change had been financially struggling for some time. Its future was finally resolved with a decision that left Mack uneasy. He was persuaded, as a fundraising strategy, to recreate it as the John E. Mack Institute, with a benefit being planned at the home of a Malibu environmentalist, Andrew Beath, who had established EarthWays, a foundation to protect the wilderness and Indigenous communities in North and South America. Shirley MacLaine had agreed to serve on the committee. Other prospects included Gary Cooper's daughter Maria, married to concert pianist Byron Janis, and two of Mack's famous Oberlin classmates, composer John Kander and financier John Gutfreund. Dominique would take a leading role in the Institute, and Mack naively asked Roz if she would partner with her.

"No, John," Roz said. "I'm harboring a little jealousy." Mack lit up with sudden pride. "That's the best news I've had in a long, long time," he said.

A part of him, though, remained dubious. In the office one day he asked Maria Talcott of PEER, "Doesn't a person need to be dead to have an Institute in their name?"[1] He wrote friends, "I'm still in good health but clearly slowing down." He had undergone cataract surgery in both eyes, which clarified his vision, but he still needed 2.0 reading glasses and had lost some peripheral eyesight. He was also seeing an herbalist, who had prescribed a mixture of Palmetto berry, nettle root, white sage, and collinsonia to treat his prostatitis.

He had been invited back to England in late September for a T. E. Lawrence commemoration at Oxford. But before he left, he said, he wanted to do whatever he could to deny George W. Bush a second term. The war in Iraq was an abomination. One Saturday he drove to Manchester, New Hampshire, to join hundreds of other activists canvassing voters for John Kerry. Mack and a teammate visited twenty homes in a struggling neighborhood. "I think that grassroots, door to door work, will win this election," he wrote. He summarized his experiences in a short report that the campaign wanted to put up on the America Votes website, provided Mack allowed use of his name. He had no objection. The answer came swiftly. "Perhaps it would be simpler to identify you just as a Massachusetts volunteer." Mack laughed. They had discovered his "infamous identity."

Mack knew his reputation had taken a battering. Now, he joked, "what would they think if I told them I've been talking with dead people?" Close associates continued to edge away, wary of damaging their careers with what Mack laughingly called "that Mack/abduction thing."

They would sometimes start their Institute meetings, remembered Maria Talcott, by "picking a Rune" from a bag of stones marked with twenty-four letters of a two-thousand-year-old mystic Germanic alphabet that Mayo-Smith had initially provided.[2] The stones were said to foretell various fates. Margaret Mead had called the Runes "remarkable—an alphabet that goes A, B, C, D . . . X, Y, God."

At the last Institute meeting before Mack's departure for England, they enacted the ritual. Mack's friend Ralph Blum, author of the popular 1983 *Book of Runes*, had given them a set of stones comprising twenty-five runes symbolizing life's verities like Joy, Partnership, Movement, Defense, Fertility, and Growth. Someone formulated a question ("How can I improve my relationship with So-and-So?"), selected a stone from the bag, and compared the image to the interpretation in his book. One stone was blank to represent the Unknowable and Divine.

Mack drew a Rune. It was the blank. Some remembered Blum's saying that the blank could portend death. Mack laughed it off. But when the meeting later grew tense, Talcott recalled, Mack covered his eyes with his hands and said, "Sometimes I think it would be a lot easier for me to do this work from the other side."[3]

Particularly disquieted was Wes Boyd, the medical student who had turned up in the audience at Cambridge Hospital when Mack spoke on anomalous experience in December 1991.[4] They had connected the following November when Boyd wrote Mack a note and came to see him in his office. They had bonded, and when Boyd joined the psychiatric faculty, Mack referred him some patients. Now, after the Institute meeting, Boyd and his wife, Theonia, a pediatric pathologist, boarded a flight to St. Petersburg, Russia, where she was to deliver a series of lectures. They landed at Pulkovo Airport, found a taxi, and were driving through heavy traffic to their hotel when Boyd, in a passenger seat, glanced to his right. To his shock, he saw a turning car run over a pedestrian crossing the street. Boyd saw the victim's head slam onto the ground and his legs crumple under the car. Their driver gave no sign of noticing and kept on going. It disturbed Boyd at the time, but it disturbed him much more later.

46

"I NEVER KNEW

IT WOULD BE SO EASY"

Mack's invitation to take part in the T. E. Lawrence Symposium at Oxford's St. John's College on the last weekend of September 2004 had come from Jeremy Wilson, a British historian and Lawrence biographer. Mack would also be appearing with Malcolm Brown, editor of Lawrence's letters. If Harvard wouldn't pay Mack's way, Wilson offered a travel stipend of five hundred pounds. Mack would stay at the "new" College of St. John the Baptist, going back to 1555 on property granted by Henry VIII.[1]

Only something untoward would prevent his participation, Mack wrote back. But Harvard paying his way? That was really funny—he'd explain when he arrived.

As the conference approached, Mack had sudden qualms. It had been nearly three decades since *A Prince of Our Disorder* had come out. He had forgotten many details. Wilson sought to reassure him. This was a friendly gathering of fans. September would find Oxford at its best, fellow panelist Malcolm Brown promised, "when Matthew Arnold's boast about it breathing the last enchantments of the Middle Ages doesn't seem too far-fetched." Mack's assistant, Pat Carr, said he should treat himself to business class. Sally offered to contribute seventy-five thousand of her frequent flyer miles. They had long since resettled into an affectionate relationship of mutual regard, Mack having written her: "You also are of such a caliber that if you truly believed another life or person could be right for me or make me happy you would accept and want that. I wonder if I have a scope like that should or when it would be required of me. This is, then, an expression of appreciation, of love. I am truly in your debt, not out of guilt but simply that. All this may bode well for our future relationship, whatever its form may be . . . You have my great respect and, always, my love."

Mack arrived in London the Thursday before the weekend conference, meeting up immediately with Veronica Keen, the widow of a prominent

British afterlife investigator, Montague Keen, who had died of a massive heart attack the previous January at seventy-eight.[2] Monty, a hero to Mack, had spent much of his life on the council of the Society for Psychical Research and had been the principal investigator of a major study of life after death experiences in the Norfolk village of Scole. Within days of his death, Veronica had told Mack, Monty was sending messages from the beyond.[3] Mack was eager to follow-up with her.

At lunch Mack told Veronica he wanted to attend some séances. He only regretted he had come to his after-death interest so late in life. Afterward, for the Lawrence seminar, a friend of Keen's dropped Mack off at Paddington Station for the train to Oxford.

The program was underway Saturday when Dominique emailed.

I hope you are having a wonderful time at Oxford! You'll tell me all about it . . . I don't know if I can find anything new to say—you know so much about my life already: my struggles, kids, frustrations and dreams . . . I think back to the era of our grand adventures and am glad we had them . . . I regard you and it is as a part of myself, like my own self. For me, it does not require examination or analysis. It is organic to me. Sometimes you speak as if there is so much more to be had together—but the fact is, I think we have had and have it. We have loved each other and achieved a depth of communication in our conversations and work together that is unparalleled, in my life at any rate . . . With very much love—meditating on your birthday (not the party but the fact itself) and see you very soon—thinking of you under the lovely trees over there—

The seminar was a big success. Mack was the star. He drew special empathy when he paid tribute to his father, Edward, killed on the road in Vermont as Mack was finishing the writing—a haunting congruence, it was noted, with Lawrence's fatal motorcycle crash in 1935.

Afterward, Mack returned to London, where he and Keen were invited for lunch by Rupert Sheldrake, a renowned cell biologist and parapsychologist who had a lot in common with Mack. He had been scorned by scientific colleagues for his unorthodox theory of "morphic resonance," holding that all nature communicated inherently, so that dogs, for example, knew when their owners were on the way home. Mack had met Sheldrake at a psychology conference ten years before. Until meeting Mack, Sheldrake had thought of himself as avant-garde.

After leaving Sheldrake's, Mack met with some financial consultants who had been trying to raise money for the Institute. They went to dinner, and the evening ran late. Then Mack headed back to Keen's, where he would stay the night. He looked forward to taking the Underground again. Keen had given him directions from the Tube station at Totteridge and Whetstone but told him to call her from the station; she would pick him up.

In an area of South London known as Crystal Palace for the great Victorian exhibition hall that stood there from 1854 until its destruction by fire in 1936, Raymond Czechowski, a fifty-year-old computer-systems manager, had arisen at his usual time of 7:00 a.m.[4] A man of simple habits who wore glasses and took a daily pill for gout, he washed, dressed, and climbed into his well-traveled silver Peugeot 306 for the drive across the city to his job at North London Collegiate School, a palatial day academy for girls founded in 1850 by the daughter of an artist friend of Charles Dickens who had produced some etchings for *The Pickwick Papers*. Czechowski started work by 8:00, cooked and ate his lunch at school, and left by 4:30 for home. He had a bath, changed his clothes, and drank some tea and coffee. At 7:15 he got back in the car and reversed direction to the London Borough of Barnet. He was raising money for the North Finchley Royal British Legion, a charity providing financial and emotional support services to veterans of the armed services by selling paper flowers to the public. That Monday night in September 2004 was devoted to sorting out the collection lists for the sale of the red poppies commemorating the fallen since the Great War. He had been doing it for almost twenty years.

As he worked with the other volunteers, Czechowski availed himself of the bitter shandy (half IPA beer and half lemonade). He might have had five or six pints of the iced glasses, he wasn't exactly sure. It was after 11:00 when he got back into his car for the drive home. The night was clear and neither cold nor warm—perfect for September.

Czechowski drove slowly along the darkened green of the North Middlesex Golf Club, through light traffic, with the radio off. The posted limit was thirty miles per hour (England using miles, not kilometers), and Czechowski was careful to keep at about twenty-five. He merged onto the Whetstone High Road and turned left on Totteridge Lane. It could be narrow and busy on occasion, but he had traveled the route countless times and knew it well.

Mack, wearing a backpack, climbed wearily out of the Underground station. It was about 11:20 p.m. From Keen's directions, it was a ten or fifteen minute walk to her home on Longland Drive. He decided to make his own way there instead of calling her. Heading west, he crossed the grassy strip of Whetstone Stray over the Dollis Valley Brook and reached the crossing of Longland. He got about halfway across when his American instinct told him to look to the right. In England, for anyone heading south, westbound traffic comes from the left.

For some reason she couldn't later explain, shortly after 11:00 p.m. Keen's grown daughter had a sudden panic attack.[5]

Czechowski shot up from behind, suddenly seeing someone in front of him looking the other way. He slammed on the brakes, but he was too late. The figure was flung into the air, striking the windshield and flying over the top of the car to land hard on the ground. Czechowski rushed over, afraid to touch the body. He pulled out his phone to call an ambulance, and immediately people came running from everywhere. The victim said he was in pain and grabbed for a passerby's shoe. A firefighter rushed up, squatted down, and asked for help in easing off the man's knapsack. He turned him onto his back while feeling his neck for a pulse. A witness heard the injured man mumble, "Please help me." He grasped the firefighter's ankle then seemed to lose consciousness as his eyes rolled upward and an ambulance screamed up.

The police arrived and took down Czechowski's account. They could smell alcohol on his breath. "He just stepped there, bang," Czechowski said numbly. He submitted to a breath test, which showed fifty micrograms of alcohol in one hundred milliliters of breath—the legal limit was forty. A later blood test showed ninety-seven milligrams of alcohol in one hundred milliliters of blood—the legal limit was eighty.

Keen had waited and waited for Mack's call and then began repeatedly calling his phone. There was no answer.[6]

Mack was rushed unconscious to Barnet General Hospital, where he was pronounced dead less than two hours later, at twenty minutes after midnight on Tuesday morning, September 28, 2004. He had sustained a fracture of the left tibia, a fracture of the spine, multiple rib fractures, and severe injury to the lungs.

At 2:30 a.m. the police, using the address Mack was carrying in his pocket, knocked on Keen's door, which is when police officers first learned his identity.

Word traveled fast. Mack's assistant Leslie Hansen was at work. Her phone rang, and suddenly coworkers came running.

"What happened?" she asked, dazed.

"I don't know, you screamed."

Dominique got a call and ran over to Mack's house to tell Karin Austin, who exploded in helpless anger. "You left without saying good-bye!"

Dominique phoned Roz, Bob Lifton, Mack's cousins Terry Liebman and Susan Butler, and John Kander. She barely knew whom she was calling.

Roz got a "supernatural feeling." After the shock waned, it was too odd, she thought. "He's writing a book about communicating with the dead, and he dies."

It was Trish Pfeiffer, Mack's coauthor of the consciousness anthology, who called Sally.

At first Sally thought there was some confusion. Pfeiffer was telling her about someone else.

"No," Sally insisted. "I'm talking about John Mack."

"I'm telling you about John Mack," Pfeiffer said.

All over the world, UFO websites lit up. Was it true?

The new John E. Mack Institute posted an ominous notice. "AN ANNOUNCEMENT WILL BE FORTHCOMING."

By shortly after noon on Tuesday, September 28, Jay Burke, chief of psychiatry at the Cambridge Hospital, emailed an urgent notice to colleagues. "We have just received the very sad news that John Mack died tragically in a motor vehicle accident in England last night."

It was Randy Nickerson who called Boyd with the news, two days after Boyd and his wife had returned from Russia. Nickerson had been Boyd's first patient, referred by Mack. Boyd immediately flashed back to the horrific accident he had witnessed from his taxi in St. Petersburg. That couldn't have been long before Mack was run down in London, Boyd thought. How strange.

The news ricocheted around Harvard and beyond, creating shock and disbelief. Bob Lifton's wife, BJ, reached Budd Hopkins at his art studio in Wellfleet on Cape Cod. Hopkins burst into tears. Gurucharan Singh Khalsa got the call while at his annual international yoga conference in New Mexico. He suspended the meeting and asked all participants to chant a powerful sound, one he had taught Mack years ago, that awakens and guides the soul in passing.

To Victor Gurewich, a Cambridge internist, Mack's death brought back memories of the sixth grade, shortly after he and his family of war refugees arrived from England. Johnny Mack was his classmate. Gurewich remembered the Macks' opulent apartment in Morningside Heights, he remembered Mack's father Edward and the way he died on the road in Vermont, and he remembered all the years Mack said he was writing his book on Lawrence, a project Gurewich was sure was going nowhere, and how surprised he was to hear that it had won a Pulitzer Prize. When Mack ran into trouble at Harvard over that abduction "craziness," which is how Gurewich thought of it, he wasn't really surprised. Mack was always doing something interesting and going overboard about it. There was no one he had known longer than Mack, Gurewich reflected, but as he thought about it, he wasn't sure he ever really knew Mack at all.

In London, Veronica Keen went to the morgue and sat with the body. She sensed she was hearing Mack say, "I never knew it would be so easy."

Sally and Kenny caught the first flight to London and took time to stand in silent tribute at the fatal intersection.

Two days after Mack's death, Keen said, she arranged a séance. With Danny's arrival, she offered to cancel it, but Danny said she should go ahead. "John came through, he described his death," Keen later reported. In answer to her question, Mack said, according to Keen, "It was as if I was touched with a feather. I did not feel a thing. I was given a choice, should I go or should I stay? I looked down at my broken body and decided to go and there was Monty waiting for me."[7]

A kickoff fundraiser for the John E. Mack Institute had been scheduled for October 1 at Roz's house in Cambridge. Plans were hurriedly changed. "Dearest Ones," Roz emailed everyone the day before, "there will be an informal gathering at John's house on Monday, this Monday, the 4th of October at 6 PM. It would have been his 75th birthday." The caterer engaged for the benefit would now provide a light supper at Mack's house, "so I don't think there will be anything for people to bring. Except our ragged hearts." Remembering Mack's love of chocolate, Roz had baked his favorite cookies for the gathering. Transporting them on a cooking sheet on the front seat of her car, she noticed with surprise that they unaccountably began jiggling. She pulled over and stopped the car. They continued jiggling. There was no reason for it, she thought, "except John was saying thank you."[8]

Sally and the boys sat shiva at Mack's house for three days afterward.

The small funeral service was held on October 13 at Hendon Cemetery in London. It had been hastily organized by Keen with Mack's London and Oxford friends.[9] Malcolm Brown and Jeremy Wilson from the Lawrence seminar were there, as was Nick Pope, a staffer at the British Defense Ministry who had taken a special interest in UFOs. In the sunny cemetery garden, forty-two acres of towering trees were strewn with bouquets of flowers and a fountain burbled.

The arrival of the hearse was heralded by a solitary walker, an undertaker in funereal black with a black top hat; he looked the very figure of death itself. Pallbearers hoisted Mack's simple casket covered in white roses and carried it into the chapel. Danny, in a powder-blue sweater, stood mute at the pulpit, prepared, as he said, to be unprepared, with no words. He tapped his heart and whispered, "I love you, Dad."

47

"JOHN MACK NOW

KNOWS EVERYTHING"

Facing Harvard's flagship Widener Library across Harvard Yard, steps from Daniel Chester French's colossal statue of the seated founder, Harvard's Memorial Church points a white steeple heavenward like the warning forefinger of God. At noon on the gloriously autumnal Saturday of November 13, 2004, its pews quickly filled with hundreds of family members, friends, and colleagues of John Mack, who had been run over in London seven weeks before.[1]

Standing at the pulpit with its traditional golden-eagle lectern, the Rev. Peter J. Gomes, the church's widely beloved gay Black Baptist minister and Divinity School professor, opened the nondenominational service. Death was no stranger in the house, Gomes said. It had claimed their friend, as it surely would claim everyone in attendance. "It will do no one any good to pretend otherwise and in my office, on this occasion, I cannot and will not permit it." But the very fact of death occasioned a celebration of life, he said, and that was why they had come.

Danny, who had carried home his father's ashes, rose first to acknowledge those all over the world who were participating from afar, lighting candles and joining them in spirit. After Czechowski had pleaded guilty to causing death by careless driving while over the prescribed limit of alcohol, Danny and the rest of the Mack family had sent an anguished appeal to the court urging leniency for the driver.[2] "Although this was a tragic event for our family, we feel Mr. Czechowski's behavior was neither malicious nor intentional and have held no ill will toward him since we learned the circumstances of the collision. From the beginning we have felt compassion for the shock and guilt we imagine he must have experienced, and thus hope that he will not have to endure further suffering." They added, "We all believe John Mack would not want Mr. Czechowski to go to jail. As for ourselves, our grief will not be lessened by knowing that he is incarcerated—in fact, we would wish that he not be." But Czechowski was nevertheless sentenced to fifteen months imprisonment and banned from driving for three years.

Rising from the church pews, Robert Lifton, Mack's comrade in arms from the picket lines and antinuclear protests, recalled how proud Mack was to demonstrate his skill at microwaving frozen ice cream.

Ed Khantzian, who had crossed the Rubicon with Mack to bring Harvard's psychiatric services to Cambridge, confessed to being skeptical of Mack's abduction theories. But Mack had inscribed a copy of *Passport* to him anyway—"For Ed, in the spirit of his continuing education." Khantzian said he treasured Mack's final words to him: "If anyone asks, tell them I am not crazy."

Mack's friend Michael Blumenthal said he had experienced love at first sight only once in his life, twenty years before at a house party in suburban Newton where he first met and fell in love with John Mack. His wife wasn't jealous—she herself saw Mack as a sex symbol, Blumenthal said. And that family—"those gorgeous Macks"! His friend John, he said, learned the meaning of loss in the gravest loss a child can suffer—the loss of a mother. But he also knew "that our woundedness can also become the source of our strength, of our compassion, of our *openness* to the world and its mysteries." Yet John rarely spoke ill of anyone, he said, with the possible exception of George W. Bush. "He is, I believe, here with us today," Blumenthal said. "And the light from his flame will light my own life until the same Unidentified Flying Object that came to get him comes to get me."

His mentor, the two-time poet laureate Howard Nemerov, Blumenthal said, had penned lines about Paul Klee that seemed applicable here to his friend.

His dream an emblem to us of the life of thought,
The same dream that flared before intelligence
When light first went forth looking for the eye.

Karin Austin, in a gray jacket over a black dress, her blonde hair cropped short, mounted the stage unsteadily, stifling sobs. "I must confess," she could barely say without convulsing, "this is not where I ever wanted to be." She was the last of their close circle to have seen him. She had dropped him off at the airport for London, and she was going to pick him up when he came home. He had helped her, she said, for she was truly an experiencer. She was not just someone who *believed* she had contact with the unknown—she actually *had*, and Mack had done her the honor of believing in her. She never got to say thank you. She turned to leave the stage and stumbled, nearly falling down the steps before catching herself and staggering back to her seat.

Randy Nickerson paid tribute at the piano with an original composition dedicated to Mack. He and Mack had last met months before by the purest happenstance in New York. Nickerson was roller-skating in Central Park and suddenly, mid-park at the Naumburg bandshell at 71st Street, there was Mack, wide-eyed and beaming. He was there, he told Nickerson, to relive his earliest childhood memory—in a baby carriage at the bandshell.

Mary Lee's two sons, Mack's nephews, Jon and David Ingbar, filled out the tributes, followed by their cousins, Ken and Tony. Kenny asked the mourners for forgiveness if he cried. It was an old habit he had picked up from his father, who mortified his family by crying at movies and ball games. A leading energy lawyer with interests in Asia and Europe, he said that when he was considering marriage to Aliya his father had encouraged him. A couple, he had said, can create more together than two people individually, and that certainly had proved true with Ken's loving parents, John and Sally.[3]

Gomes had the final word. "The transition from this life to the next is a great mystery of which we know nothing and of which John Mack now knows everything," he said. "In the face of the greatest of all mysteries we stand silent and mute." This was a house of prayer, Gomes said, and so they would pray. "Oh Lord, until the shadows lengthen and the evening comes and the busy world is hushed and the fever of life is over and our work is done, grant us a safe lodging and a holy rest."

EPILOGUE

John Mack's journey, heroic, imperfect, and human, ends here. But in another reality, if there is such a thing, it took some further twists and turns. I'm not saying this part happened. But it is, as folklorist Eddie Bullard would say, a "story" people tell.

In late October 2004, a month after Mack died, Barbara Lamb, the California psychotherapist and marriage counselor who had helped organize Mack's crop-circle tour the previous July, was visiting her daughter in Rancho Bernardo, the northernmost suburb of San Diego.[1] Lamb was allergic to her daughter's kittens, and so, during the night, she had gone outside to the patio, despite the autumn chill, to try to sleep there. Propped up in a chair with her eyes closed, she suddenly found herself struggling to breathe. Gasping for air, she feared she might choke. Then, her eyes still closed, she became aware of a presence on the patio and heard Mack's voice. It was hard to mistake after all the time they had spent together.

"Don't worry, Barbara," she heard him say. "You will be okay. You will get through this." She had the sense of a ball of light entering her chest with a soothing warmth. She could breathe again and drifted off to sleep.

The next night, in Phoenix for a crop circle conference, Shawn Randall from the crop circle trip had a dream.[2] She saw Mack walking out of a crowd toward her. She heard him say, "C'mon, let's sit down and talk." Then she was in a restaurant at a banquette, Mack to her left.

"You know you're dead," she said.

"Of course," he said.

He was wearing the kind of short-sleeve shirt he often wore, and she was in a sleeveless blouse. Their bare arms touched, and she could feel intense heat radiating off his body. Randall told him he was burning her.

"Oh," she heard him say, "that's so you'll know I'm real." Then he asked, "How's Barbara?"

Randall happened to have a photograph of her in her purse. She pulled it out to show Mack and saw to her horror that Lamb's face was disfigured by a black smear, as if by a paintbrush.

"Take care of her," Randall heard Mack say. "Watch out for her." The dream ended.

When Randall rushed to tell Lamb the story, Randall heard about Lamb's near suffocation.

Lamb had another strange experience a month later.[3] She was treating a client who was trying to give up smoking. At the end of the hypnotherapy session, the young woman patted the empty cushion next to her and said, "I don't know how you feel about these sorts of things, but someone here wants to talk to you." Lamb had had no idea her client was mediumistic but urged her to go on. "His name is John," the woman said. She appeared to have no inkling who he was.

Lamb took the occasion to ask him a question. On their crop-circle trip to England, she and Mack had discussed a mutual interest in reptilian beings. They had planned a presentation on the subject with another UFO researcher, Joe Lewels of El Paso, at the fourteenth annual International UFO Congress in Laughlin, Nevada, in March 2005. Mack's death had halted their collaboration.

Now Lamb asked Mack through her client, "Would you like Joe and me to continue with the lecture?"

"By all means," came the answer. He said Lamb should use his notes. He told her to call Karin Austin in his house, describing exactly where he had stashed them—in the bookcase closest to the old desk in the alcove between the dining room and kitchen, middle shelf, in an envelope with a circle-and-string enclosure. The envelope would have a corner sticking out.

Lamb called Austin to relay Mack's instructions, and there the notes were, just as the message had prescribed. Lamb and Lewels gave their presentation in Nevada in March. Lamb took most of her allotted time to read Mack's material.

Weeks after Mack's death, Andrew Beath, the Malibu environmental activist, hosted a memorial service for Mack's California friends. In 2001 Beath had asked Mack, say you were on your deathbed and you were searching for something to tell your grandchildren, one thing. What would you say?[4]

Mack responded,

Stay still when you're afraid. Notice fear, instead of running from fear to some addiction, like sex, food or drugs, or getting angry with somebody else. Stop and notice what it is to be with the fear. If you stay with fear, fear is a vehicle for the opening of consciousness to connected-ness and love. Fear is permeated with insecurity. All our problems really derive from our reactions to fear. I may be afraid; but if I look at fear, stay with it, examine it, be with it, go into it—it transforms. So fear is the most powerful vehicle of shifting awareness and enabling transformation that we have. Use fear rather than escaping from it, as we do in this country by giving people Librium and other tranquilizers.

Fear, Mack said, was a pathway to courage. "Courage is simply fear that is not."

Now, at the California gathering, Beath related his own series of dreams about Mack. In one, Mack described being hit by the car. "Wow, this is amazing! It's finally my turn!" In another, Mack appeared as a robust figure in his forties. He calmly approached Beath, who, remembering that Mack had died, was delighted to see him, glad that he had found a way to visit. Beath rushed over for a hug, but Mack stopped him, saying, "We're not allowed to touch."

Roberta Colasanti, PEER's clinical social worker who had been at Mack's side through many of his most trying engagements with experiencers, had lunched with Mack before he left for England. Mack had given her an outline of his afterlife book on Elisabeth Targ, with a joke. "It might be I can do better work on the other side." Colasanti told him not to say things like that.

Now, a year after Mack's death, she had arranged a meeting with Will Maney, an experiencer and intuitive who was one of the subjects of their multiple-witness study.[5] As a fifteen-year-old boy in Barrington, Rhode Island, Maney had been climbing a tree when he inadvertently grasped a 14,700-volt power line that melted his left arm and nearly electrocuted him. He fell to the ground and landed on his neck, performing an impromptu CPR that somehow restarted his heart. He had had out-of-body and other anomalous experiences as a child, but when he emerged from the hospital with one arm he found he had gained enhanced spiritual powers, an experience he illuminated in a memoir, *Letters From Adam: A Call to Remember*, cowritten with Lynda Friedman.

Maney had made his way to PEER in 1996, he and Mack collaborating on some supernatural experiments, as Mack detailed in *Passport*. For a livelihood, Maney conducted psychic readings where he sat with people and described other dimensions of their being. It was like having an old-time crystal radio set, Maney said. All the frequencies were available, you just needed to fiddle around to tune into something.

That day, he had arranged a reading with Colasanti.[6]

As Maney, sitting with Colasanti, prepared to go "on line," she got the eerie feeling that Mack had materialized. She said nothing, waiting to see how Maney would react, only to hear him say, "Oh, come on, Bobbie, what? You don't know? John's here!"

She admitted she had sensed Mack too.

Maney said Mack had come with a message for her: "It was not what we thought!"

Colasanti reeled. *Not what we thought?*

Maney did not seem surprised. To him it was obvious. Mack meant abduction, aliens, multidimensionality—all the work he had done with them. But Colasanti was not sure.

What was not what they thought?

She waited for more, but that was it.

And that was all save for one more strange episode four years later. Colasanti's husband of twenty-four years, Charles Neuhaus, had lost his struggle with cancer when another intuitive told her he had a message for her. "Charlie wanted you to know that death is not what we think."

Colasanti, amazed, couldn't help remembering Mack. He had used the same words but not, so far as she could tell, about death.

Was *anything* what they had thought? *How strange!*

AFTERWORD

An electrifying image flashed around the world on April 10, 2019, from the Harvard-Smithsonian Center for Astrophysics and other observatories. It showed a fuzzy, orange donut with fiery-yellow highlights aglow in the inkiness of space. It was the first ever capturing of nature's biggest question mark—a black hole, an incomprehensible cosmic drain where light, space, matter, and time disappear, sucked into oblivion by infinite gravity, a possible clue to the ultimate fate of all creation. The object, as massive as 6.5 billion suns, lay in a galaxy far, far away—Messier 87 in the constellation Virgo, some 58 million light years from earth. With light traveling a little over 186,282 miles per second, that's almost 5.88 trillion miles per year, multiplied by 58 million. Yet even at that unimaginable distance scientists were able to map its shadow and snap, or rather compile, the picture—"a smoke ring framing a one-way portal to eternity," in the words of *New York Times* cosmic affairs correspondent Dennis Overbye.[1] The image combined data from radio antennas spread over four continents, from the South Pole to France, from Chile and Hawaii, a telescope array as big as the earth itself. The results, too voluminous for transmission even over the internet, were recorded on hard discs for analysis in Germany and the Haystack Observatory of the Massachusetts Institute of Technology.

If that feat seemed extraordinary, consider the Large Hadron Collider, history's biggest and most expensive science experiment, scheduled to restart, after upgrades, in 2021.[2] Here, around a seventeen-mile electronic racetrack at CERN, the European Center for Nuclear Research, buried deep under the Swiss-French border near Geneva, opposing beams of protons and other hadrons composed of quarks and who knows what else are propelled to 99.99999 percent of the speed of light by 10,000 supercold electromagnets bathed in 150 tons of superfluid helium. They smash into each other up to a billion times a second as detectors take 40 million pictures a second, seeking the release of elusive particles that could illuminate the dark energy and dark matter that make up the 95 percent of the universe that is still a complete unknown and explain why there is something rather than nothing in existence. In 2012, after 3,000 trillion collisions, one of those particles was found—the Higgs boson, a visible manifestation of a field that existed within the first trillionth of a second after the Big Bang and gave the universe mass.

Couldn't technology this sophisticated help figure out the nature of UFOs and whether human beings are actually getting abducted by aliens?

Indeed, so far as we know, little if any of the taxpayer billions spent on investigating black holes and the spawn of creation have gone to understanding what so mystified abduction researchers John Mack, Budd Hopkins, and others—the otherworldly experiences of seemingly normal people that went against every known concept of reality. Cosmology, after all, is deemed a serious subject; ufology and alien abduction are not. But if standard science showed little inclination to dirty its hands in the disreputable business, scientists could be just as narrow-minded as anyone else, another upsetter of the universe told friends in 1950. "In any case, there is little pure science; most of it consists of the subjective interpretation of natural phenomena. But even if some scientists have achieved objectivity in their work, in other fields they can be just as easily misled by mass suggestions or propaganda as anyone else," said Albert Einstein.

Surely there is fertile ground for research in areas of the human brain that might harbor special powers we have yet to understand, or in studies of the cell structure and DNA of people supposedly exposed to anomalous objects and beings.

Still, we know the government has not been incurious. From Project Blue Book and its ilk going back to the 1947 crash of *something* at Roswell, the Pentagon has continued to track at least the hardware of UFOs, if not also who, or what, may be behind the wheel, pursuing some deeply classified research, including persistent if so far unconfirmed reports that it has sequestered fragments of downed nonhuman craft for reverse engineering to unlock their secrets. That the intelligence services have fomented disinformation campaigns to unnerve global adversaries and overzealous hobbyists has multiplied the confusion.

In December 2017 I and two colleagues writing in the *New York Times* broke the story of a secret Defense Department UFO unit—the Advanced Aerospace Threat Identification Program. Funded with $22 million starting in 2007, it investigated a series of close encounters with what resembled giant rounded white Tic Tacs by F-18 fighter jets from the aircraft carrier group Nimitz off the coast of San Diego in 2004. One of the objects appeared to be underwater. Ominously and mysteriously, military officers quickly scooped up the radar logs and other evidence of the encounters.

Despite a Pentagon avowal that the program ended in 2012, it later emerged that it continued under a new name, the Unidentified Aerial Phenomenon Task Force in the Office of Naval Intelligence, into at least 2020, after an even more puzzling series of encounters from 2013 to 2015 came to light through a History Channel documentary. The nuclear-powered aircraft carrier *Theodore Roosevelt* was on maneuvers along the east coast of the United States when its Navy pilots captured on radar and using their thermal-imaging systems—and in a few cases eyeballed—a menagerie of hypersonic otherworldly objects. These included what looked like a spinning top or gyroscope, a flying suitcase, and a sphere-encasing cube. Some flew so close to the F-18s that pilots feared a crash and later filed official hazard reports. Creepily, the objects seemed to follow the carrier group as it cruised into the Persian Gulf on a Syrian war mission. Credible, highly trained observers and the most sophisticated military technology confirmed, at least, that there *was* something very strange and physically real out there.

Yet after all this, I'm little closer to a satisfying explanation than I was at the beginning. Whoever said, "At last, I don't understand," I'm with you. But I might have a better idea of some things the phenomenon *isn't*.

In 2004 I was Southwest bureau chief for the *New York Times* in Houston when a slim paperback fell into my hands. I must have picked it up in a used bookstore in Texas. It was Mack's *Passport to the Cosmos*, the 1999 sequel to his 1994 *Abduction: Human Encounters with Aliens*. Mack would later say that *Passport to the Cosmos* was a better book than the first, which even he finally realized had been too credulous. I thought I might try to profile Mack myself (not realizing how famous, or infamous, he already was), and then suddenly he was dead, struck down in a suspiciously freakish demise that seemed anything but accidental. As a longtime investigative reporter, I knew the perils of jumping to conclusions, and I recognized the importance of maintaining an open mind. I also knew a good yarn when I saw one. I contacted Mack's family, who, after their bereavement, shared Mack's voluminous archives without conditions—barring, of course, his confidential treatment sessions with patients and research subjects, although their essence, too, would emerge over time.

To my surprise, I realized the Macks and I had repeatedly crossed paths. John's father, Edward, was a distinguished English professor at the City College of New York when I was an undistinguished English major there in the 1960s. Much later, Mack's stepmother, Ruth Prince Gimbel, the New Deal economist, left scholarly papers in a historic collection I came to be archiving at Baruch College, where she had once taught and where I also taught.

Mack's cousin Walter Henry Liebman 3d, known as Terry, the last brewer of his family's Rheingold beer and a rich source of biographical details along with his writer-sister, Susan, turned out to be living across the street from me in Manhattan. Then, too, I'd been spending summers teaching international high schoolers at Phillips Exeter Academy in Exeter, New Hampshire, which was the epicenter of a flying-saucer craze in the 1960s and not far from the site of abduction's lode star, Betty and Barney Hill's incomprehensible 1961 encounter in the White Mountains.

My book lawyer, constitutional scholar Leon Friedman, knew Budd Hopkins from Cape Cod. When Hopkins had needed an investigator to track down witnesses in his most sensational case, he turned to Friedman, who found him the perfect gumshoe for the job—a private eye whose own wife turned out to be an abductee!

Furthermore, I found, Mack himself had linked his estrangement from Freudianism to my exclusive *Times* science series in the 1980s that introduced Jeffrey Moussaieff Masson as the renegade scholar who highlighted Freud's rejection of the reality of sexual assault as a fateful turning point for psychoanalysis—it was really all in the head, Freud decided, against compelling documentary evidence of actual widespread societal abuse. Not to repeat Freud's mistake, Mack would later come to regard the abduction experience as some actual traumatic event rather than a mental aberration.

I spent the fifteen years after Mack's death reading, researching, interviewing, and writing, including a 2013 piece on Mack for *Vanity Fair* online ("Alien Nation: Have Humans Been Abducted by Extraterrestrials?") and, with colleagues, a series of *New York Times* pieces exposing the Pentagon's latest efforts to track UFOs. Sometimes I awoke from a restless night's sleep with a nagging insight into Mack that I absolutely had to include—a download from the cosmos?

I came to see a pattern in Mack's odyssey—a progression of passions from community health reform to Lawrence of Arabia and Middle East peace, nuclear disarmament, world peace, cosmic consciousness, and, ultimately, survival of consciousness—life after death. In the end there was something of Everyman in John Mack, with his stepmother complex, workplace conflicts, back pain, marriage woes and other romances, and weakness for UFO cartoons.

So here we have John Mack, an earthling like us who stumbled on a colossal enigma and, bravely or foolishly, decided he was the one to solve it. For didn't the blinding revelation lie within sight all the time, much like how the characters in his favorite story, *The Wizard of Oz*, found themselves in search of qualities they possessed all along? As the San Francisco Zen philosopher Alan W. Watts liked to say, "When you get the message, hang up the phone." Mack may have stayed on the line too long or taken the message too literally, underestimating its staggering complexity as he would later acknowledge. He liked to dabble widely and to "blue sky" unimagined possibilities, at least until his main benefactor, Laurance Rockefeller, warned, "I'm pulling you down, John. I'm grabbing your feet and pulling you down to earth."

Mack had little patience with people who asked if he believed in UFOs and aliens. "A silly question," Margaret Mead once wrote in *Redbook*. "Belief has to do with matters of faith. It has nothing to do with the kind of knowledge that is based on scientific inquiry." The abundant record of cryptic experiences that so enraptured Mack and the Dalai Lama and so many others speaks for itself. That impossible things actually happened in some form or realm, intruding shockingly into the physical world we call reality—"an outreach program from the cosmos to the spiritually and consciously impaired," as Mack called it—seemed undeniable. Mack liked to attribute to Freud a quote that may actually have originated with Freud's teacher Jean-Martin Charcot: "A theory is good, but that doesn't prevent things from showing up." Or, as Philip K. Dick put it, "Reality is that which, when you stop believing in it, doesn't go away." The question is what these things are, and what we draw from them. There may or may not ever be answers, leaving phenomenologists like Edmund Husserl to go back to the things themselves, the way they come to us as experiences. In any case, abduction, a corporeal thing human beings did to each other, seemed a strange way of describing transcendent encounters with the ineffable.

Mack would have had issues with the title of this book. He insisted that he was never what people called a believer; he was only following a trail of overwhelmingly powerful anecdotal evidence, the kind of eyewitness testimony that gets people convicted in court and executed. Yet I believe he believed. He believed in earthly justice, in the unquenchable human spirit, and in an infinite and benign cosmic intelligence. He believed in taking risks and breaking boundaries to boldly explore the deepest secrets of existence, which no one yet has come close to fathoming. Never mind aliens, as the pioneering transpersonal psychiatrist Stanislav Grof said; where did this table and chair—*and everything else*—come from? John Mack set forth, journeyed far, had many adventures, and returned to tell the tale around the digital firelight, for humanity's sake. It's what heroes do. It's what human beings do.

Ralph Blumenthal JULY 2020

ACKNOWLEDGMENTS

Compared to the obstinate mystery he was chasing, John Mack was an open book, compiling a voluminous record of his formative thoughts, feelings, ideas, and presentations, a good part helpfully preserved in audio and video recordings retained by the family. No words or thoughts ascribed to Mack or anyone else in this book are the author's speculation or invention; all come from interviews, articles, recordings, emails, letters, or other documentary accounts by Mack and other principals. I am deeply grateful to Danny, Kenny, and Tony Mack for making the material available through Mack's devoted archivist and adviser, Will Bueché, and for providing their recollections and encouraging others to be forthcoming as well.

I was exceptionally fortunate to have spent time with Mack's wife, Sally, at the end of her life. Despite their split, Sally remained a faithful and loving supporter of her husband and his work. Others particularly close to Mack who generously shared their recollections and insights included Dominique Callimanopulos, Karin Austin, Pat Carr, Roz Zander, David Ingbar, and Budd Hopkins, whom I was privileged to interview also shortly before his untimely death, along with Temple professor David Jacobs, the third of their triumvirate, whose academic standing, like Mack's, also took a beating.

Mack's cousins, Walter Henry (Terry) Liebman and his sister, Susan Butler, were vital sources of family history. Wes Boyd and Stan Grof opened the door to transformative chapters in Mack's story. Gurucharan Singh Khalsa and Rick Tarnas, Mack's confessors, who were party to his taped therapy sessions and other personal consultations, gave away no confidences that Mack himself hadn't already recorded for posterity, but they helpfully provided context.

Robert Jay Lifton, Bernard Lown, Daniel Ellsberg, Vivienne Simon, Anne Cuvelier, Leslie Kean, Roberta Colasanti, and David Pritchard also offered valuable perspectives.

Randall Nickerson, one of Mack's first experiencers, generously shared his memories of Mack and his extensive research into the child-witnessed 1994

UFO landing in Ruwa, Zimbabwe—the subject of a documentary film, *Ariel Phenomenon*, that he had been working on for years.

Professional photographer Stuart Conway took some of the most atmospheric photos of Mack and generously allowed their use in this book.

Jerome Clark's magisterial 2018 *The UFO Encyclopedia* is a treasure, and so, for anyone studying the phenomenon, is he. I am indebted, too, to Leon Friedman, Barbara Lamb, Whitley Strieber, Rudolph Schild, Christopher Green, Linda Napolitano, Will Maney, David Gotlib, Mike Briggs, Jeffrey Kripal, Diana Pasulka, Ann Druyan, Luise White, Susan Lepselter, Margaret Meese, David Cherniack, Phil Isenberg, Lester Grinspoon, Edward Khantzian, Artemis Joukowsky III, Amy Anglin, Eric MacLeish, Dan Sheehan, Carl Sapers, David Hufford, Jeffrey Rediger, Russell Targ, Jane Katra, Shawn Randall, Carol Rainey, Leslie Hansen, Jill Neimark, James Willwerth, Donna Bassett, Victor Gurewich, the Rockefeller Archive Center, Elizabeth Robinson, Susan Manewich, Judy Einzig, Rachael Donalds, Cheryl Costa, Linda Miller Costa, Trish Corbett and Michael Mannion, Michael Murphy, Norie Huddle, Terry Hunt, and Amy and Elliot Lawrence.

My agent, Al Zuckerman of Writer's House, was an unfailing champion and savvy guide through the literary wilderness. James Ayers of the University of New Mexico Press was a scrupulous and sensitive copy editor, an author's prayer answered. Stephen P. Hull, director of the University of New Mexico Press, was an enthusiastic and supportive publisher, and I thank his legendary author and dean of western writers, Ol' Max Evans, for pointing me his way and for regaling me with the absolutely best cowboy-UFO stories. As always, my greatest debt is to my closest friend and shrewdest critic and editor, my wife, Deborah, who has been, as John Mack might say, not only witness but cocreator.

NOTES

Because John Mack's personal archive, much of it digitized by Will Bueché for the family and John Mack Institute, is not—or is not yet—open to scholars, it will be of limited use to detail where in Mack's voluminous files any particular material was located, particularly since it may well be reorganized once the collection is professionally processed. Some of Mack's articles and links to *Abduction, Passport,* and other material are posted on the John E. Mack Institute website, johnemack institute.org. Owing to Mack's celebrity, much more can be found on the web. These notes should provide as full an accounting of my sources as possible, along with the provenance of other material in the public domain. When citations are given in the text, there may be no need for additional data in the notes.

....

Note to Epigraph: Crookes, Sir William, "Researches in the Phenomena of Spiritualism," 1874. Mack cites Crookes in *Passport to the Cosmos,* as noted in chapter 42. Crookes was a decorated British scientist of the nineteenth and early twentieth centuries, later knighted for his discoveries with cathode rays, radioactivity, and helium, who was sent to debunk a celebrated spiritualist, Daniel Dunglas Home, then astounding Europe with his mediumship. Crookes witnessed Home (pronounced "Hume") materialize body parts in séances, levitate his body, and play a locked-up accordion without ever touching it, and he returned a believer. When told that what he had seen was impossible, Crookes wrote, "The quotation occurs to me—'I never said it was possible, I only said it was true.'"

CHAPTER 1

1. A full account of the conference at MIT is available in Pritchard et al., *Alien Discussions.* See chapter 24. See also Bryan, *Close Encounters of the Fourth Kind.* Mack also kept his own files on the conference and his interviews with Bryan. Accounts of the conference also rely on the author's interviews with David Pritchard and other participants.

2. Mack's quote, from his hypnosis by Gilda Moura in Brazil, is explained in chapter 29. See chapter 29, note 3.

CHAPTER 2

1. Hufford's account of the conference at MIT comes from multiple author interviews with him as well as from the *Alien Discussions* volume. Hufford's own research into paranormal encounters is described in his book, *The Terror That Comes in the Night.*

CHAPTER 3

1. A fuller account of Mack's introduction to Grof's Holotropic Breathwork is in chapter 14.

2. Interview of Mack by his friend Andrew Beath of Earthways Foundation, July 2001 (day not specified in transcript):

> *Beath*: Well did the holographic breath work and the psychedelic experiences and other things like that expand your awareness too?
> *Mack*: They primed me. I often teasingly said they put a hole in my psyche and the UFOs flew in you know through the space but I would not have been even anything but dismissive of the whole notion of the abduction phenomena had I not had several years of working in transpersonal psychology and being able to see that psyche could travel and identify with entities and beings that were not physical . . .

3. Mack's files describe his meetings with Chavoustie and, from Hopkins's files courtesy of Hopkins's last partner, Leslie Kean, I have the mailing Chavoustie sent Hopkins on December 30, 1989, asking him to meet with Mack. The picture postcard from the Metropolitan Museum of Art (depicting "The Bodmer Oak, Fontainebleau Forest" by Claude Monet) read, "Dear Bud [sic], I'm not sure if you received the message I left for you—John, my friend the psychiatrist will be here on Jan. 10th. Could you meet with him in the afternoon? Look forward to seeing you—Blanche." Chapter 18 offers more details of Chavoustie's allegations against MKUltra. The CIA subsequently made public much historic material on MKUltra, without, of course, mentioning Chavoustie. Her MKUltra story never fully emerged before her death in 2016, but Mack had grown sufficiently uneasy about Chavoustie to ask reporter Stephen Rae, writing a magazine article on Mack for the *New York Times*, to keep her name out of his piece. "You don't want that name in there for complicated reasons," Mack said on December 7, 1993. But he credited her in the acknowledgements to *Abduction*—despite misspelling her name as "Chavonstie."

4. Mack, *Abduction*, 1.

5. Mack recalled this at his first public talk on abduction at Grof's Hollyhock Farms on August 29, 1990.

6. I interviewed Hopkins in his townhouse at 246 West 16 St. on December 17, 2010, eight months before his death of cancer at age eighty on August 21, 2011.

7. Author's multiple interviews with Gurucharan Singh Khalsa and Mack's tape-recorded therapy sessions with Khalsa, available in Mack's archives.

8. Stephen Rae's article on Mack in the *New York Times*; see chapter 27.

9. See also chapter 20. Mack gave an account of his Shop Club talk on February 21, 1990, at an Affect Seminar he was leading at Harvard on March 12, 1991:

So I presented the whole story that I know, from beginning to end, and then proceeded to withstand a bombardment of reductionistic remarks and questions. . . . So I had to respond to each of these. I'd say "yes but that leaves out all of the physical phenomenon or the deep distress or the fact that the people don't know each other," or that "to me it has an authentic quality of an experience and not a fantasy or imagination." . . . I received a letter from the wife of the president of the university a couple days afterwards, who was very excited about the evening, very moved by it, very provoked. But she in a subtle way point[ed] out that I did seem to become impatient at certain points . . . she was supportive but she noted that I become impatient at certain points, which was correct. . . . So I think I "survived" it. Now what they're saying behind my back I don't know. There's another meeting in a week or so of the group and I'll go there just to see what they say to me and get more feedback. But I think that as far as my engagement with this work is concerned I am completely out of the closet, I have no cover whatever in this community a[n]y more, which is both exhilarating and terrifying. It means that I am free.

CHAPTER 4

1. Author's multiple interviews with Wesley Boyd, who is now on the faculty at the Center for Bioethics and an associate professor of psychiatry at Harvard Medical School.

2. Interview with Sally, February 22, 2016; see chapter 8.

CHAPTER 5

1. The best overall source, by far, for the history of UFOs and alien encounters is Jerome Clark's two-volume *The UFO Encyclopedia*. CQ Researcher also has a solid database of UFO scholarship. I rely here too on an excellent historical account in a book financed by Laurance Rockefeller, *UFO Briefing Document: The*

Best Available Evidence, a 1995 collaboration by Don Berliner, Antonio Huneeus, Whitley Strieber, Marie Galbraith, and Sandy S. Wright. See also David Jacobs's authoritative debut, *The UFO Controversy in America*. Another authoritative source is Leslie Kean's *UFOs: Generals, Pilots and Government Officials Go On the Record*, which cites the Barry Goldwater-LeMay exchange. Keyhoe's classic, *The Flying Saucers are Real*, expanded from a 1949 *True* magazine article; Donald Menzel's debunking *Flying Saucers*; and Aimé Michel's book, *Flying Saucers and the Straight Line Mystery* make up the other sources for this chapter. The preeminent UFO researcher and theoretician Jacques Vallee dedicated his book, *Confrontations: A Scientist's Search for Alien Contact*, to Michel, "who taught me to 'shake the pear tree' of science." But as noted by Jerome Clark in *The UFO Encyclopedia*, even Vallee came to question Michel's "straight line" hypothesis, which remained inconclusive.

CHAPTER 6

1. The manuscript Mack was still laboring over at the end of his life and could never place with a publisher, "When Worldviews Collide: A Paradigmatic Passion Play," remains a rich source of autobiography, especially on Mack's struggle with Harvard. Useful genealogical information also comes from his grandfather Clarence's 1921 passport application. In 1944 at age fifteen, John wrote a thirty-five-page typed autobiographical fragment, "Confessing is Depressing," dedicating the opus, with pasted-in snapshots, "to my wife and children of the future who, upon reading it will become my severest critics." He noted the hour of his birth as 8:00 a.m., which would take on significance in his later efforts to interpret his astrological chart. Much later Mack also wrote an autobiographical chapter for Ellen L. Bassuk's *The Doctor-Activist: Physicians Fighting for Social Change*.

2. BeerHistory.com.

3. To resolve any question of how Eleanor died (see chapter 22), I tracked down her death certificate, which banishes all doubt. Mack's cousins Susan Butler and her brother, Walter Henry (Terry) Liebman, provided recollections of grandma Lulu.

4. See chapter 27.

CHAPTER 7

1. The Joseph C. Aub papers (1918-1974) are available online at the Harvard Library.

2. See Mack's chapter in Bassuk, *The Doctor-Activist*.

3. Taped interview with Katherine Diehl, November 24, 1993. An abbreviated version ran in the March/April 1994 issue of *Body, Mind, & Spirit* magazine.

4. Author's interview with Sally at Brigham and Women's Hospital, February 22, 2016. She died of cancer on March 24 at age eighty-two.

5. Bassuk, *The Doctor-Activist.*

CHAPTER 8

1. Bassuk, *The Doctor-Activist.*

2. Einzig, "Do You Believe in God?"; see also author's follow-up interview from 2020.

3. Records of the City College memorial service, in Mack's files.

CHAPTER 9

1. Clark, *UFO Encyclopedia.*

2. See the *New York Times* obituary of John Grant Fuller, November 9, 1990, and other press accounts.

3. Fuller, *Incident at Exeter.*

4. Fuller, *The Interrupted Journey.*

5. Friedman and Marden, *Captured!*

CHAPTER 10

1. Fuller, *Interrupted Journey.*

CHAPTER 11

1. Bassuk, *The Doctor-Activist.*

2. After returning from his trip, Mack typed out, on February 6, 1978, a five-page memo on his peace mission: "The Arab-Israeli Conflict: A Psychiatrist's View from Egypt." He followed this with a twenty-nine-page "Confidential" draft version on February 14, called "Psychology and International Relations in the Field: A Psychiatrist's Diary of two Weeks in Cairo." He also described his trip in a later interview with his friend Andrew Beath, a California philanthropist and activist who established Earthways Foundation in 1985.

3. Bassuk, *The Doctor-Activist.*

4. Mack typed out a detailed diary of his trip from April 20, 1980, through April 27, filling sixty-three pages. On May 7, 1980, he sent *New York Times* editor Mitchel Levitas a thirteen-page Q&A with Arafat, which appears not to have run, probably because *Times* correspondent Anthony Lewis happened also to be in Beirut interviewing Arafat. Lewis's piece ran in the paper's foreign news pages on May 8, 1980.

CHAPTER 12

1. Author's multiple interviews with Danny Mack, principally in February 2016.

2. Author's interview with Sally, 2016.

CHAPTER 13

1. Lown, *Prescription for Survival*. See also interviews with Lown and Robert Lifton, which are referenced throughout the chapter.

2. Caldicott, *A Desperate Passion*.

3. Author's interview with Lifton, February 1, 2016.

4. Mack later wrote up ten pages of "confidential" notes on his meeting with Teller at the Cosmos Club on May 10, 1986.

5. Mack wrote an op-ed article on the protest that ran on June 20, 1986, in the *New York Times* as "To Test Or Not to Test: That is the Nuclear Question; To Halt the Arms Race." Mack also transcribed twenty-eight pages of tape-recorded recollections of Kenny and Sally on the family's arrest experience.

6. Author's multiple interviews with Daniel Ellsberg, summer 2017 and October 4, 2017.

7. Mack taped the session on July 7, 1987, and kept a transcript.

8. Author's multiple interviews with Roz Zander, July 9, 2019, and thereafter.

CHAPTER 14

1. Kripal, *Esalen*; and the *New Yorker* profile of Michael Murphy from the January 5, 1976, issue.

2. Watts, *Joyous Cosmology*.

3. Mack's paper on Grof, May 16, 1989.

4. Author's interview with Stan Grof, March 7, 2016.

5. Author's interview with Stan Grof, March 7, 2016.

CHAPTER 15

1. Bassuk, *The Doctor-Activist*.

2. Author's interview with Stan Grof, March 7, 2016.

3. Mack filled at least eighteen journals in which he recorded his romantic anguish and thoughts on abduction and other matters.

4. Mack family video, December 25, 1988, 2 hours, 2 minutes.

CHAPTER 16

1. Hopkins, *Art, Life and UFOs*.

2. Hopkins, *Missing Time*.

3. Jacobs, *Secret Life*.

4. Letter from David Jacobs to John Mack, April 7, 1991.

5. Hopkins, *Intruders*.

CHAPTER 17

1. Mack's journal and author's multiple interviews with Daniel Ellsberg.

CHAPTER 18

1. Author's multiple interviews with Grinspoon, February 22, 2016, and thereafter.

2. The meeting was taped, and a partial transcript was made available on August 7, 2017, by Will Bueché.

3. Mack file on Affect Seminars. For one session, he recruited his former Oberlin classmate and Broadway composer, John Kander. The homework was to listen to *Cabaret*. In another session, on June 3, 1994, he called our society spiritually dead. "We're living in an Auschwitz of the soul."

4. Tape recording of Mack's presentation at the breathwork module at Hollyhock Farms.

CHAPTER 19

1. Hopkins's file on "The Abduction Syndrome," made available by Leslie Kean, included his copies of the manuscript along with his extensive critique.

2. Lawson, "Hypnosis of Imaginary CE3 Abductees."

CHAPTER 20

1. See chapter 3, note 9.

2. Based on a recording of the December 18, 1991, lecture, available in Mack's files.

3. On June 28, 2000, according to a transcript in Mack's files, Mack and his colleague Roberta Colasanti, a licensed clinical social worker, reminisced about the grand rounds with an experiencer on the tape—a woman identified as Donna (not Donna Bassett).

> *Mack*: I played a section of one of Donna's tapes. Were you there, at Grand Rounds in December of '91? Budd was up here. Just to show—
> *Colasanti*: . . . [inaudible]
> *Mack*: And it set us back five years!
> *Colasanti*: Yeah, right. I remember, we went . . . [inaudible]
> *Donna*: I know, I know.

Mack: Their attitude wasn't—it wasn't that this isn't real or to believe it. They just—

Colasanti: [inaudible]

Mack: This was in my days of "More is better," you know?

Donna: More of what's better, though?

Mack: More information to what I'm teaching, which is not true. In other words, more is not better when you're teaching.

Donna: Really?

Mack: No, because people can only stand so much.

Donna: That's right.

Colasanti: [inaudible]

Donna: That's right.

Mack: You have to know where they are, and we just flooded them. We hit them with everything, you know? Julia [last name redacted by author] was there, which totally freaked them out, because she's like Mrs. everyday whatever. And then we had Budd showing all his slides of cuts and these scoop marks. And I was presenting all the clinical stuff. We had you screaming on tape, you know? I mean—

Colasanti: And everybody was just going—

Donna: And everyone . . . [inaudible]

Mack: Yeah. And they wouldn't discuss it at the Cambridge Hospital for several years after that, you know?

Donna: You're kidding?

Mack: We flooded—we overwhelmed them, which was—We learned. I figured, how could they possibly not get excited and interested, because it was so overwhelmingly true, you know? Never mind truth. It's what I can stand that matters.

CHAPTER 21

1. See chapter 19, note 1. Other comments on "The Abduction Syndrome" are in Mack's files.

2. Author's interview with David Gotlib, September 2017.

CHAPTER 22

1. Detailed in Mack's journals.

2. As an exercise for Bly, Mack used his journal to scribble a letter to his dead father to unburden himself of ancient grievances against him and his stepmother, Ruth: "Freud had it all wrong. I battled & was afraid of you as a 3 & 4 y.o. boy, but

not in rivalry but in disappointment. My rage, then, that you, like a playboy in a Fitzgerald film did, Gatsby-like, sport yourself, always the college boy, being neither a full man nor a God. You would let her castrate us all. But I fought   Kenny says proudly it's a miracle I survived." Mack was also enthralled with Bly's "Warrior archetype," as he noted in his journal: "Men are hard-wired to be warriors. Societies which suppress it have war . . . Those who follow spiritual path are warriors; warrior disciplines the psyche; archetype of loyalty—can be carried too far. Warriors have to be disciples of a king . . . True warriors hate heroes; heroes grandstand . . . Hero breaks patterns; warriors hold patterns."

3. Nickerson's story is detailed in chapter 5 of *Abduction*.

4. Puzzlement over this suicide reference, related by Mack to Khalsa in a tape-recorded therapy session on January 8, 1992, prompted me to closely question Mack's cousins Susan Butler and Terry Liebman and finally track down Eleanor's death certificate, which resolved all doubt in favor of peritonitis, even if it failed to explain Mack's statement. See chapter 6, note 3.

5. Author's interview with Vivienne Simon, August 31, 2012.

6. Author's interview with Dominique Callimanopulos, July 22, 2012. Also follow-up interviews through 2019.

CHAPTER 23

1. This chapter is largely based on transcripts of the conference prepared by Pam Kasey and preserved in Mack's files.

2. Author's interview with David Cherniack, September 27, 2017.

CHAPTER 24

1. See chapter 1, note 1.

2. Hopkins, *Witnessed*. On April 25, 2012, Andrea Zarate, a South American correspondent for the *New York Times*, asked Javier Pérez de Cuéllar, then ninety-two, in Lima, Peru, what he knew of Budd Hopkins, Linda Napolitano, and the bodyguards "Richard" and "Dan." After a non sequitur, he said, "I never heard those, those words, those names. I don't know anything." Pressed by Zarate, he said, "Aha," suggesting he understood the questions, and then, "For those things, maybe it's better if you ask my wife," although his wife was not present during the events in question. He then added, "I wouldn't dare or I'm not interested in those events." In any case, Pérez de Cuéllar carried whatever secrets there were to his grave. He died March 4, 2020, at age one hundred.

3. Interviews with Hufford, April 25, 2018, and April 16, 2019.

4. Author's interview with David Pritchard, November 2019.

CHAPTER 25

1. Vallee, *Passport to Magonia*. See also Vallee, *Confrontations*; Vallee's numerous other books; and Clark, *UFO Encyclopedia*. See also chapter 5, note 1.
2. Strieber, *Communion*.
3. Mullis *Dancing Naked in the Mind Field*.
4. Lepselter, *Resonance of Unseen Things*.
5. Author's interview with Susan Lepselter, May 19, 2019.
6. White, *Speaking with Vampires*.
7. Author's interview with Luise White, May 9, 2019.

CHAPTER 26

1. Author's interview with David Pritchard, September 22, 2017.
2. Mack's taped therapy session with Gurucharan Singh Khalsa, June 2, 1992.
3. Mack's taped therapy session with Gurucharan Singh Khalsa, June 2, 1992.
4. Mack's taped therapy session with Gurucharan Singh Khalsa, November 27, 1992.
5. Mack's taped session with Rick Tarnas, March 3, 1993.
6. Mack's taped session with Rick Tarnas, March 3, 1993.
7. Mack would later seek a research contribution from Carter, to no evident avail.

CHAPTER 27

1. Mack's taped interview with Stephen Rae, October 27–28, and December 7, 1993.
2. Mack's taped interview with Jill Neimark, November 2, 1993.

CHAPTER 28

1. An account of the mishap is preserved in Mack's files on his abductees, some of whom were inadvertently named.
2. Letter from "Sheila" to Mack, June 19, 1993.
3. Mack kept tapes of the February 3–4, 1994, media-preparation sessions with his PEER staff and consultant Norie Huddle. See also author's interview with Huddle, March 4, 2018.

CHAPTER 29

1. Clark, *UFO Encyclopedia*.
2. Callimanopulos, Dominique, "Memo to PEER Staff Only, Notes from Brazil," February 20–March 1, 1994, in Mack's files.
3. Mack tape-recorded his extraordinary hour-and-a-half hypnotic regression by Gilda Moura in Brazil on February 24, 1994. See chapter 1, note 2.

CHAPTER 30

1. *New York Times*, March 20, 1994.
2. *Psychology Today*, March 1, 1994.
3. Author's interview with James Willwerth, November 24, 2017. I knew Willwerth from South Vietnam, where we overlapped reporting assignments. He was there for *Time* from April 1970 to May 1971 and I for the *New York Times* from November 1969 to February 1971. Mack retained a tape of the interview with Willwerth dated March 2, 1994.

CHAPTER 31

1. The show was taped in Cambridge and Chicago beginning March 22, 1994, and aired April 18, two days before the publication of *Abduction*.

CHAPTER 32

1. Author interview with Rick Tarnas, November 9, 2017.
2. See chapter 30, note 3.
3. I don't recall crossing paths with Ed Bassett in South Vietnam.
4. Author's interview with Ed and Donna Rice Bassett, January 8, 2018.
5. At a CSICOP skeptics conference in Seattle in June 1994, Mack was blindsided by Bassett, an unannounced speaker. "I faked it," she told the audience. "Women have been doing it for centuries." Afterward, Dominique recalled in a memo for the files, without identifying herself as Mack's associate, Dominique confronted Bassett to ask why she had hoaxed Mack. "Because people were being hurt," Bassett said. Such as whom? Dominique asked. Basset said he had heard about an unidentified person from Mufon. Dominique said thousands of people were hurt and dying all over the world, why focus on Mack? "Because," Bassett said, "that's how Hitler started."
6. Author's interview with Budd Hopkins, December 17, 2010.

CHAPTER 33

1. James Gleick, "The Doctor's Plot," *New Republic*, May 24, 1994.
2. Email from Mack to Will Bueché, July 31, 2004.
3. Mack, unpublished manuscript, "When Worldviews Collide."

CHAPTER 34

1. The day before, July 7, 1994, Mack scribbled three pages of notes he entitled, "Thoughts re 'superstition' of which you're accused." He ended with, "Am I bringing the demonic back in in literal (new) form, thus provoking the wrath of Christians?"

2. From an official transcript of the first day of the proceeding, July 8, 1994, sent by Mack's lawyer Roderick "Eric" MacLeish to co-counsel Daniel P. Sheehan and Mack.

CHAPTER 35

1. Author's interview with David Ingbar, April 9, 2019.

2. Author's interview with Carl Sapers, December 15, 2017.

3. Not all committee sessions were transcribed, but Mack kept his own extensive notes.

4. Mack was furnished an official copy of the committee's interview with Fred Frankel, which took place on July 12, 1994.

5. Committee's interview with Malkah Notman, July 20, 1994.

6. Committee's interview with Joseph Coyle, July 22, 1994.

7. Committee's interview with "Sheila," July 27, 1994; committee's interview with Marcy Nickerson, mother of Randy ("Scott"), August 5, 1994; committee's interview with Randy, August 1, 1994.

8. Committee's interview with Peter Faust, August 18, 1994.

9. Committee's interview with Pam Kasey, August 18, 1994.

10. Committee's interview with George Vaillant, September 8, 1994.

11. Author's interview with Daniel Sheehan, November 19, 2019.

12. Author's interview with Eric MacLeish, September 19, 2012.

13. "Proposed Litigation Plan of Dr. John E. Mack v. Harvard University," memo from Daniel Sheehan to Mack, dated September 1994.

14. Mack, "When Worldviews Collide."

CHAPTER 36

1. Notes of telephone conversation between Tim Leach and Pam Kasey, September 16, 1994, in Mack's files.

2. Transcripts of Leach phone conversations, in Mack's files.

CHAPTER 37

1. Cynthia Hind, "Down in Africa," UFO Times, January/February, 1995.

2. Mack and Dominique traveled to Zimbabwe in late November 1994, stopping in Johannesburg, where they met the Zulu shaman Credo Mutwa. By November 30 they had begun their taped interviews at the Ariel School in Ruwa, Zimbabwe, sessions that continued until December 6. The interview transcripts fill at least 104 pages and, with accompanying video, provide the basis for the accounts in this chapter. Experiencer Randall Nickerson has made a documentary

film of the Ruwa events, *Ariel Phenomenon*, which he generously allowed me to screen.

CHAPTER 38

1. "Draft Report of the Ad Hoc Harvard Medical School Committee," December 16, 1995, in Mack's files.
2. Author's interview with Daniel Sheehan, November 19, 2019.
3. "Committee Draft Report—Response," memo from Mack to Eric MacLeish and Daniel Sheehan, January 4, 1995, in Mack's files.
4. "Strategy Memorandum, John Mack v. Harvard University," memo from Daniel Sheehan to Mack, January 16. 1995, in Mack's files.
5. "Response of John E. Mack, M.D., To Draft Report of Ad Hoc Committee," March 31, 1995, in Mack's files.
6. Final report, from Arnold S. Relman, MD, Chair, Allan M. Brandt, PhD, and Miles F. Shore, MD, to Dean Daniel Tosteson and Dean S. James Adelstein, RE: John E. Mack, MD, June 8, 1995, in Mack's files.
7. Mack, "When Worldviews Collide."
8. Mary Roach, "Probed in Space," *Salon*, July 30, 1999.

CHAPTER 39

1. Author's interview with Roz Zander, July 9, 2019.
2. Dominique Callimanopulos, "Challenges of Cross-Cultural Research," article in Mack's files dated February 1996.
3. Memorial tribute to Mack by Bill Chalker, September 29, 2004.
4. BBC's videotaped interview with Mack, dated only 2000.
5. See Clark, *UFO Encyclopedia*, on Varginha incident.
6. Transcript of Mack's Interview with Kátia, May 13, 1996, in Mack's files.
7. Transcript of John Mack and Gilda Moura on May 23, 2002, in Cambridge, MA. In Mack's files.

CHAPTER 40

1. Newman and Baumeister, "Toward an Explanation."
2. McLeod, Corbisier, and Mack, "A More Parsimonious Explanation."
3. Videotape and transcript, March 7, 1997, in Mack's files.
4. A Chris Lydon program was instrumental in one of Mack's best hires: Will Bueché, a peppy young graphic designer from the Boston suburbs with family roots going back to the French Revolution, who had had some strange experiences growing up that he couldn't put a name to. Haunted by the alien cover of Whitley

Strieber's *Communion*, he ended up building an admiring fan's website, "Beyond Communion." In the process, Bueché had come across a 1996 WBUR radio dialog of Mack and Lydon and began transcribing it. Having trouble spelling some names, he researched them online, came across PEER, and ended up emailing them his transcript. As it happened, PEER's transcriber of experiencer audiotapes was retiring, and the job was open. At age thirty-one, Will Bueché was at the right place at the right time, tapped as Mack's chief archivist and media adviser. He would eventually reorganize and digitize Mack's voluminous files.

5. Audiotape and partial transcript, April 29, 1997, in Mack's files.

6. According to Karen Wesolowski's later notes on the April 30, 1997, meeting with Rockefeller, "LR was quite inspired by Karin's talk the night before; asked her for a copy of last sentence she said, including the word, 'joy.'"

7. Unsigned typed notes by someone at the meeting, in Mack's Rockefeller files. Laurance's twenty-room penthouse on the fourteenth, fifteenth, and sixteenth floors of the building he owned at 834 Fifth Ave. at 64th Street would, after his death at ninety-four in 2004, sell to Rupert Murdoch for $44 million, the highest price until then for a New York City residence.

CHAPTER 41

1. Mack, "When Worldviews Collide."

2. Mack, "When Worldviews Collide."

3. Mack summarized their objections to Relman's critique in a letter to Budd Hopkins dated October 27, 2000, in Mack, "When Worldviews Collide," appendix B.

CHAPTER 42

1. But he hadn't lost his taste for drama. In May 1998 he and PEER's Roberta Colasanti had staged a "Star Wisdom" Conference at a holistic center in Newtonville, west of Boston. It drew an unusual array of presenters from experiencers like Karin Austin and Peter Faust to astronaut Edgar Mitchell and astrophysicist Rudy Schild, including Indigenous healers and spiritual leaders like Sequoyah Trueblood, an elder of the Choctaw Nation of Oklahoma; Dhyani Ywahoo, Cherokee Chief of the Green Mountain Aniyunwiwa Band of the Tsalagi Nation of Vermont and director of a Buddhist Dharma center; and Bernardo Peixoto, a Brazilian shaman also known as Ipupiara or "Fresh Water Dolphin" from the Amazon rainforest tribe of Ureu-eu-wau-wau, the People of the Stars. Cartoonist Roz Chast poked fun at them in a comic strip called "Aliens, Ahoy!" that showed Mack peering over his spectacles and Mitchell in his moon suit.

2. See note to book epigraph.

CHAPTER 43

1. Mack's taped phone call with Shirley MacLaine, February 18, 2001, in Mack's files.

2. Mack's other favorite lines from Rilke are from "Letters to a Young Poet," when Rilke gives advice to Army recruit Franz Kappus, written August 12, 1904:

> We must accept our reality as vastly as we possibly can; everything, even the unprecedented, must be possible within it. This is in the end the only kind of courage that is required of us: the courage to face the strangest, most unusual, most inexplicable experiences that can meet us. The fact that people have in this sense been cowardly has done infinite harm to life; the experiences that are called apparitions, the whole so-called "spirit world," death, all these Things that are so closely related to us, have through our daily defensiveness been so entirely pushed out of life that the senses with which we might have been able to grasp them have atrophied. To say nothing of God.

3. As late as September 20, 2004—a week before his death—Mack was emailing his agent Tim Seldes the book proposal, with the poignant note: "There is a bit of urgency about this, as there are several people I want to send this to (not with regard to publication) who have a special interest in being helpful." Mack never completed the book.

CHAPTER 44

1. Mack family videotape of Ruth's memorial at Terrace in the Sky, March 3, 2003.

2. Barbara Lamb also told me the story at Anne Cuvelier's annual Newport experiencer retreat, July 16, 2012.

3. I also ordered a small piece of moldavite, which my wife put in a box in her dresser drawer. So far, several years later, it has stayed put.

4. Author's interview with Shawn Randall, March 14, 2018.

5. Author's interview with Karin Austin, March 17, 2018. Shortly before the crop-circle trip in 2004, Austin had sent Mack an article about the "Enigma of Namibia's 'fairy circles.'" He responded on April 2: "Ah, so its fairy circles now, is it?"

6. Author's interview with Leslie Hansen in Newport, July 16, 2012.

7. Author's interview with "Nona," July 16, 2012.

8. Author's interview with Randall Nickerson, January 11, 2011.

CHAPTER 45

1. Maria Talcott, "Dancing with the Other Side: Conversations with Dr. John E. Mack—here and in the hereafter," draft, July 28, 2013.

2. Talcott, "Dancing with the Other Side."

3. Meetings on the new John E. Mack Institute were often contentious. "This is a tough ship to keep off the rocks, as the crew is unevenly skilled, the skipper is a bit old for on line command, and the purser has to function as the first mate," Mack emailed Dominique on July 1, 2004. The last reference was obviously to her.

4. Author's interview with Wesley Boyd, March 10, 2018. Also, reminiscences written up by Boyd for Mack's memorial tributes, 2004.

CHAPTER 46

1. Emails from Malcolm Brown and other members of the British T. E. Lawrence Society, in Mack's files.

2. In an email dated September 22, 2004, Mack told a friend he would be meeting with Keen (Montague's "lovely Irish wife") "tomorrow morning in London"— September 23. Mack said Keen was already receiving "many communications from Monty" beyond the grave, including a reminder for Mack to wear a tie for lunch at the Farmer's Club.

3. "My husband Montague Keen has materialized many times," Veronica Keen told me in an email dated September 9, 2012. She also related one unnerving incident: On their way to lunch at the Farmer's Club, hosting Britain's agrarians since 1842, Keen had parked the car and was walking away when she looked back at Mack and imagined she saw him turn into her dead husband. She gaped, and then he turned into Mack again.

4. The accident narrative is based on official London police documents and court records, including the nine-page "Record of Interview" of Raymond Czechowski, November 16, 2004; the twenty-four-page Solicitors Report by William Latimer-Sayer and Irwin Mitchell, representing the Claimants (Danny and Tony Mack, executors of John Mack) against Defendant Czechowski, January 24, 2006; and various witness statements, all in the Mack family's possession.

5. Email from Jane Katra, step-mother of Elisabeth Targ, to Dominique Callimanopulos, October 1, 2004.

6. Email from Veronica Keen to author, September 8, 2012.

7. Email from Veronica Keen to author, September 8, 2012.

8. Author's interview with Roz Zander, July 9, 2019.

9. Videotape of the funeral service on October 13, 2004, taken on Veronica Keen's camera, 1 hour, 3 minutes. The video was taken at Hendon Cemetery and Crematorium, going back to 1899 in the London Borough of Barnet, not far from where Mack was run down on September 27.

CHAPTER 47

1. The Mack family's videotape of November 13, 2004, Harvard memorial service, 1 hour, 54 minutes. Also, a transcript of the eulogies.

2. Letter from Daniel, Kenneth, Tony, and Sally Mack, "To the Presiding Judge of the Wood Green Crown Court," September 30, 2005.

3. Asking for Aliya's hand had not been an easy process, Ken had informed his family. In olden times when Kazakhs were nomads living in yurts on the west Asia steppe, the male relatives of a boy would meet the male relatives of a girl and arrange their marriage, the couple often never having met. Today, the boy, accompanied by his father or other respectable male relatives, was expected to visit the girl's father to seek his permission. But Ken had had no one to go with. Still, he had dressed, as advised, in a jacket and tie and presented himself to Aliya's family, mostly relatives of her father, a prominent attorney by the name of Maidan Suleimenov, as much of her mother's family had died of starvation under Stalin. At the head of the table sat Maidan's uncle Atpai, a man in his eighties and a passionate communist and World War II hero who had survived a German bullet only because he was carrying, in his breast pocket, a sheaf of love letters from his wife-to-be—a Kazakh museum had them on display, Ken was assured. There was a deep silence at the table. Ken finally realized he was expected to speak first when one of the senior relatives declared, "Let us hear the voice of Kenneth Mack; let us hear him state his intentions; say why you have come here." Ken froze. Was he supposed to announce he was there to seek Aliya's hand, or was that assumed? Was he supposed to recite his bio? He fudged it, falteringly asking for permission and telling about himself. Then he turned to Aliya's father and asked, "What should I say?" Maidan approved. "That's fine," he said. "That's enough, you've said what's most important." Whereupon the other relatives, in a mixture of Kazakh and Russian, agreed. Aliya's great-aunt Raficah, blind and in her eighties, declared that Kenneth was brave to have come alone. Others said that if Aliya had decided to marry him, then they all approved, because she was a wise young woman with good judgment and who were they to stand in the way of love? And so it was done.

EPILOGUE

1. Author's interview with Barbara Lamb, March 16, 2018.

2. Author's interview with Shawn Randall, March 14, 2018.

3. Author's interview with Barbara Lamb, March 16, 2018.

4. Andrew Beath's interview with John Mack, July 2001.

5. Author's interview with Will Maney, March 18, 2018.

6. Author's interview with Roberta Colasanti, March 16, 2018.

1. *New York Times*, April 10, 2019. A year later, on May 14, 2020, the *Times* published a radio telescope image of X-shaped jets from a monster black hole in a galaxy even farther away, PKS 2014-55 in the constellation Telescopium, about 800 million light years from earth.

2. *New York Times*, December 21, 2018.

BIBLIOGRAPHY

Alexander, Eban. *Proof of Heaven: A Neurosurgeon's Journey in the Afterlife*. New York: Simon & Schuster, 2012.

Alexander, John B. *UFOs: Myths, Conspiracies, and Realities*. New York: Thomas Dunne Books, 2011.

Anglin, Amy. *Experience: Memoirs of an Abducted Childhood*. Telluride, CO: Sacred Peak Press, 2014.

Bader, Christopher D., F. Carson Mencken, and Joseph O. Baker. *Paranormal America: Ghost Encounters, UFO Sightings, Bigfoot Hunts, and Other Curiosities in Religion and Culture*. New York: New York University Press, 2010.

Baigent, Michael, Richard Leigh, and Henry Lincoln. *The Holy Blood and the Holy Grail*. London: Jonathan Cape, 1982.

Bassuk, Ellen L., ed. *The Doctor-Activist: Physicians Fighting for Social Change*. New York: Plenum Press, 1996.

Berliner, Don, with Marie Galbraith and Antonio Huneeus. *UFO Briefing Document: The Best Available Evidence*. New York: Dell, 1995.

Braud, William. *Distant Mental Influence: Its Contributions to Science, Healing, and Human Interactions*. Charlottesville, NC: Hampton Roads Publishing Company, 2003.

Brewer, Jack. *The Greys Have Been Framed: Exploitation in the UFO Community*. Middletown, DE: CreateSpace, 2016.

Bryan, C. D. B. *Close Encounters of the Fourth Kind: A Reporter's Notebook on Alien Abduction, UFOs, and the Conference at M.I.T.* New York: Alfred A. Knopf, 1995.

Bullard, Thomas E. *The Myth and Mystery of UFOs*. Lawrence: University Press of Kansas, 2010.

Caldicott, Helen. *A Desperate Passion: An Autobiography*. New York: W. W. Norton & Company, 1997.

Campbell, Joseph. *The Hero With A Thousand Faces*. Princeton: Princeton University Press, 1949.

Chalker, Bill. *Hair of the Alien: DNA and Other Forensic Evidence of Alien Abduction*. New York: Paraview Pocket Books, 2005.

Clancy, Susan A. *Abducted: How People Come to Believe They Were Kidnapped by Aliens*. Cambridge: Harvard University Press, 2005.

Clark, Jerome. *UFO Encounters & Beyond*. New York: Signet, 1993.

———. *The UFO Encyclopedia: The Phenomenon From the Beginning*. 2 vols. Detroit, MI: Omnigraphics, 2018.

Corso, Col. Philip J. *The Day After Roswell*. New York: Pocket Books, 1997.

Costa, Cheryl. *The UFO Beat: The New York Skies Column July 2013 to June 2019*. Syracuse: Dragon Lady Media, 2020.

Costa, Cheryl, and Linda Miller Costa. *UFO Sightings Desk Reference: United States of America 2001–2015*. Syracuse: Dragon Lady Media, 2017.

Dolan, Richard M. *UFOs & the National Security State: The Cover-up Exposed 1973–1991*. Rochester: Keyhole Publishing Company, 2009.

Druffel, Ann. *Firestorm: Dr. James E. McDonald's Fight for UFO Science*. Columbus, NC: Wild Flower Press, 2003.

Einzig, Judy. "Do You Believe in God?" 2008.

Fort, Charles. *The Books of Charles Fort*. New York: Henry Holt and Company, 1941.

Fowler, Raymond E. *The Allagash Abductions: Undeniable Evidence of Alien Intervention*. Tigard, OR: Wild Flower Press, 1993.

———. *The Andreasson Affair: The Documented Investigation of a Woman's Abduction Aboard a UFO*. Englewood Cliffs: Prentice-Hall Inc., 1979.

Friedman, Stanton T. *Flying Saucers and Science: A Scientist Investigates the Mysteries of UFOs: Interstellar Travel, Crashes, and Government Cover-Ups*. Pompton Plains, NJ: New Page Books, 2008.

———. *Top Secret/Majic: Operation Majestic-12 and the United States Government's UFO Cover-up*. Philadelphia: Da Capo Press, 1996.

Friedman, Stanton T., and Kathleen Marden. *Captured! The Betty and Barney Hill UFO Experience*. Franklin Lakes, NJ: New Page Books, 2007.

Fuller, John G. *The Ghost of Flight 401*. New York: Berkley Publishing Corporation, 1976.

———. *Incident at Exeter: Unidentified Flying Objects Over America Now*. New York: G. P. Putnam's Sons, 1966.

———. *Incident at Exeter, The Interrupted Journey: Two Landmark Investigations of UFO Encounters Together in One Volume*. New York: MJF Books, 1966.

Graham, Robbie, editor. *UFOs: Reframing the Debate*. Hove, UK: White Crow Books, 2017.

Greene, Brian. *The Elegant Universe: Superstrings, Hidden Dimensions, and the Quest for the Ultimate Theory*. New York: W. W. Norton, 1999.

———. *The Hidden Reality: Parallel Universes and the Deep Laws of the Cosmos*. New York: Alfred A. Knopf, 2011.

Grof, Stanislav, and Christina Grof, eds. *Spiritual Emergency: When Personal Transformation Becomes a Crisis.* New York: Jeremy P. Tarcher/Putnam, 1989.

Hansen, Terry. *The Missing Times: News Media Complicity in the UFO Cover-up.* Xlibris Corporation, 2000.

Hastings, Robert. *UFOs and Nukes: Extraordinary Encounters at Nuclear Weapons Sites.* Bloomington: AuthorHouse, 2008.

Hill, Paul. *Unconventional Flying Objects: A Scientific Analysis.* Charlottesville: Hampton Roads Publishing Company, 1995.

Holt, Jim. *Why Does the World Exist? An Existential Detective Story.* New York: Liveright Publishing Corporation, 2012.

Hopkins, Budd. *Art, Life and UFOs: A Memoir.* San Antonio and New York: Anomalist Books, 2009.

——. *Intruders: The Incredible Visitations at Copley Woods.* New York: Random House, 1987.

——. *Missing Time: A Documented Study of UFO Abductions.* New York: Richard Marek Publishers, 1981.

——. *Witnessed: The True Story of the Brooklyn Bridge UFO Abductions.* New York: Pocket Books, 1996.

Hufford, David J. *The Terror That Comes in the Night: An Experience-Centered Study of Supernatural Assault Traditions.* Philadelphia: University of Pennsylvania Press, 1982.

Hynek, Allen J., Philip J. Imbrogno, and Bob Pratt. *Night Siege: The Hudson Valley UFO Sightings.* St. Paul: Llewellyn Publications, 1998.

Jacobs, David M. *Secret Life: Firsthand Documented Accounts of UFO Abductions.* New York: Fireside Books, 1992.

——. *The Threat: Revealing the Secret UFO Agenda.* New York: Fireside Books, 1998.

——. *The UFO Controversy in America.* New York: Signet, 1975.

——, ed. *UFOs and Abductions: Challenging the Borders of Knowledge.* Lawrence: University Press of Kansas, 2000.

——. *Walking Among Us: The Alien Plan to Control Humanity.* San Francisco: Disinformation Books, 2015.

Jacobsen, Annie. *Area 51: An Uncensored History of America's Top Secret Military Base.* New York: Little, Brown and Company, 2011.

——. *Phenomena: The Secret History of the U.S. Government's Investigation into Extrasensory Perception and Psychokinesis.* New York: Little, Brown and Company, 2017.

Jahn, Robert G., and Brenda J. Dunne. *Consciousness and the Source of Reality: The PEAR Odyssey.* Princeton: ICRL Press, 2011.

Kean, Leslie. *Surviving Death: A Journalist Investigates Evidence for an Afterlife.* New York: Crown Archetype, 2017.

——. *UFOs: Generals, Pilots and Government Officials Go On the Record.* New York: Harmony Books, 2010.

Keel, John A. *Operation Trojan Horse.* San Antonio and Charlottesville: Anomalist Books, 1970, 1996, 2013.

Keyhoe, Donald E. *The Flying Saucers Are Real.* New York: Fawcett Publications, 1950.

——. *Flying with Lindbergh.* New York: Grosset & Dunlap, 1928.

Krauss, Lawrence M. *A Universe From Nothing: Why There is Something Rather than Nothing.* New York: Free Press, 2012.

Kripal, Jeffrey J. *Authors of the Impossible: The Paranormal and the Sacred.* Chicago and London: University of Chicago Press, 2010.

——. *Esalen: America and the Religion of No Religion.* Chicago and London: University of Chicago Press, 2007.

——. *Secret Body: Erotic and Esoteric Currents in the History of Religion.* Chicago and London: University of Chicago Press, 2017.

Lawson, Alvin H. "Hypnosis of Imaginary CE3 Abductees: History, Transcripts and Analysis." Internet Archaeology, accessed August 9, 2016. www.internet archaeology.org/6521/SA1.html.

Leininger, Bruce, and Andrea Leininger. *Soul Survivor: The Reincarnation of a World War II Fighter Pilot.* New York and Boston: Grand Central Publishing, 2009.

Lepselter, Susan. *The Resonance of Unseen Things: Poetics, Power, Captivity, and UFOs in the American Uncanny.* Ann Arbor: University of Michigan Press, 2016.

Lown, Bernard. *Prescription for Survival: A Doctor's Journey to End Nuclear Madness.* San Francisco: Berrett-Koehler Publishers, 2008.

Mack, John E. *Abduction: Human Encounters with Aliens.* New York: Charles Scribner's Sons, 1994.

——. *Borderline States in Psychiatry.* New York: Grune & Stratton, 1975.

——. *Nightmares and Human Conflict.* New York: Columbia University Press, 1989.

——. *Passport to the Cosmos: Human Transformation and Alien Encounters.* New York: Three Rivers Press, 1999.

——. *A Prince of Our Disorder: The Life of T. E. Lawrence.* Boston and Toronto: Little, Brown and Company, 1976.

Mack, John E., and Holly Hickler. *Vivienne: The Life and Suicide of an Adolescent Girl.* New York: Little, Brown and Company, 1981.

Mack, John E., with Rita S. Rogers. *The Alchemy of Survival: One Woman's Journey*. New York: Addison-Wesley Publishing Company, 1988.

Mack, Ruth P. *Planning on Uncertainty: Decision Making in Business and Government Administration*. New York: Wiley-Interscience, 1971.

Marsh, Roger, ed. *UFO Cases of Interest, 2018 Edition*. Mufon, 2018.

———, ed. *UFO Cases of Interest, 2019 Edition*. Mufon, 2019.

McLeod, Caroline, Barbara Corbisier, and John Mack. "A More Parsimonious Explanation for UFO Abduction." *Psychological Inquiry* 7, no. 2 (1996), 156-68.

Menzel, Donald H. *Flying Saucers: A Great Astronomer Explains the Facts*. Cambridge: Harvard University Press, 1953.

Michel, Aimé. *Flying Saucers and the Straight-Line Mystery*. New York: Criterion Books, 1958.

Mitchell, Edgar. *The Way of the Explorer: An Apollo Astronaut's Journey Through the Material and Mystical Worlds*. New York: G. P. Putnam's Sons, 1996.

Monroe, Robert A. *Journeys Out of the Body*. New York: Doubleday, 1971.

Mullis, Kary. *Dancing Naked in the Mind Field*. New York: Pantheon Books, 1988.

Newman, Leonard S., and Roy F. Baumeister. "Toward an Explanation of the UFO Abduction Phenomenon: Hypnotic Elaboration, Extraterrestrial Sadomasochism, and Spurious Memories." *Psychological Inquiry* 7, no. 2 (1996): 99-126.

Overbye, Dennis. *Darkness Visible, Finally: Astronomers Capture First Ever Image of a Black Hole*. New York: *The New York Times*, April 10, 2019.

———. "A Black Hole's Boomerangs." *New York Times*, May 14, 2020.

———. *It's Intermission for the Large Hadron Collider*. New York: *The New York Times* December 21, 2018.

Pasulka, D. W. *American Cosmic: UFOs, Religion, Technology: Poetics, Power, Captivity, and UFOs in the American Uncanny*. New York: Oxford University Press, 2016.

Pfeiffer, Trish, and John E. Mack, eds. *Mind Before Matter: Visions of a New Science of Consciousness*. Winchester, UK, and Washington, DC: O Books, 2007.

Pilkington, Mark. *Mirage Men: An Adventure into Paranoia, Espionage, Psychological Warfare, and UFOs*. New York: Skyhorse Publishing, 2010.

Pritchard, Andrea, David E. Pritchard, John E. Mack, Pam Kasey, and Claudia Yapp, eds. *Alien Discussions: Proceedings of the Abduction Study Conference Held at M.I.T., Cambridge, MA*. Cambridge: North Cambridge Press, 1994.

Randle, Kevin, and Russ Estes. *Faces of the Visitors: An Illustrated Reference to Alien Contact*. New York: Fireside Books, 1997.

Ring, Kenneth. *The Omega Project: Near-Death Experiences, UFO Encounters, and Mind at Large*. New York: William Morrow and Company, 1999.

Roach, Mary. *Spook: Science Tackles the Afterlife*. New York: W. W. Norton & Company, 2005.

Robinson, Elizabeth. *There Are No Goodbyes: Guidance and Comfort From Those Who Have Passed*. Carlsbad, CA: Hay House, 2017.

Roll, William, and Valerie Storey. *Unleashed: Of Poltergeists and Murder: The Curious Story of Tina Resch*. New York: Paraview Pocket Books, 2004.

Sheehan, Daniel. *The People's Advocate: The Life and Legal History of America's Most Fearless Public Interest Lawyer*. Berkeley: Counterpoint, 2013.

Sheldrake, Rupert. *Dogs That Know When Their Owners are Coming Home And Other Unexplained Powers of Animals*. New York: Crown, 1999.

Shermer, Michael. *Why People Believe Weird Things: Pseudoscience, Superstition, and Other Confusions of Our Time*. New York: W. H. Freeman and Company, 1997.

Skinner, Cornelia Otis, and Emily Kimbrough. *Our Hearts Were Young and Gay*. New York: Dodd, Mead & Company, 1942.

Smith, Susy. *ESP*. New York: Pyramid Publications, 1962.

Solomon, Grant, and Jane Solomon. *The Scole Experiment: Scientific Evidence for Life After Death*. Waltham Abbey, UK: Campion Books, 1999.

Strassman, Rick. *DMT: The Spirit Molecule: A Doctor's Revolutionary Research into the Biology of Near-Death and Mystical Experiences*. Rochester, VT: Park Street Press, 2001.

Strieber, Whitley. *Communion: A True Story*. New York: Beech Tree Books, 1987.

———. *A New World*. San Antonio: Walker & Collier, 2019.

Strieber, Whitney, and Jeffrey J. Kripal. *The Super Natural: A New Vision of the Unexplained*. New York: Jeremy P. Tarcher, 2016.

Sturrock, Peter A. *The UFO Enigma*. New York: Warner Books, 1999.

Sylvia, Claire. *A Change of Heart: A Memoir*. New York: Warner Books, 1997.

Targ, Russell. *Do You See What I See? Lasers and Love, ESP and the CIA, and the Meaning of Life*. Charlottesville: Hampton Roads Publishing Company, 2008.

———. *The Reality of ESP: A Physicist's Proof of Psychic Abilities*. Wheaton and Chennai: Quest Books, 2012.

Tarnas, Richard. *The Passion of the Western Mind: Understanding the Ideas that Have Shaped Our World View*. New York: Harmony Books, 1991.

Taylor, Eugene. *William James on Exceptional Mental States: The 1896 Lowell Lectures*. New York: Charles Scribner's Sons, 1982.

Tomkins, Peter, and Christopher Bird. *The Secret Life of Plants*. New York: Harper & Row, 1973.

Vallee, Jacques. *Anatomy of a Phenomenon*. New York: Ace Books, 1965.

——. *Confrontations: A Scientist's Search for Alien Contact.* New York: Ballantine Books, 1990.

——. *Passport to Magonia: From Folklore to Flying Saucers.* Chicago: Henry Regnery Company, 1969.

Vallee, Jacques, and Chris Aubeck. *Wonders in the Sky: Unexplained Aerial Objects From Antiquity to Modern Times and Their Impact on Human Culture, History, and Beliefs.* New York: Jeremy P. Tarcher, 2009.

Watts, Alan. *The Joyous Cosmology: Adventures in the Chemistry of Consciousness.* New York: Pantheon, 1962.

Weisberg, Barbara. *Talking to the Dead: Kate and Margaret Fox and the Rise of Spiritualism.* New York: HarperSanFrancisco, 2004.

White, Luise. *Speaking with Vampires: Rumor and History in Colonial Africa.* Berkeley, Los Angeles, and London: University of California Press, 2000.

INDEX

aliens *(continued)*
  Experience, I, L; dreams of, 87;
  environmentalism and, 242–43;
  ethics and, 212–15; exams by, 59–62,
  143–44; experiencers of, 204; at
  Harvard, 119–24; humanity and,
  90–91, 107–8, 117–18, 234–35, 244–45;
  Intelligent Life in the Universe, 101;
  narratives of, 151–57; Newport Alien
  Festival, 258–60; physiognomy
  of, 136; for popular culture, 255;
  psychology of, 214–15; purpose for,
  123; reproduction with, 107, 114–15,
  156, 182; teleportation by, 145–46;
  UFOs and, 13, 14, 109–18, 279–84;
  witness testimony of, 20, 206–15
The Allagash Abductions (Fowler), 259
Alpert, Richard, 82–83
amnesia, 55, 58, 110, 142
Anderson, Walter Truett, 81
Andrade Xavier, Kátia, 229–30
Andresen, Jeffry, 12
Andrus, Walter H., 125
Anglin, Amy, 104–5, 189
anomalous experiences, 12–14, 13
Arabs. *See* Middle East
Arafat, Yasir, 2, 66–67, 202, 291n4
Arbatov, Georgi, 74–75
Ariel Phenomenon (documentary),
  286
The Armada (Mattingly), 49
Arnold, Kenneth, 15–16, 18–19
ARPANET. *See* Advanced Research
  Projects Network
artifacts, from aliens, 21, 100–101
Ash, David, 206–7
astral travels, 1, 51, 159
astronauts, 174, 235–36
astronomy, 21, 24, 30
Atlantis, 137, 246
Atomic Energy Commission, 25

Aub, Della, 27
Aub, Joseph, 27, 35
Austin, Karin, 31, 235–36, 238, 269,
  273–74, 285; collaboration with,
  255; in public, 300n1; as roommate,
  249; support from, 242–44; travels
  with, 258
Australia, 73, 142, 153, 228–31
ayahuasca, 129–30, 229, 231
Ayers, James, 286

Bachmeier, James F., 24
Baez, Joan, 81
Balducci, Monsignor, 255
Barton, Bruce, 28
Bass, Ellen, 111
Bassett, Donna, 180, 186–91, 297n5
Bassuk, Ellen L., 290n1
Baum, L. Frank, 31
Baumeister, Roy F., 232–33
Baylor, H. W., 17
Beath, Andrew, 263, 276–77, 288n2
The Beatles, 72, 82, 88
Begin, Menachem, 64–66
behavioral science, 5
benevolence, 34
Ben-Gurion, David, 64
Bequette, Bill, 16
Bershad, Michael, 93–94
Bertrand, Eugene, 53
Bey, Hajim, 46
Bhajan, Yogi, 10
Big Bang theory, 30
Bigelow, Robert, 144
Bigfoot, 6, 147
black holes, 280, 304n1
Blanchard, William H., 19–20
Bloecher, Ted, 93–94
Blumenthal, Deborah, 286
Blumenthal, Michael, 32, 249, 273
Bly, Robert, 128–29, 294n2

children: for Bullard, 147-48; childhood trauma, 27, 31-32, 37, 87, 203-4, 235; family and, 68-69; narratives from, 125-26, 210-15; nightmares of, 39, 103; parents and, 43-44; religion for, 76

Chiten, Laurel, 255

Churchill, Winston, 46, 65

CIA. *See* Central Intelligence Agency

Civil Air Patrol, 30

civil disobedience, 78

Civilian Flying Saucer Investigators, 23

civil rights, 53-54

Clamar, Aphrodite, 93-94

Clark, Jerome, 17-18, 21, 103, 151, 286, 289n1

Clinton, Bill, 236, 262

Clinton, Hillary, 43, 262

Close Encounters of the Fourth Kind (Bryan), 140

Close Encounters of the Third Kind (film), 117, 151

Clouser, K. Danner, 222-23

Cocteau, Jean, 26

Colasanti, Roberta, 225, 277-78, 300n1, K; for PEER, 192; support from, 222, 293n3

Cold War, 8, 25, 75, 79

Coles, Robert, 70

colleagues, 2-3, 31-32, 36-37, 105, 118-19, 124, 135, 164, 166, 177, 238, 255, 266, 269, 272

collective disorders, 3

Collodi, Carlo, 31

Comings, Mark, 250-52

Committee for the Scientific Investigation of Claims of the Paranormal (CSICOP), 147, 191, 239, 297n5

communication, 58-60, 62, 114, 266-67

Communion (Strieber), 20, 152-53, 155, 228, 299n4

Community Mental Health Act, 41

conclusions, 10, 25

conferences: abduction, 1-2, 27, 200-201; "Alien Discussions," 140-50; on crop-circles, 275; experiencers at, 234; at Harvard, 64; Newport Alien Festival, 258-59; Sagan at, 148; in Soviet Union, 75; on UFOs, 255-56

consciousness, 37

contactees, 51

conventional rationality, 27

Conway, Stuart, 286

Cooper, Maria, 263

Cooper, Peter, 50

Corbisier, Barbara, 233

cosmology, 101-2

Cosmos (TV show), 102

courage, 2, 111, 120, 220, 254, 262, 277, 300n2

The Courage to Heal (Bass/Davis), 111

Coyle, Joseph, 201

crashed aircraft, 15

credibility: abduction and, 218-19; for Air Force, 21; of evidence, 198-99; of hypnosis, 55, 186; of informants, 10; of Mack, J., 195-99; of narratives, 18; professionalism and, 3-4, 216-18; research and, 119-24, 239-40; with science, 125-26; of sightings, 279-84; skeptics and, 25-26, 92-93, 200-205; UFOs and, 56-63, 209; of witness testimony, 54-55

Crenna, Richard, 127, 157

critics, 10-11, 191-94, 200-201, 223-24

Cronkite, Walter, 64-65

Crookes, William, 241, 287

crop circles, 241, 256-58, 275

Crop Circles Revealed (Lamb), 256

CSICOP. *See* Committee for the Scientific Investigation of Claims of the Paranormal

Cultural Source Hypothesis, 7
curiosity, 27, 121
Cuvelier, Anne, 19, 258–59
Czechoslovakia, 87, 97–98
Czechowski, Raymond, 267–68, 272–73, 302n4
Czech Republic, 257

Dalai Lama, 2, 129, 135–39, 255, 283
Dale, Margaret L., 193
Dancing Naked in the Mind Field (Mullis), 155
Dass, Ram, 82–83
Davidson, William D., 64–65
Davis, Laura, 111
Dean, Gordon, 25
Dean, Gwen L., 142
death, 245, 268–71, 302n4
Death in Life (Lifton, R.), 73
debunkers, 6, 52, 168, 186, 216
Defense Department UFO unit, 280–81
Dershowitz, Alan M., 225, 255
The Development and Sustenance of Self-Esteem in Childhood (anthology), 76
Dewey, John, 34
Diablo Canyon nuclear plant, 74
A Dialogue on the Alien Abduction Experience (Lydon), I, L, 234
Dick, Philip K., 152, 283
Dickens, Charles, 267
dimethyltryptamine (DMT), 83, 129–30
diplomacy, 42, 65, 73–80, 84
DMT. *See* dimethyltryptamine
The Doctor-Activist (Bassuk), 290n1
"The Doctor's Plot" (Gleick), 191
Donderi, Don, 148
Doolittle, Jimmy, 19
The Dragons of Eden (Sagan), 101
"Dream of Reality" (Loomis, V.), 69–70

dreams, 43, 77, 84, 87, 96, 103, 123, 131, 136, 191, 228, 266, 277
Druyan, Ann, 75, 77
Dunlap, George, 17
Dystel, Jane, 255
Dzangare, Praxedes, 207

Eastman, George, 1
Eastman Laboratories, 1
Ebb, Fred, 35
EBE film award. *See* Extraterrestrial Biological Entity film award
Egypt, 46, 64–66, 291n2
Einstein, Albert, 16, 147, 167, 242, 280
Einzig, Judy, 42
Der Eisenhans (Grimm Brothers), 128
Elisabeth and Mark Before and After Death (Mack, J./Comings), 252
Ellsberg, Daniel, 77, 97–99, 129, 202
Emerson, Ralph Waldo, 34, 259
England, 44–45, 49, 263–64, 267–70.
    See also specific topics
environmentalism, 115–16, 121, 133, 242–43
Erhard, Ludwig, 71
Erhard, Werner, 71–72, 76, 79–80, 88, 164, 191, 247–48
Erhard Seminars Training (EST), 71–72, 164
Erikson, Erik H., D, 69, 74, 77–78, 195
Esalen encampment, 81–85, 89, 191
EST. *See* Erhard Seminars Training
ET (film), 117
Ethical Culture School, 28
ethics, 209, 211–12
ethnoreligious culture, 27
European Center for Nuclear Research (CERN), 279–80
Evans, Max, 286
event phenomenon, 18, 34, 103, 135–39, 147–48, 217

evidence: for abduction, 141; anecdotal, 148; conclusions and, 10; credibility of, 198–99; of flying saucers, 26; from hypnosis, 136–37, 200–201; for Mack, J., 181–82; memories and, 218–19; from photographs, 116, 120; in science, 222–23; skeptics and, 157, 217; technology and, 279–80, 304n1
evil, 4, 7, 37, 43, 47, 74, 137, 212, 234, 248
Exon, Arthur, 20
experiencers, 113, 204, 234. *See also specific topics*
experiments, 8, 25, 105–6, 156, 250, 278
extraterrestrials. *See* aliens

Faisal (king), 46, 48
false memories, 110, 112, 232
family, 27–33, 261, 285; children and, 68–72; death for, 302n4; for Mack, S., 78–79, 88; psychology of, 132; support of, 166
Fantástico (TV show), 229–30
Faraday, Michael, 242
Fátima Silva, Liliane, 229–30
Fátima Silva, Valquíria, 229–30
Faust, Peter, 136–37, 168, 238, 255, 300n1; Nickerson, R., and, 182–83, 185; for popular culture, 181; support of, 201–2
FBI. *See* Federal Bureau of Investigation
fear, 48, 79, 110, 115, 120, 122, 129, 130, 132, 152, 173–75, 193, 210, 230, 236, 243, 247, 260, 276–777
Federal Bureau of Investigation (FBI), 16, 52, 162
Felony, Lawrence, 42
Feynman, Richard, 191
Fish, Marjorie, 63
flashbacks, 104–5

The Flying Saucer Conspiracy (Keyhoe), 58
flying saucers, 15–16; for Air Force, 23; evidence of, 26; flying disc, 19–20; *Flying Saucer Review*, 95; "The Flying Saucers are Real," 21–22; sounds of, 17, 20
Flying Saucers (Menzel), 26
Flying Saucers and the Straight-Line Mystery (Michel), 26
folklore, 5–6, 16–17, 55, 137–38
Foltz, Charlie, 259
Forrestal, James, 19
Fort, Charles, 18
Fowler, Raymond E., 53, 259
France, 26, 49
Frank, Anne, 69, 98
Frankel, Fred H., 169, 200–201
Franklin, Eileen, 111–12
Franklin, George, Sr., 111–12
Franklin, Girard, 93–94
Freud, Sigmund, 37, 43, 82, 84, 98, 282–83, 294n2
Friedman, Leon, 146, 282
Friedman, Stanton, 54, 61, 230
Friendly Fire (Bryan), 140
FUFOR. *See* Fund for UFO Research
Fuller, John Grant, 254; *Interrupted Journey* by, 54, 56–63, 95; narratives for, 52–55
Fund for UFO Research (FUFOR), 94

Gale, Robert Peter, 84
Gallagher, Buell G., 50
Garfield, James A., 29
Gawande, Atul, 37
Germany, 27, 46–47, 257, 279
Gestalt Therapy, 72, 82
ghosts, 6–7, 142, 147
Gibson, William, 97

GIM. *See* Guided Imagery and Music
Gimbel, Lee, 30-31
Gimbel, Mary Lee, 31
Gimbel, Ruth Allegra Prince, 30-31, 253, 282
Gleick, James, 191
The Godfather (Puzo), 249
Goldberg, Harvey, 35, 79
Goldwater, Barry M., 21, 289n1
Gomes, J., 272, 274
Gorbachev, Mikhail, 13
Gordon, Charles George, 50
Gotlib, David A., 126-27, 135-36
government, 20, 49, 85, 89, 109, 116, 137, 170, 187, 202, 205, 207, 230, 262, 280-81
GRAA. *See* Group for Research and Aid to Abductees
Granchi, Irene, 172, 175
Great Depression, 29-31
Greenberg, Dan, 71
Griffin, David Ray, 254
Grimm Brothers, 128
Grinspoon, Lester, 35, 77, 100-102
Grof, Christina, 8, 83
Grof, Stanislav, 8, 82-90, 129, 160, 178, 229, 261-62, 284; influence of, 105-8; reputation of, 197; *Spiritual Emergency* by, 89
Group for Research and Aid to Abductees (GRAA), 189, 196, 218
Guided Imagery and Music (GIM), 83
Gurewich, Victor, 270
Gutfreund, John, 35, 263
Gyatso, Tenzin (Dalai Lama), 2, 135-39

Haines, Richard F., 126
Hair of the Alien (Chalker), 228
Hansen, Leslie, 255, 259, 269
Harvard: *Abduction* for, 185; Affect Seminars at, 10, 280n9; aliens at, 119-24; for Boyd, W., 12-14; career with, 41-43, 217-18; conferences at, 64; inquisition at, 195-99, 216-24; Jews at, 35-36; legacy at, 272; Mack, J., at, 34-35, 125-27, 157-59, 161-62, 164, 192-93, 194, 224-27; psychiatry at, 8, 13, 13-14; Relman for, 75, 193; reputation of, 223-24; scholarship at, 12; Shop Clubs at, 10, 119; sightings from, 25-26; staff at, 2
Hauck, Dennis William, 221
Haut, Walter, 19
Havel, Václav, 97
Havens, Leston, 12-13, 119-20
"Have We Visitors from Space?," 23
health, 132-33, 231
Heidegger, Martin, 79-80, 90
Heisenberg, Werner, 71
Henry, Michael, 81
heroism, 45, 50
Hero's Journey (Campbell, J.), 89-90
Hickler, Holly, 69-70
Hill, Barney: narratives of, 56-63; sightings by, 53-55
Hill, Betty, 95; narratives of, 56-63; sightings by, 53-55
Hind, Cynthia, 207, 209-11
Hitler, Adolf, 25, 82, 297n5
Hofmann, Albert, 82-83
Holotropic Breathwork, 8, 83-91, 107, 197
Home, Daniel Dunglas, 241, 287n
Honan, William H., 223
Hooft, Gerar 't, 239
Hopkins, Budd, 8-10, 87, 259, 270, 282, 285; advice from, 125-26; "Hopkins Image Recognition Test," 144-45; *Intruders* by, 95, 127; investigations by, 147; Jacobs and, 185, 196-97; on *Jane Whitney Show*, 158; Mack, J., and, 32, 91, 97-100,

Maxwell, James Clerk, 242
Mayo-Smith, Richmond, 78, 256
McKenna, Terence, 83
McLeod, Caroline, 170, 178, 191-92, 233, 238-39
McNally, Richard J., 238
McNamara, Robert, 77, 188-89
MDMA (ecstasy), 88
Mead, Margaret, 264, 283
Medway Plantation, 262
Meir, Golda, 38
memories: abduction and, 58, 60, 235; evidence and, 218-19; false, 110; flashbacks, 104-5; hypnosis and, 6, 102-3, 113; narratives and, 168-69; psychology of, 111-12, 154; science of, 170-71
Men in Black, 137, 142-43, 156
mental-illness: abduction and, 116-17, 121; *Borderline States in Psychiatry* on, 43-44; experts on, 100; funding for, 41; lobotomies for, 28; for Mack, J., 12, 36; National Institute of Mental Health, 179
Mental Radio (Sinclair), 147
Menzel, Donald H., 25-26, 101
Mesopotamia, 49
Michel, Aimé, 26
Middlebrook, Samuel, 50
Middle East, 48-49, 64-67, 73, 291n2, 291n4
military. *See specific topics*
military draft, 38-39
Miller, Henry, 81
Miller, John G., 110, 143, 144
mind-control experiments, 8, 105-6, 288n3
The Miracle Worker (Gibson), 97
Missing Time (Hopkins), 94, 158
MIT. *See* Massachusetts Institute of Technology

Mitchell, Edgar, 235-36, 241, 300n1
MKUltra project, 8, 106, 288n3
modified hypnosis, 197
Monroe, Marilyn, 23
Montville, Joseph, 65, 83-84
Moore, Francis D., 36-37
"A More Parsimonious Explanation for UFO Abduction" (Mcleod, Corbisier), 233
morphic resonance, 266-67
Morrison, Philip, 140, 141
Motherwell, Robert, 92
Moura, Gilda, 172-74, 229-31, 238, 255
Moyers, Bill, 236-37
Mueller, Robert, 200
Mufon. *See* Mutual UFO Network
Muktananda (Swami), 83
Mullis, Kary Banks, 154-55
Murphy, Bridey, 10
Murphy, Dulce, 83-84
Murphy, Henry, 81
Murphy, Michael, 83-84
Murray, Joseph, 36
Muscarello, Norman, 53
Muslims, 66-67
Mutual UFO Network (Mufon), 125, 142-43, 207, 209, 221
Mutwa, Credo, 211-12, 233
Myrdal, Alva, 10
Myrdal, Gunnar, 10
mystery missiles, 16, 19
mythology, 90, 137-38, 191, 218-19

Naiman, Robert, 93
Napolitano, Linda, 102-3, 145-46, 295n2
narratives: abduction, 2-3, 256-57; from Air Force, 15-16, 19-20; of aliens, 151-57; from children, 125-26, 210-15; of contactees, 51; credibility of, 18; critics of, 10-11; for Fuller, 52-55; of

Passport to the Cosmos (Mack, J.),
  241–45, 281–82
Pazzaglini, Mario, 138
peace, 2, 12, 49, 64–67, 73, 75, 77–78, 83,
  135, 283, 291n2
Peebles, Curtis, 216, 218, 224
PEER. *See* Program for Extraordinary
  Experience Research
PEER pressure, 168–71
Peixoto, Bernardo, 300n1
Pentagon Papers, 77, 202
Penzias, Arno, 30
Pérez de Cuéllar, Javier, 146, 295n2
Perls, Fritz, 82
Peter Jennings Reporting, 261–62
pets, 7, 88, 249
Pfeiffer, Trish, 254, 269
phenomenology, 89, 283–84
photographs, 23, 63, 116, 120, 139, 182,
  203, 207, 249, 258, 259, 286
physics: aerophysics, 24, 120, 148,
  151, 199, 238, 239, 242, 250, 279; of
  aircraft, 18; speed records in, 15–16;
  of UFOs, 2
The Pickwick Papers (Dickens), 267
pilots: experiences of, 15–26, 142; during
  World War II, 18–19
Pinel, Philippe, 169
Pinocchio (Collodi), 31, 37, 87
politics: government and, 202; for
  Mack, J., 64–67, 75, 263, 273; of
  Mack, K., 78–79
Pollock, Jackson, 92
Pope, Nick, 271
popular culture: *Abduction* for, 223–24;
  abduction in, 168–71, 172–76; aliens
  for, 255; *Buck Rogers in the 25th Century*, 147; conventional rationality
  and, 27; cosmology in, 101–2; *Cosmos*, 102; debunkers in, 216; event
  phenomenon for, 34; Hopkins for,

127; humanity and, 279–84; LSD in,
  100; NICAP for, 52–53; Oprah Win-
  frey Show, 181–84; *Passport to the
  Cosmos* in, 241–45, 281–82; research
  in, 162–63; sightings in, 53–55; Simon,
  B., in, 70–71; skeptics in, 228–29,
  300n1; Strieber in, 299n4; *Time*,
  178–80, 185–90; UFOs in, 20–26
Porter, James R., 204
Price, Richard (Esalen), 81
Price, Richard (experiencer), 141
"Primitive Concepts of Illness and
  the Dilemma of the Sick Child"
  (Mack, J.), 37
Prince, Julius S., 30, 254
A Prince of Our Disorder (Mack, J.),
  44–45, 50, 256
Pritchard, David E., 2, 140, 200,
  238, 242; friendship with, 116, 166;
  at MIT, 141, 147, 150; reputation
  of, 157
probes, 94, 100–101, 143, 177
professionalism: credibility and, 3–4,
  177, 216–18; in psychiatry, 47–48,
  232–33; in science, 195–99
Program for Extraordinary Experience
  Research (PEER), 76, 164, 168–71,
  177–79, 192, 202, 207, 216, 225, 233,
  239; finances for, 234, 236; findings,
  216; representation for, 222. *See also*
  Center for Psychology and Social
  Change
Project Blue Book, 22–23, 51–52, 62,
  203, 280
Project Grudge, 21, 22
Project Saucer, 21, 22
Project Sign, 21
pseudospeciation, 74
psilocybin, 83
psychedelic research, 82–83, 100, 129–
  30, 138, 229, 231

psychiatry: in academia, 39; amnesia for, 58; anomalous experiences in, 12–14, 13; career in, 195–96; childhood trauma in, 31; at Harvard, 8, 13, 13–14; humanity and, 9–10, 42; hypnosis and, 93–94; for Mack, J., 2–3, 27, 36–38; peace and, 64–67; professionalism in, 47–48, 232–33; psychoneuroses, 69; research, 103–4; skeptics in, 117, 126–27

"The Psycho." *See* Massachusetts Mental Health Center

psychology: of abduction, 57; of aliens, 214–15; curiosity, 121; of evil, 47; of family, 132; of fear, 276–77; Gestalt Therapy, 72; of heroism, 45, 50; of memories, 111–12, 154; parapsychology, 89, 249–51; *Psychological Inquiry*, 232–33; *Psychology Today*, 177–78; skeptics in, 133; of suicide, 69–70

Puzo, Mario, 249

Quine, Willard Van Orman, 10, 119
Quintanilla, Hector, 52

Rae, Stephen, 164–65, 177, 288n3
Rainey, Carol, 259
Raleigh, Walter, 45
Ramsey, Donald James, 18–19
Ramsey, Roger M., 20
Randall, Shawn, 258, 275–76
Rapid Eye Movement, 5, 43
Reagan, Ronald, 73, 75, 78, 202
Rediger, Jeffrey, 238, 239
Red Scare, 23, 35
Reich, Wilhelm, 84–85
reincarnation, 204, 254
religion, 261, 272–74, 297n1; for children, 76; holidays and, 88; for humanity, 246; Ifá, 165; for Mack, J., 27, 34, 170;

spiritual experiences and, 32–33

Relman, Arnold S., 238–40, 255; for Harvard, 75, 193; against Mack, J., 195–201, 205, 218–19, 225

Remembering Satan (Wright), 111

reproduction, 1, 107, 114–115, 117, 119, 121–123, 156, 182–83, 185, 234, 235, 244, 245

Resch, Tina, 254

research: abduction, 105–7; career in, 130–31; credibility and, 119–24, 239–40; on experiencers, 113; on Lawrence, T. E., 42, 44–50, 64; on LSD, 106; on mass hysteria, 10; by Nickerson, R., 285–86, 298n2; parapsychology, 250; peer pressure and, 168–71; in popular culture, 162–63; psychedelic, 82–83, 129–31, 138; psychiatry, 103–4; on supernatural experiences, 70–71

"Researches in the Phenomena of Spiritualism" (Crookes), 287

The Resonance of Unseen Things (Lepselter), 155

Rice-Bassett, Donna Lee, 180, 186–90, 191, 297n5

Rich, Clara Bertha, 30

Rich, Helen, 30

Riedel, Walther, 25

Riggs, Austen Fox, 69

Rilke, Rainer Maria, 248, 301n2

Ring, Kenneth, 142

Rivera, Geraldo, 226

Roach, Mary, 227

Robertson, H. P., 22–23

Robertson, Ronald, 202

Rockefeller, Laurance, 84, 179, 236, 300n7; funding from, 202, 205, 219, 289n1; support of, 234, 236–37, 262, 283, 300n6

Rockwell, Mary, 78, 97

Rockwell, Norman, 78, 97
Rodeghier, Mark, 148
Rogers, Rita, 64–65, 70
Rojcewicz, Peter M., 137–38
Roosevelt, Franklin D., 28, 194
Rosenberg, John Paul, 71
Roswell, New Mexico, 19–21, 280
Rothko, Mark, 92
Rudenstein, Neil, 126, 159, 185, 223
Ruppelt, Edward J., 21–23
The Russia House (le Carré), 97

Sachs, Hanns, 37
Sadat, Anwar, 64–66
Sagan, Carl, 75, 77; at conferences, 148;
   expertise of, 100–102; as skeptic, 178,
   183, 191, 236
Salk, Jonas, 75
"Sane Citizen sees UFO in New Jer-
   sey" (*Village Voice*), 93
Sapers, Carl M., 200, 203, 205
Saturday Night Fever (film), 68
Schaller, Bill, 227
Schild, Rudolph E., 225, 238, 240, 242,
   300n1
scholarship: on childhood trauma, 37;
   on children nightmares, 39; in *The
   Development and Sustenance of
   Self-Esteem in Childhood*, 76; at
   Harvard, 12; recognition in, 43; on
   sibling rivalry, 39
Schulte, David A., 30
science: behavioral, 5; credibility
   with, 125–26; evidence in, 222–23;
   of LSD, 82–83; of memories, 170–71;
   nondisclosure agreements by, 1;
   professionalism in, 195–96; skeptics
   and, 119–24; soul and, 12; UFOs
   for, 126; weird, 34; during World
   War II, 25
Science Fiction Society, 2

séances, 108, 241, 266, 287n
Search for Extraterrestrial Intelligence
   (SETI), 148
Secret Life (Jacobs), 117, 120, 140
segmented psychosis, 99
Seldes, Tim, 252, 254–55, 301n3
Semrad, Elvin, 12, 37
SETI. *See* Search for Extraterrestrial
   Intelligence
Seven Pillars of Wisdom (Lawrence, T.
   E.), 47–48, 77
Shaw, George Bernard, 50
Sheaffer, Robert, 147–48
Sheehan, Daniel P., 202–5, 217–24
Sheldrake, Rupert, 266–67
Shop Club, 10, 119, 126
Shore, Miles F., 193, 196
short-wave sleep, 43
sibling rivalry, 39
sightings, 17–23; by Air Force, 24–25, 53;
   credibility of, 279–84; from Harvard,
   25–26; narratives of, 56–63; in popu-
   lar culture, 53–55; UFOs, 51, 92–96
Silkwood, Karen, 202
Silva Mind Control, 71
Silverglate, Harvey A., 203, 255
Simon, Benjamin, 55, 58–63, 70–71
Simon, Vivienne, 31, 133, 179
Sinatra, Frank, 35
Sinclair, Upton, 147
skeptics: of abductions, 151–57; credibility and, 25–26, 92–93, 200–205;
   debunkers, 168, 216; event phenomenon for, 147–48; evidence and, 157; of
   Hopkins, 232–33; of hypnosis, 191; at
   MIT, 147; in popular culture, 228–29,
   300n1; in psychiatry, 117, 126–27;
   in psychology, 133; Sagan, 178, 183,
   236; science and, 119–24; *Skeptical
   Inquirer*, 239; for Strieber, 187; Willwerth for, 185–90

Wallace, George, 21
war. *See specific wars*
War of the Worlds (Welles), 92
Watch the Skies (Peebles), 216, 224
water, 18, 281
Waterman, William, 201
Watts, Alan W., 283
Waxelbaum, Lulu, 28-29
Weiner, Jack, 259
Weiner, Jim, 259
Weinstein, Justin, 261
weird science, 34
Weizmann, Chaim, 48-49
Welles, Orson, 92
Wesolowski, Karen, 164, 178, 300n6
"When Worldviews Collide" (Mack,
    J.), 254-55, 290n1
White, Luise, 156-57
White, Paul Dudley, 35
Whitney, Jane, 158
Willwerth, James, 178-80, 185-90
Wilmot, Dan, 20
Wilson, Jeremy, 265, 271
Wilson, Robert Woodrow, 30
Winfrey, Oprah, 181-85, 201, 226
Witnessed (Hopkins), 146
witness testimony, 16; of aliens, 20, 206-
    15; credibility of, 54-55; investigators
    and, 152; similarities in, 113-14
The Wizard of Oz (Baum), 31, 174, 283
The Wolfen (Strieber), 153

women: abduction of, 110; *The Cour-
    age to Heal* for, 111; narratives from,
    113-15, 122-23, 230
World War I, 44, 46
World War II: Civil Air Patrol during,
    30; mass hysteria after, 22; pilots
    during, 18-19; science during, 25;
    sightings after, 20-21
Wright, Lawrence, 111
Wright Brothers, 16

The X-Files (TV show), 162, 229

Yankelovich, Daniel, 76
Yom Kippur War, 64
"You are What You Est" (Greenberg), 71
Ywahoo, Dhyani, 300n1

Zamora, Lonnie, 51-52
Zander, Benjamin, 80
Zander, Rosamund "Roz," 32, 80, 225,
    263, 269-71, 285; affair with, 88-89,
    97-99, 132; Mack, S., and, 228; sup-
    port from, 104, 106, 160
Zarate, Andrea, 295n2
Zen beliefs, 72, 82. *See also* Tibetan
    Buddhism
Zimbabwe, 206-15
Zimmerman, Michael, 238, 240
Zuckerman, Al, 286
Zuckerman, Mortimer, 76

ABOUT THE AUTHOR

Ralph Blumenthal was a *New York Times* reporter from 1964 to 2009, serving as a foreign correspondent in West Germany, South Vietnam, and Cambodia; a national bureau chief in the Southwest; and an investigative reporter and arts writer. He was a member of the metro desk team that won the Pulitzer Prize for breaking news coverage of the 1992 truck bombing of the World Trade Center. In 2017 he and two colleagues broke the story of a secret Pentagon program to track UFOs, with videos of encounters between the objects and Navy pilots. He is the recipient of a Guggenheim fellowship, the author of six nonfiction books, and a distinguished lecturer at Baruch College of the City University of New York. He lives in Manhattan with his wife, Deborah, a children's book author.

ALSO BY RALPH BLUMENTHAL

Miracle at Sing Sing

Stork Club

Once Through the Heart

Last Days of the Sicilians

Outrage (with Robert McFadden, M. A. Farber, Charles Strum, E. R. Shipp, and Craig Wolff)

The Gotti Tapes (with John Miller)